ROUTLEDGE LIBRARY EDITIONS:
ARTIFICIAL INTELLIGENCE

Volume 4

NOVICE PROGRAMMING ENVIRONMENTS

NOVICE PROGRAMMING ENVIRONMENTS

Explorations in Human-Computer Interaction and Artificial Intelligence

Edited by
MARC EISENSTADT, MARK T. KEANE
AND TIM RAJAN

Routledge
Taylor & Francis Group
LONDON AND NEW YORK

First published in 1992 by Lawrence Erlbaum Associates Ltd.

This edition first published in 2018
by Routledge
2 Park Square, Milton Park, Abingdon, Oxon OX14 4RN

and by Routledge
711 Third Avenue, New York, NY 10017

Routledge is an imprint of the Taylor & Francis Group, an informa business

British Library Cataloguing in Publication Data
A catalogue record for this book is available from the British Library

ISBN: 978-0-8153-8566-0 (Set)
ISBN: 978-0-429-49236-5 (Set) (ebk)
ISBN: 978-0-8153-5162-7 (Volume 4) (hbk)
ISBN: 978-1-351-14128-4 (Volume 4) (ebk)

Publisher's Note
The publisher has gone to great lengths to ensure the quality of this reprint but points out that some imperfections in the original copies may be apparent.

Disclaimer
The publisher has made every effort to trace copyright holders and would welcome correspondence from those they have been unable to trace.

Novice Programming Environments: Explorations in Human-Computer Interaction and Artificial Intelligence

Marc Eisenstadt

Human Cognition Research Laboratory
The Open University
Milton Keynes, England

Mark T. Keane

Department of Computer Science
Trinity College Dublin
Dublin, Ireland

Tim Rajan

Performance Technology
Lloyd's Register
Croydon, England

LAWRENCE ERLBAUM ASSOCIATES, PUBLISHERS
Hove (UK) Hillsdale (USA)

Lawrence Erlbaum Associates Ltd., Publishers
27 Palmeira Mansions
Church Road
Hove
East Sussex, BN3 2FA
U.K.

British Library Cataloguing in Publication Data

Novice programming environments: explorations in human-computer interaction and artificial intelligence.
I. Eisenstadt, Marc II. Keane, Mark T. III. Rajan, Tim
004.01

ISBN 0-86377-180-7 (HBK)

Cover by Joyce Chester
Typeset in the U.K. by Acorn Bookwork, Salisbury, Wilts.
Printed and bound in the U.K. by BPCC Wheatons, Exeter

To my father, Joseph, and the memory of my mother,
Adele
(M.E.)

To Ruth and Bert
(M.K.)

To Jane – A new beginning
(T.R.)

Contents

List of Contributors

Mike Brayshaw Human Cognition Research Laboratory, The Open University, Milton Keynes, England.

Joost Breuker Department of Social Science Informatics, The University of Amsterdam, Amsterdam, The Netherlands.

John Domingue Human Cognition Research Laboratory, The Open University, Milton Keynes, England.

Marc Eisenstadt Human Cognition Research Laboratory, The Open University, Milton Keynes, England.

Tony Hasemer Human Cognition Research Laboratory, The Open University, Milton Keynes, England.

Hank Kahney Human Cognition Research Laboratory, The Open University, Milton Keynes, England.

Mark T. Keane Department of Computer Science, Trinity College Dublin, Dublin, Ireland.

Joachim Laubsch Computing Systems Center, Hewlett-Packard Laboratories, Palo Alto, CA, USA.

Matthew W. Lewis Department of Psychology, Carnegie-Mellon University, Pittsburgh, PA, USA.

Rudi Lutz School of Cognitive & Computing Sciences, Sussex University, Sussex, England.

Tim Rajan Performance Technology, Lloyd's Register, Croydon, England.

Preface

Motivation

Computer programming: what's the big deal? Judging from the growing literature on the problems and misconceptions of novice programmers, it is a very big deal indeed! Newcomers to programming are distinctly prone to certain characteristic "traps" or pitfalls. There is a widespread feeling that by means of careful curriculum design, careful programming language design, careful tracing/debugging system design, careful advice, or some combination of the above, many pitfalls can either be avoided or at least diminished.

We share a strong view on what makes learning to program a satisfactory experience, this does not require that it be free of pitfalls. Indeed, as Papert and his colleagues argued persuasively in their seminal work on LOGO, learning and debugging are very tightly intertwined, therefore overcoming pitfalls ought to be a valuable experience. However, it seems clear that some pitfalls are "worthwhile" and others are "worthless". To the extent that we can identify "worthless" pitfalls, we can help eliminate them from programming languages and curricula. Similarly, "worthwhile" pitfalls once identified as such, can form the basis of good teaching examples either in standard texts or embedded in intelligent tutoring systems and automatic debugging aids.

Perhaps it is not coincidental that the co-editors of this volume are all self-taught programmers (we are collectively fluent in Prolog, Lisp, Fortran, and BASIC, and "literate" in numerous other languages). In an important sense, all programmers are self-taught. Naturally, the learning phase can be facilitated by "good" texts, "good" examples, and "good" advice. But what exactly does "good" mean in these cases? That is what this volume tries to address.

History

Broadly speaking, our motivation over the years has been to understand and improve the plight of computer programmers. The activity has been highly self-reflexive because (a) the languages we have been studying have been the languages of cognitive science and artificial intelligence, (b) the programmers we have been observing have been students of cognitive science and artificial intelligence, and (c) the remedies we have proposed have been cognitive science and artificial intelligence remedies. Our activity began in 1976 when we first faced the task of teaching AI programming to cognitive psychology students at the Open University. We wanted to do this in the first place because we thought that properly trained cognitive psychology students ought to be able to do some AI programming. The problem was that Open University courses have no formal prerequisites so we could not insist on our students having a prior computing background. We therefore had to present the fundamental ideas in a sugar coated fashion, but we still wanted students to come to grips with the primary problems of representation, reasoning, and algorithm design without being handed too much on a silver platter. This activity gave birth to our first main project: SOLO, a LOGO-like language for manipulating semantic networks.

The fact that our students were working on their own, (at first via dial-up lines to a DECsystem-20 and later on personal computers), catalysed our foray into automatic program understanding and debugging. If we could provide some sensible automated assistance to our students we could help them overcome certain difficulties in an effective manner. Moreover, the intellectual challenge of writing programs which could understand buggy student programs was very exciting to us. Although the task was too open-ended in general, we had two critical points in our favour: SOLO was a reasonably restricted language, and we knew the exact curriculum sequence the students would be working on. The seminal work of Rich and Waters on programming plans and clichés had come to our attention, and we tailored and extended their work to suit our own needs, first in the context of SOLO, and later in the context of Lisp and Pascal, which were of particular interest to some of the lab's Ph.D. students.

As the automatic debugging work was progressing, another important development took place which affected our curriculum design activities: Bob Kowalski was intrigued by the apparent success of SOLO as an overall programming environment and its superficial similarity to Prolog. He got in touch with Marc Eisenstadt and said, in effect, "Why not concentrate on providing a good environment for a well-understood language like Prolog rather than inventing a new language?" Two other events at this time proved significant. One was our observation that, although our students found SOLO easy to learn, they soon reached its limits and they felt frustrated as a result. The other event was as sabbatical trip by Marc Eisenstadt to Amsterdam, during which he observed the extensive use of Prolog by Bob Wielinga to teach AI and Cognitive Psychology. This latter observation was the catalyst which triggered our move into Prolog. Wielinga was a long-standing colleague, fellow devotee of Lisp, and a real cognitive scientist at heart, and was free of any religious conviction in favour of Prolog. Such conviction had put us off in the past, but Wielinga's unbiased support for Prolog was very convincing (we learned later that Wielinga had himself been profoundly influenced by a sabbatical visit of Alan Bundy from Edinburgh to Amsterdam a few years earlier). The end result is that we eventually abandoned SOLO in favour of Prolog for in-house teaching. We also went on to develop a graphical tracing and debugging environment for Prolog, as well as undertaking empirical studies and getting involved seriously in "visual programming" and "program visualisation". This has become the foundation for much of the current activity within the Human Cognition Research Laboratory at the Open University.

Organisation of the Book: Design, Empirical Studies, and AI

Through the iterative cycle of design, testing, and observation of programmers, we spent a lot of time thinking about the relationships between curriculum, programming language, and software environment. Concurrent activity in the emerging discipline of software psychology provided important guiding ideas, particularly the notion of a concrete execution model that beginners could really sink their teeth into. Part I of the book describes how we have taken a series of such design principles, extended and used them in the design of integrated textbook, video, and software environments for several programming languages and styles.

Design principles are not enough, they risk being too "seat-of-the-pants". Empirical studies are necessary to bring home the harsh realities of the behaviour of genuine users. Over the years we have debated the significance of seat-of-the-pants design, and have come to the following conclusions.

Good seat-of-the-pants design *is* good cognitive science, provided that:

(a) The design principles are clearly articulated.
(b) The design artifact (programming language, hardware, etc.) is subject to rigorous empirical study.

In part II of the book, we put on our collective empirical hats in order to assess the "goodness" of our design artifacts, and to understand the root causes of programmers' misconceptions. As cognitive scientists, we are never really content with lists of bugs, although these are useful, nor with studies of the form "feature X" is better than "feature Y" although these too have their role. Rather, "bug taxonomies" get us one step closer to being able to provide the relevant generalisations which articulate the nature of the difficulties faced by programmers. Even this is not enough for the inquisitive cognitive scientist, however. Each generation of researchers tries to push ever deeper towards the root cause of misconceptions with the aim of providing a good cognitive explanation of the problem, and maybe even a cure. We don't necessarily have cures to recommend, although we do have thoughts about ways to pre-empt certain kinds of misconceptions, and these surface throughout part II.

An important underlying conviction of our work has always been that if we *really* understood the root causes of programmers' problems, we could build an AI system which embodied this understanding in the form of a program to help students debug their programs. Stated more strongly, we felt that *unless* we could build such an AI system, we wouldn't really understand the root causes of programmers' problems. In other words, building the system helps foster our understanding as cognitive scientists. We find the AI activity exciting and worthwhile in its own right, and we have certainly found ourselves beaming with pride when a program of ours automatically detected a student bug, even when it could not then help the student. But underneath the AI activity is a thread which links it back to the design activity and the empirical studies: this thread is one of articulating the root causes of problems and misconceptions. To the extent that these root causes can be avoided in the first place, then the language/environment embodies good design. Where they can't be avoided, the empirical studies can help identify which ones persist, and say something about why. To the extent that they are genuinely understood by us, an AI program can help hold the hand of a baffled student. Part III of the book pursues the "hand-holding" theme in detail.

HCRL

The Human Cognition Research Laboratory is a collection of about 25 researchers (teaching staff, Ph.D. students, and research fellows) at the Open University engaged in a variety of cognitive science and AI activities. The activities concerned with understanding and improving the plight of computer programmers are covered in this volume. Another large activity within the lab falls broadly under the heading of knowledge engineering, including: automatic knowledge acquisition, knowledge acquisition methodology, knowledge engineering environments, qualitative reasoning, fault diagnosis, discovery systems, and strategic planning. Other researchers are studying the psychology of memory and ageing, cognitive models of analogical problem solving, and cognitive architectures.

HCRL has provided an exciting and supportive environment over the years for the kind of research described in this volume. We want to thank our colleagues in the lab, and also the sponsors and industrial partners who made some of the work possible:

Science and Engineering Research Council: grant funded Mike Brayshaw (Chapter 3).
A CASE studentship funded John Domingue (Chapter 12).
British Telecom: a research grant funded John Domingue (Chapter 4).
International Computers Ltd.: a CASE studentship funded John Domingue (Chapter 12).
Social Science Research Council (now Economic and Social Research Council): grant funded Joachim Laubsch (Chapter 9).
Open University: funding for Laubsch (Chapter 9); Lewis (Chapter 5); Eisenstadt's work with Breuker (Chapter 6); studentships for Kahney (Chapter 7), Hasemer (Chapter 10), and Rajan (Chapters 2 and 8).

We look forward to continuing our research in the tradition and style which has evolved within HRCL.

Marc Eisenstadt
Mark Keane
Tim Rajan
Milton Keynes, UK, March 1990.

Acknowledgements

The editors would like to thank the following publishers for permission to reproduce/adapt previously published material:

Kluwer Academic Publishers

Rajan, T. (1990). Principles for the Design of Dynamic Tracing Environments for Novice Programmers, *Instructional Science*, *19*, 1–29. (Chapter 2)

Eisenstadt, M. & Brayshaw, M. (1990). A Fine-grained Account of Prolog Execution for Teaching and Debugging, *Instructional Science*, *19*, 407–436. (Chapter 3)

Rajan, T. (1991). An Evaluation of the APT: An Animated Program Tracer for Novice Prolog Programmers, *Instructional Science*, *20*, 89–110. (Chapter 6)

Morgan Kaufmann Publishers Inc.

Domingue, J. & Eisenstadt, M. (1989). A New Metaphor for the Graphical Explanation of Rule Execution, *Proceedings of the Eleventh International Conference on Artificial Intelligence (IJCAI–89)*, 129–134. Copyright International Joint Conferences on Artificial Intelligence, Inc. Copies of this and other IJCAI Proceedings are available from Morgan Kaufmann Publishers, Inc., 2929 Campus Drive, San Mateo, CA 94403, U.S.A. (Chapter 9)

I Design Issues in Programming Environments

The first part of this book contains four chapters which look at the design issues involved in programming environments. The programming environments described vary both in their intended user group, the scope of the programming domain, and the mode of presentation.

For example, the first chapter by Eisenstadt presents an environment which combines a programming language, SOLO, and a curriculum which aims to support Psychology undergraduates who have no previous experience of programming. Although the design issues pervade all aspects of the user's interaction with the computer, the scope of the domain is small (i.e. to build simple AI models of psychological theories in a limited time period). The SOLO language is therefore very simple, and limited in its expressive power. This trade-off means that while SOLO is perfect for the task and group it was designed for, it is very limited for use elsewhere. However, the lessons learned from the design and use of this environment have been put to good use as can be seen in Chapter 3.

In Chapter 2, Rajan describes the design of an Animated Program Tracer, APT, which aims to provide a faithful story of the execution of Prolog programs. As in the previous chapter the user group is limited to novice programmers, although in this case the language being supported is a full blown artificial intelligence programming language which exhibits complex and unintuitive behaviour. The technique used by APT to explain the behaviour of Prolog programs is that of text animation, where each step of the execution repre-

sents one frame of the animated sequence. The user moves through the animation which is designed to reflect the dynamic behaviour of the Prolog interpreter.

The paper by Eisenstadt and Brayshaw presented in Chapter 3 builds on and extends the design principles detailed in the previous two chapters. It describes the Transparent Prolog Machine and its associated curriculum. Whereas SOLO and APT are limited in their intended user group and/or the scope of the language, TPM provides a "cradle to grave" environment for Prolog programmers. As such, it provides a medium both for learning Prolog, and developing and debugging complex programs. The technique used to explain execution behaviour is, as with APT, animation. However, where APT used text, TPM uses graphics as the basis for its animation. The use of graphics allows TPM to cater for all manner of Prolog users, ranging from beginners through to old hands, and are used extensively throughout the course material.

The last chapter, by Domingue and Eisenstadt, describes TRI, the Transparent Rule Interpreter. TRI is a debugging environment for the rule-based component of a knowledge engineering environment, and as such covers both forward chaining and backward chaining rule interpreters. This chapter explores not only how to present a story of the behaviour of a rule interpreter, but also how to present an execution model of two interacting programming languages. The TPM model described in the previous chapter is used as the execution story for the backward chaining rule interpreter.

In summary, the research described in this part explores the design issues involved in creating programming environments for a variety of domains, user groups, and programming languages. The chapters are presented in the chronological order of research, with the work carried out in each chapter building on the lessons learned in the earlier work. The section should therefore convey a progression in the corpus of design issues, and the presentation techniques of the programming environment whether it be computer based or book based.

1 Design Features of a Friendly Software Environment For Novice Programmers*

Marc Eisenstadt
Human Cognition Research Laboratory, The Open University, Milton Keynes, England

OVERVIEW

This paper describes a highly-friendly, software environment for novice programmers. The environment, based around a non-numerical programming language called SOLO[1], has been used extensively by Social Science students. The paper outlines several features which could benefit designers of other software environments, concentrating in particular on the interaction among three aspects of software design: the programming language itself, the user environment, and the curriculum used to introduce students to programming. The language has an "explicit flow of control" construct in conditional statements which eliminates the elementary flow of control bugs normally found in novices' programs. The environment is simple, consistent, and "visible" in that it displays all changes to the values of global variables as soon as they occur. The curriculum is non-standard: students begin with the concepts of "assertional data base" and "pattern matching", which they find highly intuitive, motivating, and relevant to their academic interests (Psychology, in this case).

---

*This research was supported by a grant from the Open University and carried out in the Human Cognition Research Laboratory.

[1]The name SOLO is derived from a combination of SOL (Norman, Rumelhart, & the LNR Research Group, 1975) and LOGO (Papert, 1980). It is also meant to convey the image of Open University students who study at home on their own. The language SOLO has no connection with Project SOLO (Dwyer & Critchfield, 1981) or the SOLO operating system (Brinch-Hansen, 1977), which came to our attention after our first primer had been printed.

1. INTRODUCTION

This paper describes the results of a six year period of design, implementation, testing, and iterative re-design of a programming language, user aids, and curriculum materials for use by Psychology students learning how to write simple computer programs. The resulting product, called "SOLO"[1] has now been used by 2000 Open University students. SOLO itself is a very simple programming language, but the design philosophy of the language, the user aids, and the curriculum materials embody many principles which could pay off if adopted in the teaching of other programming languages. The next section describes the background to the project and the reason it was undertaken. Sections 3–5 describe in turn the programming language, the surrounding "software environment", and the curriculum materials, listing the important principles underlying the design of each of these. Throughout the paper, the principles which can benefit designers of other software environments are emphasized.

2. BACKGROUND

The Open University, in existence since 1969, is a "long-distance" teaching institution. We have 70,000 undergraduates currently enrolled. Students typically hold full-time jobs, studying at home for roughly 12 hours per week. We make extensive use of correspondence text, BBC television and radio programmes, small home experimental kits, and one-week residential summer schools. Through a special arrangement with colleges and polytechnics around the country we have established 250 study centres, where students can meet with tutors, and where they can use a computer terminal via dial-up facilities to one of our main central computers. These computers run a variety of Computer Assisted Instruction packages, simulation games, and programming languages. Students attending summer school have hands-on access to a large range of microcomputers, and an increasing number of Open University courses are using microcomputers as part of their home experimental kits.

In 1976 a team of Open University lecturers under the direction of Professor Judith Greene began to design a course on Cognitive Psychology. The course was to be presented for the first time in 1978. A course such as this runs for 32 weeks every year, for approximately six to eight years, and is almost entirely pre-packaged with the exception of yearly changes to some assignments and exam questions. Thus, there is tremendous pressure on us to get the material right before it goes into print. Two important principles were agreed by the course team early in 1976: (a) the course would contain a fairly large amount of material on Artificial

Intelligence (AI), because such material was becoming increasingly relevant for Cognitive Psychologists, and (b) all the course materials would undergo two rounds of drafting and group criticism, after which a third draft of the materials would be produced and used by a trial group of thirty students in 1977 (they received credit for taking the course in this unpolished form). The comments of these "developmental testers" would then provide the basis for revisions of the material to appear in the final curriculum in 1978.

Our desire to include a lot of material on Artificial Intelligence meant that our students had to become conversant with a number of basic ideas involving computation. We felt this was essential, because it would enable our students to feel more comfortable when encountering AI articles or cognitive science theories which are expressed in some computational form. The best way to achieve this was clearly to require the students to undertake an elementary programming project. The goals of the project are summarised in this excerpt from the students' project booklet (Eisenstadt, 1978):

> By the time you finish this project you should be able to:
> 1. connect to and log in to the computer;
> 2. define the following terms, and state their relevance to models of cognitive processing:
>
> | | |
> |---|---|
> | symbol | relation |
> | computer | pattern-matching |
> | program | parameter |
> | programming language | variable |
> | procedure | flow of control |
> | subroutine | recursion |
> | data base | iteration |
> | semantic network | inference |
> | node | proposition |
>
> 3. write working computer programs using all of the above concepts;
> 4. explain the aspects of cognitive processing which are embodied in your programs;
> 5. explain why "representation" is a problem

Students at summer school used SOLO to develop some elementary models of human memory and reasoning. A typical project involved students setting up a database of "facts" about some murder mystery, and then writing a program to search through the database, exploring the motive, the alibi, the weapon, etc., to try to find the culprit.

The Open University, as one of its founding principles, has no entrance requirements, and our course has no prerequisites (though students invariably will have first taken a "foundation" course in Social Sciences, and an introductory Psychology course). Thus, we had to proceed with great caution; we had to produce a "friendly" experience of computer programming for a student who would be working alone at a remote study centre, who had no prior computing experience, and was not interested in computing in the first place. Initially, we decided to develop a software package on the central computer, encouraging remote dial-up access, because the facilities we required could not be provided cost-effectively to students on smaller computers at 1976/1977 prices. In later years, the package we developed could run on microcomputers, allowing the delivery of a complete hardware and software package direct to our students.

Our results have been very encouraging. If nothing else, we have succeeded in giving the vast majority of our students a pleasurable encounter with computers in potentially intimidating conditions. A majority of students coming to our residential summer schools consistently chose a programming project as their first choice out of four projects – and this is with the selection process weighted against the programming project, because those few students (10%–20%) who had prior programming experience were advised to choose one of the other projects. How, then, did this state of affairs come about? The short answer is that we designed a programming language which enabled students to do powerful things on the first day, embedded this language in a friendly software environment which corrected obvious errors (such as silly spelling mistakes) automatically, and developed a curriculum sequence which from start to finish tried to motivate the student by highlighting the relevance of each programming task to the student's main academic interest—cognitive psychology. One of the main messages of this chapter will be that the language, the environment, and the curriculum all warrant equal attention from would-be software designers. Sections 3–5 present a detailed discussion of each.

3. THE LANGUAGE

SOLO is primarily a data base manipulation language. User-defined procedures can invoke primitives which add, remove, retrieve, or print out structures in a relational data base. The data base is a unidirectional labelled graph, with arbitrarily-named nodes connected by arbitrarily named relations to other nodes, as in the following structure:

```
FIDO
 |
 |---ISA---> DOG
 |
 |---HAS---> FLEAS
 |
 |---LIKES---> BEER
```

Manipulation of this relational network is accomplished by means of the following primitives:

NOTE: allows relational "triples" to be added to the data base, e.g.

NOTE FIDO---EATS---> MEAT
NOTE FELIX---ISA---> CAT

FORGET: allows relational triples to be removed from the database, e.g.

FORGET FIDO---HAS---> FLEAS

CHECK: allows the user to test for the *presence* or *absence* of relational triples, e.g.

CHECK FIDO---LIKES---> BEER

would return "present", given the relational structure shown above, whereas

CHECK FIDO---LIKES---> WINE

would return "absent". This present/absent dichotomy (rather than true/false) is used as the basis for conditional branching in user-defined procedures. CHECK also allows the use of "wild cards" in the final position of the relational triple. For instance, given the above structure for FIDO.

CHECK FIDO---LIKES---> ?X

would return "present", and would also assign to X the value "BEER". SOLO uses an implicit "reverse quoting" convention so that the node whose name is "FIDO" is simply referred to by the four character string FIDO. Conversely, the value of the variable X is referred to by prefixing it with an asterisk, i.e. *X. Our students find this pattern matching style of memory retrieval, the emphasis on assertional data bases, and the use of "reverse quoting" all highly intuitive, and they have no problems performing simple pattern-matching retrieval from the data base during their first terminal session.

PRINT: allows the printing of arbitrary messages, in the form of quoted strings, interspersed with variables, if desired, e.g.

PRINT "I SEE THAT FIDO LIKES TO DRINK" *X
PRINT "I SEE THAT" *X "IS THE THING FIDO LIKES"

TO: allows the user to define his or her own procedures. Parameters may be used, indicated by enclosing them in slashes. Line numbering is similar to that used by BASIC and LOGO, e.g.

```
TO PRAISE /X/
10 NOTE /X/---IS---> PRAISEWORTHY
20 PRINT "I THINK THAT" /X/ "IS REALLY GREAT"
DONE
```

Automatic line numbering is available, as is screen-oriented editing without any line numbering. These features are discussed as "environment" issues in Section 4.

The design of the language encourages a top-down, modular style of programming. Procedures may have at most 10 main steps. No GOTOs are allowed. The present/absent dichotomy, described above, provides a standard if-then-else style of conditional with the following three restrictions: 1) no nesting of conditionals is allowed; 2) only one action (sub-procedure or primitive invocation) can be performed on each branch of the conditional; 3) the user must specify whether the interpreter is to CONTINUE on to the next main step or EXIT back to the calling procedure. Sub-line numbering, indenting, and "present/absent" prompting (illustrated in italics below) are all provided automatically by SOLO, e.g.

```
TO ASSESS /X/
10 CHECK /X/---VOTES---> LIBERAL
  10A If present: PRAISE /X/; CONTINUE
  10B If absent: CONDEMN /X/; CONTINUE
20 PRINT "I'M NOW DONE ASSESSING" /X/
DONE
```

In this case, the user may have already defined PRAISE, as in the preceding example, but can wait to define CONDEMN later on (as long as it is done before invoking ASSESS).

EDIT: allows the user to retype old lines or insert new ones within the definition of any existing procedure. Essentially, EDIT mode and DEFINE mode ("TO" mode) are identical. Lines are inserted or overwritten just by typing in the line number followed by the desired SOLO statement. A line number followed by a carriage-return deletes that particular line. EDIT mode and DEFINE mode are both terminated by typing the word DONE. A screen editor, based on the syntax-directed editing philosophy of the Cornell Program Synthesizer (Teitelbaum & Reps, 1981) is available to summer school students using our microcomputer implementation of SOLO (described below).

LIST: student-defined procedures may be listed out on the terminal by using this primitive, e.g.

```
LIST ASSESS

  TO ASSESS/X/
etc.
```

DESCRIBE: data base structures emanating from a given node may be printed out on the terminal using this primitive, e.g.

```
DESCRIBE FIDO

FIDO
 |
 |---ISA---> DOG
 |
 |---HAS---> FLEAS
 |
 |---LIKES---> BEER
```

BYE: Allows the user to log off, and automatically saves the entire data base and all user-defined procedures under a unique (invisible) directory for each SOLO user.

FOR EACH: allows the user to iterate through sets of common relation-names emanating from a given node, e.g.

```
TO ANALYZE  /X/
10 FOR EACH CASE OF /X/---DRINKS---> ?Y
  10A PRINT "HERE IS ANOTHER ONE:" *Y
DONE
```

As with CHECK, sub-line numbering is supplied automatically by SOLO.

This completes the description of the SOLO kernel. The kernel has remained unchanged over the years, although some extra facilities have been added in order to give our students improved tools in the light of empirical studies (see Chapters 5 and 7). The resulting implementations of SOLO are as follows:

1. SOLO-78: This comprised the kernel described above, plus an extensive HELP feature, illustrated in Section 3. SOLO-78 was used by over 1600 students between 1978 and 1981.

2. SOLO-82: This is an optimized version, running several times faster than SOLO-78. Its HELP facility was streamlined to take account of those

HELP features not accessed by SOLO-78 users. In addition to the kernel, this version has a BASIC-style INPUT primitive, plus a more compact syntax for searching through several successive links in the data base. SOLO-82 users can type in

```
LET *B = FIDO'S MOTHER'S BROTHER
```

instead of the more cumbersome SOLO-78 sequence shown below:

```
CHECK FIDO MOTHER ?M
  If present: CONTINUE
  If absent: EXIT
CHECK *M BROTHER ?B
  If present: CONTINUE
  If absent: EXIT
  etc.
```

A small number of extra utilities are provided for simplifying editing and book-keeping. For example, KILL gets rid of unwanted procedures and DIR gives a list of the names of all user-defined procedures and node names in current use.

3. Micro-SOLO: This UCSD-Pascal implementation of SOLO has all the features of SOLO-82, plus a simple screen editor which displays syntactic "templates" to the user in order to minimize input errors (Eisenstadt & Gawronski, 1987). It has been used by over 200 of our students at summer schools.

4. E-SOLO: This is our experimental version, containing a smarter front-end, and a tutorial package incorporating automated program-understanding and debugging aids (see Chapters 5, 9 and 10). It has been used by 40 students, all volunteer experimental subjects.

The word "SOLO" will be used throughout this paper to refer to the kernel of the language shared by all four dialects, with exceptions pointed out as appropriate.

3.1 Design Features of the SOLO Programming Language

In describing the kernel of SOLO, the only aspect of the environment which has been discussed so far is the notion of automatic numbering of sub-lines (such as 10A) within conditionals and FOR EACH loops. The environment is very important, of course, but discussion of it in this section has been minimized in order to highlight those aspects of the language itself which are crucial. Here are the design features of SOLO which we think have yielded high rewards for our students:

1. *Simple virtual machine.* The abstract "SOLO machine" is extremely simple: it is a "data base machine" consisting of two halves – data base, and a pool of procedures. Procedures are described as "autonomous experts" which know how to do things to the data base. The pool of procedures (NOTE, etc) can be augmented by user-defined procedures, which are simply new bundles of autonomous expertise. Subroutine calls are described to the student as "activations" of procedures. Activation from the top-level (e.g. typing in NOTE FIDO ISA DOG) is conceptually identical to sub-procedure activation (e.g. having step 10 of your own procedure perform NOTE FIDO ISA DOG).

The importance of a simple virtual machine has been emphasized by duBoulay, O'Shea, and Monk (1981). Their work influenced the design of SOLO, and this principle appears to have been very beneficial for novice programmers. Related to this concept is the one discussed next, consistency.

2. *Consistent use of virtual machine.* It is always possible to design a simple machine without adhering to it consistently, which is why this principle is discussed separately from the preceding one. The idea of consistency, also emphasized by duBoulay et al., is particularly reflected in the wording of error messages. For example, suppose that a student simply types in:

FIDO ISA DOG

(omitting the NOTE). Ignoring for the moment clever user-aids which can infer that the word NOTE was omitted (E-SOLO does this), what sort of error message should the student be presented with? Possibilities include such things as:

SYNTAX ERROR
???
WHAT?
I DON'T UNDERSTAND "FIDO" IN THIS CONTEXT

However, students are told that SOLO works by applying a procedure to arguments, and that the first word on a line is always the name of a procedure. Thus, we felt that the most consistent error message to provide was the following:

I DON'T HAVE A PROCEDURE CALLED "FIDO"

This consistency pays tremendous dividends, as it helps pinpoint for the students exactly what has gone wrong and why.

3. *Powerful mnemonics.* The English meanings of the primitive names NOTE, FORGET, DESCRIBE, etc, correspond very closely to the actual jobs they perform within the SOLO virtual machine. This makes them easy to remember. Good mnemonics, however, do not require a software designer to develop an "English-like" programming language, as the next design principle emphasizes.

4. *Not "English-like".* A pilot version of SOLO in 1976 was modelled closely on SOL (Norman et al. 1975) and included syntactic constructs such as the following:

CONNECT "FIDO" TO "DOG" WITH "ISA"

This was abandoned in favour of NOTE FIDO ISA DOG after a brief trial run in which it became apparent that:

- All of the extra keystrokes were an enormous burden for beginners.
- Pilot students found the syntax harder to remember, even though it was English. They were tempted to try closely related constructs such as:

  LINK "FIDO" UPTO "DOG" VIA "ISA"

- Pilot students imparted too much intelligence to other aspects of the SOLO machine, assuming it could understand English. In addition, some pilot students said that they actually felt more secure about the activity of programming if it was kept deliberately distinct from the activity of communication in English. This distinctness also applies to the use of symbols such as * (which refers back to the result of the pattern-match involving the symbol ?). Other symbols, such as the word T, could have been used to refer to the result of a pattern match, but our pilot students actually preferred a special symbol. Although the course team agonized over what symbol to use, our pilot students said in the end that they didn't care what symbol it was, as long as it was unique and easy to detect in their programs.

5. *Iconic symbols.* The data base descriptions are printed out using characters which look almost like the description one would draw on a

blackboard because of the use of "arrows" to print them out. This same notation is used in the students' own programs, e.g.

NOTE FIDO---ISA---> DOG

(Incidentally, the arrows may be omitted by the user on input. SOLO-82 supplies them as soon as the space bar is pressed. Micro-SOLO displays them in advance, as a template to be filled in. SOLO-78 and E-SOLO supply the arrows when procedures are LISTed).

The symbol used to delimit parameters is a slash, e.g. /X/, which helps to remind the students of the "slot"-like role played by parameters. The analogy of "slot" is used in the primer for the language (Section 5 discusses other issues specific to the SOLO curriculum).

6. *Distinct symbols for distinct usage.* X, "X", /X/, ?X and *X have the following meanings:

X can only be the name of a node.
"X" can only be a character string, and it can only appear as an argument of PRINT.
/X/ can only be a formal parameter of a user-defined procedure.
?X can only be an unbound variable awaiting a successful pattern-match.
*X can only be a variable bound as the result of a successful pattern-match.

These distinctions definitely win on the "consistency" issue mentioned earlier, but may lose on the "convenience" issue because students can type the wrong symbol by mistake. The context is often sufficient to determine the students' true intent, so it is up to the environment (user-aids) to cope with mundane lexical and syntactic mistakes. From the standpoint of the language alone, we feel that the use of these distinct conventions helps to clarify the different roles that X may be playing in different contexts.

7. *Entirely non-numerical.* The entire language is geared towards data base manipulation—this is not an add-on feature. This is particularly useful for those students who feel uneasy about their mathematical skills.

8. *Small number of primitives.* SOLO-78 has only 10 primitives. This reduces the cognitive load for the beginner. For those who still have trouble remembering, the entire language is neatly summarized on the back cover of the primer.

9. *Uniform syntax.* The four "workhorse" primitives (NOTE, FORGET, CHECK, FOR EACH) share the same syntax (i.e. node---

relation---> node). Of the others, only TO has an idiosyncratic syntax, i.e. TO procedure-name (optional parameters).

10. *Encourages top-down programming style.* Since SOLO is interpreted, special forward declarations are not necessary for procedures which have yet to be defined. The student is encouraged simply to put in the names of such procedures when they are needed, then define them later.

11. *Forced modularity.* By restricting SOLO-78 procedures to 10 main steps, students are forced to break problems into manageable sub-problems, and to define sub-procedures to deal with each of the sub-problems.

The number 10 is somewhat arbitrary, however, and students can have trouble keeping track of the hierarchy of subroutine calls which result from this restriction. Even so, we feel that this restriction is still generally useful. Micro-SOLO users are encouraged, but not forced, to keep procedure lengths down to less than one screenful (which turns out to be 20 lines).

Modularity is also imposed by allowing students only one action on each branch of a conditional – this must be a subroutine call if more than one action is desired.

12. *No backward jumps allowed.* SOLO imposes a weak form of structuring on students' programs by encouraging the use of FOR EACH loops and outlawing general GOTOs. Some of our students (those who have used BASIC) complain about this, but most of them find the flow of control very easy to specify. The one exception to this is the difficulty of exiting a loop after *precisely* n iterations. This is only difficult because SOLO deliberately has no numerical primitives. Students can add their own "counting" nodes into the data base, but this is cumbersome, so we have considered adding counting primitives for the students' benefit.

A restricted form of GOTO is allowed by means of the CONTINUE control-statement on conditional branches. This feature is discussed under point 14 below.

13. *Imperative-style conditionals.* We adopted an imperative-style construction for conditionals using

```
CHECK node---relation---> node
```

instead of

```
IF PRESENT (node---relation---> node)
```

This is analogous to the use of TEST in some dialects of LOGO, e.g. TEST A = B rather than IF A = B. The virtue of this style is that it allows beginners to experiment with conditional tests at the top level of the interpreter. Students can just type in such tests and have the results ("PRESENT" or "ABSENT") immediately displayed. An additional bonus for SOLO users is that the syntax for CHECK is the same as that for NOTE and FORGET.

When students begin entering conditional clauses into their own procedures, they can continue using the *same* construct, but now they get prompted directly for the extra lines which constitute the "then" and "else" branches of the conditional clause (in our case these are called "if present" and "if absent"). The fact that the prompting and indenting are done automatically is obviously an environment feature rather than a language feature, but the point here is that it is the language feature (imperative style) which makes the environment feature (automatic prompting and indenting) possible, and thus minimizes the burden of having to remember a special syntax for conditional clauses.

14. *Obligatory "then" and "else" branches on conditional clauses.* Students must specify what action is to be taken on each branch of a conditional (this includes "no action", of course). This forces students to be clear about the intended effects of their procedures, since they must always think about the case they *weren't* catering for (i.e. "what do you do just in case that relational triple is absent from the data base, unlikely as that may be?"). This feature, combined with those described in 15 and 16 below, make the flow of control in student-defined procedures exceptionally clear.

15. *Annotated conditional branches.* The labelling of SOLO's conditional clauses with "if present" and "if absent" provides an unambiguous annotation which greatly simplifies the task of program design and debugging. The provision of an (albeit simple) annotation was influenced by the work of Sime, Green, and Guest (1973), who found that explicitly labelled conditional clauses, such as the one shown below, were easier to write, easier to understand, and less error-prone than Algol-style conditional clauses.

IF LEAFY
    THEN BOIL
NOT LEAFY
    FRY
END LEAFY

The point here is that "NOT LEAFY" (like SOLO's "if absent") is much more explicit than "else" would be, as it reminds the programmer of precisely the circumstance in which "FRY" will occur.

16. *Obligatory flow-of-control specification on conditional branches.* After specifying some action (or no action) to occur on each branch of a conditional clause, students must add flow-of-control information in the form of "EXIT" (analogous to "RETURN" in FORTRAN or BASIC) or "CONTINUE" (which means continue with the next main step). This forces students to think clearly about what should be happening next in their programs, and help them to avoid the classic "falling through conditional" bug which plagues most beginners. This construct is to some extent an artifact of our desire to stick to line-at-a-time procedure entry and editing. Yet in the hundreds of student programs we have looked at, we have never seen an example of the standard beginner's flow-of-control error illustrated by the BASIC and LOGO programs below (line 20 is always executed, but the intent is to have it executed only when A=B).

BASIC:

```
10 IF A=B THEN PRINT "YES"
20 PRINT "BOO"
```

LOGO:

```
10 TEST A=B
15 IFTRUE PRINT "YES"
20 PRINT "BOO"
```

With the exception of SOLO-78, all versions of SOLO now have primitive tests for equality which use automatic prompting and indenting conventions analogous to those of CHECK. Thus, the previous BASIC and LOGO examples would look like this in SOLO-82:

10 TEST *A = *B
  10A If yes: PRINT "YES"; EXIT
  10B If no: PRINT "BOO"; EXIT

4. THE ENVIRONMENT

In order to make SOLO a relatively painless experience for novices, a great deal of effort was put into the total software environment within which these novices would be working. The important features of this environment are most easily illustrated by example. The example below is contrived to illustrate a large number of features in a short space, but is otherwise authentic, in that it will run as shown using SOLO-78. The example depicts a student logging in and adding a few nodes and relations to the data base, then trying to define the procedure ASSESS which was illustrated earlier during the discussion of the SOLO primitive "TO". Student input is shown *ITALICISED LIKE THIS*. The numbers at the left refer to the environment features which are discussed following the example. As you read through the example, keep in mind the profile of the Open University students taking the course, as described in Section 2 earlier. These are students who may have never even used a typewriter before.

1. *LOGIN D303 AI 1010*
   Good evening.
   Welcome to SOLO.
2. Student Number Please: *CO123865*
   Messages
   \------------
   Type
   HELP
   for advice. Be sure to press the "RETURN" key after every line you type.
3. Do you want a typing lesson? (YES or NO): *NO*
   SOLO: *NOTE JOHN ISA PERSON*
   OK...
   JOHN
   |---ISA--->PERSON
   SOLO: *NTE JOHN VOTES LIBERAL*
4. (NTE = NOTE)
   OK...
   JOHN
   |---ISA--->PERSON
   |---VOTES--->LIBERAL
   SOLO: *TO ASSESS /X/*
   :10CHECK /X/ VOTES LIBRAL
   (10CHECK = 10 CHECK)
5. When you typed "LIBRAL" did you mean "LIBERAL" (YES OR NO): *Y*
6. ..... 10A If present: *PRAISE /X/*
7. (Please specify EXIT or CONTINUE after the ";" below)
   ..... 10A If present: PRAISE /X/; *EXIT*
   ..... 10B If absent: *CONDEMN /X/; CONTINUE*
   ..... : *10A*
8. ..... 10A If present: *PRAISE /X/; CONTINUE*
   ..... : *20 PRINT THAT'S ALL I HAVE TO SAY ABOUT" /X/*
   (Left hand quotes assumed)
   ... : *BYE*

9. (BYE interpreted as DONE)
OK . . . I now know how to 'ASSESS' /X/
SOLO: *LIST ASSESS*
10. TO ASSESS /X/
10 CHECK /X/---VOTES ---> LIBERAL
10A If present: PRAISE /X/; CONTINUE
10B If absent: CONDEMN /X/; CONTINUE
20 PRINT "THAT'S ALL I HAVE TO SAY ABOUT" /X/
DONE
SOLO: *ASSESS MARY*
Oops . . . I don't have a procedure called 'CONDEMN'
11. SOLO: *HELP*
You've tried to use a procedure without first having defined it (see pp. 37–39 of Units 3–4 for how to do this, or else type HELP PROCEDURES). By the way, this error may simply have been caused by a spelling mistake!
12. SOLO: *SOS*
(Tutor being informed, please wait) . . .
[LINK from EISENSTADT (Advising)]
(talk): Hi, what's the problem?
(talk): *I'M WORKING ON THE 'ASSESS' EXAMPLE, AND CAN'T FIGURE OUT WHAT THE DEFINITION OF 'CONDEMN' SHOULD BE*
(talk): You're free to define your own version. If you would feel happier modifying an existing version, then you can copy mine, and edit it later. When you see the SOLO: prompt, type in COPY CONDEMN TUTORME1. Then you can LIST CONDEMN or EDIT CONDEMN, just like any other procedure.
(talk): *OK, THANKS*
(talk): See you
[Advice terminated]
13. SOLO: *COPY CONDEMN TUTORME1*
SOLO: *LIST CONDEMN*
TO CONDEMN /X/
10 PRINT /X/ "IS EVIL"
20 PRINT "EVERYONE DISLIKES" /X/
DONE
SOLO: *EDIT CONDEMN*
. . . . : *20 NOTE /X/ THINKS FUNNY*
. . . . : *DONE*
OK . . . I have re-defined how to 'CONDEMN' /X/
14. SOLO: *HELP OPTIONS*
Hold down the "CTRL" key and press the letter "O" to suppress the detailed description of available options.

Here are the options you are allowed to request (a "+" below means that this option is in effect by "default" when you initially log in to SOLO):
(Options related to spelling correction):
SPELL (+) Enables any misspellings of procedure-names to be automatically corrected.
NOSPELL (−) Completely disables spelling corrector, thereby eliminating the next 4 options shown.
TRUSTING (+) Performs most corrections without asking approval.
^*O* . . .
Type option here: *TRACE*
Do you want to select any more options (Yes or No): *NO*

15. SOLO: *ASSESS MARY*

```
(ASSESS)
  10
  10B
    (CONDEMN)
      10
MARY IS EVIL
      20
OK . . .
MARY
  |---THINKS---FUNNY
  20
THAT'S ALL I HAVE TO SAY ABOUT MARY
SOLO: BYE
```

16. Goodbye

Features of the SOLO environment which should be of interest to designers of software environments for novice programmers are listed below. The numbers correspond to the numbers on the left hand side of the sample interaction presented above.

1. *Login trap.* Timesharing users are automatically connected to SOLO upon logging in, to minimize their interactions with other systems/monitors which are totally irrelevant to their coursework. This gives them the illusion of interacting entirely with a SOLO machine, which is consistent with the way SOLO is taught.

Micro-SOLO achieves the same effect through an auto-start bootstrap facility which takes effect as soon as the power is switched on.

2. *Personalized environment.* We maintain a separate data base for each student. This helps to reinforce the idea of a personalized SOLO

machine, and encourages experimentation with changes to the data base. From the user's point of view, SOLO has an infinitely large memory, and all procedure definitions and changes to the data base are permanently stored (automatically).

3a. *Typing lesson for first time users.* Interaction via a QWERTY keyboard can be a daunting task in itself, so SOLO-78 provides a separate typing lesson for our novices. In the example shown, the user chooses to bypass the lesson. Both the typing lesson and this (possibly annoying) question are removed after the first few sessions.

3b. *Visible workings of inner machine.* The effect of any change to the data base is displayed to the user the instant that it occurs. This minimizes the possibility of hidden surprises. Experienced users can easily disable this capability.

4. *Automatic spelling correction of obvious errors.* "Obvious" refers to near-misses of procedure names, since any given student defines very few procedures. The spelling correction algorithm is a slightly modified version of the algorithm outlined in Teitelman (1978).

5. *User confirmation of tricky spelling cases.* Node names and relation names are considered "tricky", since users can have hundreds of them, and many of them differ by only one or two characters. Any near-miss results in a request for confirmation from the user.

6. and 7. *Automatic prompting and indenting for both branches of conditional clauses.* The rationale behind the conditional clause construct was discussed in section 3 as a language feature. The important aspect of the user environment in this example is the way in which it forces the student to specify some action on each branch of the conditional. Also it eliminates the need for the user to remember the idiosyncratic syntax. This feature provides an elementary syntax-directed editing capability for users with access only to hard-copy terminals.

8. *Inviolability of complex syntax by later editing.* In this example, the user has completely eliminated line 10A. Since both branches of the conditional clause are mandatory, the user is instantly re-prompted for the "then" branch of the conditional, as shown. Thus, there is no way to destroy the integrity of a multi-line clause such as 10–10A–10B, even by editing the three lines separately. This principle extends to such things as students typing in "10A if absent", which is detected as an anomaly, since all "A" sub-lines must be "if present" branches. The Micro-SOLO screen

editor imposes similar constraints, prohibiting the deletion of obligatory sub-lines.

9. *Interpretation of appropriate intentions, given the surrounding context.* This capability is very difficult to achieve in general. There are many cases, however, where the current state of the machine provides strong constraints on what the user must have meant. In this example, "BYE" only makes sense in the context of a top-level "SOLO" prompt. Given an edit-level ". . . . :" prompt, "DONE" is a more natural interpretation, so this is imposed on the user.

10. *Normalized output (prettyprinting).* Automatic indenting of the user's code on printout is an obvious benefit. SOLO-78 and E-SOLO provide a normalized version of the node---relation---> node "arrows" (on output) to help reinforce the idea of a relational data base, and to make the user's code easier to read. The user is not, however, required to include these arrows on input. In SOLO-82 and Micro-SOLO the arrows are supplied automatically during user input, so that "what you see is what you get".

11. *HELP facilities.* If a user types HELP immediately following an error message, an expanded version of that message appears. If there is no immediately preceding error message, a general index of available HELP facilities is printed. HELP followed by a keyword gives specialized advice related to that keyword. The keyword OPTIONS is explained below (14).

12. *On-Line (human) tutorial aid.* We experimented with a "talk" facility (using the DECsystem-20's LINK and ADVISE capabilities). If students typed "SOS", then a bell rang on the terminal of one of the tutors (provided that an appropriately designated tutor was logged in). This facility was only available in SOLO-78. Some students found it valuable, although communicating in this fashion was somewhat slow. It was mainly useful as a source of data about tutorial dialogues. Interestingly, when students were given the choice of explaining their problems in English vs. demonstrating them in SOLO, they typically chose English, but then had to revert to demonstrations (at the tutor's request) when they had difficulty articulating their problems clearly in English. This has led us to the view that automated debugging assistants and programmer's apprentices (e.g. Ruth, 1976; Waters, 1982) should definitely not attempt to process natural language input from the user.

13. *Ability to share code with other students.* SOLO-78 users could copy code from other students or tutors at summer school. Students

appreciated the virtues of copying to enhance group problem solving activities, and did not worry about the security or privacy of their programs. Some students used this capability to devise an "underground" mailbox utility.

14. *Options for users to modify the environment.* SOLO-78 users were able to select from a variety of options, which altered certain aspects of the environment. For instance, students could suppress the "visible machine" principle, by selecting the option "SILENCE"; they could switch off the spelling corrector by typing "NOSPELL"; and so on. We felt that these options should be embedded within a separate facility (the "HELP OPTIONS" facility) rather than directly accessible within SOLO, because options like SILENCE do something fundamentally different from SOLO primitives like NOTE and CHECK. Unfortunately, the HELP OPTIONS interaction of SOLO-78 was clumsy. An investigation of transcripts of a large sample of user interactions (see Chapter 5 and Lewis, 1980) revealed that some of the options, e.g. TRUSTING and CAUTIOUS (which fine-tuned the spelling corrector) were never used.

Later dialects of SOLO use the primitives ENABLE and DISABLE, so that students can type in ENABLE TRACE or DISABLE SPELL, etc. The keywords ENABLE and DISABLE still demarcate the special nature of the TRACE and SPELL facilities to which they are applied, but are conveniently accessible from within SOLO. This use of fundamentally distinct features of the environment violates some aspects of the guiding principle of consistency. However, this does not appear to hamper students' understanding if the feature is consistent within itself, and is explained and defined as being a different entity from the SOLO machine.

15. *Tracing of user-defined procedures.* Tracing facilities are important debugging tools. SOLO-78's tracing facility just shows the name of each procedure as it is entered, and each step number as it is executed. Sub-step numbers (such as "10B") indicate the outcome of the enclosing CHECK (B always indicates that the "absent" branch was taken). Students found even this simple SOLO-78 trace quite useful, E-SOLO's trace includes parameter-passing details and a single-step facility to clarify further the inner workings of the SOLO machine. An intelligent "skimmer" which analyzes buggy SOLO programs is described in Chapter 10.

16. *Automatic filing facilities.* All procedure definitions and changes to the data base are permanently stored when the user logs out. Upon the next login, everything is exactly the same as when the user last typed "BYE". If necessary, the data base can be cleaned up with the aid of the HELP OPTIONS. All filing details are dealt with behind the scenes, so the

beginner doesn't have to bother with "DISKOUT" or "SAVE" operations.

5. THE CURRICULUM

Students are given a primer/workbook (Eisenstadt, 1978) to introduce them to SOLO. The layout, contents, and sequencing of the primer each contribute to the overall "SOLO experience". Here are the features of the primer which could be of most benefit to designers of curriculum material to accompany other programming languages:

1. *Clear objectives.* The objectives shown earlier in this paper (section 2) are laid out for the students' benefit in a study guide at the very beginning of the primer. This ensures that students have an idea of what they are expected to achieve, and gives them a way of assessing their own progress on a long-term scale (two weeks, in this case). Progress on individual parts of the booklet is more easily ascertained by means of self-assessment questions, with answers provided at the back of the primer.

2. *Highly motivating and obviously relevant "entry point".* Traditional curriculum sequences, involving simple examples such as PRINT "HELLO" or PRINT (3 + 4), followed by variable assignment, control flow, list structures, etc., are so unrewarding for most students as to be hardly worthy of comment. Our students begin by experimenting with assertional data base and pattern matching examples. These are couched in terms of elementary models of human memory, which are directly relevant to the students' main academic interest. It is undoubtedly important for students to be able to do something powerful and exciting during the first session at a computer terminal. Turtle geometry is an example of one such activity which has been used successfully as an entry point into computing for school children (Papert, 1980). We believe that alternative entry points need to be explored, with an eye towards arousing the interest of students whose primary motivation comes from their dedication to some other discipline. Data base manipulation is one of many possibilities. Others include word processing, music synthesis, games, and laboratory simulation.

3. *Warmth without condescension.* The need to make the material non-threatening had to be balanced against the fact that the students were working adults paying hard-earned money to take an intensive course. Hand-written or cartoon-style presentations, which work well with children learning about computers, were unacceptable to our target population. The solution was to present the material in a totally serious vein, but

FIG. 1.1. FIDO.

to provide lots of hand-holding commentary for clarification, and the occasional "cuddly dog" drawing in the margin for atmosphere (see Fig. 1.1). The dog became an instant cult hero among the students, some of whom have now established a thriving Fido T-shirt business!

4. *Consistent metaphorical description of virtual machine.* Following duBoulay, O'Shea and Monk (1981) we chose a single metaphor for describing the working of the SOLO machine (a pool of autonomous "experts" waiting to be "activated" and going to work on something like a huge telephone directory). The important point here is the use of a single metaphor and a single technical term for each concept in the primer (e.g. "slot" is used as a metaphor for "parameter"). This is a difficult rule to adhere to, and we discovered some exceptions after the SOLO primer went into print. However, students seem to appreciate the clarity which results from minimizing the proliferation of metaphors and technical terms.

5. *Use of nonsense words in examples.* Beginners often attribute too much intelligence to the machine with which they are working. For instance, students tend to believe that "WORKSFOR" has some meaning

in the triple JOHN---WORKSFOR---> FRED. The primer emphasizes that "WORKSFOR" only derives its meaning from the procedures which students define, and drives home this point by working through several examples based on nonsense triples, e.g. NOTE FOO---BAZ---> GORT, CHECK FOO---BAZ--->?, etc. Future editions of the primer could rely even more on nonsense examples, since some students insist on imparting deep significance to English-like words in the database.

6. *Clearly demarcated "paper and pencil" vs. "terminal" activities.* The fashionable "try it" philosophy which has dominated some primers (e.g. Winston & Horn, 1984) is not necessarily the best way to teach all aspects of computing. Clearly, hands-on interactive exercises are very rewarding and are of utmost importance for novices, but it is important to distinguish visibly between those activities which are meant to be done while sitting at the computer and those activities which can (or should) be done using paper and pencil. Our primer highlights "study centre (computer terminal) activities" with a wide green stripe along the border of the page.

7. *Delineation of primer and reference manual functions.* Many programming instruction manuals fail to distinguish between the role of a primer and that of a reference manual. A primer provides a step-by-step introduction, while a reference manual should provide a quick answer to a specific question. The SOLO self-instruction manual is first and foremost a primer. Because of the simplicity of SOLO, the requirements of a reference manual were easily met by having a readily accessible summary chart of SOLO printed on the back cover of the primer, with the most salient page references printed in a bold box.

8. *Signposting the student's progress.* One of the most difficult aspects of teaching computing to non-computer specialists is maintaining their interest throughout the entire curriculum. They soon get bored by the "fun" examples used in the introduction, and they don't possess enough expertise to be goaded on by the promise that they will be writing "recursive inference schemas". During the development testing (pilot) phase of our curriculum design, we found students complaining that they couldn't see why they were doing all these activities. A detailed rationale presented at the beginning was too abstract for students who had no programming background at all, and presenting the rationale at the end (when they could finally understand all the terminology) was no good because students would have given up before they got that far. To circumvent this problem, "progress boxes" were introduced throughout the primer. These boxes provide a summary of what the students have

done, *why* they have done it, and where they are headed with the new tools they have acquired. Early progress boxes motivate the students with promises of future achievements, concretely tied to one or two concepts they know, while later progress boxes get increasingly specific, referring to the development of skill in writing search and inference programs.

6. CONCLUSIONS

SOLO is very simple in conception, and provides a unique combination of attributes which make it ideal as a two-week introduction to computing for non-computer specialists. The special features of the language, environment, and curriculum which have paid high dividends for Open University students are summarized below:

Language
Simple virtual machine
Consistent use of virtual machine
Powerful mnemonics
Not English-like
Iconic symbols
Distinct symbols for distinct usage
Entirely non-numerical
Small number of primitives
Uniform syntax
Encourages top-down programming style
Forced modularity
No backward jumps allowed
Imperative-style conditionals
Obligatory "then" and "else" branches
Annotated conditional branches
Obligatory flow of control specification

Environment
Login trap
Personalized environment
Typing lesson for first time users
Visible workings of inner machine
Automatic spelling correction of obvious errors
User confirmation of tricky spelling cases
Automatic prompting and indenting for both branches of conditional clauses
Forced explicitness with respect to flow of control
Inviolability of complex syntax by later editing

Interpretation of appropriate intentions, giving the surrounding context
Help facilities
On-line (human) tutorial aid
Ability to share code with other students
Ability for users to modify the environment
Tracing of user-defined procedures
Automatic filing facilities

Curriculum
Clear objectives
Highly motivating and obviously relevant entry point
Warmth without condescension
Consistent metaphorical description of virtual machine
Use of nonsense words in examples
Clearly demarcated paper and pencil vs. terminal activities
Delineation of primer and reference manual functions
Signposting of students' progress

One of the main lessons of SOLO is that software designers hoping to have any significant impact on a large population of users must pay a great deal of attention to the interaction of the language, the environment, and the curriculum. A weakness in any of the three can seriously undermine an entire project. Perhaps the best known example of an attempt to tackle all three is UCSD-Pascal (Bowles, 1977). Bowles' project was a success because he took the problems of language, environment, and curriculum quite seriously, and was unwilling to compromise in developing an entire package.

A similar uncompromising attitude has characterised the whole development cycle underlying SOLO. The constraints imposed by the combination of distance-teaching, an audience of social science students, the lack of formal prerequisites, and a two-week project timescale (for students) led my computer science colleagues around the globe to claim that the idea was unworkable from the start.

Yet our students acquired a demonstrable competence at writing programs which illustrated the concepts mentioned in section 1. Part of the secret of this success is the iterative cycle of empirical observation and ensuing refinement of language, environment, and curriculum. Our pilot students could cope with an English-like language, but found it involved too much typing, and in addition they suffered from lack of motivation. The motivation problem was tackled by modifying the primer to include examples of obvious relevance to the course at the very beginning, and the language was trimmed down to minimize typing. An in-depth study of SOLO-78 users, reported in Chapter 5 (see also Lewis, 1980) revealed an overzealous spelling corrector and hard-to-use HELP and TRACE facilities. These in turn were streamlined for later implementations of SOLO.

One of the most difficult issues over the years has been a very delicate balance between the principle of consistency, discussed in section 3, and the need to provide intelligent (albeit slightly magical) correction of user errors, so as not to burden them with needless retyping of silly mistakes. Intelligent error correction leads one to sacrifice consistency in favour of convenience. Although convenience often makes things easier in the short term, it can confuse things in the long term, especially if the student mistakenly attributes cleverness to simple cosmetics. A glaring example of this in SOLO is the use of the word "TO", which was chosen on cosmetic grounds, it seemed both convenient and cute, and LOGO had used it with apparent success for years. Nevertheless, the word "DEFINE" would have been more consistent. A modification of SOLO seems warranted as we have observed that students who use "TO" may begin thinking that all procedures must be verbs.

The issue of convenience is not to be totally ignored, however. We feel that when a user has typed something which makes his or her intentions obvious, even though the line may contain a minor error, intelligent user-aids should come to the rescue, rather than dogmatically forcing the user to re-type the offending line. Thus, E-SOLO deals with input lines such as:

SOLO: *FIDO ISA DOG*

by responding

DID YOU INTEND TO TYPE "NOTE FIDO ISA DOG"? (YES OR NO):

even though the most *consistent* response, in terms of the inner workings of the SOLO machine, would actually be

I DON'T HAVE A PROCEDURE CALLED "FIDO"

As long as the user realizes that an intelligent user-aid is distinct from the SOLO machine, it is in fact possible to achieve both consistency and convenience.

What about the drawbacks of SOLO? Its biggest strength, that it is tailor-made for a particular type of student working to a particular time-scale, turns out to be its biggest weakness. Just when students are happily constructing propositional representations and writing inference programs in SOLO, they begin to get frustrated by its limitations. They want to concatenate strings, perform arithmetic, work with n-tuples rather than triples, and so on. The exciting thing is that they develop many of these notions themselves. The frustrating thing is that SOLO cannot cater to their needs. An enhancement of the language, though technically feasible, is definitely *not* on the cards.

SOLO was designed to explore the possibility of taking students in very adverse circumstances and handing them a pleasant and moderately powerful computing environment on a silver platter to see if they could quickly learn some elementary computing concepts with a minimum of fuss. Now that this has been shown to be possible, we have taken the next logical step of applying the lessons learned from SOLO to the development of a two-week introduction to a more widely available language. In recent years, we have adopted the AI language PROLOG in our courses (see also Chapter 3).

SOLO has proven to be a very useful testbed, and its simple semantics has been ideal for the development of automated debugging aids and programmers' apprentice tools for novices, which are described elsewhere (see Chapters 9 and 10). If nothing else, it has shown that the intensive development of a language, its surrounding environment, and curriculum materials, coupled with an active series of empirical investigations, can be of tremendous benefit in developing a practical and successful software product for use by large numbers of computer-naive students.

REFERENCES

duBoulay, J. B. H., O'Shea, T., & Monk, J. (1981). The black box inside the glass box: Presenting computing concepts to novices. *International Journal of Man-Machine Studies*, *14*, 237–249.

Bowles, K. (1977). *Microcomputer problem solving using Pascal.* New York: Springer.

Brinch-Hansen, P. (1977). *The architecture of concurrent programs.* Englewood-Cliffs, New Jersey: Prentice-Hall.

Dwyer, T. & Critchfield, M. (1981). Multi-computer systems for the support of inventive learning. In P. R. Smith (Ed.), *Computer assisted learning: Selected papers for CAL'81 Symposium.* Oxford: Pergamon Press.

Eisenstadt, M. (1978). Artificial intelligence project, Units 3/4 of *Cognitive Psychology: A Third Level Course.* Milton Keynes: Open University Press.

Eisenstadt, M. & Gawronski, A. (1987). Micro-SOLO: A tool for elementary AI programming. In A. Jones, E. Scanlon & T. O'Shea, (Eds), *The computer revolution in education: New technologies for distance teaching.* Hassocks, Sussex: Harvester Press.

Lewis, M. W. (1980). Improving SOLO's user-interface: An empirical study of user behaviour and a proposal for cost effective enhancement. *Technical Report No. 7*, Computer Assisted Learning Research Group, The Open University, Milton Keynes, England.

Norman, D. A. & Rumelhart, D. E. & LNR Research Group (1975). *Explorations in Cognition.* San Francisco: Freeman.

Papert, S. (1980). *Mindstorms: Children, computers, and powerful ideas.* Harvester Press, Brighton, England.

Ruth, G. R. (1976). Intelligent program analysis. *Artificial Intelligence*, *7*, 65–85.

Sime, M. E., Green, T. R. G., & Guest, D. J. (1973). Psychological evaluation of two conditional constructions in computer languages. *International Journal of Man-Machine Studies*, *5*, 123–143.

Teitelman, W. (Ed.) (1978). *INTERLISP reference manual*. Palo Alto, CA: Xerox Palo Alto Research Center.

Teitelbaum, T. & Reps, T. (1981). The Cornell program synthesizer: A syntax-directed programming environment. *Communications of the ACM*, *24*, *9*, 563–573.

Waters, R. C. (1982). The Programmer's Apprentice: Knowledge Based Program Editing *IEEE Trans. on Software Eng. SE-8*, 1–12.

Winston, P. H. & Horn, B. K. P. (1984). *LISP*, Second Edition. Reading, MA: Addison-Wesley.

2 Principles for the Design of Dynamic Tracing Environments for Novice Programmers*

Tim Rajan
Performance Technology, Lloyd's Register, Croydon, England

OVERVIEW

This chapter describes the principled design of a computational environment which depicts an animated story of the execution of programs for novice programmers. The design principles are aimed at solving the problems that novice programmers face when learning new programming languages, and are embodied in an Animated Program Tracer (APT) for Prolog. The goal of this research is to develop a more systematic, if not yet scientific, basis for the design of animated tracing tools.

1. INTRODUCTION: THE PROGRAMMING BEHAVIOUR OF NOVICES

In most programming courses novices are introduced to concepts using traditional methods of a blackboard, or paper and pencil. Dynamic programming concepts are normally introduced either as abstract theories or by analogy to non-programming ideas. Some concepts such as the stack, the linked list, the arrays are usually taught with the aid of static graphic tools (e.g. matrices, lists and pointers). However, the programming concepts which have a dynamic nature (i.e. recursion, iteration, variable binding, flow of control, parameter passing, and search methods) are more difficult to represent using static graphics, or even "snapshot sequences", as their action is not easily conveyed with fixed images. The shortcomings of using static teaching aids to represent recursion and backtracking can be seen in many books on programming (Bratko, 1986; Clocksin & Mellish, 1981;

*This research was supported by a grant from the Open University and carried out in the Human Cognition Research Laboratory.

Hasemer, 1984; Touretzky, 1984; Winston & Horn, 1981, 1984). As we shall see from the review in the remainder of this section, there is also a growing body of research demonstrating the problems that novices have learning dynamic programming concepts (Anderson, Farrell, & Sauers, 1984a; Brooks, 1977; Eisenstadt, Breuker, & Evertsz, 1984; Kahney, 1982; Rajan, 1985, 1986; Sime, Green, & Guest, 1973; Soloway, Ehrlich, Bonar, & Greenspan, 1982; Taylor & duBoulay, 1987; van Someren, 1984, 1985; Waters, 1979).

1.1 Understanding Programs

In developing a system to understand and debug simple Pascal programs, Lukey (1980, p. 189) defines what it is to understand a program:

> Before designing a mechanism to understand programs, one must first decide what it is that constitutes an understanding of a program. This is a very difficult problem. The theory views the understanding of a program as the construction of descriptions of the program. These descriptions should indicate what the program does and how the program does it.

Although this description of program understanding is aimed at machine understanding, I believe it to be equally relevant to human understanding.

Studies of the knowledge held by expert and novice programmers (Soloway et al. 1982; Soloway & Erhlich, 1984) shed some light on how this program understanding might take place, and show the gap that exists between experts' understanding of programs and that of novices (see Chapter 8 for some further tests of these ideas).

Soloway et al. state that experts possess two types of programming knowledge, (i) "Programming Plans", and (ii) "Rules of Programming Discourse", while novice programmers have no such high-level knowledge. The first of these consists of "program fragments that represent stereotypic action sequences in programming", such as a running counter plan. This suggests that experts hold a library of program fragments which they draw upon when developing a program. The second type of knowledge concerns "rules that specify the conventions in programming", which "set up expectations in the minds of the programmers about what should be in the program". An example of a discourse rule is to use a variable name that corresponds to its function. It is these programming plans and discourse rules that experts possess that enable them to understand programs, and that novices need in order to increase their understanding of programming.

Lukey's description of program understanding essentially suggests that a novice must build up a description of the execution of the program in terms of what the program does, and how it does it.

1.2 The Model of the Language Presented to the User

The ideas mentioned above resemble closely that of a "mental model" which several researchers believe novices build when learning to program. duBoulay et al. (1981) present the concept of the "notional machine", which they describe as, "the idealized model of the computer implied by the constructs of the programming language". Norman's (1983) "system image" is essentially the same idea. This "notional machine" consists of every aspect of the computing interface that the user comes into contact with, which relates information concerning the action of the programming language. This includes the user guide, the programming language, and the programming environment on the computer, but not the hardware of the computer. In other words, the "notional machine" consists of a model of the execution of a programming language, from which the user attempts to determine how the language works and thus build their mental model of execution for the programming language they are learning.

The descriptive level at which the notional machine is presented to the user is not specified by Norman or duBoulay et al. This description could be at several different levels each of which would constitute a "notional machine". For example, a programming language may be described in terms of (i) the language it is implemented in; (ii) the programming language itself; or (iii) an analogy. Each of these descriptions will tell a different story of program execution, so care must be taken when interpreting the phrase "notional machine". For the purposes of this chapter, "notional machine" should be interpreted as a description of how a programming language executes, presented at the same cognitive level at which the language is portrayed in programming texts.

1.3 The Effect of Presenting the User with a "Notional Machine"

There is evidence to support the usefulness of presenting novices with a "notional machine" from which they may build up a mental model of program execution. Mayer (1976; 1981) conducted experiments which showed that when novices were given a description of a programming language's "notional machine", they learned to program more effectively than those who had no such aid. The description given to subjects consisted of a four foot diagram which made visible the basic operations of the computer to the subject, plus a one page description. This model presented a concrete analogy for the four major functional units of the computer, (Mayer, 1981: p. 128):

> (1) Input is represented as a ticket window at which data are lined up waiting to be processed and placed in the finished pile after being processed; (2)

output is represented as a message note pad with one message written per line; (3) memory is represented as an erasable scoreboard in which there is natural destructive read-in and non-destructive read-out; (4) executive control is represented as a recipe or shopping list with a pointer arrow to indicate the line being executed.

The model of the computer presented by Mayer is a static picture of the computer, which attempts to portray the dynamic actions at run time. Although this model improves the performance of novice programmers, it does not tell us which is the best way to portray the notional machine for novices to assimilate an understanding of the concepts of computer programming.

1.4 Concrete Examples

In studying how novices build up their mental representation of program execution, Jones (1984a: p. 777) states that "A particular problem for novices learning their first programming language, therefore, is the lack of an appropriate cognitive framework which will serve to relate new information to existing knowledge."

She shows how ideas such as the "notional machine" attempt to provide such a framework for novices to build on. Through experiments with novices learning SOLO (see Chapter 1 for an account of the language) Jones concludes that novices often build inaccurate models of program execution even when presented with the "notional machine". Jones (1984a: p. 782) states, "For example, subjects spontaneously use their own metaphors to relate new information to existing knowledge, and as we have seen, this can lead to inappropriate expectations."

Jones reports that novices have difficulty understanding the actions of the computer in executing control statements and procedure calls. This affects both their ability to write programs and their understanding of programs when they are run.

One pointer which Jones' data gives towards improving novice performance in learning to program, is that "although novices do not find it easy to abstract plans from examples that are given, programming success seems to be dependent upon doing so". It seems therefore, that it is important to present novices with concrete program examples which embody these abstract plans. The "notional machine" should be capable of presenting the abstract plans (algorithms) mentioned above in a concrete fashion. In order for the "notional machine" to present an algorithm successfully the novice must have a dynamic view of the algorithm in action. Anything less will cause misconceptions in the user's conceptual model due to the lack of detail, and mismatch between the dynamic concept and the static presentation.

1.5 Novice vs. Expert Debugging Strategies

Research looking at how novice and skilled programmers differ in their ability to debug programs (Gugerty & Olson, 1986) shows that there are differences in the strategies that each group use. In this study, both groups studied buggy programs intensively before any action was taken, the novices doing the same things as the skilled programmers. One difference between the two groups was that the novices took longer in studying the programs than did the experts. Another difference between the groups occurred in the way they attempted to solve the bugs in the programs. The novices seldom found the bug in their first attempt at changing the program, and often added bugs. The experts, on the other hand, usually found the bug at the first attempt, and almost never added bugs to the program.

According to Gugerty and Olson, the reason novices had such difficulty in correcting the buggy programs was that they generated inferior hypotheses about the behaviour of the program, and it was these that led the novices to make unnecessary changes to the program rather than to correct the original bug. The reason given for the experts' superiority in debugging programs was the "ease with which they understood what the program does and what it is supposed to do". Conversely novices did not possess sufficient programming knowledge to generate a good hypothesis for the program's behaviour. In other words, the novice did not comprehend the program whilst the expert did.

This evidence supports the research described earlier which suggests that the main obstacle novices find when learning a programming language is assimilating a model of the "notional machine". The lack of this model of how the system works is made apparent in the experimental findings of Gugerty and Olson where the lack of comprehension of program behaviour causes novices problems in debugging programs.

1.6 The Effect of Analogies upon the User's Conceptual Model

This research has shown the importance to novices of building a conceptual model of the programming language, which will allow them to make predictions about the actions of that language. It has also shown that providing the novice with a "notional machine" on which to base this conceptual model facilitates the learning of that language. What we must do now is to determine how this "notional machine" should be presented to users so that they can build their conceptual model more efficiently.

It is generally thought that using metaphors and analogies is a useful way of introducing novices to programming (Carroll & Thomas, 1980; Rumelhart & Norman, 1981), and with the advent of the desktop metaphor increasingly used as the user-interface in today's computers, this approach seems very convincing. However there is research which shows the deficiencies of using metaphors and analogies in teaching complex concepts.

The argument in favour of analogies is described thus by Halasz and Moran (1982: p. 383):

> Given the analogy, the new user can draw upon his knowledge about the familiar situation in order to reason about the workings of the mysterious new computer system. For example, if the new user wants to understand about how the computer file system works, he need only think about how an office filing cabinet works and then carry over this same way of thinking to the computer file system.

But the problem with analogies is that because they are analogies the story they tell will only be accurate some of the time, and when an analogy is used to describe a complex system it will not be specific enough to guide the user to the actual operation of the system. Halasz and Moran also point out that analogies are bound to contain many aspects which are irrelevant to the system being learned, and they will also only cover a small part of that system (the more complex the system the less the analogy will cover). The problem here is that the novice will not know which part of the analogy to believe and which to ignore. This in turn is bound to lead to misconceptions in the model of the machine which the novice is building. For the novice, there is no reliable one-to-one mapping from any part of the analogy to any part of the domain being learned.

Instead of using an analogical model, Halasz and Morgan suggest that, "the appropriate basis for teaching about a computer system is an abstract conceptual model" which will "provide a specialised framework for reasoning about the system" (p. 383). In other words this means directly presenting users with the underlying conceptual structure of the system being learned so they have an appropriate basis for reasoning about the system they are learning.

1.7 Problems with the Presentation of the "Notional Machine"

The above approach, suggested by Halasz and Moran, is similar to the idea of presenting the "notional machine" or "system image" to the novice in an attempt to help them build a conceptual model of the programming language. However, the "notional machine" still poses a problem to novices. In its present form it provides the novice with a model of the programming language drawn from the programming environment, its commands and its manuals. It may be the case that, because the examples are presented in a static printed form, novices cannot appreciate the important dynamic features being exemplified. Trying to associate these static examples with actual running programs is not easy. If the examples were presented in a fashion more in accord with program execution the novices might well glean more information from them.

Although duBoulay et al. say that wherever possible methods should be provided for the learner to see the workings of the notional machine in action, the methods they discuss do not go far enough. Novices need to be presented with a detailed description of program execution displayed at the correct level, so they may associate the notional machine with actual running programs. As Halasz and Moran (1982) say, if users are provided with a framework around which to build a mental model of program execution, and this framework is presented in terms of the underlying conceptual structures of the system being learned, then they will have an appropriate basis for reasoning about that system.

1.8 Problems Encountered by Novice Programmers

There is a growing amount of research concerned with the specific problems novices have when learning a programming language. Over the years many ideas have been adopted to improve the performance of the programmer; however, most of these aids have been adopted without knowledge of whether or not they solve any of the problems that programmers face. Sheil (1981) in a review of the empirical research studying such user aids (e.g. prettyprinting, flowcharting, variable naming, specification of data types, and commenting of code) concluded that there is no evidence to show that any of these aids actually improve the performance of programmers. Where differences have been found between experimental conditions, Sheil comments that, "many of these effects tend to disappear with practice or experience. This raises some doubt as to whether these results reflect stable differences between notations or merely learning effects and other transients that would not be significant factors in actual programming performance" (p. 108). So what are the problems which novice programmers have and which these aids have attempted to solve?

Many other studies have been conducted to investigate the type of problems that novice programmers meet in their first few weeks of programming. There are several studies on the problems novices have with control flow statements (Mayer, 1976; Miller, 1974; Sime, Arblaster, & Green, 1979). Domingue (1985) reports similar errors to those mentioned above for novices learning Lisp. Others have reported the great problem that recursion causes novices (see Chapter 7; Anderson, Pirolli, & Farrell, 1984b; Pirolli & Anderson, 1985). In Chapter 7, Kahney shows that although many novices had some model of recursion, it was an incorrect model. Their models were sometimes based on a correct model of recursion, and other times based on something more akin to iteration. Some novices had no model of recursion at all. Soloway et al. (1982) have shown that novice programming errors are not only due to "difficulty with syntax and semantics" of the language, but also to problems in "determining which constructs to use and how to coordinate them into a unified whole" (see also Chapter 8). This shows that there are two separate problems facing novice programmers. The low level problem with the syntax and semantics of the programming language, and the higher level problem of constructing meaningful units, or program fragments, when programming.

In Chapter 5, some of the errors made by novice SOLO programmers are catalogued. Setting aside language-specific errors, the main categories listed are:

Flow of control: Flow of control statement used as an argument. inappropriate use of flow of control statement. Missing control flow statement.
Side effect. Attempting to assert into the data-base facts that already exist. Attempting to delete facts that do not exist.
Recursion. Infinite loops.
Procedure call. Too many/few arguments.
Variables. Non-unique variable names used as global variables.
Modes. Users assume that they are at the top-level when in the editor, and vice versa.

Most of these errors are dynamic in nature, in the sense that they are due to misconceptions of dynamic concepts. These errors only become apparent to novices at run time, as they lie hidden in the static environment of the editor. Likewise the misconceptions novices have of dynamic concepts lie hidden with the static teaching methods used in text books, on blackboards, and in most on-line tutorial packages that are available. One way to remove these misconceptions or even prevent them arising is to provide the novice with a dynamic environment in which to present the type of dynamic concepts which at present cause them problems.

1.9 Intermediate Conclusions

The studies discussed in the above section provide valuable information in the task of determining what novices need to smooth their path through the jungle of learning a programming language.

Drawing all the threads of this previous research together provides a clear vision of how to approach the problem novices face when learning a programming language. The novice needs to be provided with a basis for understanding how programs work, both at the level of syntax and semantics and how programming constructs are used in combination to build programs.

The traditional notional machine presents the novice with a static view of the programming language because it is based on text books or disparate tracing snapshots. In order to give the novice the information to understand the dynamic concepts, it is necessary to show the notional machine in action. They should be given a dynamic view of program execution which will enable them to build a mental model of the workings of the language.

This dynamic notional machine must not be an analogy of the system in question, but a direct view of the way in which the program is executed (cf. Halasz & Moran, 1982). This will provide an accurate story with which novices can build their mental model. Also the way in which this view is presented must enable users to see concrete examples of "programming plans" so that they can abstract out the way constructs are combined to produce a program.

An animated tracing tool that shows details of the execution of programs would provide the user with a dynamic notional machine. This would directly show what a program does, and how it does it. In other words, novices would have a basis for understanding the syntax and semantics of the programming language. This type of tool would also provide a means of presenting concrete examples of "programming plans" which should facilitate the novice programmer in determining how constructs are combined to form programs that embody abstract algorithms.

2. APPLYING THE RESEARCH TO TRACERS FOR PROLOG

So, one reason novices find programming concepts difficult to learn arises from the problem of associating the abstract nature of the description of a concept, to the structure and content of the programs they are attempting to write. In other words, the difficulty lies in translating the static abstract description of a hypothetical program or programming technique into the nuts and bolts of a particular syntax and set of commands which have a dynamic/run-time meaning. For example, recursion may be described as the referencing of a function from within that function, and presented as the execution of fresh copies of that function. However, in order to understand recursion the novice must, at the very least, map this description onto program code and generate a program.

For a novice to move from being presented with a theory of programming to the practice of writing programs requires a large mental leap. It is in fact a Catch-22 situation, as the novices need to understand dynamic programming concepts before they can write useful working programs, but on the other hand they will need some experience of using such concepts in simple working programs before they can build a mental model of program execution based upon concrete examples. Even the "viewing" tools provided by programming environments only present a snapshot of a program's execution, and so fall short of providing a concrete base on which the novice may build an understanding of how the program works.

Most of the existing tracers and single steppers do not explicitly show the surface evaluation of the code that the user has written (surface evaluation means the evaluation of the user's program in terms of the code in which that program is written) but a mixture of program output, the internal evaluation of the code, the code that the user has written, and in a format that is some variant of the internal representation of the user's code. Once again this presents novices with the problem of associating the trace with the program that they have written. How can novices understand the output of a program trace when it bears no resemblance to the program they have written? Catch-22 again! The novice requires a good model/story of program execution before they can have any chance of understanding the program trace. These traditional tracers provide no help to the novice who is trying to learn a programming language, with its myriad concepts. In fact, they are just an extra cognitive burden for the novice. To illustrate the dilemma we will consider a simple Prolog program, and the output when run through a traditional tracer (see Clocksin & Mellish, 1981; Bratko, 1986; for further details on Prolog).

Prolog uses a modified predicate logic notation to express facts, rules of inference, and queries. The following program contains three facts and one rule:

```
kisses(mary,john).
kisses(john,june).

has_flu(X):-
      kisses (Y,X),
      has_flu(Y).
has_flu(mary).
```

The program has the following intuitive meaning. The first two facts state that "mary kisses john", and that "john kisses june". The rule has both a declarative and a procedural meaning. Declaratively, the rule states "for all X, if Y kisses X and Y has flu, then X has flu". Procedurally, the rule means "to prove that somebody has flu", (1) show that that person kisses someone, and also (2) show that someone has the flu. Finally, the last fact states that "mary has flu". These rules and facts together form the Prolog data base.

All the symbols inside the brackets are arbitrary tokens, so that the last fact, for example, specified "has_flu" to be a unary predicate. Upper case letters, or words beginning with an upper case letter denote a variable, while those in lower case denote constants.

Queries are addressed to the Prolog interpreter as follows:

```
?- kisses(mary,john).
?- kisses(mary,X).
```

The first query asks, "is it true that mary kisses john?", and the second query, "is it true that mary kisses anyone?". In both cases, the interpreter searches sequentially for facts or rules which can be used to deduce the truth of the query expression. In the later case, the interpreter also shows the "binding" (pattern match) of the variable "X" to the first possible item it matches against in the data base. Further matches are produced by the interpreter if requested by the user, who types a semicolon to the "More?" prompt which appears after the variable binding/s.

Here is what happens if we run the above program using the standard "spy" trace package:

```
?-  has_flu(june).
**  (1) Call : has_flu(june)?
**  (2) Call : kisses(_1, june)?
**  (2) Exit : kisses(john, june)?
**  (3) Call : has_flu(john)?
**  (4) Call : kisses(_2, john)?
**  (4) Exit : kisses(mary, john)?
**  (5) Call : has_flu, mary)?
**  (6) Call : kisses(_3, mary)?
**  (6) Fail : kisses(_3, mary)?
**  (5) Exit : has_flu(mary)?
**  (3) Exit : has_fly(john)?
**  (1) Exit : has_flu(june)?
yes
?-
```

The main problem with the above stepped output is that it is difficult to relate to the original source code. This is because it is presented in a very different format to the Prolog program, making it difficult to associate the dynamic events occurring in the trace with the static representation of the program.

The trace leaves the following important questions unanswered:

1. How are the variables instantiated; where do they get their values from?
2. How and why does the program finish?
3. How does the flow of control work?
4. How does the matching of clauses work, and in what order?

This Prolog trace is based on the "Byrd" box model of Prolog execution (Byrd, 1980). To use this tool the novice must fully understand this model of program execution to get any information from the stepper. The "Byrd" box model displays what has happened at certain important points during program execution, but not how it got to these points which is most useful to a beginner.

Remember that the example is showing a correct and simple program: just think how confusing a more complex program would look, or even a buggy one.

2.2 The Approach

Progress in a field often follows the development of a more powerful method of representing the ideas within that field. For example, advances in program and text editing have followed the development of interactive user aids. This has led to many improvements, the most commonplace of which is the screen editor in word processing. The screen editor, a vast improvement on the previous line editors, allows the material being worked on to be viewed in meaningful units as it is in everyday life, for instance paragraphs and pages, rather than a series of single lines. If the ideas used in screen editing are transferred to other parts of the programming environment such as tracing and tutorial packages then this will allow users to concentrate on developing the basics of programming rather than on the commands necessary to carry out their aims. A consistent and simple user environment working in terms of the user's code would act as a good base on which to build conceptual models of the programming language and techniques.

A possible answer to the problem of learning dynamic programming concepts is to produce an environment which contains tools that display these concepts in such a way that their dynamic nature is clear, and the representation is understood by a novice with only a few hours experience of the programming language in question. With a display of the traced code shown in terms of the code written in the editor, the user should have a more effective means by which to describe the programming techniques initially taught as an abstract theory. This will add some positive feedback to the programming environment, aiding both learning and debugging. What is needed is a way of representing dynamic concepts in a manner that is easy to understand, and at a level that requires little or no mental translation by the user. This will allow concepts such as variable binding, flow of control, and techniques like recursion and iteration to be demonstrated dynamically by stepping through example programs.

This chapter investigates a representation of program execution in an explicit dynamic form, with the intention that the user will be able to assimilate knowledge much more easily than from traditional tracers and single steppers. The proposed representation of program execution potentially offers a triple aid to novice programmers:

1. Students should be able to learn through visual examples what is actually happening in the program. These visual examples are in effect a concrete embodiment of the workings of a program (cf. Lieberman, 1982; 1984).
2. Students should be able easily to debug their mistakes by understanding them in terms of the evaluation of the code.
3. Students should be able to develop their programs more quickly due to the ease of monitoring the surface evaluation of the program.

We have concentrated on the first of these assertions in the present system (see Chapter 6, for an empirical test of the system). It is felt that this is the most important of the three assertions because the other two are dependent upon the effectiveness of the first. In other words, unless this approach to tracing is successful in communicating run-time information to the novice, then it is unlikely that it will aid novices in the debugging and development of programs. On the other hand, if this method of tracing proves successful then the improved communication of information provides the basis for both the second and third assertions. In order for novices to debug and develop programs they must understand both the current actions of that program, and the actions of any changes they propose to make. It is claimed that this understanding will be increased by an animated trace package.

In the system we propose there is a dynamic/animated representation of the execution of the code, in terms of the code that the user has written in the editor. The representation of program execution is in the form of a direct copy of the user's "edit-time" code so that the novice can see the correspondence of the "trace-time" code to the "edit-time" code (In this research "edit-time" code refers to the code that the user has written in the editor or at the top-level, whilst "trace-time" code refers to the simulated evaluation of that "edit-time" code). This animated representation or "visual model" of the language in action, which is henceforth called

"APT" (Animated Program Tracer) will enable the user to view the action of a program in a way that traditional tracers and single steppers do not allow, and will bridge the conceptual gap mentioned above. The visual model of program execution provides a basis for the novice to associate the nuts and bolts of a program to the algorithm or programming technique that the novice is attempting to learn/program.

In detail, APT shows how variables get their value; how parameters are passed; the flow of control; and the relationship between the edited code and the traced code. It is based on the model of the language that is presented in the majority of programming manuals (i.e. the surface evaluation of the program code).

3. DESIGN PRINCIPLES FOR A STORY OF PROGRAM EXECUTION

The design principles presented below are meant to be used as a set of guidelines for the production of a view of program execution that will enable novice programmers to learn dynamic programming constructs.

3.1 General Design Principles

The "a priori" principles underlying the design of an animated stepper are those of simplicity, consistency and transparency (duBoulay et al. 1981). These three principles present global guidelines which enable novices to easily understand, learn and use a computer system.

Simplicity. Simplicity refers to a system having a small number of parts which can be explained by a small number of descriptions, and interact in a way that is easily understood by the novice. This attempts to reduce the amount of information novices have to learn before they can use the system. Instead of learning how to use the system, novices can now concentrate on learning about the items that the system manipulates. In this case a programming language.

To simplify a view of program execution two things can be done. Firstly, the command structure through which the user controls the tracer should be rigid (as opposed to flexible) and contain as few commands as possible. For example, the three commands to "step", "stop stepping", and "restep" are sufficient to allow a novice user to carry out all the desired tracing actions.

Secondly, the method by which program execution is displayed should be carried out by the minimum of transactions. This means that with only a handful of information novice users can control and understand the animated tracing tool which is presenting them with a view of program execution.

Consistency. The method by which information concerning program execution is presented to users (by way of the interface) should be consistent throughout the system. This means that if a display method is used in one place to describe an event, it should also be used elsewhere in the system, allowing novices to transfer information learned in one part of the system to other parts in order to understand what is happening.

Together with the principle of "simplicity" this means that the novice only has to learn the meaning of a small number of display methods, which describe the execution of programs, and always mean the same thing wherever they occur. This all helps to reduce the amount of work users have to do in order to understand the information presented by the system.

Transparency. Transparency means viewing selected parts and processes of the "virtual machine" in action, by means of pictures and a particular story line. In order for novices to be able to build a working model of a programming language it is essential that they can see everything that happens during program execution. Many of the events that occur at run-time are dynamic so the execution view should be presented in a dynamic fashion allowing the novice to see the process by which these events take place.

A problem that crops us here is how transparent a system should be. Programming languages can be explained at various different levels of detail from the commands of the language to the way that language is implemented. It is important that the correct level of description is chosen for the user of the system. (see also section 3.2.4).

3.2 Specific Design Principles

3.2.1 Edit-time and Trace-time Code Isomorphism

The code that is used to show the run-time trace of a program should be a direct copy of what the user has typed into the editor. In other words, the trace-time animation of program execution will be built from the user's edit-time code. This means that the novice should immediately recognise the structure and meaning of the code being traced.

Both the edit-time and trace-time code should be shown together during the trace, so that the events which occur in the trace-time code can be related to the edit-time code. This will enable the novice to see the relationship between the dynamic form of the run-time code and the static form of the code written in the editor. It should also help novices develop future programs, enabling them to predict what will happen to the edit-time code at run-time.

3.2.2 *In-place Subroutine Instantiation*

This refers to the insertion into the trace-time code of any called piece of code, whether it be a procedure call in LISP or a goal call in Prolog. This will build up the animated execution of the user's program by adding new code to the trace as and when it is required. In terms of program execution, it should help the novice assimilate a model of how flow of control works in the programming language. In the same manner, if code has to be removed from the trace-time code (for instance in backtracking and the cut in Prolog, or function evaluation in LISP) the sequence of execution should be displayed explicitly.

3.2.3 *WYSIWHa – "What You See Is What Happens"*

"What you see is what happens" presents the virtual machine in operation, giving novices a concrete view of program execution which is normally taught as an abstract concept. This not only aids the previous principle in showing how flow of control works, but shows exactly what happens to that code when it is evaluated, thus providing a clear view of program execution. In essence this is making the view of program execution transparent to users (mentioned in section 3.1), allowing them to see the virtual machine in action. This idea can be split into the following principles:

Fidelity to the true evaluation sequence of the code. The instructions in the user's code are executed by the stepper in the same order as they would be executed by the interpreter. This provides a one to one mapping between what the user sees and what the interpreter is doing, and is intended to prevent the user from picking up misconceptions about program execution as can happen when analogies are used to convey information.

Side-effect visibility. This principle should allow the user to see explicitly any side effects that the traced program makes to the programming environment. These can be caused by the use of global variables in LISP (and many other languages), or by carrying out an "assert" at run-time in Prolog. Normally, the user would not see side effects happening at run-time and can therefore be confused by the effects they have on the rest of the program.

Integration of variable instantiation within the trace-time code. The assigning of values to variables should be displayed to the user in the context of the trace-time code, showing how, why and when each variable in the program gets bound to its value. The integration of variable instantiation into the program execution display means that the novice needs only one view to see what is happening, rather than several if the variable values were to be shown separately.

3.2.4 Description Level of Trace

This principle is concerned with the description level of the program execution story presented to novice programmers. It seems obvious to tell the user the truth about program execution. However, a problem arises when you ask the questions, "What is the truth?", and "How does the language work?".

Any programming language usually has many different implementations, some written in machine code, others in Assembler, while still others will be written in higher-level languages like C or Pascal. The programming language works in many different ways at the level of the implementation language. However, at a slightly higher level all implementations of a programming language work in the same way. This behaviour is normally determined by a specification of what the language is meant to do, and how it is meant to do it. The way a language works, and the behaviour of its model therefore depends on what level of description is used to describe its actions.

So the new question becomes, "What level of description should be used in a display of program execution?" The level of description used for the system being built is ultimately determined by the end-users. If the end-users are working in the field of language implementation they will want a model of the language at a very low-level of description (i.e. one that displays all the implementation-dependent features of that language). On the other hand, if the end-users are novice programmers, the model of the language presented should be independent of the specific implementation. The level of description, or "the truth", should be the outward appearance of the language stated in the language specification. This should ensure that the behaviour shown by a story of program execution is consistent, and works in all the situations that the user will come across. The aim of this "truth" is for the user to build a useful model of the language, which can be used to interact with and predict the actions of that language.

Another problem on a similar theme is that as soon as a system that models the behaviour of an environment is added to that environment, the intrusion of that system on the environment changes its behaviour. To prevent the behaviour of the environment being changed enough to require another model, it is necessary to design the system so that it has a minimal effect on the environment.

3.2.5 *Status-Line Navigation*

"Status-Line Navigation" is a method by which the user is kept informed of what is happening in the animated trace at all times. This idea has been used in some single-user workstations such as those from Symbolics™ and Perq™ to provide the user with information concerning the percentage of tasks carried out, the function of mouse buttons, and disk access.

The status line should provide a continual brief commentary on the current state of the stepper in order to clarify the stepper's action and to prevent the user from getting lost. The messages will comment on events such as variable instantiation, subroutine instantiation, input and output, and evaluation. The presence of a status line reduces the need for symbols to point out the important features being displayed by the stepper. This leaves the screen clear for displaying the text of the program. The status line will in effect be presenting the user with an English version of a model of program execution. Unlike traditional tracers, the user will not have to learn a model of program execution before being able to use the tracer to help build a working model of program execution. Having this type of information contained in a status line means that if the user understands what the display is showing, the status line can be ignored, and attention can be directed solely at the animation. This is not possible if symbols are used to flag tracing features as they are still present within the trace-time code.

3.2.6 *Trace Forwards and Backwards*

This is an important facility for novice programmers as it provides them with an easy way of reviewing the execution of a tricky piece of code. It is likely that novice programmers will find many pieces of code difficult and will want to see the execution of that code several times before being satisfied that they understand how it works. Unless a facility for reviewing program execution is provided, the novice will have to reinvoke the tracer repeatedly. Not only is this time consuming, but it interrupts the user's train of thought.

3.2.7 *Integration of the Interpreter's Error Messages*

This principle aims to provide the novice with contextual information concerning the cause of error messages. This is similar to the principle concerning variable instantiation discussed in section 3.2.3.

The error messages given by the interpreter should be integrated into the trace-time code so that the user can see the context of the process leading up to the error. If the relevant piece of code is highlighted in the edit-time code this will allow the user to see exactly which piece of code has produced the error, and provide a starting point for error correction. The error message should be as specific to the user's code as possible; for example, saying which variable is at fault, rather than being a general message presented for a particular type of error. An expansion of the error message should be available in case the user does not understand the initial message.

3.2.8 Uniformity of the Editor, Top-level and Utilities

The tracing system should be integrated with other systems, such as the editor, so that the command set and display format are the same throughout the environment. This is an attempt to make the programming environment as simple and consistent as possible at a global level. This should enable the user to learn and use the environment quickly and easily.

The novice will have to learn how to use an editor in order to write programs, and will learn the commands and environment early in their programming experience. It is therefore sensible to reduce the amount of information needed to use the tracing system by basing that system on the editor. This will reduce the cognitive load on novices when learning a language, allowing them to concentrate on learning to program rather than on how to use the different tools provided in the programming environment.

3.2.9 Demonstration Utility

This principle is aimed at providing a means of presenting users with a concrete example of programming techniques so they may be aided in abstracting out general plans for programming. Jones (1984a) has pointed out that programming success depends on this ability to abstract out plans from examples.

The stepping facilities at the most detailed level should demonstrate different features of the programming language (i.e. backtracking, cut, function calls, and programming techniques such as recursion and search). This will allow the system to be used as a teaching tool with either an automated tutoring system or lectures on programming, or simply providing a pool of on-line dynamic demonstrations available to the user through a help system. A demonstration facility should allow the novice programmer to associate concrete programs with the abstract algorithms they need to understand in order to become successful programmers.

3.2.10 Minimal Extraneous Symbols

This principle aims at reducing the number of symbols used to flag the meaning of information presented to the user in the trace. This is another attempt to keep the display of the trace simple by reducing the amount of information needed before using the system.

Only the symbols used in the syntax of the language should be used in the trace-time code of the stepper display. Using other symbols to denote particular events in the trace causes several problems. Firstly, it means that novices have to learn the meaning of all the symbols before they can use the system, and usually have to learn the model of program execution that these symbols represent. This is not helpful as the aim of animated tracing tools is to facilitate the assimilation of a working model of program execution. Secondly, the symbols clutter the display distracting the user from concentrating on what is happening to the program.

The important features and events displayed by the animated tracing system should be highlighted using inverse video or colour to augment their importance compared to the rest of the display. This concentrates users' attention on the highlighted text rather than distracting them with extraneous symbols.

3.2.11 Non-Proliferation of Views

This principle states that the number of views a novice is given to show program execution should be kept to a minimum, and is another example of keeping the system simple. Paxton and Turner (1984) have shown that novices prefer inflexible tools, with few commands so that they can concentrate their attention on understanding one view of program execution instead of spreading it across several displays. Once the novice has built a working model of the execution of programs then other views could be made available, which the user can then understand in terms of the original view. This should allow a smooth progression in the complexity and number of views provided by the system as the user becomes more adept with the programming language.

3.2.12 Detail/Speed Trade-off

Novices need an inflexible detailed story of the virtual machine allowing them to build a conceptual model of program execution, while experts want a fast flexible interface so that they can test their hypothesis about the action of the program by finding a particular piece of information quickly. When designing an animated tracing system the designer should primarily meet the needs of novice programmers, but the system should also be designed to be integrated into a larger system of programming tools that can be used by novices as they become more adept at programming. This approach should provide a smooth ascent for the novice into fast flexible tools.

3.2.13 Display Shape

The shape and placing of the windows displaying the code should be determined by the shape of the code. For example, assembly code programs which are "long and skinny" should be displayed with two windows side by side (horizontally), whereas Prolog and Lisp programs tend to be rather fat, and so should be presented in windows placed above and below each other. This approach allows more code to be seen on screen with less wasted space providing a natural interface between the language and the user.

3.3 Summary

These design principles present precise guidelines for building an animated tracing tool. They aim to provide novice programmers with a view of program execution they can use to build a dynamic model of how a programming language works. In order to demonstrate that these guidelines are both realistic and realisable it is necessary to build an animated tracer based on the principles specified above. This will also allow the design to be tested on novice users indicating whether it reaches its aims of being simple to use, and communicates the desired run-time information.

4. OVERVIEW OF APT

The principles described in the previous section have been used as the basis for constructing three prototypes and one real stepper. The representation of program execution in both the prototypes and APT are in the form of a direct copy of the user's edit-time code so that the novice can see the correspondence of the trace-time code to the edit-time code.

The three prototypes were built for Lisp, Prolog, and 6502 Assembler and are fully described elsewhere (Rajan, 1985; 1986). The prototypes took the form of canned text, constructed out of many single frames, which when displayed look like the trace of a real program. They demonstrated that the design principles are applicable to a wide range of programming languages ranging from low to high level, and procedural to declarative.

The Animated Program Tracer (APT), was constructed for Prolog because Prolog contains some very complex concepts which are difficult for novices to learn because they are not intuitive (i.e. backtracking and unification). In addition, Prolog has very few tools available to aid the view of program execution (with the recent exception of TPM described in Chapter 3). APT is written entirely in Lisp, including the Prolog interpreter, and runs on the Symbolics™ 3600 family machines under release 6 of the system. A detailed description including several scenarios using screen snapshots can be found in Rajan (1986). An evaluation demonstrating the usefulness of APT is communicating run-time information to novice Prolog programmers, and an experiment to determine the misconceptions novices have concerning the workings of the Prolog interpreter, are described in chapter 6.

APT provides novice programmers with a clear and consistent view of program execution, showing the execution sequence of a program (the trace-time code) in terms of the code the novice has written (the edit-time code). The trace-time code is associated with the edit-time code, by inverse video highlighting, so that the novice may see and understand the relationship between the static and the dynamic form of the program. All the dynamic features that occur in the program are shown in the context of the trace-time code (i.e. variable binding, unification, recursion).

The following description of APT assumes that the reader has a working knowledge of Prolog. The syntax used is standard DEC10 syntax except for the representation of variables. Variables consist of any atom whose first character is an underscore, which differs from DEC10 where a variable may either be any atom starting with a capital letter, or an underscore.

The curly brackets "{ }" in the description below contain the design principle which pertains to the part of APT being explained. This shows how the guidelines have been used in the construction of APT.

The screen consists of three areas or windows as follows (see Figure 2.1):

Editor Window: This is a normal Zmacs screen editor window in which the user can write programs. This window contains the edit/time code.

Prolog Window: The user can enter queries to the Prolog interpreter in the normal way in this window. Queries are evaluated after a "do-it" key is pressed. Any output generated by the interpreter is also printed in this window. The Prolog window is also an editor window with the same screen editing facilities as the Editor Window {Uniformity of Editor, Top-level and Utilities}. This window contains the "trace-time" code during the animated trace. The trace-time code scrolls automatically during the trace to keep the current focus of attention on the screen {Non Proliferation of Views}.

Status Line: The bottom window is a status line which is blank when the user is editing or running programs, but contains comments during a program trace.

The animated tracer works by showing novices each line of their program being executed in the same order and in the same manner as the interpreter executes the program {WYSIWHa part i}. Each step of the program's execution is shown in the trace, the user moving from one step to the next by means of a menu {Detail/speed Trade-off}. The menu also allows the user to end the tracing session at any time.

The simulated execution takes place in the Prolog Window. Outstanding goals in the trace-time code are matched against entries contained in the edit-time code (Fig. 2.1). This demonstrates how the interpreter searches through the database. The goal is highlighted in the trace-time code while

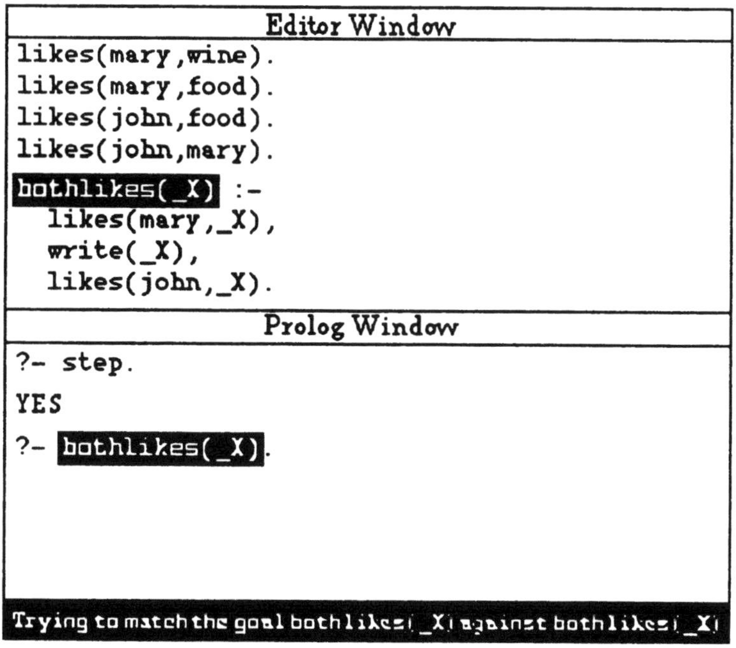

FIG. 2.1. The simulated execution of a program (part i).

each attempted match in the edit-time code is highlighted in turn. If the goal matches a rule then that rule is inserted into the trace-time code so that its subgoals may be proved and its variables instantiated accordingly. If the goal matches a fact no insertion needs to occur, only the instantiation of any unbound variables. If the match fails the tracer moves on to the next database entry in the Prolog procedure. {Description level of the trace}.

When new rules are inserted into the trace-time code (Fig. 2.2) the display grows to accommodate the rule {In-place subroutine instantiation}. Any variables that occur in the inserted code are highlighted using inverse video and replaced by the value they become instantiated to {WYSIWHa part ii}. In Fig. 2.3 the variable "_X" is highlighted in the Prolog window while the value it is being matched against "wine" is being highlighted in the Editor Window. Figure 2.4 shows what happens after the unification (i.e. "The variable _X is instantiated to wine"). Note that the variable "_X" in the trace-time code has been replaced with the value "wine".

While the trace goes on, the status line gives a running commentary on what is happening and what the display is showing {Status-line navigation}. These messages remind the novice of the terminology used in explanations commonly found in programming manuals and teaching texts,

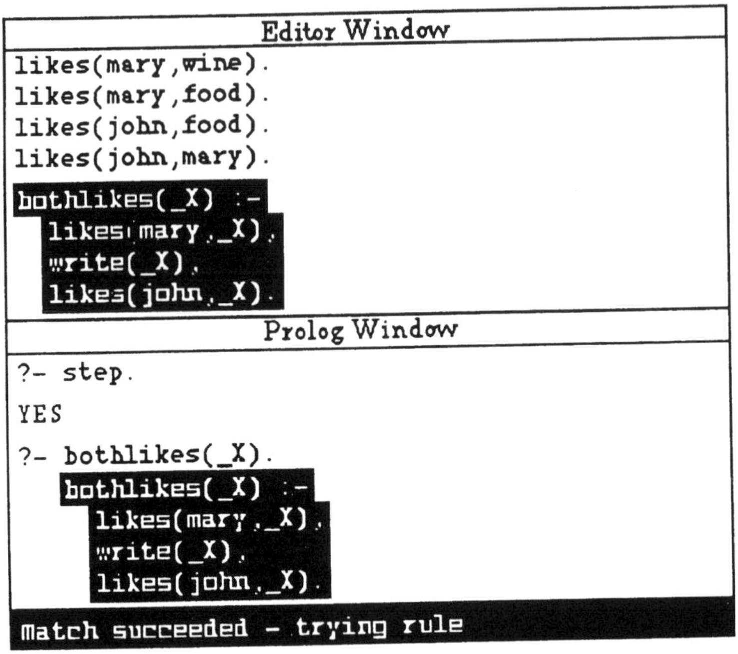

FIG. 2.2. The simulated execution of a program (part ii).

as well as reinforcing the animated display in the Prolog window. In Fig. 2.4, the status line comments "The variable_X is instantiated to wine" informing the user of the impending unification.

If a goal fails backtracking is initiated. If the failed goal has any variables that were instantiated when the goal was unified, then they are uninstantiated. The failed subgoals are then removed from the display, and the tracer then attempts to retry the goal by matching it against other database entries.

Both the edit-time and trace-time code are displayed during the trace {Edit-time and trace-time code isomorphism}. The correspondence between the edit-time code and the trace-time code is conveyed to the novice by the inverse video highlighting {Minimal extraneous symbols}. This shows novices how the static code they have written relates to the dynamic run-time action of the program. The inverse video highlighting shows such things as uninstantiated variables, where its binding is going to come from, the matching of rules and facts, and the updating of the trace-time code.

APT can also display what happens when the cut is encountered upon backtracking, and list manipulation, including the bar notation. It does not

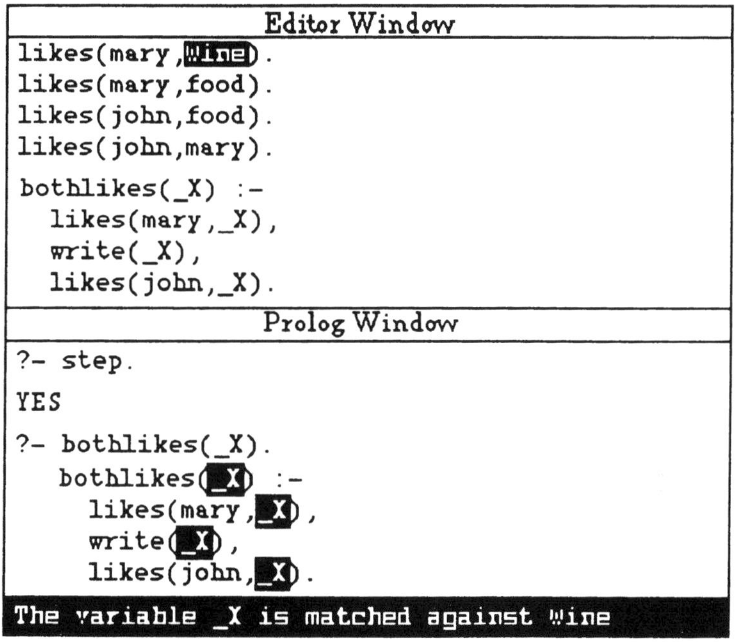

FIG. 2.3. The simulated execution of a program (part iii).

yet incorporate two of the principles listed above. These are WYSIWHa (ii) side-effect visibility, and the integration of error messages into the trace-time code. Also, the current implementation does not show the renaming of variables during program execution. However, these features could be easily added, and would improve the story of program execution that is portrayed.

5. DISCUSSION

The research described in this paper has presented a new approach to viewing program execution, which allows novice programmers to assimilate easily a conceptual model of the action of programs at run-time. Animated program tracing is aimed at solving the problems novices face when learning a programming language. The studies reported earlier show that these problems are concerned mainly with the poor conceptual model novices have of the dynamic features that occur in programs when they are run. APT's approach is to provide novices with a concrete base upon which to build a conceptual model of program execution.

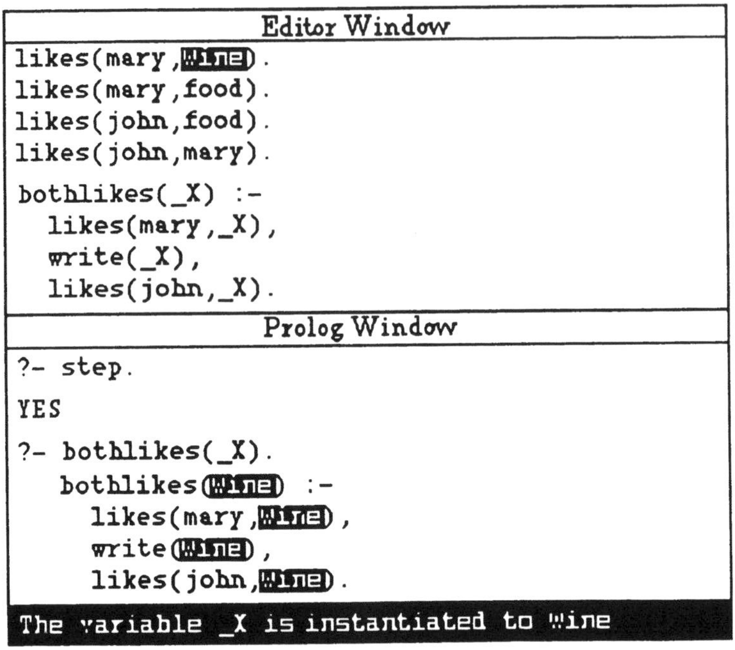

FIG. 2.4. The simulated execution of a program (part iv).

APT is based on design principles extracted both from general, systems-design principles and other tools that have made an attempt to provide a run-time view of program execution. The resulting set of design principles are directed at building animated tracing tools for novice programmers. The approach that the design principles propound is to provide the novice with a clear and consistent view of program execution, showing the evaluation sequence of a program (the trace-time code) in terms of the edit-time code. The trace-time code is associated with the edit-time code so that the novice may see and understand the relationship between the static form of the program, which is written in the editor by the user and the dynamic form of the program, which is normally run hidden with the computer. All the dynamic features that occur in the program at run time are shown in the context of the trace-time code and also associated to the edit-time code (e.g. variable binding, backtracking, unification, recursion, s-expression evaluation, and side-effecting). This approach allows the novice programmer to follow what will happen to a program when it is run after writing it into the editor, instead of hoping for the best using a trial and error paradigm.

One issue which has not been fully addressed, concerns the use of the editor window as a view of the Prolog data base (i.e. the loaded rules and facts). Specifically, what happens when a program asserts some new fact into the data base? The design principles (WYSIWHa – side-effect visibility) say that the user should be able to see all the events, including side effects, that occur during the execution of the program. It was originally intended that APT would display "asserts to", and "retracts from" the data base, by means of adding and removing the relevant fact to the editor window, along with suitable status line messages. This feature was never implemented in APT, but has since been implemented in the Transparent Rule Interpreter (see Domingue & Eisenstadt's Chapter 4) a graphical tracing environment for an integrated forward and backward chaining rule interpreter.

TPM, the Transparent Prolog Machine, has built on the foundations of the work presented in this chapter. TPM is a graphical tracing environment for Prolog, based on an AND/OR tree representation, and is aimed at both novice and expert programmers. TPM is described in detail elsewhere in this book (see Eisenstadt & Brayshaw's Chapter 3).

Another fruitful area for using the dynamic view of program execution is as a basis for explanation in automated tutoring environments. There are many tutoring systems and program analysers which have the ability to trap, analyse and understand errors made by novice programmers (Ruth, 1976; Waters, 1979; Eistenstadt & Laubsch, 1980; Domingue, 1985; Johnson & Soloway, 1985; Murray, 1986). However once they have found and analysed an error such systems tend to provide little explanation, other than canned text, from which novices have difficulty correcting both their error and their faulty conceptual model of program execution.

If a system such as APT were embedded in a tutoring environment it would provide a graphic illustration of programming language features and programming techniques to explain the correct model of program execution and demonstrate to the novice how and why a program is faulty. This approach to explanation should allow novices to understand the error made, to correct their conceptual model of program execution, and to introduce them to the debugging facilities provided for novice programmers.

Animated views of programming environments need not be confined to languages. The design principles could equally well be applied to other dynamic systems which are complex and difficult to learn; for example, operating systems, programmable robot control, and just about any interactive computer environment.

REFERENCES

Anderson, J. R., Farrell, R., & Sauers, R. (1984a). Learning to program in Lisp. *Cognitive Science*, *8*, 87–129.

Anderson, J. R., Pirolli, P., & Farrell, R. (1984b). Learning to program recursive functions. In M. Chi, R. Glaser, and M. Farr (Eds), *The Nature of Expertise*. Hillsdale, NJ: Lawrence Erlbaum Associates Inc, 153–183.

Bratko, I. (1986). *Prolog Programming for Artificial Intelligence*. Bassingstoke: Addison-Wesley.

du Boulay, J. B. H., O'Shea, T., & Monk, J. (1981). The black box inside the glass box: Presenting computing concepts to novices. *International Journal of Man-Machine Studies*, *14*, 237–249.

Brooks, R. (1977). Towards a theory of the cognitive processes in computer programming. *International Journal of Man-Machine Studies*, *9* (6), 737–742.

Byrd, L. (1980). Understanding the control flow of Prolog programs. In S-Å Tarnlund (Ed.), *Proceedings of the 1980 Logic Programming Workshop*, 127–138.

Carroll, J. M. & Thomas, J. C. (1980). Metaphor and the cognitive representation of computing systems. *Report RC 8302*, IBM Watson Research Center, May.

Clocksin, W. F. & Mellish, C. S. (1981). *Programming in Prolog*. Berlin: Springer-Verlag.

Domingue, J. (1985). Towards an automated programming advisor. *Technical Report No. 16*, Human Cognition Research Laboratory, The Open University, Milton Keynes, England.

Domingue, J. (1990). The TRI handbook. *Technical Report (in press)*, Human Cognition Research Laboratory, The Open University, Milton Keynes, England.

Eisenstadt, M., Breuker, J., & Evertsz, R. (1984). A cognitive account of "natural" looping constructs. *Proceedings of the First IFIP Conference on Human-Computer Interaction, INTERACT '84*, London, 173–177.

Eisenstadt, M. & Laubsch, J. (1980). Towards an automated debugging assistant for novice programmers. *Proceedings of the AISB-80 Conference on Artificial Intelligence*, July.

Gugerty, L. & Olson, G. M. (1986). Comprehension differences in debugging by skilled and novice programmers. In E. Soloway and S. Iyengar (Eds), *Empirical Studies of Programmers*. Norwood, NJ: Ablex.

Halasz, F. & Moran, T. (1982). Analogy considered harmful. *Proceedings of Human Factors in Computing Systems Conference*. Gaithersburg, Maryland, USA, 383–386.

Hasemer, T. (1984). A Beginner's Guide to Lisp. Basingstoke: Addison-Wesley.

Johnson, L. W. & Soloway, E. (1985). PROUST: An automatic debugger for Pascal programs. *BYTE*, *10*, 179–180.

Jones, A. (1984a). How novices learn to program. *Proceedings of the First IFIP Conference on Human Computer-Interaction, INTERACT, '84*, London, 777–782.

Jones, A. (1984b). Learning to program: Some protocol data. *Technical Report No. 41*, Computer Assisted Learning Research Group, The Open University, Milton Keynes, England.

Kahney, J. H. (1982). An in-depth study of the behaviour of novice programmers. *Technical Report No. 5*, Human Cognition Research Laboratory, The Open University, Milton Keynes, England.

Lewis, M. W. (1980). Improving SOLO's user-interface: An empirical study of user behaviour and a proposal for cost effective enhancement. *Technical Report No. 7*, Computer Assisted Learning Research Group, The Open University, Milton Keynes, England.

Lieberman, H. (1982). *Seeing what your programs are doing*, AI Memo No. 656. M.I.T. AI Laboratory, Boston, Mass.

Lieberman, H. (1984). Steps towards better debugging tools for Lisp. *Proceedings ACM Symposium on Functional Programming,* Austin, Texas, 247–255.

Lukey, F. J. (1980). Understanding and debugging programs. *International Journal of Man-Machine Studies*, *12*, 189–202.

Mayer, R. E. (1976). Some conditions of meaningful learning for computer programming: advance organizers and subject control of frame order. *Journal of Educational Psychology, 68*, 143–150.

Mayer, R. E. (1981). The psychology of how novices learn computer programming. *Computing Surveys, 13*, 121–141.

Miller, L. A. (1974). Programming by non-programmers. *International Journal of Man-Machine Studies, 6*, 237–260.

Murray, W. R. (1986). Automatic program debugging for intelligent tutoring systems. *Technical Report AI TR86-27*, The University of Texas at Austin, Texas, USA.

Norman, D. A. (1983). Some observations on mental models. In D. Gentner & A. Stevens (Eds), *Mental models*, Hillsdale, NJ: Lawrence Erlbaum Associates Inc., 7–14.

Paxton, A. L. & Turner, E. J. (1984). The application of human factors to the needs of the novice computer user. *International Journal of Man-Machine Studies, 20*, 137–156.

Pirolli, P. L. & Anderson, J. R. (1985). The role of learning from examples in the acquisition of recursive programming skills. *Canadian Journal of Psychology, 39*, 240–272.

Rajan, T. (1985). APT: The design of animated tracing tools for novice programmers. *Technical Report No. 15*, Human Cognition Research Laboratory, The Open University, Milton Keynes, England.

Rajan, T. (1986). APT: A principled design for an animated view of program execution for novice programmers. *Technical Report No. 19/19a*, Human Cognition Research Laboratory, The Open University, Milton Keynes, England.

Rumelhart, D. E. & Norman, D. A. (1981). Analogical processes in learning. In J. R. Anderson (Ed.), *Cognitive Skills and their Acquisition*, Hillsdale, NJ: Lawrence Erlbaum Associates Inc., 335–359.

Ruth, G. R. (1976). Intelligent program analysis. *Artificial Intelligence, 7*, 65–85.

Sheil, B. A. (1981). The psychological study of programming. *Computing Surveys, 13*, 101–120.

Sime, M. E., Green, T. R. G., & Guest, D. J. (1973). Psychological evaluation of two conditional constructions in computer languages. *International Journal of Man-Machine Studies, 5*, 123–143.

Sime, M. E., Arblaster, A. T., & Green, T. R. G. (1979). Reducing programming errors in nested conditionals by prescribing a writing procedure. *International Journal of Man-Machine Studies, 9*, 119–126.

Soloway, E., Bonar, J., & Ehrlich, K. (1981). Cognitive factors in programming: An empirical study of looping constructs. *Technical Report No. 81–10*, Department of Computer Science, University of Massachusetts.

Soloway, E., Ehrlich, K., Bonar, J., & Greenspan, J. (1982). What do novices know about programming? In B. Schneiderman and A. Badre (Eds), *Directions in Human-Computer Interactions*. Norwood, NJ: Ablex.

Soloway, E. & Ehrlich, K. (1984). Empirical studies of programming knowledge. *IEEE Transactions on Software Engineering. Special Issue: Reusability*, Sept.

van Someren, M. W. (1984). Misconceptions of beginning Prolog programmers. *Memorandum 30 of the Research Project "The Acquisition of Expertise"*. Dept. of Experimental Psychology. The University of Amsterdam.

van Someren, M. W. (1985). Beginners problems in learning Prolog. *Memorandum 31 of the Research Project "The Acquisition of Expertise"*. Dept. of Experimental Psychology. The University of Amsterdam.

Taylor, J. & du Boulay, B. (1987). Studying novice programmers: Why they may find learning Prolog hard. *Cognitive Studies Research Papers, Serial No. 60*. The University of Sussex, England.

Touretzky, D. S. (1984). *Lisp, a gentle introduction to symbolic computation*. New York: Harper and Row.

Waters, R. C. (1979). A method for analyzing loop programs. *IEEE Transactions on Software Engineering, SE-5 : 3*, 237–247.

Winston, P. H. & Horn, B. K. P. (1981). *Lisp*, Basingstoke: Addison-Wesley.

Winston, P. H. & Horn, B. K. P. (1984). *Lisp*, Second Edition. Basingstoke: Addison-Wesley.

3 A Fine-Grained Account of Prolog Execution for Teaching and Debugging[1]

Marc Eisenstadt & Mike Brayshaw
Human Cognition Research Laboratory, The Open University, Milton Keynes, England

OVERVIEW

A clear and consistent execution model of any programming language can lay the foundations not only for a good learning experience, but also for a smoother design/edit/run/debug cycle. In this chapter, we describe our attempt to construct precisely such a model for the logic programming language Prolog, based upon a notational extension of logic programming's traditional AND/OR trees. Our extension, called the "AORTA" diagram, is an **A**nd/**OR** **T**ree, **A**ugmented to include invocation history "status boxes" at each node. This augmentation makes it possible to present a graphical view of Prolog execution, which is very compact yet which contains complete details of unification and control history, including multiple (backtracking) invocations and extra-logical features such as the cut. The chapter describes our fine-grained view of Prolog execution in detail, and argues that this fine-grained view can readily be integrated into a coarse-grained model such as that required for understanding the execution of very large programs. Indeed, our notation is already in use across a

[1]The authors gratefully acknowledge the support of the UK Science and Engineering Research Council. AORTA diagrams were developed for teaching purposes under the aegis of the SERC Information Technology Training Initiative, which funded the development of the Open University's "Intensive Prolog" course. The graphical tracer/debugger implementation was funded by SERC grant numbers GR/C/69344 and GR/E/2333.3, as part of Alvey Project IKBS/161, undertaken collaboratively with Expert Systems Ltd. A version of the software is available from the authors.

range of media, including textbook diagrams, video animations, and a graphical tracing and debugging facility running on modern graphics workstations.

1. INTRODUCTION

1.1 Motivation

Existing Prolog textbooks (e.g. Bratko, 1986; Clocksin & Mellish, 1984; Sterling & Shapiro, 1986) provide adequate descriptions of the language, yet novices still come unstuck when having to write or debug Prolog programs that exhibit anything other than the most trivial forms of backtracking and unification (Coombs & Stell, 1985; Taylor, 1987). It could be that the language is just inherently tricky, and requires lots of practice. Alternatively, it might be the case that novices are never provided with, or at least never acquire, a clear execution model, and this leads them astray (see Chapter 2 for a review). The analysis of Bundy, Pain, Brna, and Lynch (1986) suggested that texts such as Clocksin and Mellish (1st edition, 1981) contained several different and potentially conflicting "stories" of Prolog execution, and that this was a source of possible confusion. To their credit, Clocksin and Mellish provided a much more coherent story of Prolog execution in the second edition of their book (1984). Nevertheless, there is a rather wide gulf between what is presented in any existing text and what is observed when a real Prolog program acts oddly (Taylor, 1987).

The importance of clear models of the underlying machine has been highlighted elsewhere (e.g. duBoulay, O'Shea, & Monk, 1981). Here, we present a notional machine that is based directly on a meta-level interpreter, thereby allowing us to follow execution steps in very precise detail. Far from inundating the novice with too much truth, describing the machine at such a level makes the basic concepts of the language unambiguous, more readily accessible, easier to understand, and hence less error-prone.

Our focus has been on producing an account of the language which is rich enough to satisfy the needs of experts but has the descriptive power and clarity for teaching difficult concepts to a novice programmer. Our work has developed from two ends simultaneously. That is, we were developing video-based teaching material for novice Prolog programmers at the same time as we were implementing graphics facilities for helping experts observe a 2 or 3 thousand node search space. Only by forcing these two paths to converge could we cater for the upwardly mobile student who learned about Prolog in the early phases and then went on to become a serious Prolog user.

1.2 Pedagogically-Motivated Tracers

Amongst the numerous tracing and debugging packages built for Prolog and other languages, several have been motivated explicitly by pedagogical considerations. Here we mention only the four most relevant.

Mellish has developed an animated trace which displays the run-time behaviour of small Prolog programs on VT100-style terminals connected to a machine running the Sussex University/System Designers Ltd. POPLOG environment (Hardy, 1984). This tracer was developed as part of an effort to provide a consistent execution story for the student learning Prolog, and indeed the second edition of Clocksin and Mellish (1984) conforms with the style and content of the animated tracer. Two important problems with Mellish's facility are (a) variables are destructively replaced by their instantiations on the screen in real (or slightly slowed down) time, so it can be hard to go back and see what actually happened; (b) only toy programs can be viewed. The principle of showing an animated trace in this fashion is nevertheless fundamentally important.

Rajan's (see Chapter 2) APT system works its way through Prolog code by highlighting relevant portions in the database at the appropriate moments, and by instantiating clause bodies in their entirety "in place" in the code being traced. By showing unification in painstaking detail, a very clear account of execution is presented to novices. However, Rajan's single-stepper does not fully show variable renaming, and can only deal with relatively small execution spaces. Although both the renaming and search space problems were not relevant for the class of beginners Rajan was addressing, they are problems which need to be resolved for longer-term users.

Brown and Sedgewick (1985) and Brown (1988) in their BALSA-I and BALSA-II environments have sought to use animated displays as a way of demonstrating algorithms and teaching basic computing concepts. Although they include the important notion of a replay facility in their program, the system is an algorithm viewer, rather than a true trace facility (i.e. ordinary users cannot type in arbitrary code and see a graphical trace of it).

DEWLAP is a Prolog debugger by Dewar and Cleary (1986) that graphically shows the state of the program execution by using a fisheye zoom to present detailed information about the item of current focus and gradually less about those that are further away and of less interest. The system shows individual clause head unification and allows the user to specify special ways to view individual data objects. The trace display rapidly gets very complicated even on small examples and the nature of the zooming they use means that it is not possible easily to compare parts of the tree that are a large distance apart. Although Dewar and Cleary acknowledge the desirability of seeing the program's behaviour in terms of an "AND/OR" tree (see below), they compromise in the DEWLAP diagram with a resulting loss of clarity.

PROLOGRAPH (Gunakara Sun Systems Ltd.) is a pedagogically motivated language which aims to combine features of a Prolog-like language with those of an object-oriented language. PROLOGRAPH supports a visual programming style of interface, including graphical templates in order to indicate higher order control features. Although like Prolog, any goal that fails will be taken to be an error unless the user has specified that failure is a legitimate option. The resulting dataflow diagrams can be stepped through, via an interpreter, in order to trace execution.

1.3 A Way Forward

Our work has goals in common with that of Rajan and Bundy et al. (1986). We share with Rajan the desire to tell the truth about Prolog execution in great detail, and to show unification details in terms which map directly onto the user's source code. We differ from Rajan in preferring to show large execution spaces graphically rather than textually. The work of Bundy et al. has cogently highlighted the virtues (for novices) of sticking firmly with an AND/OR tree execution model in preference to other possible models, including OR trees and "Byrd Box" models (Byrd, 1980). For readers unfamiliar with AND/OR trees, the idea is that a simple graphical convention (usually a horizontal bar) is used to indicate a conjunction of goals, whereas the absence of this convention means a disjunction of goals. Figure 3.1, for example, can be read as follows: "a is true if b, c, AND d are all true, OR alternatively a is true if e AND f are true. A more detailed discussion of AND/OR trees is provided in Kowalski (1979).

Our work differs from that of Bundy et al. in three important respects: (i) in our fine-grained account we display much more detail about clause head matching and unification, but without sacrificing the basic clarity of

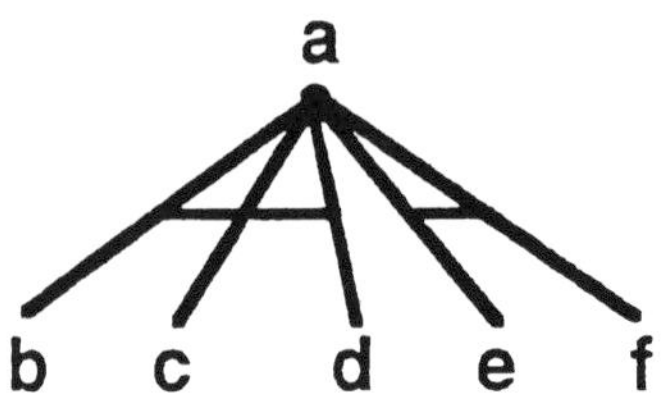

FIG. 3.1. A basic AND/OR tree, with the reading "a is true either if b, c, AND d are all true, OR else if e and f are true".

an AND/OR tree representation; (ii) our coarse-grained account is consistent with our fine-grained account, and is not only suitable for machine implementation, but is also capable of displaying the execution of large Prolog programs; (iii) we do not require separate resolution tables or database displays, although in our running implementation the user can trivially display a window showing relevant source code highlighted, as appropriate, at run time.

We begin with the following two premises; (i) it is essential both for teaching and debugging purposes to show the full execution space of large Prolog programs; (ii) it is essential to base both teaching material and a working trace package on an execution model which discriminates between clause head matching and clause body execution.

We have stuck with these two premises partly because of the challenge of resolving their underlying contradiction: premise (i) involves a global view of things, while premise (ii) involves a very close-up view. Our aim has been to reconcile these differences without losing the advantages provided by either. We feel strongly that different levels of detail (i.e. different grain-sizes of analysis) involve different conceptual views of what is happening, and therefore a simple aerial view/close-up zoom facility does not provide a magical solution. It is nevertheless possible to accommodate both premises, despite the commonly held misconception that both are too hard or too messy to achieve. The key insights which enable this accommodation, and which drive the whole of the work described in this chapter, are the following:

It is possible to display an execution space involving thousands of nodes on today's graphics workstations.

When a Prolog programmer is debugging a program which he or she has personally been developing over a period of weeks or months, an overall graphical view of the execution space of that program is highly meaningful to that programmer, because it conveys its own gestalt.

The concept of a node in a traditional AND/OR tree is needlessly impoverished. With just a few enhancements, and for a very small computational overhead, a simple node can become a status box which concisely encapsulates a goal's history, including detailed clause-head matching information.

The traditional AND/OR tree does not reveal the difference between one clause containing a disjunction and two separate clauses. More specifically, the distinction between clause head and clause body is not shown in AND/OR trees, despite the overwhelming importance of the head/body distinction to the debugging of Prolog programs. A minor notational variant enables us to overcome this problem.

The main purpose of this chapter is to provide the details of the graphical AORTA notation which serves as the basis for our fine-grained account of

Prolog execution, and to provide an overview of a teaching curriculum based almost entirely on this fine-grained account. We therefore omit certain related issues which are discussed elsewhere. In particular, the full user environment of the graphical tracer, with its replay buttons, and hierarchical zoom, is described in detail in Eisenstadt and Brayshaw (1988); extensions to handle large search spaces and scale up to full size programs, is described in Brayshaw and Eisenstadt (1991), whilst methods for user definable abstractions of the execution space, as well as customised data abstractions are contained in Brayshaw and Eisenstadt (1988). Section 2 provides full details of the fine-grained execution model. Section 3 discusses related curriculum issues. Section 4 describes the way in which our execution model can be scaled-up to provide coarse-grained views of very large programs. Section 5 concludes by restating the main findings of our current research.

2. A MODEL OF PROLOG EXECUTION

The sub-sections which follow introduce an idealised model of the Prolog machine which we dub the "Transparent Prolog Machine" (TPM). We begin with a description of the "procedure status box", which is the kernel of our representation. Subsequent sub-sections then illustrate goal/subgoal processing, unification details, and difficult invocation histories. We also show how our approach can be scaled up to a coarse-grained view for helping Prolog programmers follow the execution of very large programs.

2.1 The Procedure Status Box

We follow the common practice of using the name *procedure* to refer to the collection of clauses defining a given relation (i.e. a functor of a certain arity). The cornerstone of our notation convention, illustrated in Fig. 3.2, is the *procedure status box*. This box replaces the simple AND/OR tree node in our display of Prolog program execution. The upper part indicates the goal status, and informs us whether the goal is currently being processed (a question-mark), whether it has succeeded (a tick, sometimes called a "check"), whether it has failed (a cross, sometimes called an "X"), or whether an earlier success was followed by failure upon backtracking (a tick/cross combination). The number in the lower half of the procedure status box is a *clause counter* which tells us which of several clauses for a given procedure is currently being processed.

The small "legs" dangling down underneath the procedure status box are called *clause branches*, and correspond one-for-one to the individual clauses comprising the definition of a relation in the data base. The leftmost branch corresponds to the first clause, and the next branch

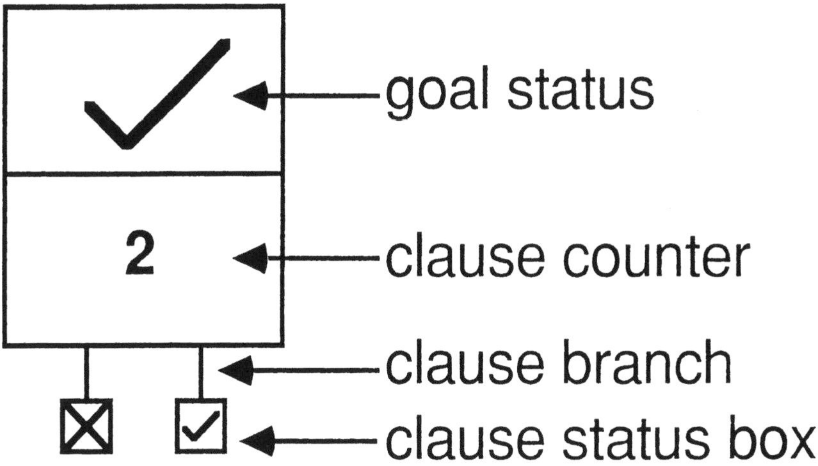

FIG. 3.2. A procedure status box.

corresponds to the second clause, etc. The small boxes at the bottom of Fig. 3.2 are *clause status boxes*, used to indicate the outcome of processing of each individual clause. The clause status box may contain any of the four symbols used to indicate the main goal status (question mark, tick, cross, and tick/cross combination). Alternatively, a clause branch may simply terminate in a horizontal dead-end bar when the head of that clause fails to unify with the current goal.

Let's now observe the execution of a trival Prolog program in slow motion to see how the procedure status box is used. Consider the following data basc:

```
eats(joe, hamburgers).
eats(fred, X).             % fred eats anything
eats(X, bread).            % everyone (actually anything) eats bread
```

Now suppose that the following query, corresponding to "Who eats rubbish?", is posed:

```
?- eats (X, rubbish).
```

Figures 3.3(a)–3.3(d) show the innards of execution. In Fig. 3.3(a), we see the main goal displayed alongside the procedure status box. The goal status symbol is a question-mark, there are three clause branches corresponding to the clauses in the definition of **eats**, and the "0" indicates that no clauses have yet been inspected. Whenever a clause is inspected, it is

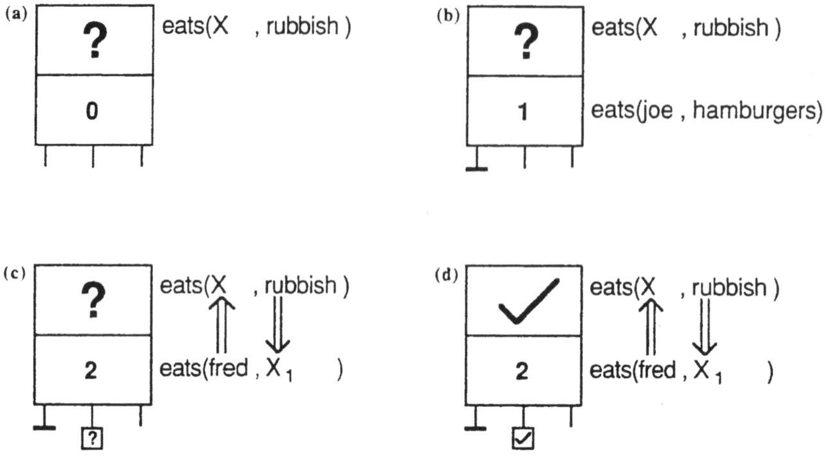

FIG. 3.3. Four-step detailed execution snapshots, given the query:
?- eats(X, rubbish).
(a) Initial pending goal.
(b) A copy of clause 1 of **eats** is inspected, but the head does not unify with the goal (because **rubbish** does not match **hamburgers**).
(c) A copy of clause 2 is inspected, and its head does unify, as shown. Variables in clauses which are copied and inspected are automatically renamed by adding an appropriately-numbered subscript. At this instant, the interpreter does not know that clause 2 is a winner.
(d) End of processing. The clause status box for clause 2 shows that it is a winner (trivially), and thus the main goal wins.

first copied, and any variables are renamed by adding an appropriately-numbered subscript. Then an attempt is made to unify the head of that clause with the current goal. Figure 3.3(b) depicts the moment when clause 1 of **eats** is inspected. The head of this clause fails to unify with the current goal, so the first clause branch has just been marked with a horizontal dead-end bar. Next, clause 2 is inspected, as shown in Fig. 3.3(c). There are three important things to note even in this simple example. Firstly, in the copy of clause 2 being inspected, the variable **X** has been appropriately renamed by adding a subscript, so that $\mathbf{X_1}$ is distinct from the **X** in the query (which is, in essence, $\mathbf{X_0}$). Secondly, the arrows in Fig. 3.3(c) are unification arrows which form an intrinsic part of our execution model. They indicate not only that **X** is instantiated to **fred** and $\mathbf{X_1}$ is instantiated to **rubbish**, but also (at a glance) that **X** is an output variable and $\mathbf{X_1}$ is an input variable. Thirdly, the clause status box at this instant has a question-mark in it, meaning that the interpreter technically needs to pursue the body of this clause. We can see that the clause is an ordinary Prolog fact, and therefore has no body, but technically it has the implicit body **true**, which is trivially satisfiable. If there had been one or more subgoals in the body, then the interpreter would need to process the subgoal(s) in order to determine the outcome of this particular clause.

Figure 3.3(d) shows the moment when processing is complete. The clause status box for clause 2 has been marked with a tick. Precisely because there are no descendants emanating from this clause status box, we can tell at a glance that this was a trivial success (i.e. an ordinary Prolog fact). The clause branches formally correspond to disjunctive choices, so if any of them succeeds, the procedure as a whole succeeds. Therefore, the goal status indicator becomes a tick as well, indicating that the goal has succeeded.

The four-step unification sequence depicted in Fig. 3.3(a)–3.3(d) is of most use to us in teaching Prolog. Once this account has been shown to students (both in textual form and in an animation in our accompanying video material), we ask them to fill in the details in empty "status boxes" alongside various examples. Because such details are not normally of interest to experienced Prolog programmers, our graphical tracing package presents final snapshot views corresponding to that of Fig. 3.3(d), with the other details being made available upon request.

2.2 AORTA Diagrams and "Execution Spaces"

AND/OR trees are a frequently used and highly expressive way of describing the execution of logic programs, and Prolog programs in particular. An investigation of notation formalisms by Bundy and his colleagues at the University of Edinburgh (e.g. Pain and Bundy, 1987) concluded that AND/OR trees offered the greatest potential in terms of clarity of explanation, but that they suffered from several deficiencies, particularly when it came to displaying different environments of recursive calls, variable renaming, and output substitution (variable instantiation). We reasoned that the node in a traditional AND/OR tree was a needlessly impoverished representation, and that by enriching it in appropriate ways we could have our cake and eat it too. In other words, we wanted to have an intuitively clear AND/OR-style account of execution while providing all the details that a traditional AND/OR tree leaves out. The missing link is precisely the procedure status box described in section 2. These boxes can be used in place of simple AND/OR tree nodes, with the clause branches representing OR choices, and subgoal branches (borrowed from the standard AND/OR tree notation) representing conjunctions of subgoals. The combination has led us to refer to our diagrams as "AORTA Diagrams" (**A**nd/**OR** **T**ree, **A**ugmented). We use a family relationship metaphor to refer to different elements of the diagram, where goals and subgoals are "parents" and "children" respectively, and conjuncts are termed siblings (e.g. **e** and **f** in Fig. 3.1). **f** is the younger sibling because it was last to be processed.

Rather than show the full search space for Prolog programs, our model concerns itself with the execution space, i.e. those goals and subgoals which are actually attempted during the processing of a given query. When a given procedure has alternative clauses which are never inspected during a particular execution, these are simply left as dangling clause branches to provide a visually meaningful context in which to view the whole execution space. Consider the following program and sample interaction:

```
older(X, Y) :-
    age(X, AgeOfX),
    age(Y, AgeOfY),
    AgeOfX > AgeOfY.
age(john, 27).
age(tom, 18).
age(sue, 24).
?- older (john, sue).
yes
```

Figure 3.4 shows the AORTA diagram corresponding to the final snapshot of execution. The small italic letters *a–i* are used as time-stamps to label the ticks, dead-end bars, and crosses in the precise order in which they appear (these are for the reader's benefit only, and do not form part of the AORTA diagram itself).

Four additional notation conventions are introduced in Figure 3.4:

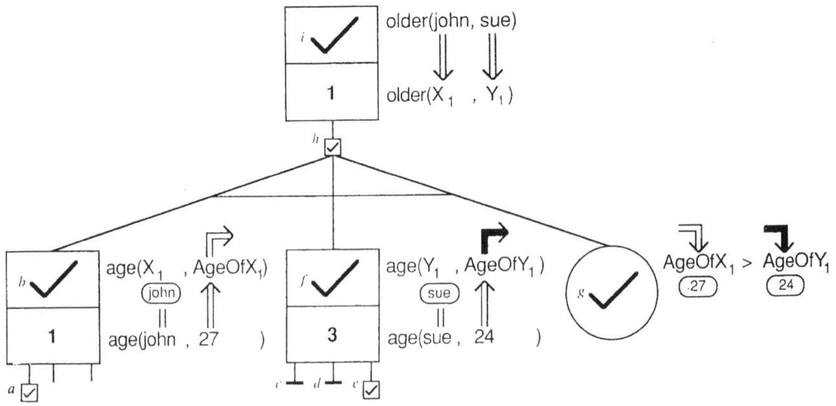

FIG. 3.4. Final snapshot after processing the query **?- older(john, sue)**. The small letters in italics indicate the order in which the status symbols appeared. Primitives are displayed as circular nodes.

The circular status box. This is used to display system primitives in a distinctive manner. In Fig. 3.4, the primitive ">" appears this way.

Right-angle arrows. When a variable appears more than once in a given clause, a right-angle arrow can be used to show how its instantiation is "passed across" from one occurrence to another. In Fig. 3.4, we see that $\mathbf{AgeOfX_1}$ is an output variable where it first appears in the goal $\mathbf{age(X_1, AgeOfX_1)}$, and that it becomes instantiated to **27** (just before time-stamp *a*, in fact). In its second appearance, $\mathbf{AgeOfX_1}$ is already instantiated by the time the subgoal $\mathbf{AgeOfX_1 > AgeOfY_1}$ is processed (time-stamp *g*), and notice that the right-angle arrow shows it correctly as an input variable at this point. The variable $\mathbf{AgeOfY_1}$ is handled analogously, and shading is used just to keep the matching pairs of arrows visually distinct.

Lozenges. In an AORTA diagram, every variable in principle has a little lozenge underneath it which shows the variable's current instantiation. In practice, we adopt a "tidying" convention which allows us to omit a lozenge whenever there is a straight up-arrow or down-arrow that lets us see the actual instantiation at a glance. We have found that the lozenges are absolutely vital for showing the details of unification, but that without the tidying convention the diagrams become needlessly cluttered. In effect, the appearance of a lozenge means that a given instantiation has come "from elsewhere". We deliberately avoid the inclusion of linking arrows depicting exactly what "from elsewhere" means, because such arrows not only become unwieldy in complex diagrams, but are actually redundant. The reader may wish to confirm that the lozenge underneath the $\mathbf{X_1}$ in the lower left-hand part of Fig. 3.4 can only mean that $\mathbf{X_1}$ was an input variable in that situation, and therefore a down-arrow above that $\mathbf{X_1}$ is unnecessary.

Headless arrows. This is actually a sideways "=", which conveniently shows a direct match between two terms. This can also be used to show when two uninstantiated variables share a value.

Because it is inherently difficult to capture the dynamic nature of AORTA diagrams in a static medium such as printed text, the reader may find it useful to work through time-stamps *a*–*i* of Fig. 3.4, and to confirm the following two observations: 1. The lozenges containing **john** and **27** are filled (i.e. the variables $\mathbf{X_1}$ and $\mathbf{AgeOfX_1}$ are instantiated) just before the tick labelled with time-stamp *a* appears; 2. The lozenges containing **sue** and **24** are filled (i.e. the variables $\mathbf{Y_1}$ and $\mathbf{AgeOfY_1}$ are instantiated) just between time-stamps *d* and *e*. In our textual presentation of AORTA diagrams (Eisenstadt, 1988), we include numerous execution snapshot sequences, with unfilled lozenges left for our students to fill in. The replay facility of our graphical tracer (as well as the video animation sequences used in our course materials) allows us to show the dynamics of program execution in a more suitable manner (Eisenstadt & Brayshaw, 1988).

To illustrate some of the finer points of our notation, consider the classic definition of **member**, which involves relatively uninteresting flow of control but much more interesting unification. Here is the definition, followed by a sample query:

```
member(X, [X | Tail]).           % case 1: X is identical to head of list
member(X, [Head | Tail]) :-      % case 2: X is a member if . . .
    member(X, Tail).             % it's recursively a member of the tail
?- member(joe, [tom,joe,sue]).
yes
```

Figure 3.5 shows the AORTA execution snapshot at the moment this query has succeeded.

There are three subtleties to note about Fig. 3.5:

Lists are expanded to show the head and tail explicitly just in those places where it is critical to reveal the precise correspondence for unification purposes. For instance, the second argument of the goal is displayed as **[tom | [joe,sue]]** rather than **[tom,joe,sue]**, thereby making the instantiations of $\mathbf{Head_2}$ and $\mathbf{Tail_2}$ obvious at a glance.

A thin horizontal line is drawn at the base of unification arrows to encompass entire compound terms (structures), thereby showing that it is the whole term, (rather than a single atom within it), which has been unified.

When an arrow points down from below (or up towards) a lozenge as a whole, then the full content of that lozenge is involved. On the other hand, when part of the arrow crosses the border of a lozenge, then only the particular term being pointed from (or to) is involved.

2.3 Esoteric Flow of Control: Backtracking and Invocation Histories

The overall structure of AORTA diagrams (and indeed the AND/OR trees from which they evolved) is inherently simple when the chronology of execution maps trivially onto the left-to-right/top-to-bottom branching structure of the diagrams. In other words, as long as control flow is straightforward, graphical representation of control flow is also straightforward. In Prolog, backtracking immediately alters this trivial mapping. Nevertheless, AORTA diagrams offer a solution. A procedure status box concisely encapsulates in one (two-dimensional) place the execution his-

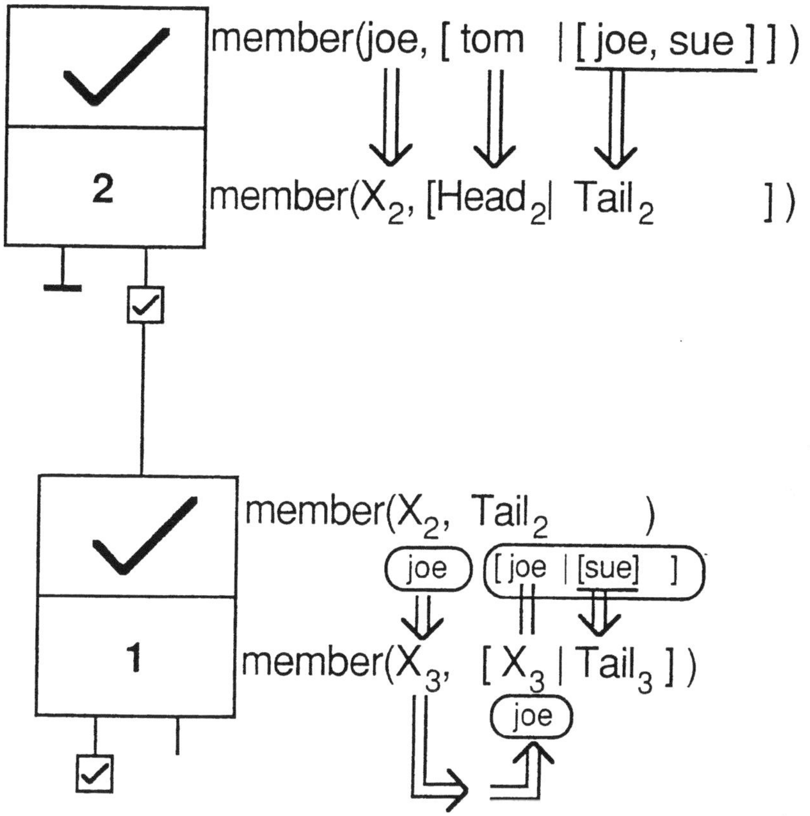

FIG. 3.5. AORTA diagram corresponding to solution of the query:
?- member(joe, [tom, joe, sue]).

tory of a single invocation of a procedure. During the course of that invocation, all sorts of things may happen, but the net result maintained in the individual clause status boxes. If a goal fails, it may be re-invoked later at what amounts to the same location in the execution space. We can use a third dimension (i.e. depth) to cater for the distinction between older and newer invocations at the same place in the execution space. When there are two or more such invocations, the latest invocation appears normally, but prior invocations are depicted schematically in the form of a shaded *ghost* status box underneath the latest invocation. In effect, the ghost is just an icon meaning "there was (at least) one prior invocation here". In our textual displays, the ghost just serves as a reminder, but in our graphical tracer implementation, the ghost is actually a mouse-sensitive item which allows the user to examine what happened at the appropriate point in the execution history.

A good example involving multiple invocations comes from the work of Coombs and Stell (1985). Here is an isomorphic variant of a program they used to investigate common misconceptions held by novices about backtracking in Prolog:

```
desperate(X):                 % We can call someone "desperate" if . . .
     name_dropper(X),         % they have a habit of name dropping
     unemployed(X).           % and also happen to be out of work.
name_dropper(X) :-            % someone is a "name dropper" if. . .
     knows(X, Y),             % they know someone . . .
     famous(Y).               % who is famous
name_dropper(X) :-            % or, alternatively,
     knows(Y, X),             % if a famous person knows them
     famous(Y).
knows(joe, mick).
knows(charles, fred).
famous(mick).                 % say, Mick Jagger
famous(charles).              % say, Prince Charles
unemployed(mick).
unemployed(fred).
```

Figures 3.6(a)–3.6(c) show isolated snapshots at critical moments in the execution history, given the top-level query **?- desperate(Who)**. The first snapshot, Fig. 3.6(a), depicts the first time **unemployed** fails, attempting to prove **unemployed(joe)**.

Let's now work through the processing. We provide only a verbal description of the micro-structure of events between Figs 3.6(a) and 3.6(b), because it would require a large number of AORTA snapshots (nine, in fact) to illustrate diagrammatically. As soon as **unemployed(joe)** fails (Fig. 3.6(a)), the interpreter backtracks to the previous choice point, attempting to see whether there are any more ways of satisfying **famous(Y_2)**, given that Y_2 is instantiated to **mick** (notice this instantiation has come from elsewhere, namely **knows(X_2, Y_2)**, so cannot be undone). There are no other ways to satisfy **famous(Y_2)** with Y_2 instantiated to **mick**, so **famous(Y_2)** fails. Following the failure of **famous(Y_2)**, the interpreter backtracks into the previous subgoal, i.e. **knows(X_2, Y_2)**. Clause 1 of **knows** receives a tick/cross, and the instantiations of X_2 (and therefore X_1 and **Who**) are undone, as is the instantiation of Y_2. Clause 2 of **knows** [i.e. **knows(charles, fred)**] succeeds, at which point X_2 is instantiated to **charles** and Y_2 is instantiated to **fred**. A new invocation of **famous** is then attempted for the goal

famous(Y_2), but **famous(fred)** doesn't unify with either of the two clauses of **famous**. Therefore, **famous(Y_2)** fails, and the interpreter backtracks to **knows(X_2, Y_2)** again. Now clause 2 of **knows** receives a tick/cross combination, and X_2 and Y_2 are uninstantiated. There are no more clauses of **knows** left to try, so **knows(X_2, Y_2)** fails, thereby failing the first clause of **name_dropper**. Clause 2 of **name_dropper** is then processed. The subscript counter is bumped up, and the variables in this clause are renamed by subscripting them with a 3.

Figure 3.6(b) depicts the beginning of the processing of clause 2 of **name_dropper**. We can see from the headless unification arrows that the variables X_3, X_1 and **Who** share. The procedure status box for **famous** shows the result of its latest invocation: both clauses failed to unify when Y_2 was instantiated to **fred**. The ghost status box partially hidden behind the procedure status box for **famous** indicates only that there was a prior invocation of **famous** at that particular point in the execution space. Each of the invocations shown corresponds to one of the former successes of **knows**, indicated by the two tick/cross combinations in the clause status boxes for **knows(X_2, Y_2)**. Technically, each of the successes associated with **knows(X_2, Y_2)** happened on a different OR choice, and since these correspond to different clause branches, they can be displayed appropriately as belonging to the fate of a single invocation of the **knows** procedure. Therefore a ghost status box is not necessary for **knows**. The goal **famous(Y_2)** has been invoked twice at the same point in the search space, and therefore requires a ghost status box to show the former invocation.

The final execution snapshot is shown in Fig. 3.6(c). Notice the new ghost status boxes for **unemployed(X_1)** and **famous(Y_3)**, indicating failure on prior invocations of the respective goals. In the case of **unemployed**, the ghost invocation is the one we witnessed in Fig. 3.6(a) following the initial success of **name_dropper(X_1)**, when X_1 was instantiated to **joe**. In the case of **famous(Y_3)**, the ghost invocation was due to the initial success of clause 1 of **knows**, i.e. **knows(joe, mick)**, nested as a subgoal within clause 2 of **name_dropper**. At that point, Y_3 would have been instantiated to **joe**, so neither of the two clauses of **famous** could have unified with **famous(Y_3)**. In our graphical tracer implementation, if any goal has more than one prior invocation (still indicated by a single ghost status box), it is possible for the user to step through them individually by mouse-clicking on the ghost. This rewinds the execution replay to the time point when the previous invocation occurred, and ensures that the simple unification history of a variable is observable. The previous invocation may of course have its own ghost (i.e. an even earlier invocation) which in turn will be selectable by the user. An alternative method is to re-observe the complete execution sequence from the beginning, using the fast-forward and single-step capabilities described in Eisenstadt and Brayshaw (1988).

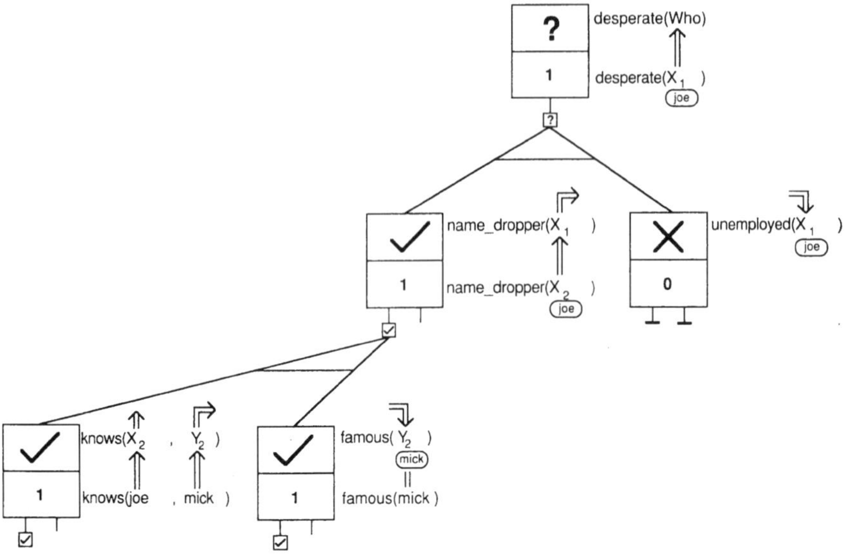

FIG. 3.6. Execution snapshot following query **?- desperate(Who)**. The definitions of desperate and its subordinates are presented in the text.
(a) The moment of first failure of **unemployed**.

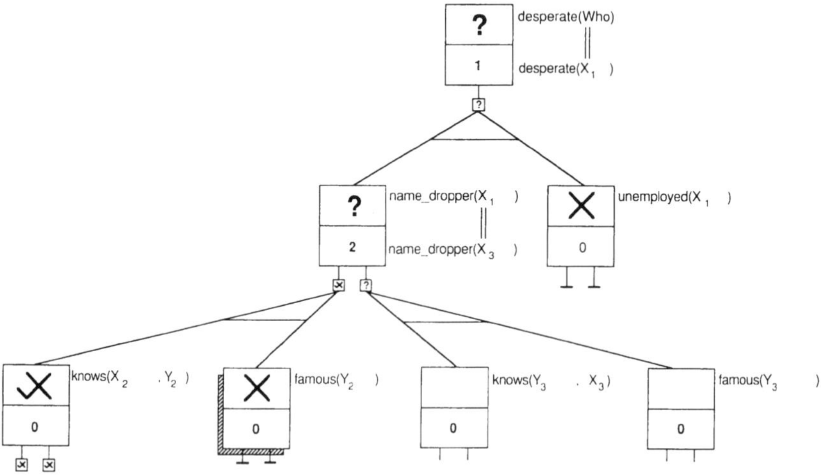

(b) Just about to attempt second clause of **name_dropper**. Notice that **famous** had a prior invocation which succeeded but then failed on backtracking. The current invocation of **famous** failed because no clause heads matched.

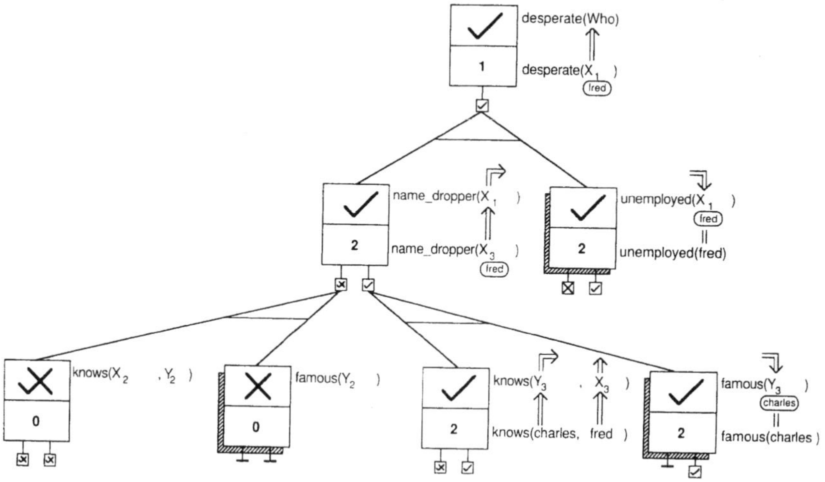

(c) Final snapshot. Both **famous** and **unemployed** failed on prior invocations.

2.4 The Cut

In addition to handling multiple invocations of a goal, the other major extra-logical control problem to deal with is the cut. Using AORTA diagram notation, this is surprisingly easy. Bearing in mind that the cut is itself a subgoal which has ancestors and (typically) siblings, the following three things happen when a cut is encountered:

1. Prior sibling (conjoined) goals and their descendants are "frozen" (enshrouded in a small cloud which makes them unalterable on back-tracking).
2. Upcoming clause branches of the cut's parent goal are chopped.
3. The cut succeeds, just like any ordinary Prolog goal.

Consider the following program, which depicts the circumstances in which some X has a party.

```
party(X):-                 % party if happy & birthday
    happy(X),
    birthday(X).
party(X):-                 % or to cheer up sad friend
    friends(X,Y),
    sad(Y).
```

```
happy(X):-                    % X is happy provided that . . .
    hot,                      % it's hot
    humid,                    % and it's humid
    !,                        % but only if it's also the case that . . .
    swimming(X).              % X is swimming
happy(X):-
    cloudy,
    watching_tv(X).
happy(X):-
    cloudy,
    having_fun(X).
cloudy.
humid.
hot.
having_fun(tom).
having_fun(sam).
swimming(john).
watching_tv(john).
sad(bill).
sad(sam).
birthday(tom).
birthday(sam).
friends(tom,john).
friends(tom,sam).
```

Figure 3.7 shows the AORTA diagram corresponding to the final snapshot of execution following the query **?- party(Name)**. The solution is **Name = tom**.

We can see in Fig. 3.7 that **happy** succeeded initially on clause 1, but unification with either clause of birthday was not possible. This failure caused the backtracking into **swimming**, which itself failed upon backtracking (no further clauses to attempt), as indicated by the tick/cross combination appearing in the top of its status box. This is also the case with the **!** goal, displayed as a circular node just like any system primitive would be. Notice the frozen cloud around the cut's older siblings **hot** and **humid** and the scissors-plus-jagged-edge icon showing the elimination of the remaining clause branches under the procedure status box of the parent goal **happy**. The parent's failure is further indicated by the tick/cross in the top part of its status box. The failure of clause 1 of **party** led to clause 2 being attempted. The **friends** goal succeeded on clause 1 [i.e. **friends(tom, john)**] but **sad(john)** failed in its first invocation. Upon backtracking, **friends** succeeded on the second clause, namely **friends(tom, sam)**, and a brand

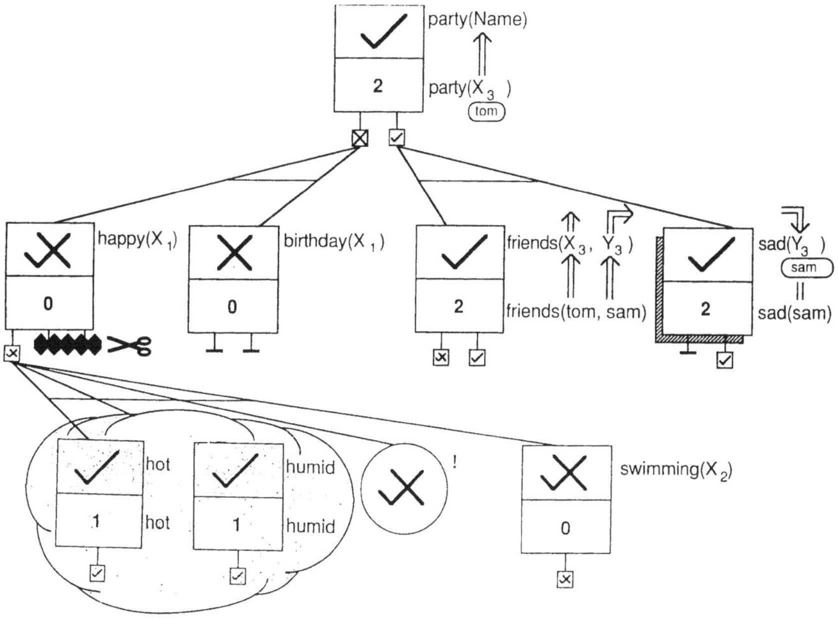

FIG. 3.7. AORTA snapshot after processing the query **?- party(Name)**, given the definitions of party and its subordinates shown in the text.

new invocation of the **sad** goal occurred, hence the ghost status box showing the previous invocation of **sad**. We can also see in Fig. 3.7 that $\mathbf{X_3}$ was instantiated to **tom,** $\mathbf{Y_3}$ was instantiated to **sam** and that this instantiation was passed to the goal **sad**. The goal **sad($\mathbf{Y_3}$)**, with $\mathbf{Y_3}$ instantiated to **sam**, matched directly against the fact **sad(sam)** in the data base. This led to the success of the goal **sad** and consequently of the main goal **party**, at precisely the moment captured in Fig. 3.7.

3. A TEXTBOOK, VIDEO, AND WORKBOOK CURRICULUM

The AORTA diagram representation was developed to fulfil a dual need, as stated in section 1. In this section, we want to focus on the way the notation is integrated into our teaching material.

3.1 Curriculum Motivation

We have developed a Prolog course (Eisenstadt, 1988) as part of an Alvey/SERC initiative. This initiative identified a need among computing professionals to learn about Prolog in a distance-teaching setting (i.e. in their own environment). We felt that since the essentials of Prolog were adequately covered in Bratko's *Prolog Programming for Artificial Intelligence* (Bratko, 1986), the most appropriate thing to do would be to build upon it by providing detailed diagrammatic execution snapshots, reworking some of the more difficult examples, and adding our own emphasis on program design and sophisticated Prolog techniques. We thus concentrated our efforts on clarifying the inner workings of the interpreter, and helping students evolve an execution model which would lead to a clearer (and hopefully less bug-riddled) understanding of Prolog execution. The AORTA notation we had been developing for our advanced graphical debugger appeared to fit the bill, particularly since conceptual clarity was already a high priority objective for that research project.

To encourage wide acceptability of the course, the teaching material works with all the most popular implementations of Prolog, including Quintus Prolog, C-Prolog, LPA MacPROLOG, Arity Prolog, Prolog-2, and even (up to the point where we discuss meta-interpreters and infix notation) Turbo Prolog. For those students who have not yet decided which commercial Prolog to buy, we include an Edinburgh syntax Prolog interpreter on a floppy disk so that they can get started immediately. We also include full source code listings of all the examples used in the course, both in hard copy and on the course disk.

3.2 Course Objectives

Students completing our 80-hour study package are expected to achieve the following objectives:

- Use any of a range of hardware/software configurations to enter, run, and debug sophisticated Prolog programs.
- Explain the practical significance of logic programming terminology (e.g. "functor", "unification", "backtracking").
- Implement a program to determine whether a person is eligible to receive free prescriptions.
- Implement a travel planning program which can propose times, flights, and routes for an airline trip from city A to city B via intermediate cities.
- Improve existing planning programs so that they avoid endless loops.
- Implement an expert system shell which can answer "why" and "how" queries about its own reasoning process.

These objectives are addressed through a graded series of presentations and exercises contained in the material outlined in the next section and the Appendix.

3.3 Course Contents

The course comprises a set of course notes, a workbook, a set book, a 120-minute video cassette, and a floppy disk. The main study material is 160 pages in length, and is accompanied by a workbook of exercise material, 136 pages in length. Appendix A presents a detailed course outline, including a summary of the pedagogical motivation of each main section and some sample diagrams illustrating the way that the course materials rely extensively on the fine-grained execution model presented above.

The course workbook includes a "how to get started" guide, which summarizes the differences among the 10 most popular implementations of Prolog. There are lots of "unfilled" AORTA diagrams for the students to fill in as part of their worked exercises, as shown in the appendix in Fig. A2. The accompanying video material relies extensively on AORTA diagram notation, and presents numerous animated sequences. A separate 16-page set of video notes is used to help the students to work through some of the exemplary problems contained in several stop/start video sequences.

4. SCALING UP FROM THE FINE-GRAINED ACCOUNT: HANDLING LARGE PROGRAMS

For a Prolog execution notation to be of practical use when dealing with real Prolog applications, it must be capable of scaling up to deal with a large amount of information while still being able to show the close-up detail. In particular, there are three issues to be dealt with: (a) unification of large terms, (b) large data bases, (c) large execution spaces. We discuss each of these in turn.

4.1 Unification of Large Terms

While compound terms can in general be dealt with in the manner described in section 2, the sheer size of certain terms in real Prolog programs necessitates the use of special collapsing conventions. We use hand-crafted (i.e. carefully-positioned) ellipsis dots ("...") in our textual displays as and when appropriate, and a special small font in our graphical tracer implementation to show the unification of very large terms. We also allow the user of our graphical tracer to specify an ellipsis template for the display of large terms, which works much like Prolog's **portray** primitive, except the user can create the necessary meta-logical declarations by manipulating a sample term. This manipulation is based on a hierarchical structure editor in the spirit of Teitelbaum and Reps (1981). The user can expand and contract arbitrarily nested terms to his or her satisfaction using simple mouse operations, and the outcome is used as a prototype for displaying future occurrences of terms involving the same predicate.

4.2 Large Data Bases

Large terms are not the only practical problem we have to face: large data bases may contain hundreds (or even thousands) of clauses in the definition of a given procedure. To cater for this, we adopt a collapsing convention in the procedure status box. Rather than showing all clause branches, we only show the current (unifying) clause, and its predecessor, with ellipsis dots on either side to indicate that there are both higher and lower number clauses of the same predicate. This will be updated appropriately during replay to reflect the search through large data bases. Figure 3.8 contains an example, using a large airline timetable data base.

4.3 Large Execution Spaces

Prolog execution can involve tens of thousands of nodes even in quite mundane applications. In our graphical implementation, we allow the expert to view the program as a whole from a distance in order to gain an overall perspective, while at the same time providing facilities for viewing program execution (control flow and unification details) from close up. In order to achieve this we eliminate the clause counter and detailed clause head information of the AORTA diagrams. What we end up with is a schematised AND/OR tree in which an individual node summarises the outcome of a call to a particular procedure. Far from being yet another notation convention, these nodes are in fact just procedure status boxes (as introduced in section 2) collapsed so that only their top half is showing. We refer to this collapsed representation as the Coarse Grained View (CGV). In earlier papers we called this the Long Distance View (LDV), but the current terminology more appropriately reflects the emphasis on granularity rather than simple scaling.

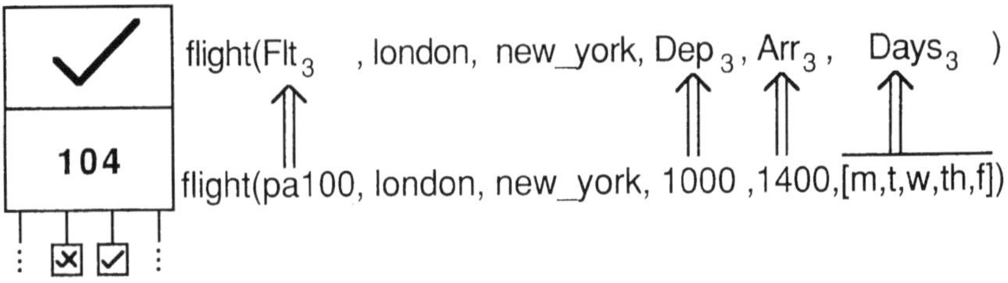

FIG. 3.8. A procedure status box to cater for large databases.

To provide the most meaningful display of information in the smallest space, we rely on colour in our colour-workstation implementation and shading in our black-and-white implementation. In the colour display, ticks are green, indicating success, crosses are red, indicating failure, and tick/cross combinations are pink (nearly red). In the collapsed status box of the CGV, it is sufficient to display just the colour (e.g. a very small fully-shaded green box instead of a box with a hard-to-see green tick in it). We simulate this in our black and white display using white to indicate success, black to indicate failure, grey shading to indicate success followed by failure on backtracking, and thickened lines to indicate "currently pending goal". Another convention we introduce in the CGV is the *compressed node*. This appears as a triangle (evocative of a sub-tree shape), and indicates that a given Prolog goal is being treated for the moment as a "black box" primitive, i.e. a goal whose inner details are not shown at the moment, but which can be expanded later upon request. Users are free to choose arbitrary predicates for compression or un-compression.

Figure 3.9 shows a snapshot taken in the middle of the execution of a moderate size Prolog program. Users of our graphical tracer/debugger implementation have the option of visualising program execution retrospectively, i.e. following a behind-the-scenes analysis, or live, i.e. interactively, or in a combination of the two styles. In the case of Fig. 3.9, the program is being executed retrospectively. This means that it is possible to say in advance (from the user's point of view) precisely which nodes will be

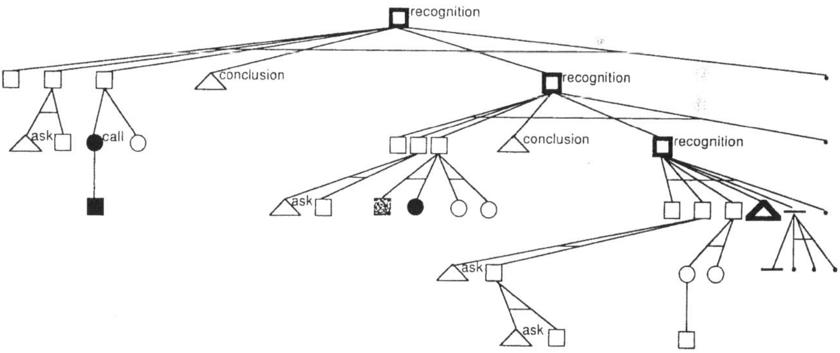

FIG. 3.9. A coarse grained view (CGV) in the middle of (re-)execution replay. The CGV is part of a graphical tracer implementation in which both CGV and AORTA views may be displayed. Only certain nodes are labelled, at the user's discretion. Triangular nodes are compressed sub-trees, which may be expanded upon request. White = success, black = failure; grey = succeeded earlier but failed on backtracking; very thick line = currently pending goal. "Dash" and "dot" (far right hand side) are user-defined procedures and system primitives, respectively, which have not yet been executed at the moment depicted by this snapshot.

traversed. The thin horizontal line indicates a user-defined procedure in the so-called "pre-ordained execution space"; that is, a call which has not yet happened at the moment the snapshot is taken, but which the program analyser can guarantee will eventually happen. Analogously, a small dot indicates a system primitive which has not yet been executed, but which will eventually be executed.

The succinct manner of CGV representation allows for the analysis of very large Prolog programs. Even if the execution space is too large to be meaningfully displayed within a single graphics pane, the user is able to scroll around the pane, selecting the area of the tree which he or she wishes to look at. A facility to monitor which part of the tree is being observed ensures that the user maintains a global perspective on the whole tree.

4.4 Seeing the Wood for the Trees: Four Navigation Methods

We feel very strongly that simple physical (machine-provided) zoom facilities are insufficient for providing a comprehensive view of Prolog execution. Indeed, such physical facilities, which manipulate the scale of the display, account for just one of four different ways of manipulating the navigational space produced by large Prolog programs. These four manipulations correspond to the following concepts in our philosophy of program tracing:

Granularity: this is our distinction between coarse-grained (CGV) and fine-grained (AORTA) presentations.

Scale: a given coarse-grained presentation may itself need to be re-scaled for a "far-away" look, as in the moving viewport feature which we use for extremely large programs.

Compression: this technique, in general, is the use of a single compact display region or symbol to indicate additional territory, at a given granularity and scale. Our compressed nodes (triangular-shaped subtrees) are an example of this technique, and allow the user to treat large lumps of code as a black box.

Abstraction: user-defined representations provide a movement away from fidelity to the raw Prolog code and towards a representation closer to the programmer's own plans and intentions (see Brayshaw & Eisenstadt, 1988).

The collection of facilities mentioned above allows the user, whether novice or expert, to be told a detailed story about the history of program execution. Based on our own experience of using TPM to debug Prolog programs, we assume that debugging begins with a coarse-grained view of execution, which may contain both compressed and abstracted nodes, reflecting the manner in which the user has chosen to manage the available information. Predicates that are reliable, i.e. tried and trusted code in which the user isn't really interested, are typically compressed by the user to avoid cluttering the display. AORTA diagrams are used as and when more fine-grained information is required. Since zooming and highlighting requests always begin with the CGV, all the perspective information associated with the CGV is available at the point of choice, allowing the user clearly to understand the context of the code which is being observed close up. This approach removes the wood-vs.-trees problem associated with conventional spy packages. The contextual information associated with the fine-grained view is naturally produced from the coarse grained view. By the combination of the CGV, AORTA, zooming, selective highlighting and replay facilities, the user may more readily understand the state of the program, and thus arrive rapidly at the source of problematic bugs.

5. CONCLUSIONS

We have developed an augmented AND/OR tree notation which enables a visual presentation of the fine-grained truth about Prolog program execution, including unification, clause selection, flow of control, and other extra-logical language features such as the cut. A collapsed long distance view, based on the same notation, enables us to display very large search spaces in a working graphical tracer implementation.

Our aim has been to satisfy both the needs of novices learning Prolog and the needs of expert Prolog users writing and debugging very large programs. These intentions have, in turn, led us along a pathway of creative tension to satisfy somewhat contradictory constraints. The key ingredients of our approach have been the following:

- Enhancement of AND/OR tree nodes with goal status boxes.
- Enhancement of traditional AND/OR tree branches with individual clause details.
- Use of lozenges and unification arrows to show unification details.
- Recognition of the need (and the ability) to display thousands of collapsed nodes at a time in a working graphical tracer.
- Ability to vary the type of detail being investigated with the particular grain size, rather than using a physical zoom.

An objection raised by first-time users of AORTA diagrams is that the diagrams are more difficult to understand than Prolog itself. We have anecdotal evidence that this difficulty is short-lived, and that an expressive visual representation eventually carries the day, particularly when non-trivial Prolog programs are involved. We know from the work of Taylor (1987) and others that the apparent naturalness and simplicity of Prolog are deceptive, and that users suddenly experience great difficulty writing and debugging programs intended to solve other than toy problems. Pain and Bundy (1987) put forward a cogent argument that a clear and consistent story describing the inner workings of the Prolog interpreter would help to alleviate some of the difficulties, and it was precisely such an argument which inspired the work described herein. Based on informal observations of our own students, we know that there is a cross-over point, after which Prolog programming becomes tricky, and students spontaneously revert to scribbling AORTA diagrams on paper in order to understand what their programs are doing. To the extent that AORTA diagrams are clear and consistent, then their use can make logic programming more accessible, and thereby contribute to its growth and appreciation as an emerging discipline. We are excited by the fact that we can now offer newcomers to Prolog a complete cradle-to-grave environment in the form of text, video, and a computer-implemented trace package. The integrated environment conveys a consistent format that makes execution intuitively clear and at the same time provides real hands-on debugging power for experienced users.

REFERENCES

duBoulay, J. B. H., O'Shea, T., & Monk, J. (1981). The black box inside the glass box: Presenting computing concepts to novices. *International Journal of Man Machine Studies, 14* (3), 237–249.

Bratko, I. (1986). *Prolog programming for artificial intelligence.* Reading, MA: Addison-Wesley.

Brayshaw, M. & Eisenstadt, M. (1988). Adding data and procedure abstraction to the Transparent Prolog Machine. In R. A. Kowalski & K. A. Bowen (Eds), *Logic Programming, Volume 1*, Cambridge, MA: MIT Press, 532–547.

Brayshaw, M. & Eisenstadt, M. (1991). A practical graphical tracer for Prolog. *International Journal of Man-Machine Studies, 35*, (5).

Brown, M. H. (1988). *Algorithm animation.* Cambridge, MA: MIT Press.

Brown, M. H. & Sedgewick, R. (1985). Techniques for algorithm animation. *IFFE Software 2*, (1), 28–39.

Bundy, A., Pain, H., Brna, P., & Lynch, L. (1986). A proposed Prolog story. *DAI Research Paper 283*, Department of Artificial Intelligence, University of Edinburgh.

Byrd, L. (1980). Understanding the control flow of Prolog programs. In S.-Å. Tarnlund (Ed.), *Proceedings of the 1980 Logic Programming Workshop*, 127–138.

Clocksin, W. F. & Mellish, C. S. (1981). *Programming in Prolog (First Edition)*, New York: Springer-Verlag.

Clocksin, W. F. & Mellish, C. S. (1984). *Programming in Prolog (Second Edition)*, New York: Springer-Verlag.

Coombs, M. J. & Stell, J. G. (1985). A model for debugging Prolog by symbolic execution: The separation of specification and procedure. *Research Report MMIGR137*, Department of Computer Science, University of Strathclyde.

Dewar, A. D. & Cleary, J. G. (1986). Graphical display of complex information within a Prolog debugger. *International Journal of Man Machine Studies, 25* (4), 503–521.

Eisenstadt, M. (Ed.). (1988). *Intensive Prolog.* Associate Student Central Office (Course PD622), The Open University, Milton Keynes, U.K.: Open University Press.

Eisenstadt, M. & Brayshaw, M. (1988). The Transparent Prolog Machine (TPM): An execution model and graphical debugger for logic programming. *Journal of Logic Programming*, *5*, 277–342.

Gunakara Sun Systems Limited, (1988). PROLOGRAPH: *Programming in Pictures, personal demonstration*.

Hardy, S. (1984). A new software enviroment for list-processing and logic programming. In T. O'Shea & M. Eisenstadt (Eds), *Artificial intelligence: tools, techniques, and applications*. New York: Harper & Row.

Kowalski, R. (1979). *Logic for problem solving*. New York: Elsevier, North Holland.

Pain, H. & Bundy, A. (1987). What stories should we tell novice Prolog programmers? In R. Hawley (Ed.), *Artificial intelligence programming evironments*. New York: Wiley.

Rajan, T. (1987). The design of animated tracing tools for novice programmers. In H. J. Bullinger & B. Shackel (Eds), *Human-computer interaction – Proc. Interact '87*. Amsterdam: Elsevier, North Holland.

Sterling, L. & Shapiro, E. Y. (1986). *The art of Prolog: advanced programming techniques*, Cambridge, MA: MIT Press.

Taylor, J. (1987). *Programming in Prolog: An in-depth study of problems for beginners learning to program in Prolog*. PhD Thesis. Cognitive Studies Programme, University of Sussex.

Teitelbaum, T. & Reps, T. (1981). The Cornell Program Synthesizer: a syntax-directed programming environment. *Comm. ACM.*, *24*, 563–573.

APPENDIX A. OPEN UNIVERSITY PROLOG COURSE CONTENTS OUTLINE

In the outline presented here, only the top-level headings are shown, along with comments about the underlying pedagogical principles. Sample diagrams from the course are included to show how the fine-grained account of Prolog execution is used in the text and in the accompanying exercises.

Part I: Essential Prolog

1. *Prolog in Sixty Minutes.* The basics of Prolog are easy, so students are launched into examples based on airline flight reservations straight away.

2. *Program Development.* Here we introduce the concept of a conservative "design/edit/invoke Prolog/load/pose queries" cycle.

3. *Behind the Scenes.* The declarative and procedural views of Prolog are presented, and a model of Prolog execution, based on AORTA diagrams, is introduced. Exercises include such things as identifying backtracking points by locating nodes in an AORTA diagram, and working through a series of unification problems. Figures A1 and A2 are representative examples.

4. *Building Problem Solving Programs from Scratch.* We provide a handle for getting into a good mental style for solving problems in Prolog. A suggested technique involves a series of steps including: identify problem area; consider an elementary concrete case; sketch objects and relations; invent functors and arguments; encode the sketch in terms of functors/arguments; invent problem query; decompose problem into easy and hard variants; add facts or rules to cope with easy variants; add rules to cope with main subproblem; generalise query to take more variables; test program; use richer structures; etc.

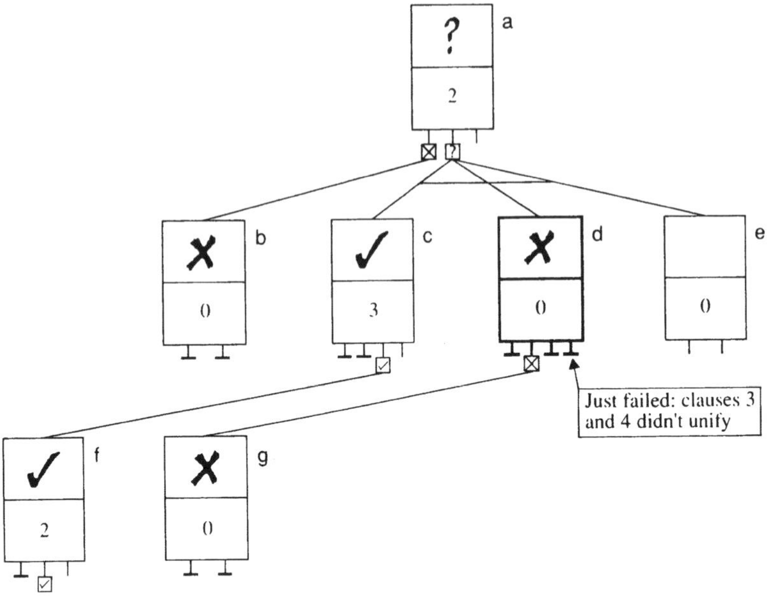

FIG. A1. A sample exercise, in which students are asked to identify backtracking points purely on the basis of the graphical layout. The exercise reads as follows: "Identify (i) the clause status box which receives a cross (or tick/cross) and (ii) the next clause to be processed in the AORTA diagram. The highlighted procedure status box has just failed."

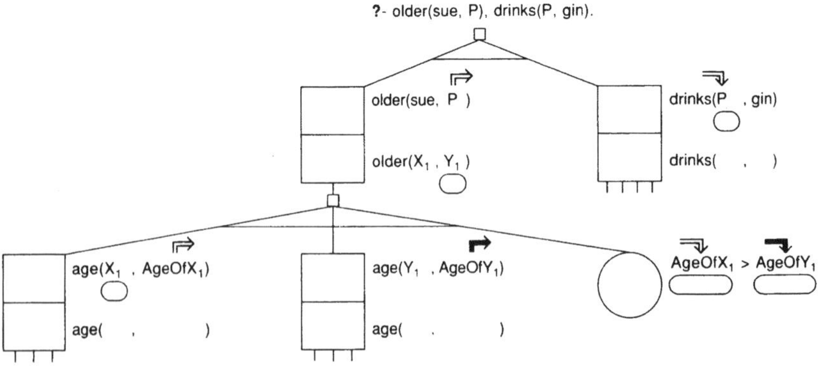

FIG.A2. A sample exercise, in which students are asked to fill in the missing parts of an AORTA diagram. This includes both filling in the appropriate lozenges and completing the outcomes of clause and status boxes.

5. *Understanding Recursion.* The concept of procedure invocation is explored in detail, and a series of AORTA snapshots is used to explain recursion. Video 1 follows this up in an animated sequence.

Part II: The Power of Prolog Representation

6. *Representation Style and Deductive Reasoning.* We discuss problems of choosing good functors and arguments, and links to logical deduction.

7. *Elementary List Manipulation.* Basic list processing, member/2, and lots of unification exercises are presented.

8. *Using Structures.* We describe more stylistic issues such as data abstraction and good representation involving the structures.

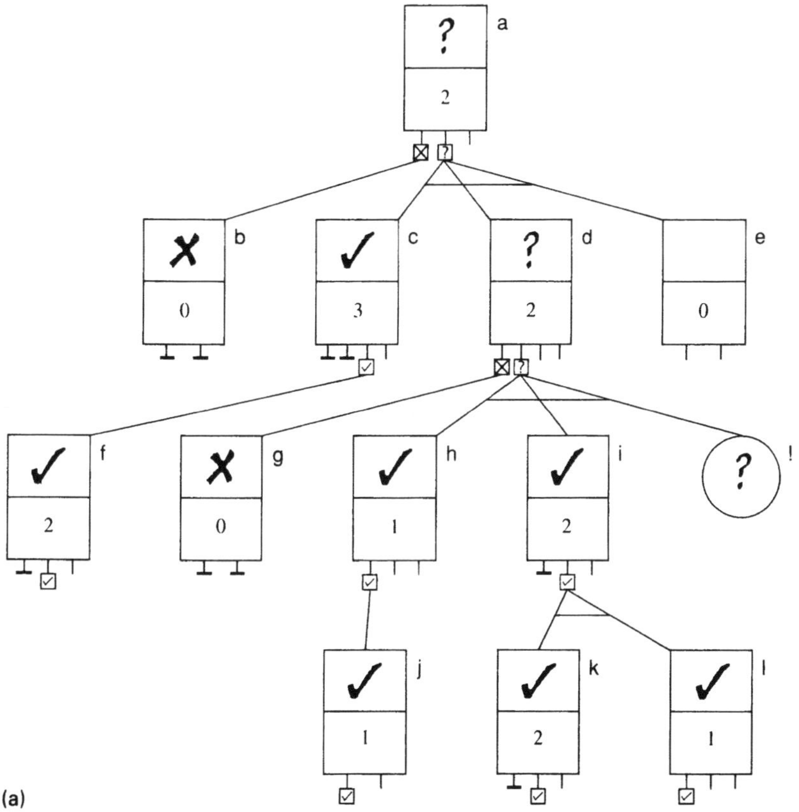

(a)

FIG. A3. Here students are asked to "draw" the effect of the cut at the moment it is executed a) The problem as presented to students.

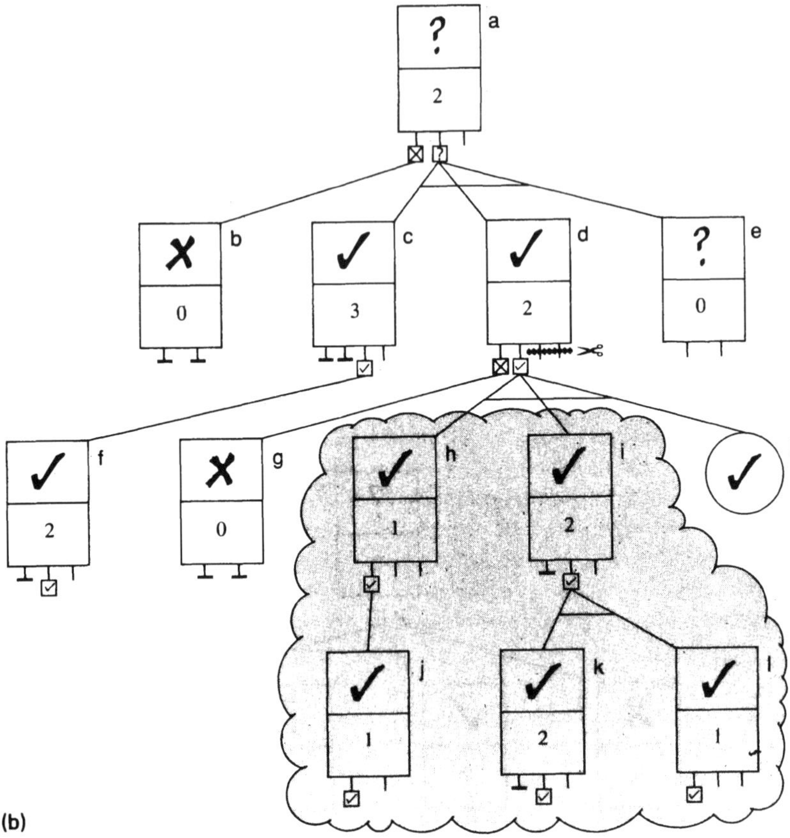

(b)

FIG. A3. b) The solution.

9. *A Closer Look at Unification.* Some subtle cases of unification are described in detail. Bratko's "Monkey and Banana" problem is illustrated step-by-step to show a particularly tricky case of shared variables becoming instantiated in a counter-intuitive way. Lots of AORTA snapshots are used here.

10. *Special List Processing Techniques.* We show how to use an accumulator argument to perform cycle detection, and how to use successive instantiation (building up a list structure in the clause head) to return results. Video 2 amplifies these points with extensive AORTA diagram animations. Students are asked to augment Bratko's travel-planning program so that it deals correctly with cycle detection.

11. *Generators and Failure-Driven Loops.* A specific set of programming cliches is introduced and explicated.

12. *Reshaping the Search Space: The cut, not/1, and once/1.* We use AORTA diagrams and the family metaphor to show precisely what happens when a cut is encountered, and how this can be used to implement (a form of) negation. Exercises require students to draw frozen clouds and to chop off clause branches on AORTA diagrams to see precisely the effect and scope of the cut. A representative example is shown in Fig. A3. Video 3 uses more AORTA animations to reinforce these concepts.

Part III: An Expert System Shell

13. *Choosing a Representation and Building a Basic Shell.* A rational reconstruction of Bratko's expert system shell is presented, starting from a minimal meta-level interpreter. The accompanying Video 4 shows an expert travel planning program (developed by Expert Systems Ltd. for Thomas Cook) in action, and relates it to the shell and travel planning programs used in the course.

14. *"How" Explanations and Truth Values.* The primitive shell is augmented to deal with "how" explanations and explicitly-stored negative facts.

15. *Other Enhancements: Query-the-User and "Why".* The shell is spruced up to deal with interactions with the user and a sensible "why" explanation facility.

4 A New Metaphor for the Graphical Explanation of Forward-Chaining Rule Execution

John Domingue & Marc Eisenstadt
Human Cognition Research Laboratory, The Open University, Milton Keynes, England.

OVERVIEW

This chapter describes a novel method for displaying and examining the execution space of a rule interpreter. This method provides both high-level (coarse-grained) and low-level (fine-grained) views. The coarse-grained view, based on temporal rather than logical dependencies, provides an abstraction of the execution history not available from text or tree-based traces. The fine-grained views allow the user to examine sections of the execution history in detail. A detailed scenario with screen snapshots is presented.

1. INTRODUCTION

This chapter presents the Transparent Rule Interpreter (TRI) a system that provides a graphical explanation of rule execution. TRI is one part of KEATS-II (Motta, Eisenstadt, Pitman, & West, 1988; Motta, Rajan, & Eisenstadt, 1990), a project with the overall aim of providing methodological and software support for all the stages of building very large, knowledge-based systems. Such support includes the provision of a suite of tools for maintaining knowledge bases, collectively known as Knowledge Base Maintenance Tools (KBMTs). In a host of different applications (see Chapters 2 and 3; duBoulay, O'Shea & Monk, 1981), the provision of a clear execution model has proved to be an essential tool for understanding a computational process. In the same vein, TRI presents a clear graphical execution model to the user.

TRI, implemented in Symbolics™ Common Lisp, has been built on top of the KEATS-II forward and backward chaining production system interpreter. The forward chaining part uses a Rete network (Forgy, 1982), and the backward chaining part has a Prolog like inference mechanism.

The rest of this chapter is structured as follows. Section 2 discusses the motivation for TRI, that is the problems found when programming with rules, previous attempts at solving the problems and our approach. Section 3 gives a brief tour of the system using an example, section 4 reviews the principles behind TRI and its extendability, and section 5 contains the conclusions.

2. TRACING RULE EXECUTION

2.1 Problems

There are two types of problem in rule-based programming. The first emerges from the nature of rule based programming (i.e. the basic program coding unit is the rule). Unlike other forms of programming, forward chaining rules do not facilitate any functional or procedural abstraction. The highest level of abstraction is a single rule. We will call these rule-unit problems. This abstraction issue results in serious problems with control. On the one hand, taking rules from the existing rule set can have apparently no effect on how the program runs, while on the other, even when the rule base is very simple, it is not easy to predict which rule will fire next. This is because rules are an unordered, declarative way of expressing knowledge, and by their very nature are inherently non-procedural. The rule-unit problems listed above can lead to buggy programs. An antidote to these problems is to provide a transparent execution model. However, this is the very area where the other class of problems arise.

The second class of problems proceed from the typical manner in which rule execution is presented to the user, which we call problems with execution transparency. There are two ways one might wish to view a program in order to debug it. In a coarse-grained (global) view, one requires some idea of the overall pattern of execution of the rules in the program. From a fine-grained (low-level) point of view, one requires detailed information about unification, instantiation and the state of working memory. Both views are required and if either is absent, two difficulties may occur. First, without a global view of execution, it is very difficult to pinpoint the part of the execution space in which a bug has occurred. Second, without a fine-grained view of execution, it is impossible to answer detailed questions about why a certain rule did not fire in a certain cycle.

2.2 Previous Attempts to Address Problems

Two main approaches have been used in the past to present the execution space of rule systems: text-based traces, e.g. OPS5, (Forgy, 1981) and tree-based traces GEETREE, (Lewis, 1983) Arboretum, (Mott & Brooke, 1987) Guidon-Watch, (Richer & Clancy, 1985) ORBS, (Fickas, 1987) KEE™ and NEXPERT™.

Both tree- and text-based traces provide a medium-level view of forward chaining. Generally they do not display fine-grained information such as showing which conflict resolution strategy ruled out a particular rule instantiation, or why a particular rule failed to fire in a particular cycle, yet both types of traces are too detailed to be considered coarse-grained (a plain scale-factor zoom is not the same as a coarse-grained view).

Text-based traces are difficult to read, because the different types of information displayed are not immediately distinguishable (e.g. information on which rules fired, the state of working memory and the state of the conflict resolution set). The display provides little (via indenting) or no information on the overall shape of the execution space (coarse-grained information). Typically the user, who has a specific query, is given a large amount of information at once, most of which will not be appropriate to the query.

Although tree-based traces are suitable for backward chaining, we believe that they are not appropriate for displaying the execution of forward chaining because the dependencies among forward chaining rules are frequently temporal as well as (or instead of) logical. We therefore opt for a metaphor which is not tree-oriented, as described in section 2.3.

The Oregon Rule Based System, ORBS (Fickas, 1987) is a rapid prototyping environment for experienced, rule-based programmers, and relies heavily on an Interlisp (Teitelman, 1978) style break package. Programmers can insert breaks at various points in their programs, which when encountered allow them to use various tools to inspect, in detail, parts of the environment. ORBS does not have any facilities for displaying a more abstract representation of the execution space. ORBS may therefore be described as transparent from a fine-grained viewpoint, but not transparent from a coarse-grained viewpoint.

The KEE tree-based rule tracer displays rules that were tickled by the rule interpreter. A rule is said to be tickled if it partially matches a new working memory element. In the trace each tickled rule is connected to the rule that deposited the matching working memory element. This provides a spreading effect trace, which we believe is inappropriate for forward chaining. A typical trace of four or five rules over ten cycles will fill a landscape screen. KEE allows the user to access low-level information such as the bindings of variables in the antecedent of a rule from the graph.

KEE is thus transparent on a fine-grained level but not on a coarse-grained level.

GEETREE (Lewis, 1983) provides the programmer with an AND/OR tree representation of the knowledge base. The terminal nodes of the tree represent facts, while the non-terminal nodes represent subgoals. The tree can be used for writing rules by direct manipulation, or for tracing forward and backward chaining programs. Lewis states some of the shortcomings of the tree-based representation (pp. 141): "In some applications, the AND/OR trees are actually highly-interconnected acyclic digraphs with many high indegree nodes. If all node interconnections were displayed simultaneously, the resulting spaghetti-like displays would be difficult to construct and impossible to interpret."

In order to prevent spaghetti-like displays GEETREE allows the user to select a subset of the links to be displayed in a tree. Although this solution can result in an uncluttered screen it does not provide a true coarse-grained view. The real problem is that trees are not really a suitable abstraction for forward chaining. The tree does not provide access to fine-grained information such as why ruleA failed to match, the state of working memory when ruleA fired, or which conflict resolution strategy ruled out ruleA.

Aboretum (Mott & Brook, 1987) is another system that uses a tree-based representation for rules, and is designed to enable naive users to build knowledge bases. Each node on the tree contains a feature and a colour. Features are global predicates which may be true or false, and the colour is either yes (+) or no (−). A link between two nodes signifies an unless clause, while disjunctions are represented by branches. The execution trace in Arboretum simply consists of a display containing the tree of each rule that fires, with adjacently firing rules attached to each other. The system does not provide coarse-grained or fine-grained information, the latter being of little use to novice users anyway.

Guidon-Watch (Richer & Clancey, 1985) is a graphic interface to NEOMYCIN which displays multiple views of a knowledge base and the reasoning process during diagnostic problem solving. Each view is displayed in a separate window. For example, the taxonomy window contains a tree of the possible diagnoses in NEOMYCIN, and the evidence window all the potential evidence for a hypothesis. Guidon-Watch provides both coarse-grained and fine-grained views of program execution. The execution space is displayed using trees which is appropriate for the heuristic classification problem solving process that NEOMYCIN uses.

2.3 The TRI Approach

Our solution to representing the coarse-grained behaviour of a forward-chaining rule interpreter is to have an explicit representation of the time

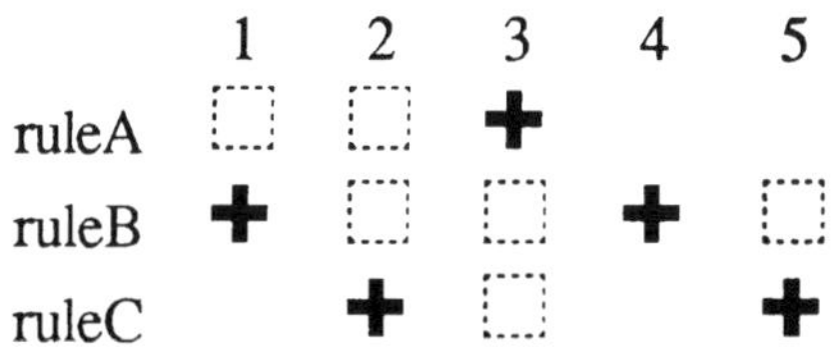

FIG. 4.1. A graph showing the execution of the rules ruleA, ruleB and ruleC over five cycles. The + means that a rule fired, a box means that a rule entered the conflict resolution set but did not fire. The rules fired in the order: ruleB, ruleC, ruleA, ruleB, ruleC. RuleA entered the conflict resolution set during the first 3 cycles only.

dimension, based on a simple musical score metaphor. A simple example is shown in Fig. 4.1.

Given the style of display shown in Fig. 4.1, we can then provide facilities for the user to replay execution, or to focus on particular moments of time and then to examine the fine-grained view to answer particular questions.

The issue of what to display at a fine-grained level is much simpler (e.g. variable bindings, working memory contents), and has been addressed by generations of textual-based tracers for production systems such as OPS5. However, TRI provides two novel extensions to earlier (textual-based) fine-grained displays:

High Selectivity: The user can select elements for fine-grained viewing in a range of ways, depending upon the time, the rule, or the working memory pattern, or any combination of these.

Synchronization with coarse-grained view: Both views can be presented simultaneously, so that as the coarse-grained view is manipulated (e.g. "played forward"), the fine-grained view changes appropriately.

3. SCENARIO

3.1 The Rulebase and Desktop

A TRI user has loaded a rulebase based on Poltreck, Steiner, and Tarlton (1986) which finds all the routes between two cities. The rules, shown in Fig. 4.2, are forward-chaining, with the exception of *b1* and *b2*, which are backward-chaining.

The rules were run with initial working memory [[origin austin] [destination dallas]] producing the output:

Using Highway 35
Austin ---> 60 ---> Temple ---> 34 ---> Waco ---> 41 ---> Hillsboro ---> 48 ---> Dallas
Total Mileage: 183

```
fact-1: if then
   (highway 35
      ((san-antonio austin 74) (austin temple 60)
       (temple waco 34) (waco hillsboro 41)
       (hillsboro dallas 48))))

fact-2: if then
   (highway 10
      ((austin san-antonio 10)
       (san-antonio fredericksburg 20)
       (fredericksburg dallas 50))))

b1 <backward>: (adjcities ?h ?c1 ?c2 ?d) if
      (highway ?h ?list)
      (:lisp (member-of (?c2 ?c1 ?d) ?list)))

b2 <backward>: (adjcities ?h ?c1 ?c2 ?d) if
      (highway ?h ?list)
      (:lisp (member-of (?c1 ?c2 ?d) ?list)))

start: if (origin ?start)
          (destination ?end)
          (highway ?h ?list)
     then (find-route ?start ?end () ?h 0))

add-city-to-route:
   if (find-route ?start ?end ?path ?road ?n)
   then (:lisp (establish ((adjcities ?road ?start
                    ?next ?new distance)) :all t)))

;;;the above establish invokes backward-chainer (& finds all sol'ns)

route-simple:
   if (adjcities ?road ?start ?next ?new-distance)
   then (route ?start ?next ?road ?new-distance))

add-city-to-route2:
   if (find-route ?start ?end ?path ?road ?n)
      (route ?start ?next ?road ?new-distance)
           ?any-total)
   then
    ?path := (append  ?path (?start ?new-distance))
    ?total :=  (+ ?n ?new-distance)
    (route ?start ?next ?road ?total)
    (find-route ?next ?end ?path ?road ?total))

end: if (find-route ?x ?x ?path ?road ?n)
        (destination ?x)
  then <print route>
```

FIG. 4.2. The rulebase taken from Poltreck, Steiner and Tarlton (1986).

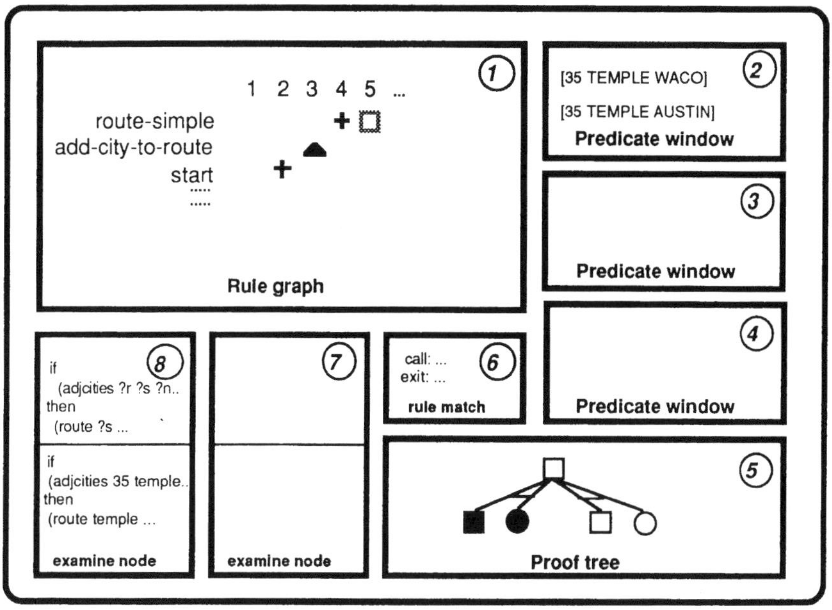

FIG. 4.3. Schematic overview of typical TRI layout.

Using Highway 10
Austin ---> 10 ---> San-Antonio ---> 20 ---> Fredricksburg ---> 50 ---> Dallas
Total Mileage: 80

The user then examines the execution history and after a few operations the TRI is in the state shown in Fig. 4.3.

For clarity of exposition, Fig. 4.3 is only schematic showing in outline form the contents of 8 separate windows, the actual window is shown in the appendix. Details of specific windows are described in turn.

3.2 Providing a Coarse-Grained View of the Execution

The coarse-grained view is provided by window 1 (the rule graph frame) in the top left of the screen. As well as an abstract view the rule graph frame provides two other facilities: a) the ability to focus on various slices of the execution space in detail, b) the ability to replay the execution. The actual appearance of window 1 is shown in Fig. 4.4.

The largest pane in the rule graph frame shows a graph of the execution history, which we call the rule graph. The rule graph enables the user to

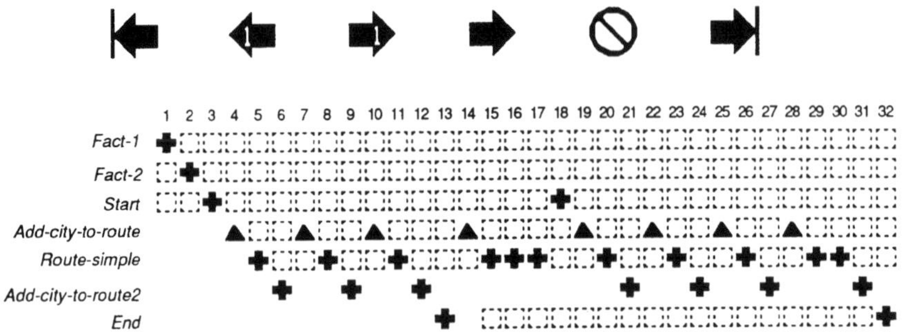

FIG. 4.4. Close-up of the rule graph frame (window 1 in Fig. 4.3).

view around fifty rules for fifty cycles at a glance (this could trivially be increased to one hundred cycles by decreasing the inter-cycle gap). Horizontal and vertical scrolling extend the practical limits to hundreds of rules and hundreds of cycles. TRI allows the user to collapse any set of rules into a single row, allowing robust forward chaining rules to be "black boxed" away. Each row then represents the execution space of one or more rules with each of the symbols ⬚, ✚ and ▲ indicating a particular type of event happening to one instantiation. Each set of rules contains a corresponding set of instantiations created from working memory and the set of rules. The symbols denote the following:

- ▲ one of the instantiations in the set fired and backward chaining occurred,
- ✚ one of the instantiations in the set fired, and
- ⬚ at least one instantiation entered the conflict resolution set and none of the instantiations in the set fired,

Where there is no symbol all of the rules in the set failed to match against working memory and no instantiations were created.

The rule graph presents a picture of the overall shape of the execution; we can see clumps consisting of the three symbols ▲, ✚ and ✚ and we can also see two diagonal lines consisting of ✚, ▲, ✚ and ✚. It is hoped that a programmer using TRI would recognise these patterns as cliches in the program and would be able to notice missing friendly cliches and spot unwanted unfriendly cliches. The rule *route-simple* fires immediately after the rule *add-city-to-route*, sometimes firing once, sometimes firing several times in succession. The rule *add-city-to-route2* always fires immediately after the rule *route-simple* has fired one or more times. The two initialisation rules *fact-1* and *fact-2* fire in the first two cycles and then never fire again. We see that the rule graph provides answers to coarse-grained questions such as "When is a rule likely to fire?", "Which rules fire together?". This sort of information is not readily available from text- or tree-based traces.

3.3 Fine-Grained Views of the Execution

The view windows, of which there are several types, provide very detailed information (a fine-grained view) of selected slices of the history. This detailed display is similar to what one might see in a normal text trace. All remaining windows in Fig. 4.3 are view windows.

A slice of working memory is chosen by selecting some predicates from a menu and then selecting the current cycle by clicking on one of the numbers in the rule graph. The predicate of a working memory pattern is the first part of the pattern, so *foo* is the predicate of the working memory pattern [*foo x y z*]. Windows 2, 3, and 4 (called predicate windows) at the right of Fig. 4.3 show three slices of working memory for the three predicates *adjcities, find-route* and *route*. Each predicate window shows all the working memory patterns present at the current cycle, for the predicate. Figure 4.5 shows the actual appearance of window 2 in detail.

The predicate has been omitted from each of the displayed working memory patterns as it is redundant (it is displayed as the title of the predicate window). The number before each of the patterns is the cycle during which the pattern was deposited in working memory. Each pattern

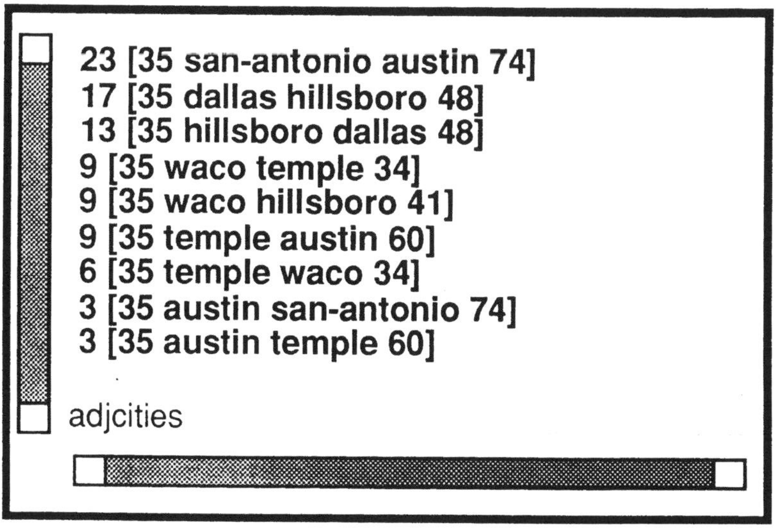

FIG. 4.5. Close-up of the adjcities predicate window (window 2 in Fig. 4.3).

is mouse sensitive, enabling either the relevant node in the rule graph to be highlighted, or a more detailed description of the pattern to be displayed.

A slice of the conflict resolution set is chosen by clicking one of the nodes in the rule graph. Windows 7 and 8 at the bottom left of Fig. 4.3 show two slices of the conflict resolution set. Figure 4.6 shows the actual appearance of window 8.

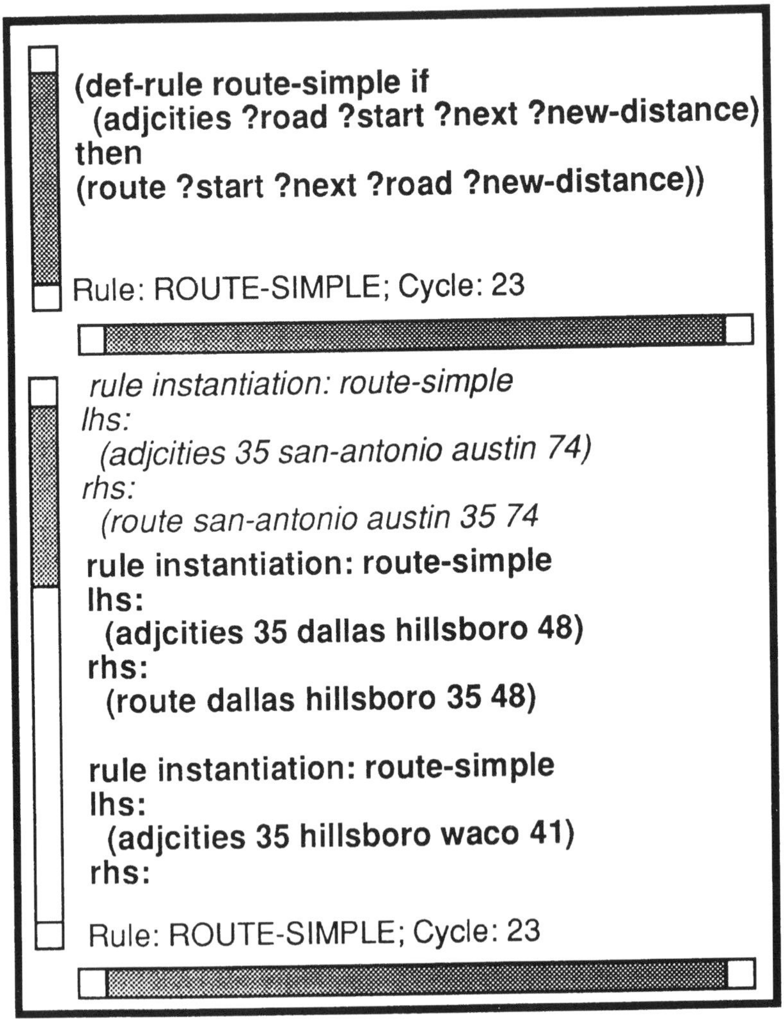

FIG. 4.6. Close-up of node examination frame for rule route-simple (window 8 in Fig. 4.3).

Each frame (called a node examination frame) has two components. The top part of the frame contains the definition of the rule; the bottom part shows all the instantiations the rule had in the conflict set. This allows easy comparison of the instantiated rule with the source code. The bottom left frame created by clicking on the + node in cycle 23 in the rule graph; it contains all the instantiations in the conflict resolution set at cycle 23 for the rule *route-simple*. The top instantiation is in italics indicating that this instantiation fired in cycle 23. Each instantiation is mouse sensitive, allowing operations such as displaying or editing the deleting conflict resolution strategy. The second node examination frame (window 7), shown in detail in Fig. 4.7, was created by clicking the triangle under the number 22 in the rule graph.

We can see that the top (firing) instantiation is in italics. We can also see that the first (and only) clause in the consequent of the instantiation is in bold. The bolding indicates that, when the rule fired, backward chaining occurred. Clicking this clause displays the proof tree, shown by the bottom right frame in Fig. 4.3, and in detail in Fig. 4.8.

The tree represents the execution history of backward chaining rules. Each node in the tree corresponds to a goal, which may or may not have been successful, within the execution. The display of proof trees is based on TPM (Eisenstadt & Brayshaw, 1988): a white node indicates a success, a black node indicates a failure. It is possible to abstract the tree both by zooming out (it is possible to zoom in again, as has been done in Fig. 4.8) and by collapsing a predicate. When a predicate is collapsed the subtree of the predicate is not shown, allowing robust backward chaining rules to be "black boxed" away, facilitating the display of thousands of nodes in a large proof tree.

Each node in the tree is mouse sensitive. Clicking a node displays more detailed information (as can be seen in window 6 above the proof tree in Fig. 4.3) including the rule the goal was called from, the source code version of the call, and the actual call, in which variables are likely to have been renamed. A screen snapshot of window 6 is reproduced below as Fig. 4.9.

3.4 Replaying the Execution

The execution can be replayed using the replay panel (the menu containing the symbol ⇤). Using the replay panel the user can choose to single-step forwards or backwards, or to replay the history. As the execution is replayed each cycle column in the rule graph is highlighted in turn and all the currently displayed view windows are updated. Each view window acts

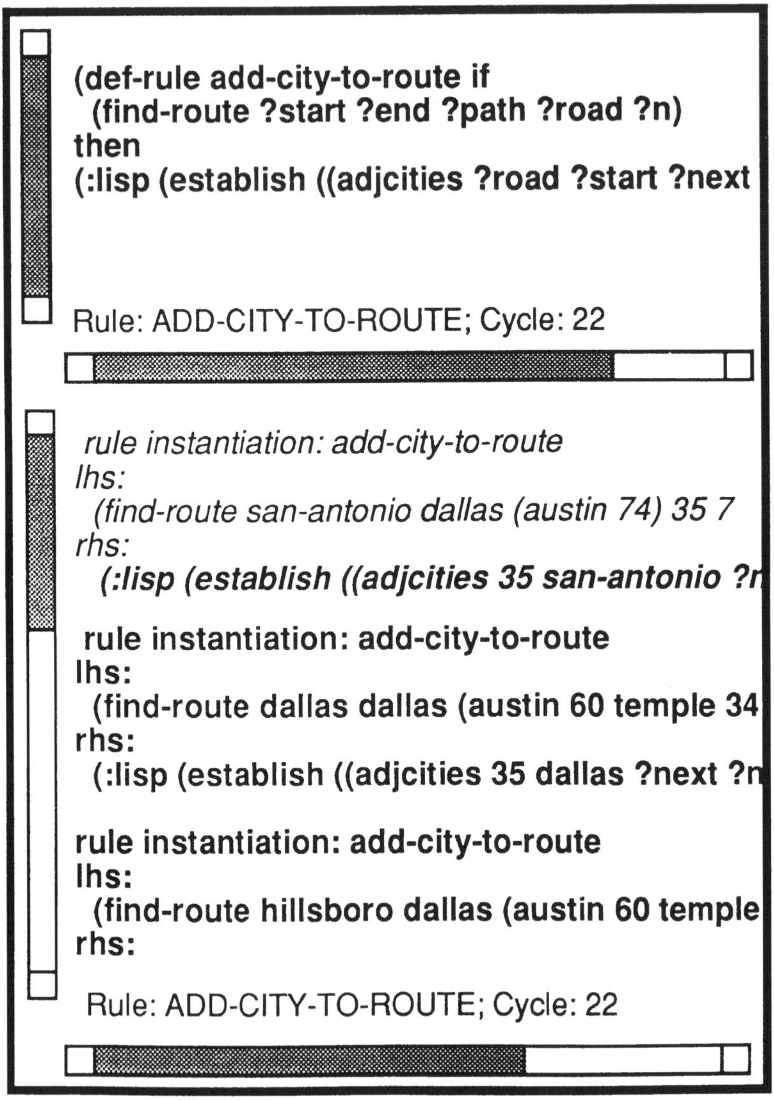

FIG. 4.7. Close-up of node examination frame for rule add-city-to-route (window 7 in Fig. 4.3).

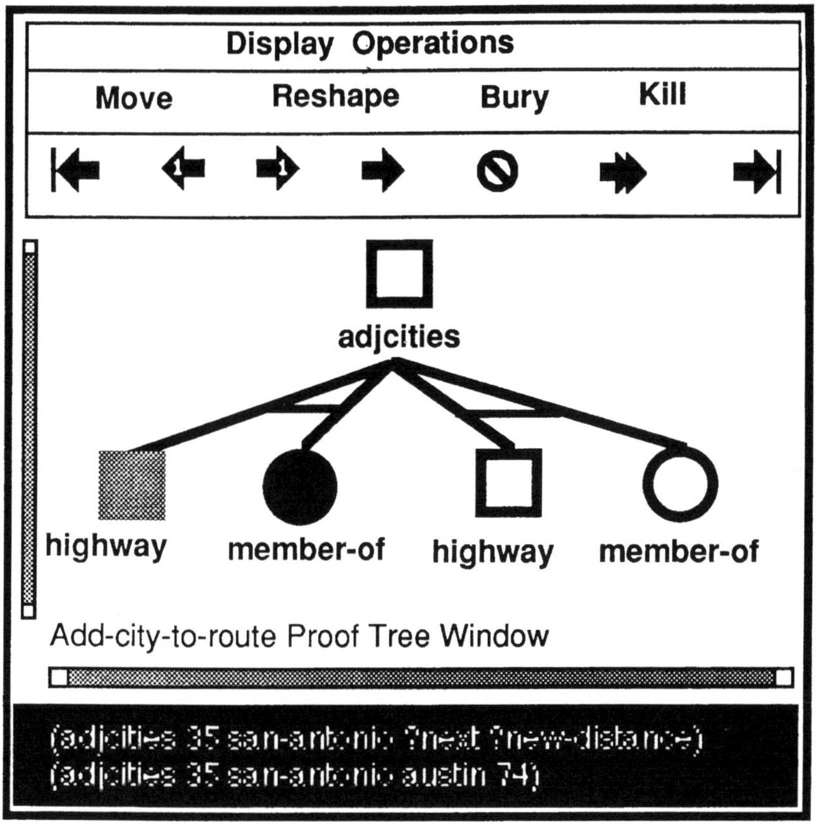

FIG. 4.8. Close-up of backward-chaining proof tree for adjcites (window 5 in Fig. 4.3).

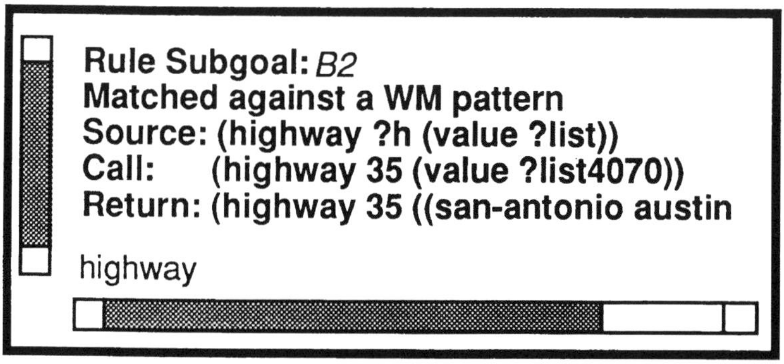

FIG. 4.9. Close-up of detailed expansion of backward-chaining tree node, showing variable bindings (window 6 in Fig. 4.3).

as a detailed measuring device, providing very detailed information on a specific part of the execution.

4. ASSESSING TRI

4.1 Temporal Dependencies vs. Logical Dependencies

The key insight underlying TRI has been the emphasis on temporal dependencies during forward chaining, providing in essence a musical score metaphor for the coarse-grained view. This contrasts directly with an emphasis on logical dependencies, the display of which relies typically on a tree/net/link metaphor. It would be foolish for TRI to ignore logical dependencies, especially in those cases where they are highly meaningful to an individual user, or simply more appropriate in a particular context. Therefore, TRI facilitates the display of logical dependencies in three ways: (a) the dependency between any working memory element (as shown in a specific predicate window, for instance) and the rule responsible for depositing that element can be highlighted by clicking the chosen working memory element, resulting in a blink of the "+" symbol at the appropriate culprit spot in the rule graph display; (b) a dependency tree for any working memory element, including those deposited during forward chaining, can be displayed upon request, the appearance is that of an AND/OR tree much like the one we use for backward chaining; (c) the backward chaining proof tree itself is of course a tree of logical dependencies, made easy for TRI because of the restriction that backward chaining rules be expressed (like Prolog) as pure Horn clauses.

Logical dependencies have been de-emphasised in this paper, because AND/OR trees are not new. Clearly, the individual user needs to have the freedom to choose the right abstraction for the right purpose, and that is precisely the mixture that TRI was designed to provide.

4.2 Scaling Up to Large Programs

The acid test of a tracing/monitoring environment is its performance on real programs. TRI is used daily on the KEATS project, and its very conception and design is meant to facilitate the handling of very large programs. A recent TRI run in KEATS (which mostly uses frames rather than rules) yielded the following statistics:

Number of rules: 63
Number of working memory elements: 157
Number of forward-chaining cycles: 504
Number of backward-chaining "history" steps: 4388
Number of nodes in backward-chaining proof tree: 199

The large number of backward-chaining history steps is due to the detailed record of backtracking which is kept by TRI, where a step corresponds to a call, exit, fail or redo operation analogous to those of Prolog.

The following features enable TRI to scale up to large problems:

Clear conceptual distinction between coarse-grained and fine-grained views: The abstractions provided are genuinely different, not just those obtainable via physical scale factor zooming.

Chunking of rules into sets: Entire rule sets may be expanded and collapsed in the left-hand column of the rule graph display, analogous to the operations of a hierarchical file directory browser. Chunking can be provided automatically, according to rules which co-exist in separate rule contexts, or manually, at the user's discretion. This allows the aggregate behaviour of many hundreds of rules to be seen at a glance.

Collapsing of details into one node: In the backward-chaining proof trees, entire sub-trees which are either uninteresting or too space-consuming can be collapsed into a single node, which itself may be expanded and explored in a separate window. This enables trees with thousands of nodes and tens of thousands of execution steps to be explored in a meaningful way.

Global view: The coarse-grained view of proof trees can itself be physically scaled (zoomed) in a separate window which provides a broader navigational perspective, this is the zoom typical of existing environments, and is therefore not new to TRI, but is provided for convenience and completeness.

Performance overheads of TRI's monitoring facilities are low (approximately 5% increase in execution time), which seems a reasonable price to pay for being able to obtain a thorough view of execution for complete rule sets. The monitoring facilities can be disabled at the user's discretion. We are looking forward to future tests of TRI's power on very large rule bases.

5. CONCLUSIONS AND FUTURE WORK

In this paper we have described TRI, a system that provides a graphical explanation of both forward and backward chaining. Our main aim in designing TRI was to overcome the difficulty of providing an abstract view of execution with easy access to low level views. Our hope is that providing the rule based programmer with these two views will greatly decrease the time taken to discover the cause of bugs. We have witnessed this informally in our lab, and are planning a series of empirical studies to demonstrate the effect in a robust fashion. A further spinoff, consistent with other ongoing work in our lab (e.g. Hasemer & Domingue, 1989), is the provision of a transparent view of the inner workings of a machine ideally suited for helping to teach rule-based programming to novices. Toward this end, we have incorporated the rule graph notation into an Open University course on Knowledge Engineering (Kahney, 1989).

We are currently extending TRI to provide information on the performance as well as the behaviour oıf rule based programs in a unified display (Brayshaw, Domingue & Rajan, 1989). In particular, iconic metering tools are being provided for both forward and backward chaining. KEATS has a truth maintenance system, and TRI is being extended to show dynamically the way in which making an "in" assertion "out" (for instance) propagates effects through a network of dependency links. We eagerly await the results of this new research.

REFERENCES

Brayshaw, M., Domingue, J., & Rajan, T. (1989). An integrated approach to monitoring the behaviour and performance of inference systems. In A. Sutcliffe & L. Macaulay (Eds), *People and Computers V*. Cambridge: Cambridge University Press 409–425.

duBoulay, B., O'Shea, T., & Monk, J. (1981). The black box inside the glass box: Presenting computing concepts to novices. *International Journal of Man-Machine Studies, 14*, 237–249.

Eisenstadt, M. & Brayshaw, M. (1988). The Transparent Prolog Machine (TPM): An execution model and graphical debugger for logic programming. *Journal of Logic Programming, 5*, 1–66.

Fickas, S. (1987). Supporting the programmer of a rule based language. *Expert Systems, 4*, 74–87.

Forgy, C. L. (1981). OPS5 user's manual. *Technical Report CMU-CS-81-135*. Department of Computer Science, Carnegie-Mellon University, July 1981.

Forgy, C. L. (1982). Rete: A fast algorithm for the many pattern/many object pattern matching problem. *Artificial Intelligence, 19*, 17–37.

Hasemer, T. & Domingue, J. (1989). *Common Lisp programming for artificial intelligence*. London: Addison-Wesley.

Kahney, H. (Ed.) (1989). *Knowledge engineering*. (Open University study pack PD624, Learning materials service office, the Open University), Open University Press.

Knowledge Engineering Environment (v 3.1) – © Intellicorp 1987, USA.

Lewis, J. W. (1983). An effective graphics user interface for rules and inference mechanisms. *Proceedings of the ACM Conference on Computer and Human Interaction*, 139–143.

Mott, P. & Brooke, S. (1987). A graphical inference mechanism. *Expert Systems, 4*, 106–117.

Motta, E., Eisenstadt, M., Pitman, K., & West, M. (1988). KEATS: Support for knowledge acquisition in the Knowledge Engineer's Assistant (KEATS). *Expert Systems, 5*, 6–28.

Motta, E., Rajan, T., & Eisenstadt, M. (1990). Knowledge acquisition as a process of model refinement. *Knowledge Acqusition, 2*, 21–49.

NEXPERT is a registered trademark from Neuron Data Inc.

Poltreck, S. E., Steiner, D. D., & Tarlton, P. N. (1986). Graphic interfaces for knowledge-based system development. *Proceedings of the ACM Conference on Computer Human Interaction*.

Richer, M. & Clancey, W. (1985). Guidon-Watch: A graphic interface for viewing a knowledge-based system. *IEEE Computer Graphics and Applications, 5*, 51–64.

Teitelman, W. (1978). *INTERLISP reference manual*. Palo Alto: Xerox PARC.

II Empirical Studies & Cognitive Models

Part II moves on from the consideration of design issues (see Part I) to empirical studies of novice programmers. Here, the emphasis is on (i) the classification of the sorts of errors made by novice programmers in several different programming languages, (ii) the attempt to model the knowledge underlying the misconceptions that produce these errors, (iii) the evaluation, using this corpus of knowledge, of environments that are designed to aid novice programmers.

The empirical studies in this section come in several different guises. Some are fairly open exploratory studies designed to catalogue the errors made by novices. Others involve the use of traditional, experimental techniques to assess the relative merits of support systems. A third type of study tests aspects of novices' knowledge of programming constructs by systematically manipulating various experimental variables, supported by simulation models of this knowledge. The hallmark of the work at HCRL has perhaps been the synthesis of these empirical methods along with the design and development of support systems in a single research program (see Parts I and III).

We see this sort of mix in Chapter 5, where Eisenstadt and Lewis carry out an observational study on the errors made by novice programmers using a version of the SOLO environment (see Chapter 1). They track down the main causes of errors and propose some modifications to the environment to preclude their occurrence.

Historically, the Eisenstadt and Lewis work came before Chapter 6 by Rajan. This gives us some indication of the direction that later studies at the Laboratory have taken. Rajan uses a combination of observational study and controlled experimentation to assess the facilitatory effects of the APT system on novice Prolog programmers' performance. APT was, of course, based on the design principles elucidated in Part I (see Chapter 2).

Chapters 7 and 8 concentrate more on the flawed or inappropriate mental models that novices bring to programming tasks. In Chapter 7, Kahney proposes computational models of novice conceptions of recursion using SOLO. Most of this chapter is concerned with outlining the different mental models of recursion which novices possess. As such, it provides a very useful, in-depth consideration of the diversity of misconceptions which may exist in a population of novice programmers.

In Chapter 8 Eisenstadt and Breuker report on novice-expert differences in looping constructs with respect to the Pascal language. They show that the natural cognitive model of looping based on everyday experience of iterative tasks is at variance with that found in Pascal. One view, therefore, of the novice-expert shift is that experts have aligned their models with that demanded by the programming language, while novices have not. In a classic cognitive science vein, Eisenstadt and Breuker also present a computational simulation of subjects' behaviour in the experiment.

In summary, this part of the book looks at a different strand of the HCRL effort. In one sense, it is a more pure strand; it attempts to establish the theoretical bases for a deep understanding of the psychology of programmers. However, in another sense it has a very applied aim when this knowledge is used to assess the adequacy of designed systems.

5 Errors In An Interactive Programming Environment: Causes and Cures

Marc Eisenstadt
Human Cognition Research Laboratory, The Open University, Milton Keynes, England

Matthew W. Lewis
Department of Psychology, Carnegie-Mellon University, Pittsburgh, PA, USA

OVERVIEW

This chapter describes an in-depth analysis of the errors made by novice programmers learning to write programs in a language called SOLO (see Chapter 1). Although the language is embedded in a helpful environment intended to minimize the difficulties often encountered by novice computer users, a variety of problems still arise. These problems are described in detail with the aim of analysing their true causes. In fact, four main culprits account for three-quarters of all problems: spelling (including unbalanced quotes), using the wrong number of arguments, invoking a non-existent procedure and omitting line numbers. Recommendations for improving novices' computing environments are made, based upon the principle of pre-emptive design. This principle argues that users can profit from an environment in which it is not possible to make syntax errors, and that such an environment need neither be unduly restrictive nor overly demanding of computational resources.

1. INTRODUCTION

The study of errors in computer programming has shifted in the last two decades from an emphasis on syntactic errors (e.g. Boies & Gould, 1974) to an emphasis on semantic and conceptual errors, particularly for novice programmers (e.g. Soloway, Bonar, & Ehrlich, 1983). Syntax errors represent trivial rule violations which either cause code not to be execut-

Primitive	*Example*	*Comments*
NOTE	NOTE FIDO ---EATS--->MEAT	{adds new triple to the data base}
FORGET	FORGET FIDO---HAS--->FLEAS	{deletes triple from the data base}
	TO INSULT /X/	{create new procedure called 'insult'}
	10 CHECK /X/---VOTES--->?Y	{conditional pattern-match}
	10A If present: PRINT "ONLY FOOLS VOTE" *Y; EXIT	{i.e. return}
	10B If absent : CONTINUE	{i.e. perform next main step}
	20 CHECK /X/---DRINKS--->?D	
	20A If present: PRINT "YUK..." *D "IS CRUMMY"; EXIT	
	20B If absent: CONTINUE	
	30 PRINT /X/ "IS NUTS"	
	DONE	

FIG. 5.1. Some SOLO examples.

able at all or, in their more sinister manifestations, cause executable code to produce hard-to-detect erroneous results[1]. Semantic and conceptual errors can be characterized by the presence of ill-formed plans in a programmer's emerging repertoire of skills.

The relative importance of different types of error is very hard to assess, particularly across different languages, programmer skill levels, and types of programming environment (e.g. batch vs. interactive, presence or absence of dynamic trace facilities, etc.). The seminal work of Boies and Gould (1974) argued that "syntactic errors do not appear to be a significant bottle-neck in programming". However, the Boies and Gould study, like the studies of Moulton and Muller (1967) and Youngs (1974), was based primarily on frequencies of errors occurring at compile-time: that is, errors detected by a compiler after the complete programs had been written. We decided to re-open the issue of error classification typified by the work of Youngs, and to look a little more deeply at the underlying causes of such errors. Our aim was to identify major sources of difficulty, investigate them in some detail, and provide concrete recommendations for alleviating as

[1]A classic example of a sinister error, which leaves code executable, is the following line of FORTRAN code, which assigns the value 1.10 to a mysterious variable called "DO8I" rather than initiating an iteration (for I from 1 to 10): DO 8 I = 1.10.

many of the difficulties as possible. In particular, we wanted to address the following questions:

What are the patterns of occurrence of errors in a highly interactive environment?
What are the root causes of such errors from the programmer's point of view (as opposed to the category assigned by the error-handler)?
Can these errors be prevented by the design of a better user interface?

To shed some light on these questions, we undertook a case study of novice programmers using a purpose-built language called SOLO-78 (see Chapter 1 for a full treatment of the SOLO language and Fig. 5.1 for several examples of code).

We first describe the specific errors which users make. Treating these errors as symptoms, we then describe our analyses of the underlying causes of these errors, based upon in-depth analyses of session transcripts. The analyses for SOLO errors are compared with error data from a popular language used in education: LOGO. We close with notes on the principle of pre-emptive design; an approach derived from our empirical studies and which we have used in revised implementations of SOLO (see Chapter 1).

2. ERRORS MADE BY SOLO USERS

Using "dribble files" collected with the aid of the DECsystem-20's PHOTO facility, we analysed the terminal activities of 96 students at a hands-on residential summer school. The students worked in 24 groups of four students, and provided us with data covering over 800 hours of connect time. During this time, students entered a total of 9428 lines of input. Of these 2468 (26%) resulted in some error-handling activity on the part of the SOLO interpreter. Error-handling activity includes automatic error correction (as in the case of spelling correction) as well as more traditional syntactic (compile-time) and semantic (run-time) error messages.

On the basis of the error messages generated, we have grouped the observed errors into major categories which we call *symptoms*. Nine symptoms account for 96.6% of all error handling activity. The symptoms are described in Table 5.1.

An important thesis of this work is that symptom frequencies alone, while useful in pin-pointing potential sources of difficulty, do not necessarily tell us the true reason for the occurrence of each error. This is because any given symptom may have more than one underlying cause. For each symptom, therefore, we took the relevant transcripts and analysed them by looking at the context surrounding the occurrence of the error message. Occurrences were then grouped into categories according to our view of

TABLE 5.1
Observed Error Symptoms

Symptom		Number	% of All Observed Errors
1.	Spelling correction and quote balancing	849	34.4
2.	Wrong number of arguments passed	633	25.4
3.	Invocation of non-existent procedure	235	9.5
4.	No line number	184	7.5
5.	Storage clash (e.g. attempt to assert FIDO---EATS--->BISCUITS without first erasing the triple FIDO---EATS--->MEAT)	183	7.4
6.	Omission of obligatory control-flow indicator ("CONTINUE" or "EXIT")	118	4.8
7.	Non-terminating recursion	64	2.6
8.	Attempt to re-define (rather than edit) existing procedure	63	2.6
9.	Unbound variable	59	2.4

what the true cause of the error message appeared to be. The appearance of multiple underlying causes was most evident for the first four symptoms mentioned above. The discussion below highlights the major causes which we believe are responsible for the first four symptoms. We then briefly discuss the causes of the other five symptoms. This discussion represents a considerable condensation of the raw data, which is available in Lewis (1980).

2.1 Symptom 1: Spelling Correction and Quote Balancing (849 Occurrences)

This symptom involved automatic correction of near misses of procedure names, user-confirmation of correction of node and relation names, and automatic balancing of quotation marks in PRINT statements. The actual causes of the observed messages, according to our hand inspection of the dribble files, are shown below. Each cause is identified, and the number of occurrences is shown in parentheses, separated by an "=" from the percentage of occurrence of this symptom accounted for by each cause. For example, the term "(229 = 27.0%)" below means the 229 lines accounted for by a particular cause represent 27% of the 849 lines exhibiting symptom 1. Examples and commentary are given, as appropriate:

a. Over-zealous algorithm notices substring match (229 = 27.0%)
(e.g. "When you typed TOTAL did you mean TO TAL?")

This is clearly a flaw in the design of the spelling corrector, and has been corrected in subsequent implementations which take the surrounding context into account. Of these 229 false alarms, 190 were caused by node-name near misses, while 39 were caused by procedure-name near misses.

b. Near-miss of node name (correctly detected) (179 = 21.1%)
(e.g. "When you typed FIOD did you mean FIDO?")

c. No space after line number (automatically corrected) (154 = 18.1%)
(e.g. 10NOTE = > 10 NOTE)

d. Near-miss of procedure name (automatically corrected) (117 = 13.8%)

e. Attempt to use control word or second procedure on single line (76 = 9.0%)
(e.g. 10 PRINT "HELLO"; CONTINUE =>
10 PRINT "HELLO; CONTINUE").
In this case the student has inserted the control-flow indicator CONTINUE in a main step, where it is not necessary. This is another case of over-zealousness on the part of the quote-balancing algorithm. The use of redundant control-flow indicators is a particular problem which can be specifically trapped.

f. Unbalanced or missing quotes (automatically corrected) (75 = 8.8%)
(e.g. PRINT "HELLO => PRINT "HELLO")

g. Miscellaneous (19 = 2.2%).
This included such oddities as (PRINT OPTIONS = PRINT "OPTIONS"), where the student actually meant to type HELP OPTIONS in order to display a special list of user-options.

The spelling corrector algorithm is a modified version of the one described in Teitelman (1978). The modifications caused the overzealousness which led to so many false alarms. The "sensibleness" rate of the spelling corrector was 521/849 = 61.4%. This is not quite the same as the "hit rate", which was 472/849 = 55.6%, because some near-misses which cause the corrector to ask for confirmation from the user (sensibly, in our opinion) nevertheless led to a rejection. For example, suppose that the database contained the node MARIE and the user wanted to add a new mode MARIEL by typing:

```
NOTE MARIEL---ISA---> WOMAN
```

SOLO would then respond

```
When you typed MARIEL did you mean MARIE?  (Y/N):
```

We would regard this as the result of sensible analysis by the spelling correction algorithm, although it would not count as a hit.

In the final section of the paper, we describe some minor SOLO-specific changes which take the surrounding context into account and hence drastically cut down the over-zealousness. A spelling corrector incorporating these changes, when run over the same sample of data, cuts out 221 of the false alarms. Of the remaining 628 cases, the new corrector has a sensibleness rate of 613/628 = 97.6%, with an actual hit rate of 564/628 = 89.8% (the remainder once again being sensible requests for confirmation which happen to lead to a rejection).

2.2 Symptom 2: Wrong Format Used (633 Occurrences)

This symptom superficially appeared to involve simple cases, such as NOTE FIDO (i.e. only one argument to NOTE instead of three). Upon close inspection, however, the following underlying causes became apparent:

a. Wrong number of arguments passed, with no deeper cause (276 = 43.6%)
   This category was pretty evenly split between misuse of SOLO primitives (141 occurrences) and misuse of user-defined procedures (135 occurrences). One of the researchers in our laboratory, Hank Kahney, has pointed out to us that many of the students he has observed appear to use the "RETURN" key as a "bail out" option when they change their minds in mid-line and are too lazy to look up the appropriate keystroke for line-deletion (CTRL-U). This would account for the appearance of strange lines such as NOTE FIDO in the middle of a session where the student clearly knows the syntax of NOTE.
b. Undetected split or join of node and relation names (102 = 16.1%)
   These were simple lexical errors, caused either by missing spaces (e.g. NOTE FIDO DRINKSBEER) or extra spaces (e.g. NOTE FIDO DRINK S BEER).
c. Typehead and illegal characters (98 = 15.5%)
   A surprising number of errors are artifacts of students typing ahead when the response from the DEC-20 is very slow (i.e. characters are not immediately echoed to the terminal). If students forget to insert a carriage return while typing ahead, they end up with a line like this:

   30 NOTE FIDO ISA DOG DONE.
d. Omission of obvious items or insertion of redundant items (62 = 9.8%)

The following examples are typical of this category:

20 NOTE A B C; CONTINUE {the "CONTINUE" is unnecessary}
LIST TO FOO {the "TO" is unnecessary}

e. Knock-on effect of spelling correction (43 = 6.8%)
If a student types NOTEW DOG ISA ANIMAL, the spelling corrector successfully splits off the "W" from "NOTE" but then foolishly passes 4 arguments to NOTE (W, DOG, ISA, ANIMAL) causing this error.

f. Wild-card convention mis-used (36 = 5.7%)
In these cases, the student types NOTE ?X HAS WINGS instead of NOTE *X HAS WINGS. The number of arguments is correct, but the use of a wild card is illegal in that context, so a "wrong format" error is generated.

g. Attempt to expand power of SOLO machine (16 = 2.3%)
These were cases in which students tried to do things which may have seemed like natural extensions of SOLO's capabilities, but they don't work. An example is:

NOTE FIDO LOVE*Y MARY

In this case *Y has an intended value such as INVERSE, and the student is trying to perform string concatenation in order to create a brand new relation name (LOVE + INVERSE = LOVEINVERSE). This is a nice idea, but it won't work in SOLO.

2.3 Symptom 3: Invocation of Non-Existent Procedure (235 Occurrences)

The dribble files revealed the following underlying causes of this symptom:

a. Missing referent, or call to as-yet-undefined procedure (95 = 40.4%)
These were cases where line 10 of procedure FOO looked like this:

10 FIE

and FIE had not yet been defined, causing a run-time error when FOO was invoked. These 95 cases did not involve any spelling errors, as far as we could determine. This message sometimes used by students as a top-down programming aid. Writing one procedure correctly at a time leaves this message as a signal that the (outer) procedure runs.

b. Undetected spelling error, or artifact of algorithm (60 = 25.5%)
These either involved cases which were too difficult for our existing spelling corrector (although detectable by the human observer), or

simply artificats of the way in which the SOLO-78 scanner works. For example a line such as:

10A PRINT "HI"

gets converted to

10 A PRINT "HI"

in the case where sub-stem "A" is not required, and then the error:

Oops, I have no procedure called "A", occurs at run time.

c. Omission of obvious item or use of synonym (44 = 18.7%)
If the student types in a line such as:

SOLO: FIDO ISA DOG

(omitting the obvious "NOTE") then SOLO will respond with the error message:

Oops, I don't have a procedure called FIDO.

Similarly, if the student had typed in ASSERT FIDO ISA DOG instead of NOTE FIDO ISA DOG, SOLO would respond:

Oops, I don't have a procedure called ASSERT.

d. Mode error (23 = 9.9%)
The student may have assumed that they were in the editor, rather than at top-level, or attempted to type input into a running program (which was not allowed in this implementation of SOLO). In the latter case, trying to answer a question by typing, say, YES would be met with the message:

Oops, I don't have a procedure called YES.

Line numbers were ignored at the top-level of the SOLO implementation for which this data applies, so if a student tried edit line 10A of a procedure by typing in:

SOLO: 10A PRINT "OK"; EXIT

the 10 would have been ignored and SOLO would have responded:

Oops, I don't have a procedure called "A".

The current implementation traps this type of error specifically by refusing to accept line numbers at the top-level of the interpreter. An appropriate warning message is displayed as soon as the first suspect keystroke ("1") occurs.

e. Data/procedure confusion (13 = 5.5%)
In these cases, the student attempts to apply EDIT or LIST to a node

name, e.g. LIST FIDO. In SOLO-78 this results in the error message:

Oops, I don't have a procedure called FIDO.

One could argue that the student saying LIST FIDO has the right intuitions, and should not be presented with any error (or even warning) message at all. In a language such as LISP, for instance, there is no such distinction between data and procedures. Nevertheless, we get some mileage out of emphasizing the simple architecture of the SOLO virtual machine, which does distinguish between data and procedures. Our compromise solution in the current implementation of SOLO is to remind the student of this distinction with the message:

"You should use DESCRIBE rather than LIST with a node such as FIDO, but I'll DESCRIBE it for you anyway".

2.4 Symptom 4: No Line Number (184 Occurrences)

Our analysis revealed four major underlying causes of this symptom:

a. Student genuinely forgot the line number (116 = 63.0%)
The frequency of this cause indicates that an automatic line-numbering facility, or a screen-based editing facility which did not depend on line numbers, would have been useful features to incorporate into SOLO-78. In fact, both of these features are available in later implementations of SOLO.

b. Wrong mode (39 = 21.2%)
In these cases, the student assumed he or she was at the top-level of SOLO, rather than still in edit/define mode, and typed in something like:

. . .:FOO FRED

(This was meant to be a trial invocation of FOO, but the student has forgotten to type DONE, so SOLO responds with the message:

Oops, you forgot the line number.

These errors are non-trivial to deal with automatically since the student might actually have meant to include a line such as FOO FRED as line 30 of the definition of FOO. A clearly delineated editing mode has been built into our microcomputer implementation of SOLO (Eisenstadt & Gawronski, 1987). We believe that this delineation makes users less prone to mode errors, but our conjecture remains to be tested empirically.

c. Number outside legal range (27 = 14.7%)
Line numbers were restricted to the range of 1-100. This was related to the fact that SOLO-78 had a limit of 10 main steps per procedure (to force modularity). This restriction occasionally backfired when a student was in the mood to use large line numbers. This range restriction has been removed from later implementations.

d. Undetected misspelling of "DONE" (2 = 1.1%)
The line containing DONE itself is not numbered in SOLO. Thus, if the student misspelled DONE in a manner which eluded our spelling corrector, then SOLO could only think that this was yet another line of the procedure, and therefore that the line number had been omitted.

2.5 Symptom 5: Storage Clash (183 Occurrences)

This symptom is a peculiarity of the SOLO architecture we present to our students: a given relation can only be used *once* emanating from a given node. Thus, if the triple FIDO---DRINKS---> BEER is already in the database and the student types in NOTE FIDO---DRINKS---> WINE, the following message is displayed:

Oops, FIDO---DRINKS---> BEER already! Sorry.

At a later point in the SOLO-78 primer, the student is informed that there is a special multiple mode, which allows the same relation to be used many times with a given node. An iterative retrieval mechanism is also available, so that the student can type in:

FOR EACH CASE OF FIDO---DRINKS--->?Y

instead of

CHECK FIDO---DRINKS--->?Y.

Students not in this advanced mode must first use FORGET with a particular triple before using NOTE if they wish to avoid this symptom. The underlying cause is invariably the same – students simply overlook the fact that a clash might occur in the database because of an earlier invocation of the procedure which they are currently debugging. Later implementations of SOLO automatically allow the use of multiple relations emanating from a given node. FOR EACH retrieves them all, in chronological order, whereas CHECK retrieves the latest one added.

2.6 Symptom 6: Omission of Control Flow Indicator (118 Occurrences)

This symptom has just one underlying cause: the student forgets to type CONTINUE or EXIT at the relevant point. The occurrence of this error automatically returns the student to the point in the line at which CONTINUE or EXIT needs to be inserted by reprinting the line. Thus, it really acts as a reminder to prevent later flow-of-control bugs from occurring.

2.7 Symptom 7: Non-Terminating Recursion (64 Occurrences)

Symptom 7 is one which occurs in other programming languages as well. Our students are encouraged to think up a case in which recursion should be terminated due to the way they are prompted for the IF PRESENT and IF ABSENT branches of conditionals. However, they may fail to take advantage of this and the non-termination error occurs. This error is detected by a SOLO stack overflow. Since the stack is very short (10) we can't be sure that the recursion would not have terminated after just a few more invocations. This stack size was set arbitrarily, and should perhaps be increased for those students who build substantial data bases requiring many levels of recursion to propagate some inference procedure through it. Unfortunately, hand analysis of the dribble files was not able to reveal which cases were on the verge of terminating, and which were genuinely non-terminating, though we know from personal tutoring experience that genuine non-termination is the predominant cause of symptom 7.

2.8 Symptom 8: Attempt to Re-Define (Rather than Edit) Existing Procedure (63 Occurrences)

This symptom is in effect a warning message. If a student types in TO FOO, when FOO already exists, then SOLO responds:

> Oops, I already have a procedure called FOO.
> Would you like to re-define it now?

If the number of parameters in the new version is different from the number on the old version, the student is made aware of this as well. Students over the years expressed anxiety about the inability to get rid of unwanted procedures in SOLO-78. They often felt it was more convenient to start with a clean slate than either to edit or re-define an existing procedure. By popular demand, all later dialects of SOLO therefore have a primitive called KILL, so that students can type, e.g. KILL FOO.

2.9 Symptom 9: Unbound Variable (59 Occurrences)

This is run-time error which can only occur when a student uses a variable (e.g. *A) which was not bound during an earlier invocation of CHECK (e.g. CHECK FIDO LOVES ?A). Hand inspection of the dribble files could not provide deeper analysis than this, but we know from our earlier inspection of other programs that the inevitable cause of the error is the use of CONTINUE as a control-flow indicator on an IF ABSENT branch, in the expectation that the branch will never be taken. When that branch finally is taken, then later steps which refer to, say, *A (wrongly presupposing that it was bound and the IF PRESENT branch was taken), will generate this error. This points to a difficulty in the semantics of CHECK. It is actually doing several things simultaneously and one of the more important is the provision of variable binding on the IF PRESENT branch only. Students who use CONTINUE on both IF PRESENT and IF ABSENT branches will ultimately find this error occurring. Some students have reported (Jones, 1987) that they use CONTINUE all the time out of laziness, so they don't have to think too far ahead about what will be happening in the different cases. This, of course, defeats the very purpose of requiring students to type CONTINUE or EXIT, which was meant to eliminate simple flow-of-control bugs. We don't know how prevalent this is as an underlying cause, but the symptom itself does not appear to be a major worry of our students.

3. DISCUSSION

What conclusions of general interest can software designers, implementors, and educators draw from the analyses presented in the preceding section? We believe the following to be of greatest general interest:

One quarter of all lines input in this friendly environment were problematic. This finding needs to be reconciled with that of Boies and Gould (1974), who argued that "syntactic errors do not appear to be a significant bottleneck in programming". Our numbers are not in fact very different, since Boies and Gould found that 16% of batch-compiled FORTRAN programs had known syntax errors, and a further 6% were terminated by users for unknown reasons. The difference may have to do with (a) the target user population in the respective studies, and (b) the interpretation of the phrase "significant bottle-neck". Boies and Gould were studying on-site users at the IBM Research Centre; we were looking at Psychology students with no prior experience of computing. Their system was a commercial "unforgiving" one; ours had already been tuned through developmental testing to catch and correct a range of user errors. Our view is that if one quarter of beginner's input lines are vulnerable to relatively mundane mistakes, then this is unacceptably high. Naturally, users of interactive computing environments, especially beginners, are destined to make some mistakes. But computing is confusing enough already, problematic lines should be dealt with in an understandable way. Classic solutions include clear error messages, help messages, and automatic correction. Although each of these has its merits, we now argue that prevention is better than cure.

Four Symptoms Account for Three-quarters of All Problems. These are: spelling (including unbalanced quotes), wrong number of arguments, invocation of non-existent procedure, and no line number. We were surprised to find such a small number of major culprits. This means that a concerted effort aimed at eliminating just these culprits would, if successful, cut down the proportion of problematic input lines from one-quarter to one-sixteenth (i.e. from 25% to 6.25%).

Symptom and Cause are Not the Same Thing. Raw summaries of error data are of interest, but do not tell us much about why particular errors occur. Therefore, the context in which particular errors occur needs in-depth analysis.

70% of All Problems Involve Either Trivial Keyboard Errors or Pragmatically Correct Lines. By pragmatically correct we mean lines which were well-intentioned and which indicated that the user clearly knew what they were doing. This includes lines such as "FIDO ISA DOG" instead of "NOTE FIDO ISA DOG", and the mode errors referred to in the preceding section. Thus, simple slips of the pen and slips of the mind are the most frequent causes of error, and are those to which we should devote most of our attention.

This summary raises two important questions. First, to what extent are these data (and conclusions) SOLO-specific? Second, how can the observed errors, and in particular the causes of those errors, be intelligently handled or even avoided? To address the first of these questions, we compare our results with those of a similar study involving the language LOGO. Following that, we turn our attention to a technique for avoiding the major sources of difficulty for beginners.

4. COMPARISON WITH A STUDY OF ERRORS MADE BY LOGO USERS

duBoulay (1979) looked in depth at programming errors made by school teachers learning the language LOGO (Papert, 1980). Due to the similarities in the ages/backgrounds of our respective students, and the resem-

TABLE 5.2
LOGO User Error Frequencies (from DuBoulay, 1979)

Symptom	*% of All Errors*
Call undefined procedure	28
Insufficient arguments	16
No line number	11
Extra test	10
Turtle off drawing area	10
Variables misused	6
Wrong type of argument	4
Command leaves a value	3
Device claiming violation	3
Number too large	3
Stack overflow	2

NOTE: Total input lines = 19,675; total error lines = 2447.

blance between SOLO and LOGO, we decided to analyse duBoulay's results in some detail.

Table 5.2 gives a summary of the frequency of occurrence of errors found in duBoulay's study.

A comparison of SOLO and LOGO error frequencies requires us to examine the underlying causes, because the symptom frequencies are not directly comparable. duBoulay's analysis goes into some detail about the underlying causes, and points out that many occurrences are due to simple typing/spelling errors, or are deliberate errors caused by students following instructions to learn about error messages.

duBoulay presented enough detail for us to re-compute his figures assuming (a) that LOGO had a spelling/typing corrector and (b) that the instructions to generate deliberate errors were removed from his primer. Since duBoulay's hand analysis of the errors relied upon his own skills as an idealised spelling corrector, it seemed only fair to re-compute the SOLO figures as well, assuming an idealised spelling corrector based upon our own hand analysis. This meant eliminating not only the false alarms produced by our over-zealous spelling corrector, but also undesirable knock-on effects, such as those detailed in cause "e" of symptom "2" in Section 2.2 (e.g. NOTEW DOG ISA ANIMAL = NOTE W DOG ISA ANIMAL). Similarly, we assumed that cause "b" of symptom 2 (e.g. NOTE FIDO DRINKSBEER) would be picked up by the spelling corrector, and that cause "d" (e.g. LIST TO FOO) was not appropriate to count at all in our comparison. Table 5.3 gives a side-by-side comparison of SOLO and LOGO error frequencies, with duBoulay's terminology mod-

TABLE 5.3
Four Most Frequent Errors Recalculated for LOGO and SOLO, Assuming Comparable Spelling Correctors

	Symptom	*% of All Errors*	
		LOGO	SOLO
1.	Spelling/typing/misquoting	28	34
2.	Wrong number of arguments passed	18	18
3.	No line number	12	9
4.	Call to undefined procedure	12	9

ified to be consistent with the terminology used in this paper. The table shows the four largest SOLO and LOGO error frequencies side by side, but this time assuming that both SOLO and LOGO had identical (intelligent) spelling correction algorithms.

The interesting point of this analysis is that the four major culprits in both languages are the same, and occur in the same relative ordering. This has implications for both the design of curriculum materials (i.e. greater emphasis on explanations of argument passing to avoid culprit number 2), and the design of intelligent user interfaces to help trap or pre-empt the most commonly occurring errors. We take up this point in detail in the next section.

5. ERROR PREVENTION

Our investigation of user errors and our comparison with the results of duBoulay's study of LOGO users have led us to conclude that the overwhelming majority of errors can be handled intelligently by a good user-interface. In cases where a human observer can look at the user's input and say "aha, the user obviously meant . . .", we believe that the user-interface should be capable of doing the same thing.

Readers who are experienced computer users might object that the number of errors we observed was quite low, and therefore there is nothing to worry about. Remember that we are talking about the experiences of novices who are fairly timid about using computers. Given that one quarter of their input lines contained some kind of error, we believe there is cause for concern. Anyone who has taught novices programming will be aware of the serious confusion which can result from a seemingly trivial input error. Indeed, even for expert programmers, a simple mistake or the omission of an obvious item can sometimes take hours to track down. Software designers have an obligation to study the errors which occur in their community of users, and to try to improve user-interfaces accordingly.

There are two possible paths to improving a user-interface in response to empirically observed difficulties: (a) try to trap errors in an intelligent fashion after the line is entered in the style of Teitleman's "Do What I Mean" analyser (Teitelman, 1977), or (b) pre-empt the possible occurrence of errors, using syntax-directed editing tools in the style of Teitelbaum and Reps (1981), before the lines are entered. We discuss each of these approaches in turn.

5.1 Intelligent Error Traps

The trap philosophy allows the user to enter nearly-correct lines of a program, and then relies on the user-interface to make sense of obvious errors. SOLO-78 already exhibits intelligent error trapping especially in its spelling corrector and quote balancer. The spelling corrector generates far too many false alarms, however, and our aim is to improve its performance drastically by addressing the problems observed in our analysis. As it turns out, most of the false alarms generated by the spelling corrector can be handled with the incorporation of a few SOLO-specific changes. Here are three:

Assume the input item is correct if it differs from the target item only by numeric characters (e.g. FOO and FOO1).

Only compare the input item against candidates of the same syntactic category (e.g. if the input is FOO FIDO, then FOO only gets matched against procedure names, and FIOD only gets matched against node names).

If the procedure name is known, but there are the wrong number of arguments, try segmenting (or merging) arguments, using known dictionary items as candidates, assuming that these are spelled correctly (e.g. NOTE FIDO IS A DOG = NOTE FIDO ISA DOG). A line such as NOTE FIOD IS A DOG would not be handled, as it requires both merging and spelling correction, which is simply too expensive.

A spelling corrector incorporating these (and several other) SOLO-specific changes has been incorporated into E-SOLO, our experimental version of SOLO. When run over the same input as that analyzed in section 3, the spelling corrector has a sensibleness rate of 97.6% and a hit rate of 89.8%. In order to improve the SOLO environment in the light of our empirical studies, we adopt the following strategy:

Look at all the causes underlying each observed symptom and then, for each cause, design an algorithm which will eliminate all of its occurrences. For example, symptom 3 (invocation of non-existent procedure) has as one of its underlying causes (c) "omission of obvious item". A typical case of this is a student typing in:

SOLO: FIDO ISA DOG

instead of

SOLO: NOTE FIDO ISA DOG.

The algorithm to trap occurrences such as this is straightforward:
IF the procedure is unknown,
and the number of input items = 3
and the first item is a known node-name
THEN assume that the keyword "NOTE" was omitted from the beginning of the input line.

This algorithm does not try to cope with combinations of errors, such as misspelling in addition to omitted procedure names. Thus, an input line such as:

SOLO: FIOD ISADOG

would not be trapped by our algorithm, despite the fact that it is easy to deal separately with (a) omitted procedure names, (b) misspelled node names, and (c) missing spaces between node names and relation names. Handling multiple errors on a single input line would be combinatorially explosive, and in any event would only yield a trivial increase in the number of occurrences which could be handled.

Table 5.4 below is a summary of those observed causes (discussed earlier) which could ideally be trapped automatically, and thereby eliminated as potential sources of delay and frustration for future users.

Our revised algorithms can realistically (i.e. cheaply) catch 552 of the above 658 ideally trappable causes. Trapping just the realistic ones would thus eliminate 552 problematic lines from the 2468 observed in our sample, a reduction of 22.4%.

The trap philosophy is based on the premise that a large number of errors can be sensibly analyzed by fairly inexpensive algorithms which take some account of the surrounding context to make sense of the user's input. A greater investment is clearly needed to provide assistance such as automatic bug-detection and correction. We have in fact provided such facilities in experimental versions of SOLO (see chapters 9 and 10; Laubsch & Eisenstadt, 1981; Hasemer, 1984). Although it is possible that intelligent error trapping might lead the user to become lazy or to develop an erroneous mental model of how the computer functions, we believe that

TABLE 5.4
Trappable Causes of the Four Most Frequently-Observed Symptoms

Symptom 1.	*Spelling correction*
Cause a:	over-zealous substring match (229 occurrences)
Cause e:	extraneous control word (76 occurrences)
Symptom 2.	*Wrong format*
Cause b:	merge of node/rel names (102 occurrences)
Cause d:	omit obvious item (62 occurrences)
Cause e:	knock-on effect of spelling corrector (43 occurrences)
Symptom 3.	*Invocation of non-existent procedure*
Cause b:	spelling error (60 occurrences)
Cause c:	omit obvious procedure name (44 occurrences)
Cause e:	data/procedure confusion (13 occurrences)
Symptom 4.	*No line number*
Cause c:	Illegal number (27 occurrences)
Cause d:	misspelling (2 occurrences)

the advantages of intelligent error trapping far outweigh the disadvantages, and welcome further empirical research to help address such issues.

An interesting alternative to the trap philosophy is that of pre-emptive design, which attempts to prevent users from making nonsensical errors in the first place. We describe this approach next.

5.2 Pre-Emptive Design

It is possible to create a software environment in which users write programs by filling in templates which already contain keywords, delimiters, and appropriate indentation. In such an environment, errors such as "missing control-flow indicator" or "wrong number of arguments to a procedure" are not even possible. This is easily illustrated in the context of SOLO. Let us assume that the user's terminal has a function keypad, and that one of these keys is labelled "NOTE". When the user presses the NOTE key, the display shown in Fig. 5.2 appears:

```
NOTE [    ]---[    ]--->[    ]
```

FIG. 5.2. Template for NOTE.

The cursor is positioned at the first box (first template position), so that if the user types in FIDO, followed immediately by a space, the cursor then moves to the second box. A carriage return after FIDO would result in a bleep from the terminal, and a blinking cursor in the middle template box would remind the user that the template was unfilled. Thus it becomes impossible for the user to enter a line such as NOTE FIDO.

Admittedly, this approach could lead to problems for novices who never look at the screen. We assume that much more work on the ergonomics of such a system is needed. Users would need well thought out combinations of auditory and visual cues to get them to pay attention to obligatory syntactic constraints. In such a system, some errors obviously will still occur (e.g. the bleep heralding an unfilled template in Fig. 5.2). However, such errors tend to be single keystroke errors, and are resolved with much less effort than resolving a completely typed erroneous line (since the good part of the line remains intact). In effect, this form-filling style of editing makes it impossible to enter syntactically incorrect input.

This approach, known as "syntax-directed editing" has been used as the design philosophy underlying the front ends of several systems used by novice PL/1 and PASCAL programmers (Teitelbaum & Reps, 1981). Indeed, the template-filling example comes from our own screen-based version of SOLO (Eisenstadt & Gawronski, 1987). Syntax-directed editing exemplifies what we like to call pre-emptive design: the software designer tries to pre-empt all of the common problems which might potentially plague the user. This philosophy is exhibited in SOLO-78 in the design of its conditional construct: users are prompted for both branches of the conditional, so that they don't need to remember any special syntax. They must fill in an explicit flow-of-control marker so that the interpreter doesn't fall through to reach other steps unexpectedly. We feel that this approach has paid enormous dividends in making the learning of conditionals particularly easy for our students. The full pre-emptive design philosophy requires us to look carefully at the observed error symptoms and all of their causes. Enhancements to the software environment must then be proposed which would prevent those errors from occurring in the first place. For example, symptom 4 (No line number) has as its most usual cause (a) "student genuinely forgot". This could be pre-empted in two ways: (a) for users of hard-copy terminals, supply the line number automatically; (b) for users of display terminals, encourage them to use a screen-based editor in which the line numbers are not necessary.

Table 5.5 shows the observed error causes which could be pre-empted, thereby saving users the worry of having to process extra error messages, and also saving the user-interface from having to make sense of erroneous input as in the error trapping scenarios discussed earlier.

Pre-empting the above causes would eliminate 1069 problematic lines from the 2468 observed in our sample, a reduction of 43.3%. An alternative way to describe this is as an increase in the proportion of trouble-free lines of input, from 6960/9428 (73.8%) to 8029/9428 (85.2%).

Combining the two techniques (smart error-trapping and pre-emptive design), we would end up eliminating 1069 + 552 = 1621 problematic lines,

TABLE 5.5
Pre-Emptable Causes of the Four Most Frequently Observed Symptoms

Symptom 1. *Spelling correction*
Cause c: no space after line number (154 occurrences)
Cause f: unbalanced or missing quotes (75 occurrences)

Symptom 2. *Wrong format*
All causes would be pre-emptable: (633 occurrences)

Symptom 3. *Invocation of non-existent procedure*
Cause d: mode error (23 occurrences)

Symptom 4. *No line number*
All causes would be pre-emptable: (184 occurrences)

leaving the users in a correct state for a grand total of 8581/9428 = 91.0% of the total input lines. This represents a combined elimination of 65.7% of the problematic lines.

6. CONCLUSIONS

We believe that giving novice programmers a positive introduction to computing is of critical importance. We have presented a methodology for identifying flaws in the design of user environments, and introduced pre-emptive design as an approach to create a friendly computing environment for novice programmers. Virtually all the unnecessary and confusing problems which are the bane of the novice can be pre-empted or trapped and intelligently handled by a friendly environment. We feel that this design stance fosters more acceptance and participation by marginally motivated novices.

Even though the specifics of the SOLO domain are limited, the concepts of flow of control, procedures, and variables are fundamental to most programming languages. Hence the lessons learned from studying SOLO as well as the methodology have a wider applicability. Indeed many of these ideas helped to form the design of an enhanced environment for the more widely available Prolog language (see Chapter 3).

REFERENCES

Boies, S. J. & Gould, J. D. (1974). Syntactic errors in computing programming. *Human Factors*, *16*, 253–257.

duBoulay, J. B. H. (1979). *LOGO learning by school teachers*. Edinburgh: Doctoral dissertation, Dept. of Artificial Intelligence, University of Edinburgh, 1979.

Eisenstadt, M. & Gawronski, A. (1987). Micro-SOLO: a tool for elementary AI programming. In A. Jones, E. Scanlon, & T. O'Shea (Eds), *The computer revolution in education: New technologies for distance teaching*. Hassocks, Sussex: Harvester Press.

Hasemer, T. (1984). A very friendly software environment for SOLO. In M. Yazdani (Ed.), *New Horizons in Educational Computing*. Chichester, U.K.: Ellis Horwood.

Jones, A. (1987). Beginners' mental models of a programming language. In A. Jones, E. Scanlon, & T. O'Shea (Eds), *The computer revolution in education: New technologies for distance teaching*. Hassocks, Sussex: Harvester Press.

Laubsch, J. & Eisenstadt, M. (1981). Domain specific debugging aids for novice programmers. *Proceedings of the Seventh International Joint Conference on Artificial Intelligence (IJCAI-81)*, San Mateo, CA: Morgan Kaufmann, 964–969.

Lewis, M. (1980). Improving SOLO's user-interface: an empirical study of user behaviour and proposals for cost-effective enhancements to SOLO. *Technical report no. 7*, Computer Assisted Learning Research Group, The Open University, Milton Keynes, U.K.

Moulton, P. G. & Muller, M. E. (1967). DITRAN: a compiler emphasizing diagnostics. *Communications of the ACM*, *10*, 45–52.

Papert, S. (1980). *Mindstorms: children, computers, and powerful ideas*. Harvester Press, Brighton: England.

Soloway, E., Bonar, J., & Ehrlich, K. (1983). Cognitive strategies and looping constructs: An empirical study. *Communications of the ACM*, *26*, 853–860.

Teitelman, W. (1977). *A display-oriented programmer's assistant*. Palo Alto, CA: Xerox Palo Alto Research Center.

Teitelman, W. (1978). *INTERLISP Reference Manual*. Palo Alto, CA: Xerox Palo Alto Research Center.

Teitelbaum, T. & Reps, T. (1981). The Cornell program synthesizer: A syntax-directed programming environment. *Communications of the ACM*, *24*, 563–573.

Youngs, E. A. (1974). Human errors in programming. *International Journal of Man-Machine Studies*, *6*, 361–376.

6 An Evaluation of APT: An Animated Program Tracer for Novice Prolog Programmers*

Tim Rajan
Performance Technology, Lloyd's Register, Croydon, England

OVERVIEW

This chapter describes an approach to evaluating the usefulness of an Animated Program Tracer (APT) in communicating run-time information to novice Prolog programmers. The method used in the evaluation consists of a set of programs which have been specially designed to elicit novices' models of program execution, and thus to reveal how accurate their model of program execution is. Two experiments are reported. The first determines the misconceptions that novices hold about the run-time actions of the Prolog interpreter, and produces six different categories of misconception. The second experiment investigates the ability of APT to communicate run-time information to novice Prolog programmers. A scoring technique was used to interpret subjects' answers, and shows that there was a significant improvement in the scores of the group who saw programs traced by APT as opposed to a control group who saw no trace. This chapter requires a working knowledge of Prolog.

1. INTRODUCTION

This chapter presents an evaluation of APT, a dynamic tracing tool for novice Prolog programmers. APT was designed with the specific aim of communicating the dynamic run-time action of the Prolog interpreter to novice programmers, in order to facilitate their understanding of the fundamental concepts of the language (see Chapter 2, Rajan, 1987). Prolog is a particularly difficult programming language for novices to learn. This is firstly because most of the action in the execution of Prolog

*This research was supported by a grant from the Open University and carried out in the Human Cognition Research Laboratory.

programs, the deduction mechanisms, is hidden from the user, and secondly, several of these mechanisms, such as backtracking and the cut, are far from intuitive in the way they work. Communicating the execution of Prolog programs in a visual manner should provide a concrete basis on which novices can build a model of the language, which may then be used to create, understand and debug new programs (see e.g. Chapter 3). The experiments reported here look at the misconceptions that novices have concerning the workings of the Prolog interpreter and whether the tracing approach of APT helps to overcome these misconceptions.

The chapter is organised as follows: Section 2 describes the problems associated with learning to program using traditional methods, discusses the types of information that novices require to learn a programming language, presents an approach to addressing these issues, and finally takes a brief look at APT. Section 3 presents the two experimental studies. The first aims to determine the type of misconceptions that novices have concerning the action of the Prolog interpreter, the second attempts to evaluate the success of APT in communicating the dynamic run-time action of the Prolog interpreter. Section 4 presents conclusions from the two experiments, and finally suggests further experiments with APT.

2. LEARNING TO PROGRAM

It has been shown that when novices learn a programming language, the concepts they find most difficult to learn are those which are dynamic in nature (see Chapter 2; Anderson, Farrel, & Sauers, 1984; Brooks, 1977; Eisenstadt, Breuker, & Evertsz, 1984; Kahney, 1982; Sime, Green, & Guest, 1973; Soloway, Bonar, & Ehrlich, 1981). This problem arises because novices are normally taught dynamic programming concepts in a static abstract manner. Novices then face the difficulty of translating this static abstract information, which describes a hypothetical program or technique, into the nuts and bolts of a particular syntax and set of programming instructions which have a run-time meaning.

To move from being presented with the theory of programming to the practice of writing programs is a large step. In fact it is a Catch-22, as novices need to understand these dynamic concepts before they can write useful working programs, yet they will need some experience of using such concepts in simple working programs before they can build a mental model of program execution based on concrete examples.

2.1 The Approach

The present approach to the problem of conveying dynamic programming concepts to novices, assumes that they need to be provided with a basis for understanding how programs work, both at the level of the syntax and semantics, and how programming constructs are combined to build programs.

Instead of showing the novice a static view of program execution (i.e. a static notional machine) a dynamic view of program execution should communicate the type of information required to build a mental model of the workings of a language and understand dynamic concepts. This dynamic view must not be an analogy but a direct view of the way in which the program is executed (see Chapter 2).

The traditional tools available in programming environments only present the user with a static or snapshot presentation of a program's execution, and so fall short of providing a concrete base on which novices may build a model of program execution. Another problem that novices face with existing tracers is that they do not show the surface evaluation of the code the user has written (surface evaluation means the evaluation of the user's program in terms of the code the program is written in) but a mixture of program output, the internal evaluation of the code and the code the user has written. This means it is an uphill struggle for novices to understand the output of a trace because it bears no resemblance to the program they have written.

To provide a clear and informative view of program execution users should be shown the order in which the program is executed and what happens to each part of the program as execution occurs. Furthermore, in order for novices to recognise this sequential execution of their program the information should be represented in terms of the code written in the editor by users. In order to relate the dynamic action of the program to the view of program execution both the edited code and the trace should be visible at the same time. To strengthen the association between the two forms of novices' programs (the static and the dynamic), relevant pieces of code should be highlighted in the edited code and in the trace as each part of the program is executed.

The trace display should contain enough detail to show why, how, and when things happen (e.g. variable bindings and rule calling). The trace should show the current, outstanding, and previous states of the program's execution so that novices can see the context of the current focus of attention in the trace. The focus of attention on the current action of the trace should not be shown with symbols, because not only do they clutter the display, but their meaning must be learnt by novices before they can understand and use the tracer.

In summary, novice programmers should benefit from the presentation of information about program execution if it is presented (i) in a dynamic fashion, in terms of the programming code the novice have written; and (ii) in a manner that is much the same as the text editor in which the program is written.

2.2 APT an Implementation of the Approach

APT was built to present novice programmers with a clear and consistent story of program execution so that they may build an accurate model of what happens to programs when they run. APT was implemented from a set of design principles extracted from programming environment design principles and a review of dynamic tracing tools (see Chapter 2; Rajan, 1985; 1986).

The APT system was constructed for Prolog because Prolog contains some complex, non-intuitive concepts for novices (e.g. backtracking and unification). APT is written entirely in Lisp (including the Prolog interpreter, modified Edinburgh syntax) and runs on the Symbolics™ 3600 family of machines under release 6.1 of the system. See Chapter 2 and Rajan (1986), for an extensive description of APT including several scenarios using screen snapshots tracing the behaviour of backtracking, the cut, and list manipulation.

APT provides novice programmers with a clear and consistent view of program execution, showing the execution sequence of a program (the trace-time code) in terms of the code the novice has written (the edit-time code). The trace-time code is associated with the edit-time code by inverse video highlighting, so that the novice may see and understand the relationship between the static and the dynamic form of the program. All the dynamic features that occur in the program are shown in the context of the trace-time code (i.e. variable binding, unification, recursion).

3. THE EXPERIMENTS

This section describes two experiments aimed at evaluating the usefulness of APT in communicating run-time information about Prolog to novice programmers. The first looks at the type of misconceptions novices have concerning the action of the Prolog interpreter on simple programs, while the second tests the effect of using APT on novices' understanding of Prolog programs.

Both the experiments presented here are based upon the same experimental technique, utilising specially designed questionnaires aimed at eliciting subjects' understanding of the way Prolog executes programs. The questionnaire is described below. The subsequent sections describe the two experiments dealing with (i) the misconceptions novice programmers hold concerning Prolog program execution, and (ii) the ability of APT to communicate the run-time action of the Prolog interpreter.

3.1 Questionnaire Materials in Both Experiments

Both experiments use a questionnaire consisting of Prolog programs. These programs were specially designed to become progressively more complex in their action at run-time, ranging from simple data base search to the more complex action of backtracking. The programs contain print statements (PP or write) which are carefully placed in order to extract information concerning the way that novices think about the action of the Prolog interpreter on programs. The output from these print statements is designed to elucidate what subjects think the values of variables are at different points in the program, providing an insight into the execution path used. Subjects were given a one-page written tutorial on the use of the print statements with each questionnaire.

With each program the subject was given a query to solve which contained either variables, constants or just consisted of a fact (with no arguments). Sometimes, subjects were required to provide all the solutions, while at other times only one solution was asked for.

The programs used in the questionnaire are detailed below, together with their model answers which follow each query:

Program 1 – "Warm up"

```
likes(mary  wine).
likes(mary  food).
likes(john  food).
likes(john  mary).

bothlike(_X)  if
     likes(mary  _X)  &
     PP(_X)  &
     likes(john  _X).

Q:  bothlike(_X).
wine
food
_X = food
yes
```

The first program was very short and simple consisting of a simple search through a small data base. This provided the subject with an easy problem to warm up on, getting used to the experimental procedure.

Program 2 – "likes"

```
has(fred  money).
has(joe  money).
has(james  money).

kisses(jane  fred).
kisses(june  james).

likes(_X  _Y)  if
    has(_Y  money)  &
    PP(_Y  )  &
    kisses(_X  _Y).

Q:  likes(_X  _Y).
fred
_X = jane  _Y = fred
joe
james
_X = june  _Y = james
no
```

"likes" is a similar program to the first with a simple search through a small data base. The difference here is that the query, "Q: likes(_X _Y)", asks for all solutions to be given, requiring the subject to use backtracking to find alternative solutions.

Program 3 – "connected"

```
origin(BA137  Chicago).
origin(TWA194  Dallas).
origin(PA100  London).
origin(AZ129  London).

destination(TWA194  Paris).
destination(PA100  Rome).
destination(AZ129  Pisa).

stopover(BA137  Washington).
stopover(TWA194  Boston).
stopover(AZ129  Rome).

connected(_F1  _F2)  if
    destination(_F1  _X)  &
    PP(_F1)  &
    origin(_F2  _X).
```

```
connected(_F1  _F2)  if
     destination(_F1  _X)  &
     PP(_X)  &
     stopover(_F2  _X).

Q:  connected(_F1  _F2).
TWA194
PA100
AZ129
Paris
Rome
_F1 = PA100 _F2 = AZ129
yes
```

This program is slightly more complex and longer than the previous two. It contains two rules capable of solving the same goal; that is, which two flights have airport connections? This requires subjects to look for alternative solutions to the first goal, with backtracking, before moving on to the second rule. The second rule succeeds with its second alternative solution.

Program 4 – "hasflu"

```
kisses(mary  john).
kisses(john  june).

hasflu(_X)  if
     PP(_X)  &
     kisses(_Y  _X)  &
     hasflu(_Y).
hasflu(mary).

Q:  hasflu(june).
june
john
mary
yes
```

"hasflu" is recursive, with a tail-recursive call. This requires the subject to have some knowledge of recursion in order to solve the problem, which goes through two recursive calls before succeeding.

Program 5 – "sisters1"

```
sisters(_X  _Y)  if
     female(_X)  &
     parents(_X  _M  _F)  &
     parents(_Y  _M  _F).

female(alice).
female(june).
female(mary).

parents(sue  victoria  fred).
parents(alice  victoria  albert).
parents(mary  susan  edward).
parents(june  victoria  albert).
parents(jenny  jill  roy).

Q:  sisters(_X  _Y).
_X = alice  _Y = alice
_X = alice  _Y = june
_X = june  _Y = alice
_X = june  _Y = june
_X = mary  _Y = mary
no
```

This program is the classic "sisters" problem, in which X is the sister of Y, if X is female and both X and Y have the same parents. This requires subjects to use simple data base search to provide all the solutions in the same way as program 2. If they use this method they should get the correct answer, or at least the fact that X can be X's sister using this definition. However if they try to solve the problems semantically with a bottom-up approach, or have an incorrect notion of data base search, they will get an incorrect answer.

Program 6 – "sisters2"

```
sisters(_X  _Y)  if
     female(_X)  &
     parents(_X  _M  _F)  &
     parents(_Y  _M  _F).

female(alice).
female(june).
female(mary).
```

```
parents(sue   victoria   fred).
parents(alice   victoria   albert).
parents(mary   susan   edward).
parents(june   victoria   albert).
parents(jenny   jill   roy).

Q:  sisters(alice   alice).
yes
```

Program 6 is the same as program 5 but with a different query. The query is as follows "sisters(alice, alice).". This program is aimed at determining whether subjects realise that this solution is possible.

Program 7 – "abstract1"

```
a(_X)  if
        b(_X)   &
        c(_X).

b(_X)  if
        h(_X   _Y)   &
        PP(_X _Y) &
        i(_Y).

b(_X)  if
        h(_Y   _X)   &
        PP(_Y   _X)   &
        i(_Y).

h(john   mary).
h(jim   sue).
i(mary).
i(jim).

c(mary).
c(sue).
c(fred).
c(jane).

Q:  a(_X).
john   mary
jim   sue
john   mary
jim   sue
_X = sue
yes
```

This is a program from a paper by Coombs, Hartley, and Stell (1986) which has been slightly modified. This program, like program 3, contains two rules to solve the same goal. As in the previous program the first rule fails with all the alternative combinations of data, causing backtracking to the second rule, which succeeds with the second alternative set of data. This program requires subjects to understand both the order of data base search and backtracking. Instead of using rules with everyday meanings this program uses letters, and so the novice will have to realise that such programs work in the same way as the others.

Program 8 – "abstract2"

```
a if
        b &
        loves(John  Mary).
a if c.

b if
        d &
        e.

b if f.
c if PP(foo).
d if PP(bar).
e if PP(baz).
e if PP(gort).
f if PP(fez).

loves(John  Sue).

Q: a.
bar
baz
gort
fez
foo
yes
```

Program 8 was the last program in the questionnaire. This program consists of a simple data base search with failure-driven backtracking. However the predicates contain no arguments which makes them look strange, and gives them no everyday meaning in their description.

These materials were used in both experiments, albeit in slightly different ways. In the first study they were used to elicit the types of errors subjects make in Prolog programs. In the second experiment they were used in a more constrained transfer paradigm.

3.2 Experiment 1: Novice Misconceptions

The first experiment classified the types of misconceptions that novices hold concerning the events occurring when Prolog programs are executed. This categorisation is based on the workings of the Prolog interpreter rather than on the bugs made in programming (van Someren, 1984; 1985).

3.2.1 Subjects

Subjects were recruited from the Open University Cognitive Psychology Summer School. All the subjects were novice Prolog programmers, having no previous experience of Prolog other than this course. The extent of their Prolog programming knowledge consisted of a 95 page Prolog primer (Eisenstadt, 1986) which teaches the following concepts: facts and queries, the query interpreter, conjunctive queries, rules, pattern matching, data base search, the processing of rules by the interpreter including variable instantiation and uninstantiation, and backtracking. It also included a dayschool which provided the subjects with their first hands on experience of Prolog, and lastly a two day Artificial Intelligence project at Summer School.

The project consists of an algorithm specifying a psychological model which is to be built, and a Prolog program embodying the algorithm. Students generally spend around one and a half days developing the program with the constant help of a tutor.

There were 33 subjects used for this experiment from the Summer School, all of whom responded to the postal questionnaire.

3.2.2 Materials

The questionnaire described above consisted of eight Prolog programs, two model answers, an instruction sheet, and a tutorial on the use of the print statement PP.

3.2.3 Method

This experiment was conducted by post. The subjects were sent the questionnaire and told to read the instructions carefully and take notice of the model answers. They were allowed to solve the queries in their own time.

3.2.4 Categorisation and Scoring

The results from this study were analysed in the following way. The different answers given by subjects to each program in the questionnaire were categorized. Each group of answers was analysed by looking at the solutions given by subjects, along with the bindings of variables shown via the "PP" statement. This information provides an insight into the strategy used by subjects to simulate execution of the programs and gives us a glimpse of their mental models of Prolog execution.

The results of the analysis were then studied to explain how the subjects arrived at each group of solutions given. Explanations were produced using two methods, both of which attempted to provide a rationale for the solutions given to the queries. The first was to alter the action of the Prolog interpreter in an attempt to find the model of the interpreter the student had in order to produce the buggy solution. The second method attempted to impose real world constraints on the program, which the subject would use as an alternative to a model of the Prolog interpreter to determine the solution to a query.

The following categories were constructed to explain the answers given by subjects to the programs in the questionnaire. Included in the results are categories for correct answers, answers that cannot be interpreted in terms of a misconception of program execution, subjects who gave the correct answer but no printed output, and those subjects who did not attempt to answer the query.

Correct. This category represents correct answers.

Correct – No Printing. Here the correct bindings are given, but no printed output. There is not enough information to determine whether a misconception concerning program execution has arisen, or not.

Static Match/All Subgoals Must Succeed. This category of answer can be explained either by a "static match" approach, or by "all subgoals must succeed". The static match is an approach where novices attempt to use a rule as a template into which they try to fit the facts contained in the data base. This is done in a static manner where the facts either fit and the rule succeeds, or they do not and the rule fails. No account is taken of partial matches within the rule, and the side effects that can thus be caused. This method can be useful for experts to estimate the action of a program at a glance but misses out many events which occur at run-time.

The "all subgoals must succeed" explanation is as follows. Unless all the subgoals of a parent goal succeed, none of the subgoals can be executed. The misconception here is that all the subgoals of a clause must be unified before any of the subgoals can succeed, rather than that each subgoal must be unified before it can succeed.

The difference between "static match" and "all subgoals must succeed" is that with the former the user works in a bottom-up static fashion, fitting the facts into the rules, ignoring such things as backtracking and correct data base search order. With the latter the user works through the program in a dynamic top-down manner. This is similar to the Prolog interpreter, but differs in the belief that all the subgoals of a rule must succeed in order for any one of them to succeed and be executed. This appears to be a misconception concerning unification.

Real World Fallacy. This is where novices understand the everyday meaning of a Prolog rule, but do not understand how the program will work given a query at run-time. Novices answer the query by using their real-world knowledge to interpret the rules, and then fit the facts into this real-world knowledge. So the novices are substituting real-world knowledge for the Prolog interpreter. This approach will nearly always cause problems, because the way Prolog works very often gives counter-intuitive answers to queries.

Do Not Search From the Top. With this misconception novices do not start searching the data base from the top each time there is a fresh goal call, but instead carry on from where they are. This will cut out large chunks of the search space preventing certain solutions, and side effects.

Only Try the First Rule. When there is more than one clause with the same head in the data base, novices will try the first one and if it fails they will stop there and give up. The other rules with the same name are not tried. As with the last misconception, this approach will cut down the search space, and result in no answer where one or more solutions may exist.

No Backtracking. If in unification a rule fails to match, do not attempt to find an alternative solution by backtracking, but move on to the next rule with the same predicate name.

Miscellaneous. This category represents all the answers which cannot be explained in terms of a misconception about program execution. This includes answers of "no".

No Attempted Answer. This category represents those subjects who did not attempt to provide a solution.

3.2.5 Results and Discussion

The answers that the subjects provided to the questionnaire have pointed out some possible misconceptions held concerning the action of the Prolog interpreter on fairly simple programs at run-time. Table 6.1 provides a summary of the occurrences of the main response categories in the various programs of Experiment 1.

TABLE 6.1
Summary of the Response Categories Found in Experiment 1

Category	*Program*							
	1	2	3	4	5	6	7	8
Correct	•	•	•			•	•	
Correct-no printing	•	•	•	•			•	
All subgoals must succeed/static match	•	•	•	•			•	•
Real world fallacy			•	•	•			
Do not search from the top				•	•			
Only try the first rule							•	
No backtracking							•	•
Miscellaneous	•	•	•	•	•	•	•	•
No attempted answer				•	•		•	•

Table 6.2 shows the percentage of subjects who responded in each category for every program used in the questionnaire. The misconceptions in Table 6.2 show that novice programmers have problems with program execution in three areas. *All subgoals must succeed* and *static match* are due to an inaccurate model of what happens in unification. *Do not search from the top*, *only try the first rule*, and *no backtracking* show a problem with the control structure of the Prolog interpreter. Lastly, *real world fallacy* demonstrates that if the program has a real world meaning, then the subject will impose this meaning on the program to produce a solution, rather than follow the mechanism of the interpreter.

Besides the misconceptions described by the categories shown, the results contain other misconceptions which have no clear interpretation. These misconceptions are contained in the miscellaneous category. Explanations have been suggested concerning how these answers may have been

TABLE 6.2
The Percentage of Subjects For Each Response Category in Experiment 1

Category	*Program*							
	1	2	3	4	5	6	7	8
Correct	49	70	9	0	0	61	30	0
Correct-no printing	24	6	9	9	0	0	9	0
All subgoals must succeed/static match	24	12	64	12	0	0	3	24
Real world fallacy	0	0	6	30	73	0	0	0
Do not search from the top	0	0	0	12	21	0	0	0
Only try the first rule	0	0	0	0	0	0	12	0
No backtracking	0	0	0	0	0	0	3	9
Miscellaneous	3	12	12	33	3	39	33	58
No attempted answer	0	0	0	3	3	0	9	9

produced, but it is felt that they are too loose to provide a useful misconception category. However, the answers contained in the miscellaneous category show that the subjects do not understand many of the concepts inherent in the execution of Prolog programs. The concepts concerned are unification, data base search, variable binding, and backtracking. These misconceptions show that novice programmers need special help to learn such dynamic features as unification and search.

3.3 Experiment 2: Evaluation APT

The aim of Experiment 2 was to determine whether APT improved the way novice programmers think about the execution of Prolog programs. This was tested by measuring the ability of novices to solve queries to Prolog programs. In the study, subjects were either allowed to see an animated trace showing the run-time action of Prolog programs or just the solution to the programs. The subjects who saw the animated demonstration are called the APT group, while the subjects who saw only the solutions are called the control group.

The experiment consisted of two questionnaires and a demonstration. The first questionnaire (as in Experiment 1) tested the ability of novice programmers to solve queries to Prolog programs. This was followed by a demonstration, using APT, showing subjects the process of execution of the programs and queries contained in the first questionnaire. The second questionnaire consisted of a set of Prolog programs and queries which were isomorphs to those used in the first questionnaire. Two examples of the programs which are isomorphs to the first and third programs in the first questionnaire are shown below (see also Rajan, 1986).

Isomorph 1 – "Warm-up"

```
colour(cat  blue).
colour(cat  black).
colour(coal  black).
colour(sea  green).

samecolour(_X)  if
    colour(cat  _X)  &
    write(_X)  &
    colour(coal  _X).

Q:  samecolour(_X).
blue
black
_X = black
yes
```

Isomorph 3 – "playswith"

```
playswith(Jim  Phil).
playswith(Sue  Mark).
playswith(Fred  Jon).
playswith(Doreen  Jon).

likes(Sue  Mike).
likes(Fred  Anne).
likes(Doreen  Simon).

talksto(Jim  Pat).
talksto(Sue  Hank).
talksto(Doreen  Anne).

friends(_P1  _P2)  if
    likes(_P1  _X)  &
    write(_P1)  &
    playswith(_P2  _X).
friends(_P1  _P2)  if
    likes(_P1  _X)  &
    write(_X)  &
    talksto(_P2  _X).

Q:  friends(_P1  _P2).
Sue
Fred
Doreen
Mike
Anne
_P1 = Doreen  _P2 = Anne
yes
```

3.3.1 Subjects

Six subjects were used in the APT group. These subjects were drawn from the same population used in the misconceptions experiment. None of these subjects took part in the misconceptions experiment. Six subjects were used in the control group. These subjects are members of the Open University staff, all of whom are novice programmers. The reason that the control group was drawn from a different population was due to the unavailability of subjects from the population used for the experimental group. The programming experience of the control group consisted of reading the same 95 page Prolog primer that the APT group used. So the programming experience of both groups was matched as far as possible.

3.3.2 Procedure

The experiment consisted of three parts, two questionnaires on solving Prolog programs separated by either the animated demonstrations for the APT group, or the solution to the programs for the control group.

Both groups of subjects were given the first questionnaire which consisted of eight Prolog programs each with a query. The questionnaire also contained a tutorial on the use of the print statement to remind the subjects how the print statement works, and for reference by the subject during the experiment. The subjects were asked to answer these Prolog queries as best they could, in their own time, writing down the output of the print statements and the final bindings of the variables given in the query.

The APT group were then given a three page introduction to the APT system before being shown a demonstration, using APT, of the way Prolog would solve each of the eight programs in the first questionnaire. Only one demonstration of each program was allowed, due to the considerable length of the experiment, which subjects could step through at their own pace.

The control group were allowed to run the programs (in Prolog on a Macintosh) from the first questionnaire, so that they could see the solution to each program. The subjects could see the source code of each program as they ran it, allowing both source code and solution to be viewed simultaneously. However they were not allowed to trace the programs at any time. Directly after running the programs the second questionnaire was given to each group of subjects.

3.3.3 Materials

The first questionnaire was the same as the one used in Experiment 1. The second questionnaire consisted of programs and queries that were isomorphs of the programs in the first questionnaires. This was to prevent the subjects from simply recalling their answers to the first questionnaire, or from the APT demonstration of these programs, when answering the second questionnaire. Isomorphs were used so that the complexity and type of programs remain the same as for the programs used in the first test.

3.3.4 Scoring

Both questionnaires were scored to determine how well the subjects answered the questions and these scores were used as a measure of their understanding of the Prolog interpreter in action at run-time on the given programs. The following method was used to score the answers to the questionnaires in order to take account of all the aspects of the program output, and subjects' answers. One point was awarded for:

a. Any correct item subjects wrote down that should be printed out by a print statement.
b. Any two items from print statements that occurred in the correct order.
c. Any correct final binding for the variable/s given in the query.
d. Any two sets of bindings that occurred in the correct order, where all solutions were asked for.

A point was deducted for any item that the subject wrote down that should not be in the program output. The maximum score on each questionnaire was 67.

3.3.5 Results & Discussion

The total marks that each group of subjects scored on each questionnaire is shown in Tables 6.3 and 6.4 below.

The results for the APT group show that all the subjects improved their scores on the questionnaire after they had seen the demonstrations of program execution provided by APT. To determine the significance of any difference between pre- and post-questionnaire scores for each condition a t-test was applied to the mean scores of each questionnaire. The reason a t-test was chosen was due to its robustness with respect to deviation from a normal distribution and homogeneity of variance for the population under study. The difference between the experimental pre- and post-scores is reliable [$t(5) = 2.58$, $p < 0.025$, one-tailed]. The results for the control group show no significant difference between the mean scores of the questionnaires [$t(5) = 0.148$, $p < 0.05$, one-tailed]. A t-test also showed

TABLE 6.3
The Cumulative Scores For Each of the Subjects in the Experimental ATP Group

APT group subjects	RP	RM	VC	TJ	PP	DP	Mean
Pre-APT Questionnaire	12	41	9	9	41	31	23.8
Post-APT Questionnaire	13	46	28	17	44	56	34.0

TABLE 6.4
The Cumulative Scores for Each of the Subjects in the Control Group

Control group subjects	LC	MD	NP	TG	DM	CR	Mean
Pre-solution Questionnaire	16	18	13	17	15	9	14.6
Post-solution Questionnaire	16	21	12	15	11	12	14.5

that the difference between the difference in scores for the APT and control groups was significant [t (10) = 2.44, $p < 0.025$, one-tailed]. In other words, there was a significant difference between the improvement in scores for the APT group compared to the control group.

Hence, the results show that there is a statistically-significant improvement in the ability of novices to solve queries to Prolog programs after seeing an animated demonstration of program execution. The control group shows that this improvement is not due to the effects of other variables such as practice or seeing the solution to programs.

Some subjects in the APT group showed a greater improvement, than others. For example, RP showed only a very tiny improvement in her score. It should be noted that RP stated prior to the experiment that she was having some difficulty with learning Prolog. This may point to the fact that APT might not help certain categories of user, suggesting that APT users need to have some basic knowledge concerning Prolog before APT will be of any use in comunicating information about Prolog execution. However, there is no general evidence for this amongst the other subjects in the groups.

In summary, this experiment shows that APT has improved the ability of subjects to answer the questions in the questionnaire. This suggests that APT has improved subjects' conceptual model of how the Prolog interpreter works in these classes of programs. It remains to be seen if this knowledge generalises to other non-isomorphic programs. In addition, this experiment has shown that further work is needed to determine how APT helps different categories of user, and which concepts of Prolog execution it clarifies and which it does not.

4. CONCLUSION AND FUTURE DIRECTIONS

Subjects in these experiments clearly lack understanding of several basic concepts in Prolog which are dynamic in nature. These concepts involve the nature of variable binding, the order of data base search, and the unification of goals to the use of rules at run-time. This evidence corroborates the reported findings that many of the problems novices face in learning programming concepts are due to an incomplete or non-existent conceptual model of the dynamic nature of these concepts.

Experiment 2 on the effects of APT demonstrates that after being given a view of program execution, an improvement can be seen in the ability of novices to solve queries to Prolog programs. The results from the control group show that this improvement is probably due to the animated view of program execution rather than any other factor. Overall this suggests that these novices also have an improved conceptual model of the action of the Prolog interpreter due to the view of program execution provided by the

APT demonstrations. The success of APT also provides indirect support for the design principles upon which it is built.

With respect to individual subjects the results show that APT may not help all novice users and may not clarify all the concepts inherent in Prolog execution. Also the results do not show what effect APT has on the novice's conceptual model of Prolog execution. Therefore, more detailed experiments are necessary in order to determine (i) how the conceptual model changed after the demonstrations had been seen; (ii) which categories of user APT helps; (iii) which features of Prolog execution APT clarifies.

A further study could be carried out comparing novice programmers perception of dynamically traced programs versus a static trace of programs. The static trace could be based on the Byrd box model of the execution of Prolog programs. This study would determine the impact of the animated features of APT on the comprehension of program execution by novices as opposed to the static approach used traditionally.

Since the work presented in this paper was completed, another Prolog tracer, the Transparent Prolog Machine has been developed at the Open University. The Transparent Prolog Machine (see Chapter 3) is a dynamic graphical tracer, which shows the execution of Prolog programs in terms of an AND/OR tree. A comparison of APT and TPM in respect of the communicative power of the dynamic aspects of the Prolog interpreter for novices would provide useful data for the design of future generations of Prolog trace packages.

REFERENCES

Anderson, J. R., Farrell, R., & Sauers, R. (1984). Learning to program in Lisp. *Cognitive Science*, *8*, 87–129.

Brooks, R. (1977). Towards a theory of the cognitive processes in computer programming. *International Journal of Man-Machine Studies*, *9*, 737–742.

Coombs, M. J., Hartley, R. T., & Stell, J. G. (1986). Debugging user conceptions of interpretation processes. *Proceedings of AAAI-86*, Philadelphia, PA.

Eisenstadt, M. (1986). *D309 Artificial Intelligence project. Unit of cognitive psychology: A third level course.* Milton Keynes: Open University Press.

Eisenstadt, M., Breuker, J., & Evertsz, R. (1984). A cognitive account of "natural" looping constructs. *Proceedings of the First IFIP Conference on Human-Computer Interaction, INTERACT '84.* Amsterdam: North Holland, 173–177.

Kahney, J. H. (1982). An in-depth study of the behaviour of novice programmers. *Technical Report No. 5.* Human Cognition Research Laboratory, The Open University, England.

Rajan, T. (1985). APT: The design of animated tracing tools for novice programmers. *Technical Report No. 15.* Human Cognition Research Laboratory, The Open University, Milton Keynes, England.

Rajan, T. (1986). APT: A principled design for an animated view of program execution for novice programmers. *Technical Report No. 19/19a.* Human Cognition Research Laboratory, The Open University, Milton Keynes, England.

Rajan, T. (1987). APT: A principled design of an animated view of program execution for novice programmers. *Proceedings of INTERACT '87 2nd. IFIP Conference on Human-Computer Interaction*. Amsterdam: North Holland, 291–296.

Sime, M. E., Green, T. R. G., & Guest, D. J. (1973). Psychological evaluation of two conditional constructions in computer languages. *International Journal of Man-Machine Studies*, *5*, 123–143.

Soloway, E., Bonar, J., & Ehrlich, K. (1981). Cognitive factors in programming: An empirical study of looping constructs. Amherst, MA: *Technical Report No. 81-10*, Department of Computer Science, University of Massachusetts.

van Someren, M. W. (1984). Misconceptions of beginning Prolog programmers. *Memorandum 30 of the Research Project "The Acquisition of Expertise"*. Department of Experimental Psychology. The University of Amsterdam.

van Someren, M. W. (1985). Beginners problems in learning Prolog. *Memorandum 31 of the Research Project "The Acquisition of Expertise"*. Department of Experimental Psychology. The University of Amsterdam.

7 Some Pitfalls in Learning About Recursion

Hank Kahney
Human Cognition Research Laboratory, The Open University, Milton Keynes, England

OVERVIEW

This chapter examines some of the errors produced by subjects in trying to write recursive functions in the programming language SOLO. Through a detailed analysis of the sorts of errors produced by learners, several proposals are made about the possible mental models underlying novices' understanding of recursion. The role of various factors in learning is also discussed.

1. INTRODUCTION

This chapter describes our on-going research into the behaviour of novice programmers. We are interested in the mental processes which occur when novices are confronted with a problem statement, and the mechanisms by which they understand the problem, design an algorithm, code it, and (if necessary) debug it. Our research is a development of earlier work on problem understanding (Hayes & Simon, 1974), models of programmers' coding processes (Brooks, 1977), and debugging (see Chapter 9; Sussman, 1975; Goldstein, 1975; Laubsch & Eisenstadt, 1981).

We investigate students attempting to write recursive inference programs using a LOGO-like data base manipulation language called SOLO (see Chapter 1; Eisenstadt, 1978; Eisenstadt, Laubsch, & Kahney, 1981). Students are presented with a prototypical problem and its solution couched in everyday terms in order to simplify the explanation of recursion: "Imagine a chain of 'KISSES' relations (e.g. JOHN KISSES MARY

KISSES FRED KISSES JANE, etc). A procedure called INFECT can propagate FLU all the way through the chain of KISSES relations, so we end up with JOHN HAS FLU, MARY HAS FLU, etc." The example is explained to the students in great detail, including several pages of text, diagrams, and a worked through trace of a sample invocation of INFECT.

As one might expect, some students "get it" (i.e. understand this simple form of tail-recursion and the notion of propagating side-effects through the data base), and some don't. The difference between those who get it and those who do not can be accounted for by differences in (a) the abstractions they make from their first detailed example, and (b) the evaluation rules inherent in the mental models they use to run through trial solutions.

2. A SAMPLE PROBLEM AND SOLUTION

We investigated students solving several recursive inference problems, including one based on a real-world example so compelling that we could be certain the nature of the task was perfectly understood. Here is a concise summary of the problem.

Given a data base describing objects piled up on one another as follows:

```
SANDWICH      ON       PLATE      ON      NEWSPAPER
          -------▶            -------▶
```

write a program which simulates the effect of someone firing a very powerful pistol aimed downwards at the topmost object (SANDWICH), yielding the final data base shown below:

```
SANDWICH        ON         PLATE        ON        NEWSPAPER
            ------▶                 ------▶

   HAS                      HAS                      HAS

    ▼                        ▼                        ▼
BULLETHOLE              BULLETHOLE              BULLETHOLE
```

As it turns out, even our crystal clear example (fleshed out in considerably more detail) causes difficulty – it appears that those students who get it can cope with either crystal clear or muddy recursive inference problems, whereas those who do not are stuck in either case.

```
TO SHOOT /X/

1 NOTE /X/ HAS BULLETHOLE

2 CHECK /X/ ON ?

   2A If Present: SHOOT * ; EXIT

   2B If Absent: EXIT

DONE
```

FIG. 7.1. S8's solution (the "*" and "?" are co-referential).

Figure 7.1 shows the solution eventually produced by subject S8, one of the subjects who got it. Below is a summary of the protocol of subject S8 during the course of reading and solving this problem, but before any attempt to write the code shown in Fig. 7.1. Problem statements are in italics. The numbers are segments from the actual protocol. It has been condensed for expository purposes, but captures the highlights of the protocol. A complete version is described in Kahney (1982).

"On page 80 of Units 3 to 4 we looked at a method for making a particular inference keep on happening."

2 Is that called "iteration"? No, "recursion" . . . I think this is going to say something about what happens when you keep on applying a function . . . through a data base.

"In this option you are asked to imagine a state of the world in which there are six objects: . . . this hypothetical world is highly structured: the sandwich is lying in the centre of the plate, which is sitting on the newspaper, which is lying on the book . . ."

4 . . . well you could also get out things like . . . sort of making inferences about "if the sandwich is on the plate which is on the newspaper [then] the sandwich is on the newspaper."

"A data base representing this state of affairs looks like this [see above]. Now imagine someone standing beside the table with a .357 magnum pistol."

8 Well, I would expect him to shoot through all that lot then. I don't know why he wants to do it though . . .

S8 began with a working knowledge of recursive procedures. At successive sentences S8 set up expectations about what would come next and usually predicted the information contained in the next sentence or two; she was always just slightly ahead of the game. S8 is apparently using a recursion schema to direct her attention during the reading process to important aspects of the problem statement. The first line of the problem statement has clearly triggered off an expectation of recursion [protocol segment 2], with a concomitant expectation of some "function to be applied through a data base" [segment 2]. The data base structure (we met earlier) is consistent with her expectation of a standard transitivity problem [segment 4], even though this is not the problem to be posed. Her real-world knowledge about pistols and the spatial relationship of the objects in the problem combines with her expectations about transitivity problems to yield an expectation about what the protagonist in the problem statement will do [segment 8]. This expectation does not mesh with her knowledge of human motivations and intentions [segment 8].

Figure 7.2 depicts our representation of S8's internalized schema for recursion. The details of the schema are derived from a variety of sources: transcription tasks, concept rating and sorting tasks, problem-solving tasks, and verbal protocols.

Bearing in mind that slot-names are displayed against the left-hand margin (e.g. GOAL, ACTION, etc.), and that the function "my" is a cross-reference to a slot-filler (e.g. (my action)) we can paraphrase S8's schema for recursion as follows:

The GOAL of a recursive procedure is to perpetrate a side-effect on every element of the data structure to which it is applied, i.e. a "transitive" chain. (Knowledge about such structures is contained in S8's TRANSITIVE-CHAIN schema, not depicted here, which indicates that a collection of nodes standing in a particular relation to one another is an essential component of recursive processing – S8 has abstracted this notion, although KISSES is not a transitive relation.) The ACTION involved is typically the application of a NOTE primitive (which performs a data base "ASSERT"). The SURFACE-TEMPLATE depicts raw SOLO code, with its own slots to be filled in during actual coding. It is based upon an exemplar given in the textbook, and corresponds to rote learning of "how to do it", rather than understanding "how it works". (Subjects like S5, discussed below, have a poorer grasp of recursion and need only have a mental pointer to a place in the textbook where they can find a typical example to copy).

"How it works" understanding is reflected primarily in the GOAL and EVALUATION-RULES slots. The GOAL slot captures the essence of the "generator plan" used in the program-understanding plan-libraries of Waters (1979) and Laubsch and Eisenstadt (see Chapter 9). The EVALUATION-RULES slot depicts S8's technique for working through a

```
                    RECURSIVE-PROCEDURE
...
GOAL: (ForEvery x In (my applies-to) do (achieve (my action) x))
ACTION: (a side-effect {default (a NOTE) } )
APPLIES-TO: (a transitive-chain)
SURFACE-TEMPLATE:
        TO (name1 = (a name)) (a parameter {default: X})
        (my action)
        CHECK (a node) (a relation) (a wild-card)
        IF PRESENT: (a procedure
                            with name = name1
                            with parameter = '*') ; EXIT
        IF ABSENT: EXIT
        DONE
EVALUATION-RULES:
        1) (let parameter = the startnode from (my applies-to))
        2) (apply (my action) parameter)
        3) assert '(ACHIEVED , (my action) , parameter ))
        4) (let parameter = (GetNextNode))
        5) (ForEvery x In (GetRestOfNodes) (assert '(ACHIEVED , (my action)s , x))
TRIGGERS: 'keep on happening' ; re-apply
```

FIG. 7.2. S8's schema for recursion.

mental model of the succession of effects carried out by a body of SOLO code. The rules are clearly not sufficient to work as a SOLO interpreter, but rather depict the subject's own naive strategy for convincing herself that the code works. The rules behave as follows:

1. Instantiate the parameter, pretending that it's the first node in the chain (i.e. SANDWICH).
2. Imagine the main action being performed on that node.
3. Make a mental note that the action has been achieved.
4. See what node is next in the data base, traversing the crucial "transitive" relation.
5. Make a mental node that the action is achieved on every node reachable along the "transitive" chain.

Below we present S8's protocol corresponding to the above evaluation rules, along with the relevant rules listed in square brackets, e.g. [ER1],

[ER2], etc. These protocol segments were recorded after S8 had written the program, but before she ran it.

208 TO SHOOT . . . X, let's say X is a SANDWICH . . . [ER1]
210 First of all it NOTEs in the data base . . . X HAS BULLETHOLE [ER2, ER3]
211 It then checks whether X is ON anything . . . [ER4]
213 X is ON PLATE so it will do that to PLATE . . . So that should keep doing that, PLATEs ON . . . something, so on and so on . . . [ER5]

3. A SECOND SOLUTION

Figure 7.3 shows the solution eventually developed by subject S5, who didn't get it. Below are extracts from S5's protocol. Whereas S8 was able to develop the solution in her head, S5's solution evolved during code writing:

46 I'm going to follow that example [= INFECT].
51 [Reads from INFECT example in SOLO primer] . . . NOTE, um, X HAS FLU . . . SANDWICH HAS BULLETHOLE . . .
54 SANDWICH ON PLATE, um . . . NOTE . . . um . . .
63 I've got to get the SHOOT in somewhere haven't I?
65 CHECK . . . X SHOOTS SANDWICH. IF PRESENT . . . SHOOTUP . . .
83 Well, I hope it will go all the way through the sequence and shoot the floor. The data base is in and I've copied that program [= INFECT] exactly.

```
TO SHOOTUP /X/

1 NOTE /X/ HAS BULLETHOLE

2 CHECK /X/ SHOOTS ?

   2A If Present: SHOOTUP * ; EXIT

   2B If Absent: EXIT

DONE
```

FIG. 7.3. The solution of S5.

S5 has a recursion schema which differs from that of S8 in several respects. First, S5's schema does not have a filled SURFACE-TEMPLATE slot, but rather (a) a pointer to the place in the SOLO primer where a typical recursive procedure, i.e. INFECT, is described, and (b) a method for filling the SURFACE-TEMPLATE slot by copying the INFECT program's structure and providing arguments from the current problem. Second, S5's schema has a restriction that the relationship between objects in the data base must be active for recursion to work. That is, from the original INFECT teaching problem with JOHN KISSES MARY KISSES FRED, S5 had abstracted the rule that a start-node has to do something to a successor-node before a side-effect can be perpetrated on the successor-node. (S8, on the other hand, had abstracted transitivity from previous study of the INFECT program – neither view, of course, is perfectly correct).

For example, ON is not an active relationship between the objects (SANDWICH, PLATE, etc.) given in the problem statement. ON is passive and thus does not support S5's notion of recursion. SHOOTS is an active relation, and S5 is convinced that somehow SHOOTS must be brought into the pattern-matching segment of the program in order to make the program work at all [segments 63 and 65 of S5's protocol]. This conviction precludes solving the problem, unless careful re-analysis of the example program leads to reformulation of the rule about relationships between data base objects. S5 never relinquishes her belief that an active relationship need exist between the nodes for recursion to work, and her reformulations of the program are all guided by this single important but wrong-headed principle. S5's protocol continues:

> 156 This one about the BULLETHOLE and this one with the KISSES are different. I need to say that the first X, the first parameter does something actively . . . to the second parameter. All I've got is BULLETHOLE. In the example it's got KISSES, which is an active thing.

Although S5 made several subsequent attempts to map the BULLETHOLE problem onto the INFECT framework, the point of view from which the mapping occurred never changed and no solution resulted (see Keane, Kahney, & Brayshaw, 1989 for further details on this issue).

4. OTHER MENTAL MODELS OF RECURSION

Obviously, there are large differences between the kinds of models different students acquire when learning about a process like recursion. In order to learn more about the range of models that might be abstracted from the worked example in the SOLO primer (the INFECT program) we devised an experimental task which we presented to a number of expert and novice SOLO programmers (the reader is referred to Kahney, 1982, for details of the performance of experts on this task, and a fuller discussion of the results presented below). We presumed that few students would acquire notions as idiosyncratic as those manifest in S5's behaviour. The conceptual model presented to students in the SOLO primer defines recursion as a process that is capable of triggering new instantiations of itself, with control passing forward to successive instantiations and back from terminated ones. This is the copies model of recursion, the model that experts, and novices who got it, were hypothesized to have. Most novices, on the other hand, were hypothesized to have a looping model, with the following features (see Fig. 7.4):

1. An entry point, the constituents of which are the program's name and a parameter slot.
2. An action part, which is designed to add information to the data base by way of the SOLO primitive NOTE.
3. A propagation mechanism for generating successive data base nodes and feeding the values of these nodes back to the entry point of the program.

This hypothesis was tested by presenting subjects with the questionnaire below. The questionnaire contains a statement of the INFECT problem (with which all subjects were already familiar from their introduction to the problem in the SOLO primer) and three program solutions, called

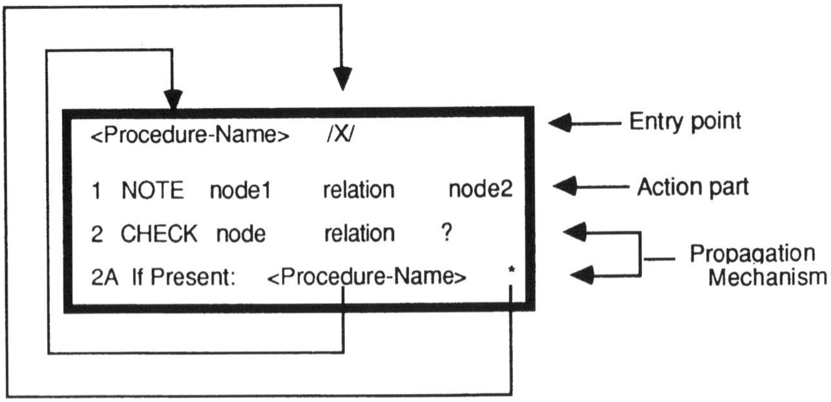

FIG. 7.4. The looping model of recursion.

SOLUTION-1, SOLUTION-2 and SOLUTION-3, respectively. Two of these solutions are critical in determining a subject's model of recursion. To make the predictions clear to the reader, we shall demonstrate the presumed reasoning processes that occur when subjects with different models of recursion are confronted with the two critical programs in the questionnaire. The text of the questionnaire was:

> Recently, I needed a programme which would make the following inference: if somebody "X" has 'flu, then whoever "X" kisses also has 'flu, and whoever is infected spreads the infection to the person he or she kisses, and so on. Starting with the data base given in Figure A, I needed a program which would change the Figure A data base into the Figure B data base (see Fig. 7.5).

```
JOHN ISA MAN                    JOHN ISA MAN
 I                               I
 I...KISSES MARY                 I...KISSES MARY
                                 I
                                 I...HAS FLU
MARY ISA WOMAN                  MARY ISA WOMAN
 I                               I
 I...KISSES TIM                  I...KISSES TIM
                                 I
                                 I...HAS FLU
TIM ISA MAN                     TIM ISA MAN
 I                               I
 I...KISSES JOAN                 I...KISSES JOAN
                                 I
                                 I...HAS FLU
JOAN ISA WOMAN                  JOAN ISA WOMAN
                                 I
                                 I...HAS FLU

       A                               B
```

FIG. 7.5. The figures used in the questionnaire.

I have been provided with three solutions to the problem (see below), all called "TO INFECT /X/" and these are labelled SOLUTION-1, SOLUTION-2 and SOLUTION-3, I want you to consider each program in turn and say (a) whether or not the program will do what I want it to do, and (b) if it will, say how it does it (in your own words), or, if it won't, why it doesn't (again in your own words).

Please write your answers on the pages provided overleaf. Thank you for cooperating.

SOLUTION-1

```
TO INFEXT /X/
1 CHECK /X/ KISSES ?
1A If Present: NOTE * HAS FLU; EXIT
1B If Absent: EXIT
DONE
```

SOLUTION-2

```
TO INFECT /X/
1 NOTE /X/ HAS FLU
2 CHECK /X/ KISSES ?
2A If Present: INFECT * ; EXIT
2B If Absent: EXIT
DONE
```

SOLUTION-3

```
TO INFECT /X/
1 CHECK /X/ KISSES ?
1A If Present: INFECT * ; CONTINUE
1B If Absent: CONTINUE
2 NOTE /X/ HAS FLU
DONE
```

SOLUTION-1 will not achieve the required effect. Its outcome would be to add "HAS FLU" to the node MARY, after which the program would be terminated. SOLUTION-2 and SOLUTION-3 would both achieve the required changes to the data base. SOLUTION-2 works by side-effecting the data base on the node first given as the argument to INFECT (= JOHN), and then generating the next node on the "KISSES" list, which triggers the recursion. SOLUTION-3 works by creating a stack of bindings for /X/, i.e. (JOHN, MARY, TIM, JOAN) and side-effecting each on return from the recursive creation of the list (i.e. side-effects the listed nodes in reverse order).

Strong evidence for possession of the copies model of recursion would be selection of both SOLUTION-2 and SOLUTION-3 as correctly designed programs for the task in hand, plus some comment on the order in which the side-effect occurs when SOLUTION-3 is run; as the side-effect occurs as the recursion unwinds, one would expect anyone who recognized this fact would mention it.

Strong evidence for possession of the loop model would be selection of SOLUTION-2 as a correctly designed program and rejection of SOLUTION-3 on the grounds that only JOAN would get 'flu when this program was run. Consider SOLUTION-2. Under the loop model, the parameter slot is first instantiated with JOHN. At step 1 of the program, the side-effect to that node is accomplished, and at step 2 the wild-card pattern match succeeds, binding the value MARY to the variable. As a result, at step 2A recursion is triggered, which, in terms of the loop model means looping back to the beginning of the program, taking along the value of the wild-card variable as the new value of the parameter slot. As the parameter can contain only one value, the previous value is swept aside.

Now consider SOLUTION-3. Under the loop model, the parameter slot is again first instantiated with JOHN. Then, at step 1 of the program MARY is generated by the wild-card pattern match, triggering recursion at step 1A. The result of this is that the value MARY is fed back to the beginning of the program. Now the value JOHN is swept aside. When the program next generates TIM and the recursive process begins again, MARY gets swept aside. Then, when JOAN is generated, TIM gets swept aside. At this point, the end of the KISSES chain has been reached, and step 1B contains the instruction to CONTINUE to step 2. At this point the triple JOAN HAS FLU would be added to the data base.

4.1 The Evidence For the Copies Model

Only three out of thirty novices chose both SOLUTION-2 and SOLUTION-3 as successful programs, indicating that just 10% of the subjects had the copies model of recursion. Unfortunately, even this assumption may not be soundly based. The reasons for selecting SOLUTION-2 and SOLUTION-3 by these three subjects were the following:

S23 (commenting on SOLUTION-2): Yes, this programme will solve the problem, but will try to INFECT all but JOAN twice, so step 2 is unnecessary. (And commenting on SOLUTION-3): Yes, this is the correct solution for this problem but could be achieved more easily by just using "NOTE /X/ HAS FLU" because the "KISSES" CHECK is not vital to the change, e.g. "JOAN HAS FLU" but does not KISS anyone. It's a "Heads you win, tails I lose" flu situation!

Whatever S23 might mean by his comments on SOLUTION-2, we are not convinced he understands the program at all. Step 2 is, of course, necessary as it carries the recursion. An explanation for this subject's misconception that all nodes would be side-effected twice by the operation of SOLUTION-2, and that the KISSES CHECK in SOLUTION-3 is unnecessary would be purely speculative and therefore no explanation will be attempted.

Here are S24's comments on both SOLUTION-2 and SOLUTION-3:

S24 Solution 2 and 3 look okay but I don't know if just typing in causes SOLO to change the data base or whether the operator has to put in the new data – after which SOLO will INFECT new nodes who are kissed? P.S. Well, I was told that 2 & 3 were okay! Before that I was wondering how JOAN got infected, but looking carefully I see TIM KISSES JOAN. As my favourite sport is jumping (to conclusions) I'm not very good at AI.

This subject's response should fail to convince anybody that he has any understanding of the behaviour of either program. The last subject in this group, S29, made these comments:

S29 (SOLUTION-2): Yes. Infects first argument, finds link, infects second argument, and follows chain of infection.
(SOLUTIOn-3): Yes. Infects first argument and follows link as above. Only difference is order of carrying out instructions. (And, incidentally, of infectings.)

Only this subject, of the three in this group, has a convincing story to tell, convincing especially in his determination of the order of the side-effects that occur as a result of running the program.

4.2 The Evidence For the Loop Model

Most of the subjects chose Solution-2 as the only program that behaved as required, which we considered to be only weak evidence that the loop model had been acquired. Unfortunately, most of the comments made by these subjects were less informative than necessary to work out their model in detail. Only a few subjects made comments longer than a couple of sentences, and only one of these made specific reference to looping as a mechanism of recursion (this alone does not mean that the subject had the looping model, of course), e.g. "This does solve the problem. When asked to infect John it adds the relation 'has flu' to John, checks who he kisses, loops back to infect that person, noting first that the person has flu and looking for any person that this new person kisses. It continues to loop the routine until all the nodes that attach the kisses relation have been infected. This will change the data base in figure one to that in figure two."

4.3 The Strong Evidence For the Loop Model

Of the sixteen subjects who selected Solution-2, four rejected Solution-3 on the grounds that only JOAN would get flu. Since it has been argued that this is the strong evidence for possession of the loop model, the figures indicate that just 13% of all subjects had this model of recursion. Here are some of the comments of those who thought only JOAN would be infected by the operation of Solution-3:

S7 Won't work because of sequence – SOLO is short-sighted – follows one line at a time. Infect John and Step 1A proceeds to Check Mary for "kisses", finds it, Checks Tim, then Joan. Only then, when Joan Kisses question mark is not present will step 1B activate Step 2 and give 'flu to Joan, then stop. John, Mary and Tim remain 'flu-less.

S13 This does not solve the problem. The program will loop its way through the data base in a similar fashion to solution two but will only Note that Joan has flu.

S14 The procedure will search through the data base repeatedly checking who /X/ kisses? However, the procedure will not use the data base to note who has flu when kissed by /X/ because of the position in the procedure of NOTE /X/ has flu. Only the last value of /X/ will be infected.

In summary, the copies model is not a viable candidate for what our students have learned about recursion. Only three out of thirty subjects showed evidence for the copies model, and two thirds of this evidence did not stand up to scrutiny. On the other hand, only four subjects appear to have acquired a loop model, on the evidence of the strong indicants of this model. Thus, what subjects know about recursion can be accounted in terms of either the copies or the loop model in only five out of thirty cases.

4.4 "Null", "Odd", and "Syntactic" Models of Recursion

A possibility not yet considered is that novices (or some of them) have no model of recursion, or a model different from those considered thus far. Some of the subjects clearly do not understand recursion at all. The evidence for this will be discussed in section 4.5 on the null model. Some of the protocol evidence suggests that a few subjects have slightly idiosyncratic copies or loop models, and this will be discussed in the section on odd models. Another possibility, for which there are fragments of evidence in the protocols, is that there is a sort of "magic" model of recursion – that a program having a particular structure simply is a recursive program and it performs a sequence of operations, although the actual behaviour of the process is a complete mystery. This model will be discussed in the section on the syntactic or magic model of recursion.

4.5 The Null Model

Some students said that none of the test programs would work. Typical comments made by these students were:

S16 Won't work. This is because as a definition of the procedure "infect", it can hardly use that very procedure as part of the initial definition. This would probably be refused by the computer.
S11 No. The procedure is cyclic (i.e. it uses itself) and hence illegal.

One of the subjects rejected SOLUTION-2 on the grounds:

Will not work. Fans out from /X/ i.e. iteration.

The same subject selected SOLUTION-3 on the grounds:

Will work. Goes in depth through the kissing, i.e. recursion.

The subject is correct in the latter statement but not correct in the former. A possible explanation for these comments is that the subject understood the behaviour of neither program, and perhaps thought he was being tested on his ability to discriminate recursive and iterative processes and just made a guess.

4.6 The Odd Model

Some protocol comments (and the protocol statements of subject S5 in the programming task described above) suggest that many novices acquire odd notions about recursion. The comments suggest that some novices have models of the behaviour of the programs given in the questionnaire, but because they have idiosyncratic ideas about some features of the programs they do not correctly predict the behaviour of the programs.

It sounds as though he has the copies model when talking about SOLUTION-3:
S27 Yes. Programme will go through Infection process till last person kissing anybody has been found – then will note all four as having flu.

But, when discussing SOLUTION-2, S27 has this to say:

> No. The programme would add 2 persons who had flu to the data base, but EXIT prevents further infection occurring.

An unimpeachable interpretation of S27's model of recursion is not possible, but this last comment provides us with a clue. S27 apparently believes that step 2A of SOLUTION-2:

> If Present: INFECT *; EXIT

is read by SOLO as:

> "INFECTS *" and then EXIT immediately.

That is, the stopping rule for the recursion is not the absence of a pattern in the data base but the flow of control statement EXIT. The subject's model of the behaviour of SOLUTION-2 is something like:

> INFECT JOHN
> INFECT MARY and EXIT

If so, his model of the behaviour of SOLUTION-3 would be:

> INFECT JOHN
> INFECT MARY and CONTINUE (the INFECT process)
> INFECT TIM and CONTINUE
> INFECT JOAN

Other subjects also seem to have S27's problem about the stopping rule. Here are a couple of their comments:

S1 (commenting on SOLUTION-2): It's not this solution, because it would only infect one person, then EXIT).

S25 (commenting on SOLUTION-2): Solution 2 will not do the job either. Althugh /X/ has flu, the EXIT in 1A and 1B stops the infection process.

In all these cases, the notion acquired is that the flow of control statement, rather than properties of the data base, acts as the stopping rule for recursion.

4.7 The Syntactic or Magic Model

The evidence to be considered next suggests that there is a syntactic or magic model of recursion based on memorizing the structure of the "Infect" program presented in the SOLO primer (and also used as SOLUTION-2 in the Questionnaire). Any program having the same structure as the Infect program would be recognized as a recursive procedure. It is a magic model in that, although the student may know what the procedure does, they have no idea how it achieves its effects.

The memorized framework for recursive procedures would look something like that in Fig. 7.6. The single quotation marks indicate the variable features, such as PROCEDURE-NAME, which the novice would have to fill in from elements of different problems.

```
'PROCEDURE-NAME' /X/
1 NOTE /X/ '<relation1> <node>'
2 CHECK /X/ '<relation2>' ?
        2A If Present: 'PROCEDURE-NAME' * ; EXIT
        2B If Absent: EXIT
DONE
```

FIG. 7.6. The memorised framework for the syntactic model.

Hints that some students base their judgements about the behaviour of programs on the syntactic structure of programs come from comments such as the following:

S12 (commenting on SOLUTION-3): The procedure will search through the data base repeatedly checking who /X/ kisses. However, the procedure will not use the data base to note who has flu when kissed by /X/ because of the position of NOTE /X/ has flu.

S14 (commenting on SOLUTION-3): Won't work. When at 2, /X/ has flu, it is after the event at 1, therefore cannot affect it.

S17 (commenting on SOLUTION-3): This will not give correct printout because the triple /X/ has flu needs to be before the Check procedure.

These students appear to be sensitive to the position of program segments, and if they have no model of the actual behaviour of recursion, such indicants may be vitally important in their judgements about programs.

5. CONCLUSION

As our programming problems use real-world examples rather than abstract programming tasks, the subjects' knowledge of programming interacts with their real-world knowledge during the reading, coding, and debugging processes. We have indicated the way (often imperfect) knowledge of programming concepts pervades problem solving even in its earliest stages.

Our subjects develop schemas for recursion which are variously adequate for solving the problems we devise. This adequacy ranges from that of subject S5 (who cannot solve any of the recursion problems we have devised) to that of subject S8 (who can solve many, but not all, of our recursion problems). When a problem maps onto an adequate set of schemas in a novice's store of knowledge, the novice can tackle the tasks of problem understanding, method finding, coding, and informal verification in a productive and efficient manner. When a problem is mapped to an inadequate set of schemas, the problem statement is often poorly understood, as much from world knowledge as from the basic elements of the implementation language.

A range of abilities is demonstrated in the program identification results. Novices can be distributed into different classes according to the internal structure of the individual concepts they have acquired. The data show that at least some novices – probably a quarter – can, after a fairly brief training period in SOLO programming, identify and mentally simulate the behaviour of recursive procedures or program segments. That is, they have mental models of the way recursion behaves. The notion that concretization of abstract concepts is an essential component of successful problem solving is suggested by the experimental results of Mayer (1981), who was able to show that less able novice BASIC programmers performed better on a variety of tasks if they were given a concrete system model before they began to learn about the system. Able novices, in Mayer's study, did not improve their performance as a result of being given such a model, they presumably had their own means of devising such models.

These results indicate that different knowledge bases need to be plugged in to an adequate model of novice programming behaviour. The average novice with a copies model of recursion and a novice with a null or magic model is not the novice with a loop model. On a given task some performances will be severely memory data-limited (Bobrow & Norman, 1975), such as those by novices with null, syntactic or other models of recursion. Students who are able to develop a loop model of recursion will be able to design procedures in terms of the model and understand unfamiliar programs by mentally simulating their behaviour in terms of the model. More importantly, possession of a model provides a person with a basis for correcting misunderstandings when confronted with a counterexample.

REFERENCES

Bobrow, D. G. & Norman, D. A. (1975). Some principles of memory schemata. In D. G. Bobrow & A. M. Collins (Eds), *Representation and understanding: Studies in cognitive science*. New York: Academic Press.

Brooks, R. (1977). Towards a theory of the cognitive processes in computer programming. *International Journal of Man-Machine Studies*, *9*, 737–742.

Eisenstadt, M. (1978). Artificial intelligence project, Units 3/4 of *Cognitive psychology: A third level course*. Milton Keynes: Open University Press.

Eisentstadt, M., Laubsch, J., & Kahney, H. (1981). Creating pleasant programming environments for cognitive science students. *Proceedings of the Third Annual Cognitive Science Society Conference*, Berkeley, California.

Goldstein, I. P. (1975). Summary of MYCROFT: A system for understanding simple picture programs. *Artificial Intelligence*, *6*, 249–288.

Hayes, J. R. & Simon, H. A. (1974). Understanding written problem instructions. In L. W. Gregg (Ed.), *Knowledge and cognition*, Hillsdale, N.J.: Lawrence Erlbaum Associates Inc.

Kahney, H. (1982). *An in-depth study of the cognitive behaviour of novice programmers*. Technical Report No. 5, Human Cognition Research Group, The Open University, Milton Keynes, England.

Keane, M., Kahney, H., & Brayshaw, M. (1989). Simulating analogical mapping difficulties in recursion problems. In A. Cohn (Ed.), *Proceedings of Annual Conference of the Society for the Study of Artificial Intelligence and Simulation of Behaviour*. London: Pitman.

Laubsch, J. & Eisenstadt, M. (1981). Domain specific debugging aids for novice programmers. *Proceedings of the Seventh International Joint Conference on Artificial Intelligence, (IJCAI-81)*. Vancouver, B.C., Canada.

Mayer, R. E. (1981). The psychology of how novices learn computer programming. *Computing Surveys*, *13*, 121–141.

Sussman, G. J. (1975). *A computer model of skill acquisition*. New York: American Elsevier.

Waters, R. C. (1979). A method for analyzing loop programs. *IEEE Transactions on Software Engineering*, *SE-5:3*, 237–247.

8 Naive Iteration: An Account of the Conceptualizations Underlying Buggy Looping Programs

Marc Eisenstadt
Human Cognition Research Laboratory, The Open University, Milton Keynes, England

Joost Breuker
Department of Social Science Informatics, The University of Amsterdam, Amsterdam, The Netherlands

OVERVIEW

Empirical studies of programmers' use of looping constructs indicate that novices have difficulty mapping their own particular view of repetitive sequences onto the constructs of typical modern programming languages (e.g. Pascal). Our goal is to try to explain where such a view comes from in the first place, and exactly how a mapping onto programming language constructs might take place. We describe a framework, 'Naive Iteration", which accounts for the conceptualizations underlying the construction of buggy looping programs. The framework embodies notions of control and data abstraction which we claim are self-evident to non-programmers. The framework is implemented in the form of a production rule-model. To test aspects of the framework, we develop a novel paradigm for investigating the algorithmic strategies used by programmers and non-programmers. The paradigm, based on observations of subjects performing iterative tasks, supports the existence of control and data abstractions which account on the one hand for the simplicity of performing everyday iterative tasks, and on the other hand for the difficulty of performing isomorphic tasks under the constraints imposed by working with a computer.

1. INTRODUCTION

Should iterative programs be hard to write? The data of Soloway, Bonar, and Ehrlich (1983) indicate that only 39% of their Pascal students could solve an elementary iterative programming problem after a full term of study. Their detailed analysis suggests that the source of difficulty is the mismatch between the way certain flow of control constructs work and the way novices think they ought to work. Consider the Pascal program in Fig. 8.1, which repeatedly reads in numbers, stopping when the number 99999 is encountered, and finally prints out the average of the numbers.

In this Pascal cliché, there is an initial read (line 7), after which the processing (lines 10 and 11) is one step out of synch with the further reading (line 12). That is, the X on line 11 refers to the *ith* item, whereas the X on line 12 refers to the $(i + 1)$th item. Soloway et al. present evidence that novice programmers prefer to use a strategy which preserves the natural sequence of reading the *ith* item, then processing the *ith* item within the same cycle of the loop (abbreviated "read/process"), in contrast to the out-of-synch process-then-read strategy (abbreviated "process/read") required by the Pascal WHILE loop shown in Fig. 8.1. But where does such a preference come from? Is a read/process strategy really the most natural way of performing the task?

An inspection of the data of Soloway et al. reveals that although the 38 subjects they analysed did indeed prefer read/process to process/read, a further 77 subjects, who exhibited various miscellaneous strategies, were

```
1    PROGRAM average;
2    VAR sum,count,x: integer;
3      average          : real;
4    BEGIN
5      sum:=0;
6      count:=0;
7      read(x);
8        WHILE x<>99999 do
9        BEGIN
10           count := count + 1;
11           sum := sum + x;
12           read(x);
13       END;
14     average := sum/count;
15     write(average);
16   END.
```

FIG. 8.1. Pascal program to compute average. Note that line 14 should actually test that count > 0 in order to avoid a run-time error! (Adapted from Soloway et al. 1983).

discarded from the comparison. The discarded subjects are potentially of great interest, because any systematic alternative strategy employed by those subjects could well emerge as the clear majority choice. Our aim is to find out what those novices really had in mind, i.e. to find what it is that people know about looping and flow of control that makes them think a programming construct ought to work in some particular way in the first place.

Our guiding principle is a firm belief that novice programmers construct a mental model of the programming task at hand, putting themselves in the computer's shoes and mapping their own experiences onto the artificially constrained world of the computer in such a way as to generate a plausible solution. In the case of iterative programs, these experiences stem from the repeated application of actions encountered in a non-computing context, such as dealing cards, keeping track of the number of points earned in a card game, or even more mundane iterative actions such as climbing up a staircase. This view is consonant with that of Soloway et al., but we take a more extreme view: we believe that the novice programmer projects his or her everyday experiences onto the programming task to such an extent that in many cases the programming problem is not perceived as a problem at all.

"To find the average of all the numbers which are read in up to some point," the insightful novice might say, "you simply read in the numbers up to the crucial point and then compute their average." Such a description is precisely the kind of non-algorithmic, non-plan-like description which had to be scored as miscellaneous in the analysis of Soloway et al. and indeed we have observed such descriptions in our own pilot studies. The current folk-wisdom argues that such naive re-statements of the problem reflect a lack of rigorous thinking on the part of the subject, and moreover that a course in programming will help to inculate such rigour. In contrast to this, we contend that such problem re-statements reflect not only a good understanding of the problem, but also an ability on the part of novice programmers to apply powerful (and rigorous) functional operations to the elements of the problem in order to derive a solution. In the following sections we outline what these powerful operations are, and then describe a computer implementation and empirical investigation of our theory.

In order to study these issues we asked subjects to perform several iterative tasks in a real-life context: finding the average value of a pile of bank cheques. We collected detailed behavioural protocols of subjects performing the task, then constructed a simulation model of their behaviour by decomposing the knowledge required to perform the task into several discrete components: knowledge of how to generate sequences of items, knowledge of how to select items which meet a certain criterion, knowledge of how to find the sum of a set of numbers, and knowledge about how to tally the number of items in a set. We examine the difference between naive and experienced programmers on this task, to see how distinct components of knowledge are composed together.

In order to study how everyday knowledge of iteration maps onto code-writing behaviour, we asked the same subjects to perform iterative tasks in a computer-like context: finding the average value of a pile of bank cheques with the constraint that only one card may be processed at a time, after which it must be thrown away. The purpose of this constraint is to approximate the constraints about which programmers have to reason when considering how their programs will perform related programming tasks. Our analysis of subjects' performance on this task allows us in turn to account in a principled way for the errors people make when writing iterative programs.

2. THE EXPERIMENT

2.1 Subjects

Sixteen University of Amsterdam undergraduate and graduate psychology students with less than 20 hours of programming experience and ten University of Amsterdam graduate students and staff members with more than 600 hours of programming experience were selected to take part in the experiment. Programming expertise was determined without consulting the subjects, and was confirmed by the subjects following the experiment, so that knowledge of programming was not considered by the subjects to be a factor.

2.2 Method

The experimental task consisted of computing the mean of a set of numbers printed on index cards with the help of a calculator. Before this task, subjects were given three warm-up problems involving the use of a simple four-function calculator (CASIO M-1) to compute means.

They were then asked to solve four averaging problems which involved either "behaving naturally" (mapping Real World Actions onto the Real World) or "behaving naturally in computerland" (mapping Real World Actions onto a Virtual Machine). The Real World Actions involved selecting, tallying, and totalling numbers printed on index cards. The Real World scenario involved a pile of cards meant to represent bank cheques, while the Virtual Machine scenario required that these same cards be processed strictly sequentially, with each card lost forever once it had been processed.

The problems involved either simple generation of a sequence of cards (e.g. all cards with the year 1981), or a combination of generation and filtering according to some criterion (e.g. all 1981 cards with the name Jan Hoekman). The instruction sequence was counterbalanced for order effects, so that half the subjects received each of the following sequences:

Sequence 1	*Sequence 2*
Generate/Real World	Generate/Virtual Machine
Generate/Virtual Machine	Generate/Real World
Generate+Filter/Real World	Generate+Filter/Virtual Machine
Generate+Filter/Virtual Machine	Generate+Filter/Real World

The actual instructions presented to subjects are shown below, assuming the order outlined in sequence 2:

The index cards on this table are meant to represent a pile of "bank cheques". Each cheque shows the Payee, Date, and Amount. The cheques cover the period 1/1/79–31/12/82, and are arranged in strict chronological order (that is, the dates follow in sequence).
Here, with the example of the *Generate/Virtual Problem*, they were asked:

How much was the average ("mean") cheque in 1979?

Rules:

---

1. You may look at only one cheque at a time. Put each one into the "discard box" as you finish it. (Once cheques are put into the "discard box" they may not be retrieved.)

---

2. You may use the pen, paper, and calculator to write down and/or calculate anything you wish along the way.

---

3. Remember: only cheques from 1979 are relevant.

Subjects were asked to read the instructions aloud, and proceed when ready. They were encouraged (but not required) to think out loud into a tape recorder microphone while working on the problem. Their sequence of steps was monitored in real-time using a coding algorithm described in the next section.
After solving problem Generate/Virtual, subjects were shown the next

problem, in this case the *Generate/Real Problem*, which referred to the remaining cards on the pile:

How much was the average ("mean") cheque in 1980?

Rules:

---

1. This time, you may pick up and handle the pile of cheques completely freely.

---

2. As before, you may use the pen, paper, and calculator to write down and/or calculate anything you wish along the way.

---

3. Remember: only cheques from 1980 are relevant.

Problem Generate/Real proceeded in the same way as problem Generate/Virtual. Then the next problem followed, the *Generate+Filter/Virtual*:

How much was the average ("mean") cheque payed to Jan Hoekmann in 1981?

The rules for problem Generate+Filter/Virtual were analogous to those for problem Generate/Virtual, with the appropriate reminder (rule 3) that only 1981 cheques were relevant. The final problem, the *Generate+Filter/Real* looked like this:

How much was the average ("mean") cheque payed to Jan Janssen in 1982?

The rules for problem Generate+Filter/Real were analogous to those for problem Generate/Real. A summary of the problems is presented in Table 8.1.

In case of a false start (e.g. when the subject realized that they had forgotten to tally the number of cards) the pile of cards was re-initialized by the experimenter and the subject started the task again.

TABLE 8.1
Problem Summary

	Year Only	*Year + Name*
ONE AT A TIME	Generate/Virtual	Generate+Filter/Virtual
FREE HANDLING	Generate/Real	Generate+Filter/Real

2.3 Coding Algorithm

The subject's behaviour was coded in real-time by one of the experimenters who sat across the table from the subject, and ticked off arcs in a transition network diagram according to the subject's actions. These diagrams represented all possible sequences of behaviour in this task. The transition network included arcs for errors and false starts, so that anomalies could be coded as well.

As this study does not aim to construct a keystroke-level model of the subjects behaviour (cf. Card, Moran, & Newell, 1983), we perform a coarser analysis than the network coding would allow for, by grouping together sequences of arcs into one of the four categories shown in Table 8.2.

TABLE 8.2
The Coding System for Responses in the Study

Symbol	*Category*	*Meaning*
. . .	Generate	Generate a sequence of cards.
V	Filter	Filter out cards which do not have the appropriate payee name.
#	Tally	Tally, i.e. count the number of cards. (The original coding distinguished between 'tally-in-thehead' and 'tally-on-paper'.)
+	Sum	Enter amount in calculator and add up.

We use square brackets to indicate one looping sentence, so that [. . . # +] means that for each card generated, the tally is incremented by one and the amount is added to the running total.

In contrast, the behaviour denoted by [. . .] [#] [+] means that first the entire sequence of cards is generated up to a new year, the number of cards is successively tallied, and the amounts on the cards are summed by going over the generated set of cards again. We omit the actual calculation of the mean (SUM/TALLY), as this invariably occurred as a last step and is of no interest for this study.

2.4 Results

Table 8.3 shows the raw data obtained from our coding. The "/" symbol means that the subject had a false start (i.e. forgot to keep a running total), and started again. Redundant passes are not counted so that the coding [. . .] [#] [+] [#], which means that the subject cautiously tallied the cards

TABLE 8.3
Codified Subjects Responses in the Study

S	*Generate Virtual*	*Generate Real*	*Generate+Filter Virtual*	*Generate+Filter Real*
NAIVE				
1	[..+#]	[..][#][+]	[..V+#]	[..][V][#][+]
2	[..+#]	[..][+][#]	[..V+]/[..V+#]	[..V][+][#]
3	[..+#]/[..][+][#]	[..][+][#]	[..V][+][#]	[..V][+][#]
4	[..#+]	[..][+][#]	[..V+]/[..V+#]	[..][V][+][#]
5	[..+#]	[..][#][+]	[..V+#]	[..][V][#][+]
6	[..+#]	[..][+][#]	[..V+#]	[..V][#][+]
7	[..+#]	[..][+][#]	[..V+#]	[..][V][#][+]
8	[..+#]	[..][+][#]	[..V+#]	[..V+][#]
9	[..+#]	[..][#][+]	[..V#+]	[..V][#][+]
10	[..#+]	[..][+][#]	[..V#+]	[..][V#][+]
11	[..+#]	[..][+][#]	[..V+#]	[..V][+][#]
12	[..+#]/[..][+][#]	[..][+][#]	[..V][+][#]	[..][V][#][+]
13	[..+]/[..+#]	[..][#][+]	[..V#+]	[..V][+][#]
14	[..+#]	[..][#][+]	[..V+#]	[..V+]/[..V+][+][#]
15	[..][+][#]	[..+][#]	[..V][+][#]	[..V][+][#]
16	[..#+]	[..][#][+]	[..V#+]	[..V+#]
EXPERIENCED				
17	[..+#]	[..+#]	[..V+#]	[..V+#]
18	[..+#]	[..#][+]	[..V+#]	[..V][#][+]
19	[..+#]	[..#][+]	[..V#+]	[..V#][+]
20	[..+#]	[..+][#]	[..V+#]	[..V][+][#]
21	[..+#]	[..+][#]	[..V+#]	[..V][#][+]
22	[..+]/[..+#]	[..][+][#]	[..V+#]	[..V][+][#]
23	[..+#]	[..][+][#]	[..V+#]	[..][V][#][+]
24	[..#+]	[..#][+]	[..V#+]	[..V+][#]
25	[..+#]	[..#][+]	[..V+#]	[..V#][+]
26	[..#+]	[..][#][+]	[..V+#]	[..V+][#]

twice, is considered to indicate 3 passes rather than 4. As our analysis revealed no effect of presentation order of the tasks this factor has been collapsed for expository purposes.

The number of passes made is the dependent variable in this study and is indicated by the number of pairs of brackets in Table 8.3. In case writing occurred on a pass of its own (i.e. first the pile of relevant cards was generated, and then the values were written down), this was also considered to be a redundant pass. By eliminating passes, we ensure that each of the categories 1, 2, 3, or 4 passes really has a unique meaning, and thus provides a nominal scale. The category "4 passes" invariably means generation followed by filtering, followed by either tally-then-sum or sum-then-tally. Three passes means generation, tallying, and summing in separate passes (summing may precede tallying).

Two passes means that as each card is generated, it is also tallied or summed at the same time, and the left over operation (tallying or summing) is saved for a final independent pass. One pass means a single (Pascal-like) loop, involving generation of the next card, filtering (if appropriate), increasing the tally, and increasing the sum (or possibly sum-then-tally), before going on to the following card.

Table 8.4 shows the frequency of occurrences of these four categories on each of the four tasks for experienced programmers and naive programmers. In this table, the last trials are taken into account; it shows, not surprisingly, that every subject can correctly perform the task, albeit sometimes after an incorrect start.

Most obvious is the expected overall difference in number of passes between the Virtual and Real Conditions ($\chi^2 = 110.24$, df = 3, $p < 0.001$). In general, in the Virtual Condition only one pass is taken; in the Real Condition the modal category is 3 passes. There is a clear difference between experienced and naive subjects, both overall ($\chi^2 = 18.72$, df = 3, $p < 0.01$) and, particularly, in the Real Condition ($\chi^2 = 5.72$, df = 1, $p < 0.05$), (because some cell frequencies are very small here, the 2×4 matrix is collapsed into a 2×2 matrix). In this condition, experienced programmers tend to take fewer passes than naive programmers.

Three of the 16 naive subjects preferred to perform the Virtual problems in multiple passes, writing down the numbers on the first pass so that later passes could be performed. For two of these subjects this was the consequence of a false start in which they realized half-way that they had forgotten to tally; a clear indication of a buggy model of the Virtual version of the task. Three other naive subjects, who chose not to write down the numbers had similar false starts, which means that in total 5 out of 16 naive subjects started with an inappropriate mental model of one or other of the Virtual

TABLE 8.4
Frequency of Occurrence of the Possible Strategies: 1, 2, 3, or 4 Passes

	NAIVE				*EXPERIENCED*			
Number of passes	1	2	3	4	1	2	3	4
Generate Virtual	13	—	3	—	10	—	—	—
Generate+Filter Virtual	13	—	3	—	10	—	—	—
Generate Real	—	1	15	—	1	6	3	—
Generate+Filter Real	1	1	9	5	1	4	4	1

problems. For the experienced subjects this ratio is 1 out of 10. In total, there are 6 of the 36 subjects (5 naive, 1 experienced) who did not start out with a correct one-loop plan on the Virtual problems.

3. DISCUSSION

We initiated this study with the belief that many, but not all, problems that novices have in writing simple computer programs are due to the fact that there is a discrepancy between their real world models of the task and constraints imposed by the virtual model of the computer, or the computer language. There is little doubt, and our experiment confirms this, that many typical novice programming tasks pose no problems at all in terms of real world actions, but such solutions are not acceptable in computer terms. It should be noted that these constraints are not so much imposed by the inner workings of the mechanism itself, the Turing machine, but by the design and intentions behind a particular programming language. In this study we compared solving extremely simple iteration problems in a real world environment, with solving the same problems in an environment that mimics the philosophy of iteration in typical block structured languages like Pascal. In this philosophy, there is a clear preference to subsume many actions under one looping control structure and to avoid — redundant storage. This philosophy is not only motivated by considerations of efficiency in processing and storage, but also by beliefs on clear, structured thinking.

This philosophy, or intended virtual machine, is clearly not in accordance with the results obtained in the Real World iteration task. Both naive and experienced programmers prefer a multiple loop solution. Also, in the task that should mimic the block-structured-language virtual machine, some 3 of the 16 naive subjects prefer to circumvent the "read and process-one-at-a-time constraint" by laboriously writing down a list of data. Creating an external memory by writing down the data is computationally equivalent to the use of arrays for intermediary data storage. Actually, we expected this percentage to be higher on the basis of some informal try-outs, in which subjects invariably wrote down the data. We believe that this percentage may increase when the number of actions that have to be combined gets larger.

On the other hand, our results also clearly indicate that subjects can solve the Virtual Problems. They (particularly the naive programmers) may have some false starts, but all subjects were able to perform this task. This means that our Virtual problems only partly represent the problems that a novice programmer may face when trying to write simple looping constructs. For example, a well-known bug in such programs is forgetting to initialize the running total and tally variables (Soloway et al. 1983). This does not occur in our experiments, because subjects may interrupt their activity at the moment they discover that they have not cleared the entry of the pocket calculator. Programming does not allow for such unplanned events. (From our observations we cannot deduce how often the initialization was not part of the plan, but we have a strong impression that subjects only cleared the calculator at the moment they wanted to enter the first amount).

Naive programmers more often have problems coping with the virtual tasks. There is strong evidence suggesting that experienced programmers may have acquired a view of iteration which has influenced their real-world thinking about it. This may be taken as support for the notion that programming may provide powerful ideas that are transferred to real-world thinking (cf. Papert, 1980), although the actual power of this construct is of dubious merit. Nonetheless, this is a clear empirical demonstration of the transfer of programming concepts to real-world problem solving.

Although all subjects succeeded in solving the Virtual problems, this does not mean that these solutions were arrived at easily. There is the paradoxical phenomenon that the solution for the highly constrained, obviously sequential iterative task involves the activation of highly parallel sub-tasks. In order properly to understand the potential interaction among the conflicting sub-tasks required to solve our experimental problems (and by extension the analogous programming problems), we have constructed a production rule simulation, to which we now turn.

4. SIMULATION MODEL

We postulate that the four processing operations described above (generate, filter, sum, tally) can be modelled as autonomous bundles of expertise, and combined in principled ways to account for all the observed behaviour. To do this, we model each of the operations as a self-contained *packet* of production rules (Newell & Simon, 1972). Packets are either active in which case they occupy processing resources, or inactive in which case they simply reside in long-term memory. In the sense that packets restrict the currently active productions, enabling the use of a hierarchical control structure, our interpreter is akin to goal-oriented production system interpreters such as GRAPES (Sauers & Farrell, 1983); however, we do not refer to packets as goals because, in our system, there is no notion of the success or failure of an invoked packet. For expository purposes, we present a simplified English-like version of the rules. Note that if a rule has several actions on the right hand side (separated by semi-colons), the actions are applied sequentially in the order shown.

Here are the four packets needed to model performance in our task domain:

PACKET G: "GENERATE"

G1:	terminating symbol visible	=>	pop
G2:	cards remaining & terminating symbol not visible	=>	remove top card
NC:	no cards remaining	=>	pop

PACKET F: "FILTER"

F1:	criterion met	=>	remove top card
F2:	criterion not met	=>	discard top card
NC:	no cards remaining	=>	pop

PACKET S: "SUM"

S1:	just begun	=>	press "all clear"
S2:	(amount is A)	=>	enter A; press "+"; remove top card
NC:	no cards remaining	=>	pop

PACKET T: "TALLY"

T1:	just begun	=>	(counter is 0)
T2:	cards remaining & (counter is C)	=>	(counter is (C + 1)); remove top card
NC:	no cards remaining	=>	pop

In addition, we assume that subjects' understanding of the problem statement causes him to formulate a simple plan specifying the sequence of packet execution. This sequence is stored in working memory as an ordered list, e.g. (G F S T).

This representation places a very minimal load on working memory: only the symbols denoting the packet sequence and the current packet need to be active at any one time. When a given packet is finished, the packet sequence order stored in working memory is sufficient to ensure that the next packet gets instantiated appropriately to carry out the next phase of the plan.

A three-pass strategy on the Generate/Real problem and a four-pass strategy on the Generate+Filter/Real problem can be modelled simply by invoking each of the relevant packets in the appropriate sequence. In fact, these rules are sufficient to account for the card-moving actions and calculator keystrokes of all subjects on the Real tasks who used the three- or four-pass pass strategies.

How, then do we account for the performance of experts on the Real problems, for which they required fewer passes? We hypothesize that the programming expert can merge together several packets by application of the following rule: If packets X's output is packet Y's input, then instead of first applying X to all of X's input then Y to all of Y's input (two passes) we can apply the sequence (X Y) to the same input (one pass). In other words, if you can do on one pass what you've been doing on two, then do so. Experienced programmers will have seen multi-statement blocks of code with iterative loops many times in their careers, and this can be regarded as a well-known schema or single "compiled away" chunk of expertise. Our model predicts that this expertise will therefore influence their performance on a real-world (non-programming) task. The experiment supports the prediction: experts perform the Real task in fewer passes than naives ($\chi^2 = 5.72$, df $= 1$, $p < 0.05$).

We now need to model the one pass performance of our naive subjects on the Virtual task. Once again, we assume that during the interval between reading and performing the task, a subject decides that knowledge of GENERATE, FILTER, SUM and TALLY are relevant. This time, however, the rules of the Virtual task specify that once processed a card must be thrown away forever. In our model, we represent this constraint as a requirement that rules which pertain to dealing with the contents of a given index card must all be active at once. In other words, formulating a plan is no longer a matter of straightforward sequencing of relatively simple packets: rather it is now a question of imposing some order on the firing sequence of production rules. The end result of this planning is a single active packet with the following rules (notice especially the symbols in quotes which are arbitrary sequencing symbols which get added into working memory):

G1:	terminating symbol visible	=>	pop
NC:	no cards remaining	=>	pop
F1:	new card visible & criterion met	=>	"good"
F2:	new card visible and criterion not met	=>	discard top card
S2:	"good" & (amount is A)	=>	enter A; press "+"; "just did sum"
T2:	"just did sum" & (counter is C)	=>	(counter is (C + 1))

The need to keep this entire packet active throughout the performance of the experimental task is precisely the extra processing burden which brings about false starts by our naive subjects (e.g. forgetting rule T2, which performs the tally). We believe that it also accounts for much of the difficulty non-programmers have in visualizing an iterative programming task with the precision required for error-free computer implementation. Experienced programmers, in contrast, can use their familiarity with iterative constructs, conditionals, and subroutines, to collapse together the cumbersome signalling sequence which is used to trigger the actions associated with rules F1, S2, and T2; these can all be composed to form a single rule, with a consequent reduction in processing load.

5. CONCLUSIONS

Of primary importance to us is an understanding of the nature of the strategies employed by our subjects, and the way in which these strategies might influence how the same subjects would write a *program* to perform a comparable task. We argue that a novice programmer faced with a coding task involving iteration first goes through a planning phase in which a mental model of the execution sequence must be constructed. This mental model will be guided by the novice programmer's everyday experiences with iterative tasks. In trying to force such experiences into the appropriate (constrained) framework of a programming language, the programmer will have to go through reasoning closely related to that involved in performing a real-world iterative task under restrictions such as those imposed by our Virtual experimental condition. This process is cumbersome and unnatural precisely because of the idiosyncracies of the virtual machine underlying iterative constructs in Pascal-like programming languages.

Soloway et al. (1983) have shown convincingly that there is an inherent mis-match between the way novice programmers think about repeating a "read-then process" sequence and how the typical Pascal WHILE loop imposes a "process-then-read" ordering. We take their argument one step further: rather than enhancing the WHILE construct to provide a better cognitive fit, we feel that the entire underlying virtual machine needs rethinking. Iterative loops in programming languages such as Pascal are traditionally thought of in terms of a sequence of steps, performed repeatedly over time. An alternative view, exemplified by the work of Wulf, London, and Shaw (1976), Waters (1979), and Rich (1981), is that the temporal sequence is really irrelevant to the essential meaning of most loops. This meaning is more properly characterized in terms of performing some operation on a set of objects, without regard to the (boring) detail of how that set is sequentially generated. The notion of operations applied to a set is referred to by Waters and Rich as "temporal abstraction", because it abstracts out the meaning, in declarative terms, without worrying about precise implementation details.

We contend that novices tend to think naturally in terms of temporal abstraction, and that the use of generators and aggregate data objects (without the terminology, of course) is far simpler for them than the confusing detail required by having to specify temporal sequence. This view enables us to pin-point an important source of confusion in students learning to write iterative Pascal programs: the natural sequence of function application to aggregate data objects is totally destroyed by iterative constructs – destroyed in a way which forces the novice to pull out orthogonal slices of each successive function to be applied.

Our experiments show that subjects overwhelmingly prefer to perform an iterative task in multiple passes over successively smaller sets of data. Each of the observed processing operations (GENERATE, FILTER SUM, and TALLY) can easily be mapped onto a function which can be applied to an appropriate aggregate data object. Consider the task of finding the mean of all 1981 cheques paid to Jones. A functional representation of the solution looks like this:

MEAN(CHOOSE("JONES",(READTILL("1982",CARDS))))
MEAN(X)=SUM(X)/TALLY(X)

The function CHOOSE(ITEM,SET) is a filter which extracts only those elements of SET containing ITEM. READTILL(ITEM,SET) is a generator function which returns a subset of SET (i.e. the first elements of SET up to, but not including, the one containing ITEM). Since function application proceeds from the inside out, this solution is isomorphic to the modal strategy used by our naive subjects on the Real problems.

Our point is that iterative operators such as WHILE and REPEAT force people to merge together isolated snippets of their mundane expertise in such a way that tasks for which algorithm-design ought to be easy suddenly become very hard. Planning and imagining the execution of a Pascal WHILE loop ought to involve most of the same processes we posited for performing mundane iterative tasks, and is therefore vulnerable to the same kinds of processing overload as our simulation model. Additional programming errors arise because of the inherent difficulty of mapping interrupt-driven termination, (e.g. our rule G1) onto WHILE loop termination, with the result that such loops often cycle once too often (cf. Sime, Green, & Guest, 1973). Our experiment suggests that the powerful abstractions being studied by Waters, Wulf et al. and others are the most natural way of expressing iteration. Our intuition is that such abstractions can be presented in a form which is palatable to novices, and we look forward to empirical studies which pursue this train of thought.

Much work still needs to be done on understanding the processes involved in code generation. We see the work of Brooks (1977) and

Anderson, Farrel, and Sauers (1984) as important steps in this direction. Kahney (Chapter 7, 1983; Kahney & Eisenstadt, 1982) has explored the way in which complicated world knowledge influences novices' understanding and solution of recursive programming problems. We see all this research leading ultimately to the point where we can state with confidence what people do when they plan, write, and debug programs. This in turn will help us to provide languages and environments which mesh appropriately with their users' preferred manner of thinking.

REFERENCES

Anderson, J. R., Farrell, R., & Sauers, R. (1984). Learning to plan Lisp. *Cognitive Science*, *8*, 87–129.

Brooks, R. (1977). Towards a theory of the cognitive processes in computer programming. *International Journal of Man-Machine Studies*, *9*, 737–742.

Card, S., Moran, T. P., & Newell, A. (1983). *The psychology of human-computer interaction*. Hillsdale, N.J.: Lawrence Erlbaum Associates Inc.

Kahney, J. H. (1983). Problem solving by novice programmers. In T. R. G. Green, S. J. Payne, & G. C. van der Veer (Eds), *The psychology of computer use*. London: Academic Press.

Kahney, J. H. & Eisenstadt, M. (1982). Programmers' mental models of their programming tasks: The interaction of real-world knowledge and programming knowledge. *Proceedings of the Fourth Annual Cognitive Science Society Conference*, Ann Arbor, Michigan, 143–145.

Newell, A. & Simon, H. A. (1972). *Human problem solving*. Englewood Cliffs, N.J.: Prentice-Hall.

Papert, S. (1980). *Mindstorms: Children, computers, and powerful ideas*. Brighton, England: Harvester Press.

Rich, C. (1981). Inspection methods in programming. *Technical Report AI-TR-604*. Cambridge, MA: MIT Artificial Intelligence Laboratory.

Sauers, R. & Farrell, R. (1983). *GRAPES reference manual*. Pittsburgh, PA: Department of Psychology, Carnegie-Mellon University.

Sime, M. E., Green, T. R. G., & Guest, D. J. (1973). Psychological evaluation of two conditional constructions in computer languages. *International Journal of Man-Machine Studies*, *5*, 123–143.

Soloway, E., Bonar, J., & Ehrlich, K. (1983). Cognitive strategies and looping constructs: An empirical study. *Communications of the ACM*, *26*, 853–860.

Waters, R. A. (1979). A method for analyzing loop programs. *IEEE Transactions on Software Engineering*, *SE-5 : 3*, 237–247.

Wulf, W. A., London, R. L., & Shaw, M. (1976). An introduction to the construction and verification of Alphard programs. *IEEE Transaction on Software Engineering*, *SE-2:4*.

III Artificial Intelligence User Aids

A great challenge which lay behind our work with novice programmers was the dream of building automatic debuggers. We believed that automatic program debuggers, aside from being exciting in their own right, could provide detailed and principled assistance for novice programmers. Moreover, this seemed especially pertinent in the context of the Open University courses, where students had reasonably good access to computers (domestic microcomputers and/or dial-up access to mainframe computers), but poor access to dedicated tutorial provision.

Our first foray into this area is described by Laubsch and Eisenstadt in Chapter 9. Their system (DAN: Debugging Assistant for Novices), like all the chapters in this section, builds upon the influential Programmer's Apprentice project of Rich and Waters at M.I.T. DAN uses "plan diagrams" to capture generalized programming clichés which serve as a common thread underneath a variety of SOLO programs. The plan diagrams are used to facilitate symbolic evaluation of a student's program, so that the net effect of the program can be computed, and compared against an idealised effect description. Of special interest here is DAN's ability to deal with recursive programs involving side-effects, which is typical of the class of programs developed by SOLO students.

Hasemer's AURAC system (Chapter 10) looks at an alternative use of programming clichés: namely, syntactic clichés which can be recognized automatically according to their surface form, and used collectively to characterize and diagnose a variety of student programs. AURAC, like DAN, works on SOLO programs, and demonstrates the power of a debugging system which does not *need to understand the programmer's intentions, but rather concentrates on what they ought to have done.*

In Chapter 11, Lutz describes a Pascal debugger based on the plan diagram formalism. The novelty of Lutz's approach is that he constructs a graphical (two-dimensional) chart parser which, instead of working on strings (like a linguistic chart parser), works directly on plan diagrams. This allows him to convert students' Pascal programs into plan diagram notation, and then parse that notation directly using a combination of top-down and bottom-up algorithms. The top-down algorithms allow Lutz to search for programming plans which ought to have occurred in the students' programs, while the bottom-up algorithms facilitate recognition of partial (potentially buggy) plans, from which near-misses can be detected.

Domingue's ITSY system (Chapter 12) adds yet another twist to plan diagram and cliché analysis: he introduces error clichés *which can be used to home in directly on a variety of common, student errors. The class of programs he is analysing come from the first 30 hours of Lisp tuition. An important difference between Domingue's ITSY and Anderson's influential "GREATERP" Lisp Tutor is that ITSY allows the students to engage in completely free-form interaction with the editor and Lisp interpreter, and only provides automatic debugging assistance upon request.*

9 The Automatic Debugging of Recursive Side-Effecting Programs*

Joachim Laubsch
Computer Systems Center, Hewlett-Packard Laboratories, Palo Alto, CA, USA

Marc Eisenstadt
Human Cognition Research Laboratory, The Open University, Milton Keynes, England.

OVERVIEW

This chapter describes DAN (Debugging Assistant for Novices), a suite of program analysis routines which can debug computer programs in the domain of labelled-directed-graph ("semantic network") manipulation. The analysis routines aim to account for the behaviour of both working and buggy programs written in a semantic-network variant of LOGO (Papert, 1980) called SOLO (see Chapter 1).

1. INTRODUCTION

Based in part on existing programmer's apprentice and debugging projects (especially Rich and Waters), our system, called DAN, makes several novel contributions: it is oriented towards a large audience (several hundred per year) of computer-naive users; the system deals with argument passing, recursion, and side-effects. Symbolic evaluation of the user's code produces an effect description which is compared with an idealised effect

*This research was supported by grants from the UK Social Science Research Council (HR7372/1) and the German Academic Exchange Service.

description (derived from a library plan). The library plan uses domain-specific knowledge to allow the user a great deal of freedom to invent alternate approaches to the programming task at hand. By using effect description mismatches, a variety of hints for correcting the code can be given to the student. Moreover, the system can generate counter-examples to code which appears to the student to be working correctly.

1.1 The SOLO Problem-Solving Context

Our students work mostly on their own at home, but have access to SOLO either on microcomputers at a 1-week residential summer school, or via terminals at one of over 250 regional study centres connected to a network of DEC system-20 computers. A range of extensive user aids, described in detail in Chapter 1, help students to enter lexically and syntactically correct programs with a minimum of fuss. Students are presented with a handful of cognitive modelling tasks to challenge their skills as cognitive scientists.

For instance, they are asked to solve the following problem: Define a procedure INFECT which would convert a data base such as the one shown in Fig. 9.1a to the one shown in Fig. 9.1b if invoked as INFECT ANDY.

Here is a sample solution:

```
% SOLUTION -1:

TO INFECT /X/
1 EXAMINE /X/
2 CHECK /X/ KISSES ?Y
  2A If present: INFECT *Y; EXIT
  2B If absent: EXIT
DONE

TO EXAMINE /X/
1 CHECK /X/ IS INOCULATED
  1A If present: EXIT
  1B If absent: NOTE /X/ GETS FLU; EXIT
DONE
```

INFECT recursively generates successive nodes along the thread of "kisses" relations (steps 2 and 2A), and invokes EXAMINE at each node. EXAMINE conditionally side-effects each node, i.e. asserting that /X/ GETS FLU only when the triple /X/ IS INOCULATED is absent. We will return to this example in detail in section 3, after an in-depth study of a non-recursive example which illustrates the reasoning and notational conventions used by DAN.

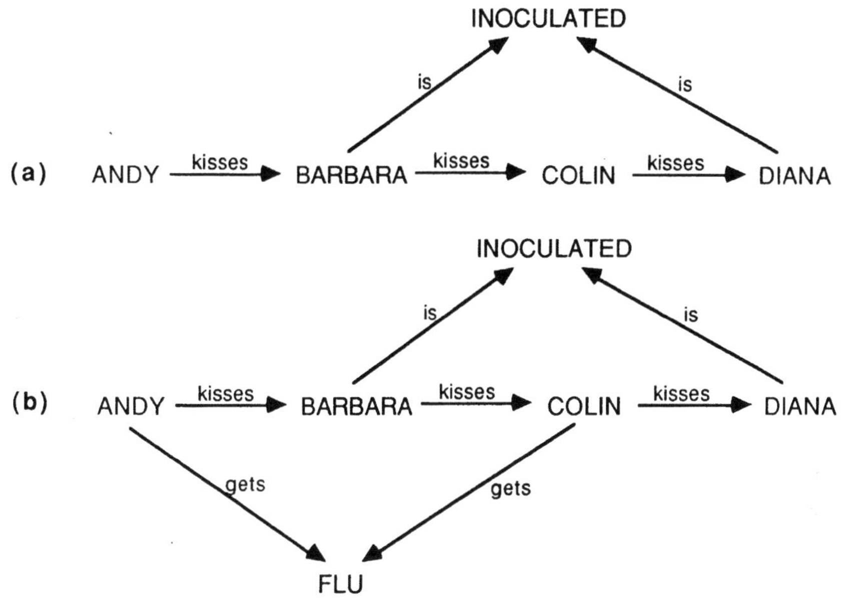

FIG. 9.1. (a) Initial data base and (b) final data base if INFECT ANDY is invoked.

1.2 A Second SOLO Problem: Two-Column Subtraction

A second problem posed to our students is that of writing a program to perform two-column subtraction. This problem provides a good testbed in which our students can develop models of children's arithmetic skills and compare their models with others reported in the literature (e.g. Young, 1981; du Boulay, O'Shea, & Monk, 1981). As SOLO has no numerical primitives, the students must invent a representation for numbers in the data base, invent all the primitive operations for working with pairs of numbers, and tackle the problem of borrowing which arises in multi-column subtraction.

To make things a little easier for the students, and to provide some standard notation for our program analyser to work with, we provide students with the definitions of some of the procedures to use as part of the subtraction problem.

To begin with, we assume that the top level procedure is named SUBTRACT, and that it has four parameters, /A/, /B/, /C/, and /D/. The parameters correspond to the following problem layout:

```
  /A/  /B/
- /C/  /D/
----------
   E    F
```

The final answer is stored in the data base on nodes E and F, using the relation VAL. For example, if the solution were the number 34, then somewhere within SUBTRACT we would have to achieve the following:

```
NOTE E---VAL---> 3
NOTE F---VAL---> 4
```

Finally, we assume that the solution is always printed out using the procedure RESPOND, whose definition is as follows:

```
TO RESPOND
10 CHECK E---VAL--->?X
  10A If present: CONTINUE
  10B If absent: PRINT "UH OH -- E HAS NO VALUE!!"; EXIT
20 CHECK F---VAL--->?Y
  20A If present: CONTINUE
  20B If absent: PRINT "UH OH -- F HAS NO VALUE!!"; EXIT
30 PRINT "THE ANSWER IS: " *X *Y
DONE
```

The final sequence of interactions with SOLO is thus meant to look something like this:

```
SOLO: SUBTRACT 3 4 1 5
THE ANSWER IS: 1 9
```

The students definition of SUBTRACT will therefore be a fleshed-out version of the following:

```
TO SUBTRACT /A/ /B/ /C/ /D/
10  ..................
20  ..................
30  ..................
40  ..................
50  ..................
60  ..................
70  ..................
80  RESPOND
DONE
```

We impose this structure only because our analyser needs to examine programs in terms of the *net change* made to the data base. Nodes E and F are thus really targets upon which some net change will be perpetrated.

Even within these guidelines the student has a great deal of freedom to select a variety of representations and algorithms. In fact, the actual code turns out to be relatively straightforward once the student has decided upon a data representation. The representation itself is by no means obvious, especially for beginners. One solution, arrived at by some of our students, is to use SOLO's relational network to construct subtraction *tables*.

For instance, here is the network structure for the node "7":

```
7
'---0---> 7
'---1---> 6
'---2---> 5
'---3---> 4
'---etc.---> etc.
```

Given the above representations, here is a buggy attempt to solve the problem:

```
%SUBTRACT SOLUTION-1

TO SUBTRACT /A/ /B/ /C/ /D/
10 CHECK /B/---/D/--->?DIFF1
  10A If present: NOTE F---VAL--->*DIFF1; CONTINUE
  10B If absent: EXIT
20 CHECK /A/---/C/--->?DIFF2
  20A If present: NOTE E---VAL--->*DIFF2; CONTINUE
  20B If absent: EXIT
30 RESPOND
DONE
```

Suppose that this procedure is used to find the difference of 77 and 32. It would be invoked as follows:

```
SOLO: SUBTRACT 7 7 3 2
```

At Step 10, the triple 7---2---> 5 would be found in the data base, matching ?DIFF1 with 5, and thus Step 10A would cause F---VAL---> 5 to be added to the data base (incidentally overwriting F---VAL---> anything else, in case such a triple had been left over from a previous example).

Step 20 would work analogously for the triple 7---3---> 4. So step 20A would cause E---VAL--->4 to be added to the data base. Finally,

RESPOND (see its canned definition earlier) would print THE ANSWER IS: 4 3.

The bug in the above version of SUBTRACT is that it fails to cope with borrowing. That is, if invoked as say, SUBTRACT 3 2 7 7, it would simply EXIT at step 10B. The next solution copes adequately with borrowing:

```
TO SUBTRACT /A/ /B/ /C/ /D/
10 CHECK /B/---/D/--->?DIFF1
  10A If present: NOTE F---VAL--->*DIFF1; CONTINUE
  10B If absent: DOBORROW /A/ /B/ /C/ /D/; EXIT
20 CHECK /A/---/C/--->DIFF2
  20A If present: NOTE E---VAL--->*DIFF2; CONTINUE
  20B If absent: PRINT "CAN'T COPE WITH NEGATIVES";
    EXIT
30 RESPOND
DONE

TO DOBORROW /A/ /B/ /C/ /D/
10 CHECK /D/---/B/--->? TEMP       %TEMP :- (D - B)
  10A If present: CONTINUE
  10B If absent: PRINT "UH OH"; EXIT
20 CHECK 10---*TEMP--->?DIFF1;
  20A If present: NOTE F---VAL--->*DIFF1; CONTINUE
       %DIFF1 = 10-TEMP
  20B If absent: PRINT "UH OH"; EXIT
30 CHECK /A/---1--->?NEWVAL        %NEWVAL :- (A - 1)
  30A If present: CONTINUE
  30B If absent: PRINT "UH OH"; EXIT
40 CHECK *NEWVAL---/C/--->?DIFF2;
  40A If present: NOTE E---VAL--->*DIFF2; CONTINUE
  40B If absent: PRINT "UH OH"; EXIT
50 RESPOND
DONE
```

This approach results in a completely self-contained arm (i.e. DOBORROW) being followed if borrowing proves necessary. This means that there is necessarily some redundancy, because this tens column must be dealt with both in SUBTRACT and in DOBORROW. A modular approach might involve setting some sort of flag if borrowing is necessary, and having a subroutine called DIFF to worry about the details of table-lookup and answer-storage for each column. This workhorse procedure, DIFF, is of course sensitive to the particular data representation the student has chosen.

Some students realize that using numbers as relation names can be rather limiting in the long run, because they may also want to start writing procedures to do addition. In this case, they need a way to discriminate between addition and subtraction tables. One solution is to use nodes such as "7SUBTBL" and "7ADDTBL" as follows:

```
7SUBTBL                 7ADDTBL
'---0---> 7             '---0---> 7
'---1---> 6             '---1---> 8
'---2---> 5             '---2---> 9
'---etc.---> etc.       '---etc.---> etc.
```

The only trick is to get from a number to the appropriate table. This can be done with the following representation:

```
7                             6
'---SUBTBL--->7SUBTBL         '---SUBTBL---> 6SUBTBL
'---ADDTBL--->7ADDTBL         '---ADDTBL---> 6ADDTBL
```

As an extra link must be traversed to get from a node (e.g. "7") to the appropriate table (e.g. "7SUBTBL"), we will call this representation an "indirect table", in contrast to the "direct table" representation presented first.

Here is how a subprocedure variant of DIFF would cope with this indirect representation:

```
TO DIFF-IND /X/ /Y/ /ANS/
10 CHECK /X/---SUBTBL--->?T                       %fetch tablename
  10A If present: CONTINUE                        %found it
  10B If absent: PRINT "UH OH"; EXIT              %oops, it's not there!
20 CHECK *T---/Y/--->?R                           %e.g.7SUBTBL---6--->1
  20A If Present: CONTINUE                        %go on to step 30
  20B If absent: ADD10DIFF /X/ /Y/ /ANS/; EXIT    %invoke user subroutine
30 NOTE /ANS/---VAL--->*R                         %e.g. F---VAL--->1
DONE
```

Notice the call to another user-defined subprocedure at step 20B, which is invoked precisely in case table-lookup fails. In such cases, borrowing must be necessary. Although some students may come up with an elegant solution which deals correctly with borrowing and generalises appropriately to multi-column subtraction for any number of columns, most students in fact begin with an ad hoc solution which does not generalize, but which DAN must nevertheless cope with. The issue of whether and how we should be teaching our students more elegant program design is important, but beyond the scope of this chapter. Instead, we focus on the debugging of actual programs developed by our students. In the above example, an ad hoc solution to the borrowing situation may be arrived at by adding 10 to the first parameter, and setting a global flag in the data base so that another routine can determine whether or not to decrement one of its variables accordingly (to simulate the borrow). Here is a definition of ADD10DIFF which behaves accordingly:

```
TO ADD10DIFF /X/ /Y/ /ANS/
10 CHECK /X/---ADDTBL--->?A                %fetch tablename
  10A If present: CONTINUE                 %found it
  10B If absent: PRINT "UH OH"; EXIT       %oops, it's not there!
20 CHECK *A---10--->?T                     %e.g. 7ADDTBL---10 --->17
  20A If present: CONTINUE                 %carry on
  20B If absent: PRINT "UH OH"; EXIT       %oops, it's not there!
30 CHECK *T---SUBTBL--->?S                 %e.g.17---SUBTBL--->17SUBTBL
  30A If present: CONTINUE                 %carry on
  30B If absent: PRINT "UH OH"; EXIT       %oops, it's not there!
40 CHECK *S---/Y/--->?R                    %e.g. 17SUBTBL---9--->8
  40A If present: CONTINUE                 %carry on
  40B If absent: PRINT "UH OH"; EXIT       %oops, it's not there!
50 NOTE /ANS/---VAL--->*R                  %e.g. F---VAL--->8
60 NOTE BORROWFLAG---IS--->SET             %global flag
DONE
```

The above sub-procedures would then be incorporated into the main SUBTRACT procedure as follows:

```
TO SUBTRACT /A/ /B/ /C/ /D/
10 DIFF-IND /B/ /D/ F
20 CHECK BORROWFLAG---IS--->SET
  20A If present: DECREMENT /A/; CONTINUE
  20B If absent: CONTINUE
30 DIFF-IND /A/ /C/ E
30 RESPOND
DONE
```

Another sub-procedure is invoked at step 20A, to decrement the tens digit (typically) if the relevant flag has been set. The code for DECREMENT (including the un-setting of the global flag) is as follows:

```
TO DECREMENT /X/
10 CHECK /X/---VAL--->?V                    %get current value V
  10A If present: CONTINUE
  10B If absent: PRINT "UH OH"; EXIT
20 CHECK *V---SUBTBL--->?T                  %find relevant table
  20A If present: CONTINUE
  20B If absent: PRINT "UH OH"; EXIT
30 CHECK *T---1--->?N                       %take away 1
  30A If present: CONTINUE
  30B If absent: PRINT "UH OH"; EXIT
40 NOTE /X/---VAL--->*N                     %this overwrites old val
50 FORGET BORROWFLAG---IS--->SET   %clean up side effect!
```

These examples are just meant to illustrate the diversity of approaches the student may follow while trying to solve a particular problem. Even clearer approaches exist: for example the DIFF subroutine may assume a very simple data base of "predecessor" and "successor" relations between digits, and use a recursive counting-up algorithm to compute the result for a given column. This approach and others can all be dealt with by our analysis program, because it is provided with detailed knowledge of a wide range of possible data structures which could be used to represent subtraction tables, along with an abstract description of effects to be achieved by a subtraction program. Only after examining the student's representation does DAN decide what the "idealised effect description" for that student's code should be, i.e. what changes to the assertional data base ought to occur as a result of a successful run of his or her program.

2. DAN: DEBUGGING ASSISTANT FOR NOVICES

2.1 An Overview

DAN relies extensively on a language-independent "plan diagram" representation developed by Waters (1979) and Rich (1981). The latter is the basis for computing the effects of programs and program segments, which in turn gives DAN a way to understand what the program achieves, and a way to compare this with what the program should have achieved. In the case of small mismatches, it is possible to recommend a particular patch to the student. More importantly, however (since we don't want to write the entire program for the student), is the generation of tailor-made counter-examples to provoke the student into thinking up his or her own solution.

When a student gets stuck, they can invoke DAN by typing HELP DEBUG. DAN investigates the student's code and data base in several phases, as outlined below:

TRANSLATION: User programs are translated (as they are entered) into a language independent "plan diagram" notation (PDN) (Waters, 1979; Rich, 1981) which encodes the control flow, the data flow, and a declarative description of each program's overall effect. During translation, three kinds of irrational code can be detected (cf. Wertz, 1982): (1) unreached code; (2) an unbound CHECK variable used following the absent branch of a CHECK statement; (3) useless code, which includes variable binding without later reference, assertion and deletion of the same data-base triple, and superfluous CHECKs. The translation phase is described in Section 2.2.

SYMBOLIC EVALUATION: An analysis is made of all possible pathways which the program might have explored, and an effect description is generated, providing a declarative account of what the program achieves in terms of changes to the data base. This is especially important for those pieces of the program which did not appear to match any known plans in the plan library. This phase is described in Section 2.3.

EFFECT DESCRIPTION MATCHING: The effect description of the student's program is now compared with an idealised effect description to find mismatches. The idealised effect description is computed by expanding a domain-specific library plan in a top-down fashion to mesh with the student's own chosen data base representation (which we analyze bottom-up).

DAN has criteria for detecting near misses, and heuristics for suggesting how to repair a program. If this fails, the effect description can still provide the basis for generating useful counterexamples which may help the student to focus more clearly on the underlying cause of the bug. Section 2.4 discusses effect description matching in some detail, and gives examples of the kinds of bugs which our system deals with.

2.2 Translation Into Plan Diagrams

The translation into plan diagrams is implemented in an object-oriented extension of Lisp, Objtalk, (Laubsch, 1979) similar to FRL (Roberts & Goldstein, 1977). Objects are organised into a class hierarchy and communicate by message-passing. The objects occurring in SOLO programs are procedures, steps, triples and variables. Procedures have steps as parts. The steps are classified into SOLO primitives and calls of user-defined procedures. The SOLO primitives CHECK, NOTE, and FORGET take triples as arguments (see Chapter 1). There are also implicit steps such as the binding and unbinding of variables that take place as the effect of

CHECK statements or the (internal) INIT, EXIT, and JOIN steps which are used to describe control flow. Most steps have successors and predecessors. Some steps side-effect the data base and others produce local binding of variables. All objects have attached procedures that handle the translation into the internal, plan-diagram notation (as well as the later phases of symbolic evaluation and plan recognition). The resulting representation facilitates reasoning about control and data flow, and also maintains back references to the sources code.

Figure 9.2 depicts DAN's representation of the DIFF-IND procedure described above. Control flow is indicated by thin black arrows, while data flow is shown by thick gray arrows. Each box in Fig. 9.2 depicts what is known as a segment, these are modules with behavioural descriptions which specify their effects. The diagrams are expressed in a frame-like notation, resembling KRL (Bobrow & Winograd, 1978). Here, for instance, is the internal representation of DIFF-IND:

```
DIFF-IND ==
(a procedure with
  name: DIFF-IND
  invars: {x y ans}   check-bound-vars: {r t}
  constants: {SUBTBL VAL}
  argmap: {[x. (check-23)]  [y. (check-24)]  [ans. (note-15)]
           [t. (check-bind-23 check-bind-24)]  [r. (check-bind-24
           note-15)]}
  steps: {check-23 check-bind-23 check-24 check-bind-24 print-12
         user-pc-49 note-15 join-5 join-6}
  init-step: check-23
  exit-step: join-6
  called-at: {user-pc-12 user-pc-17}   calls: { }
  effect: <filled in by symbolic evaluation>
  schema: <filled in by plan recognition>
  complaints: <warnings and error-messages>
)
```

The translation phase also accomplishes a limited static-program analysis that maintains a data base of the static-calling structure and will detect bugs in syntactically correct SOLO programs. These bugs are collected in the complaints slot of the internal frame representation of the procedure. Examples of complaints found during translation (and their meaning, shown in italics) are:

(double-exit <source-step> <unreached-step>)

This arises if code follows a check-step which specifies that control should leave this procedure.

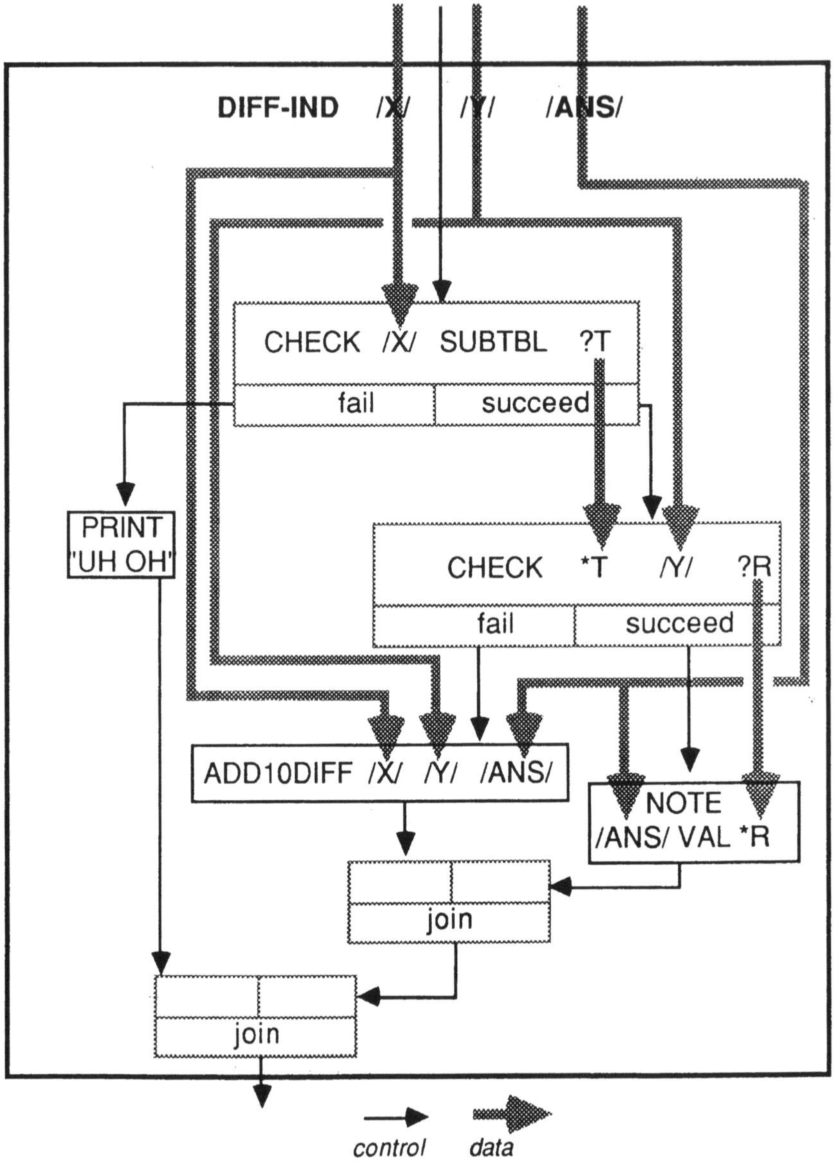

FIG. 9.2. Plan diagram representation of DIFF-IND procedure.

(unbound-check-variable <variable> <step>)
*A closed variable (e.g. *X) was not bound at any proceeding check-step. A similar complaint is made if a procedure variable (e.g. /X/) is used without being mentioned in the title line of that procedure.*

(wrong-number-of-args <user-procedure> <calling-step>)
If the procedure is still undefined, this checking is postponed to let the user incrementally add definitions.

(unreferenced-variables <list of variables>)
The argmap-slot of the procedure is screened to see whether input parameters and variables bound in check statements get referenced in the body.

2.3 Symbolic Evaluation

2.3.1 Accumulating Effect Descriptions

Symbolic evaluation serves as a tool for deriving a canonical description of the effect that a user program will have, when run in some environment with a symbolically described rather than an actual input. In contrast to evaluation, all possible paths that could be taken given the symbolically described environment and inputs are explored. The result is usually a symbolic evaluation tree rather than a single result. This tree can then be simplified into a canonical form that we call effect description. This description can be compared with the effect description of known (library) plans. Such a comparison will show that the program either behaves as intended by the tutor, deviates slightly (in which case we can suggest a patch), or deviates grossly (in which case we can derive counter-examples).

SOLO programs typically modify a global data base by side-effects. A procedure receives arguments and implicitly an input data base (db-in), and produces an output data base (db-out). The effect of a procedure is computed by an if-needed method associated with the effect-slot of the class "procedure". This method starts at the procedure's exit-step and collects the effects of each preceding step. Some steps, called join-steps, have multiple predecessors which will cause the formation of a cases-statement if the joining paths had different effects, as in:

```
effect: [cases { (present triple-1) => NIL)
               { (absent triple-1) (present triple-2) =>
                           (added triple-2) (added triple-4) }
               { (absent triple-1) (absent triple-3) =>
                           (added triple-2) } ]
```

Steps are connected by predecessor and successor links. The effect slot is inherited along these links. If bound variables occur in effect descriptions, the binding is expressed in terms of the procedure's input variables and constants, by tracing back the data-flow.

The effect of a segment is symbolically derived from the effects of its parts by accumulating effects along the control links (predecessor and successor slots) and subsequent simplification. The effect description is used by DAN in several ways: (a) interaction with the user can be more declarative, (b) we can derive the circumstances under which a segment produces a given effect, (c) the effect of a call to a user-defined procedure can be computed without re-analysing the actual code, often producing simplified expressions, (d) together with the class description of triples and symbols of the data base, the effect description assists in recognition of the user's plan, (e) we can recognise that a particular effect is achieved in the (pre-stored) library plan, but not in the user's program, and use this to generate a counter-example for the student.

The effect of a program is described by a tree which at its root has db-in and at its leaves has db-out for each possible condition. The data base consists of a set of triples, each having the form:

triple = [<source> <link> <target>]

We represent a data base as an association list of bindings, where each binding is:

binding = [bind (<source> <link>) <target>]

The data base after the student typed in the subtraction tables can then be represented as such an association list:

db0 = { [bind (9 8) 1] [bind (9 7) 2] . . . }

By the binding of (a b) in e (abbreviated as "(get a b)") we refer to the target of the first binding whose left part is (a b) in a data base e. A deletion of a triple [a b c] from the data base will add the entry [absent (a b)] to the front of the environment.

Symbolic evaluation of a procedure produces a symbolic evaluation tree which has as its root an input environment (db-in) and as its branches additions or deletions which possibly are conditional on some predicate. These branches are represented by a cases expression of the form:

```
(cases [<predicate 1> <change to data base>. . .]
       [<predicate 2> <change to data base>. . .]
```

The predicate can refer to node identity or presence of a binding. Node identity is expressed as:

(= (get a b) c)

which is interpreted as true in an evironment if there is a binding [bind (a b) c] which is not preceded by [absent (a b)]. Analogously, presence of a binding is expressed as:

[present a b]

which is interpreted true in an environment e if there is a binding of (a b) in e which is not preceded by [absent (a b)].

Consider the DIFF-IND procedure presented earlier (section 1.2). A procedure is symbolically evaluated independent of its input data-base. Here are the key events which occur in the DIFF-IND procedure:

At step 10A, T is bound to (get /X/ SUBTBL).
At step 20A, R is bound to (get (get /X/ SUBTBL) /Y/).
At step 30, db-in is augmented by [bind (/ANS/ VAL) (get (get /X/ SUBTBL) /Y/].

Symbolic evaluation produces the following: (1) augmentations to db-in (for FORGET and NOTE steps); (2) a local binding environment; (3) a cases statement (for CHECK steps).

2.3.2 Converting CHECK Steps to CASES Statements

CHECK steps come in two varieties: with an open variable (e.g. ?X, unbound) or a closed variable (e.g. *X, already bound) as the target. A CHECK with an open variable produces a local binding to that variable. The local binding environment does not enter the effect description since it does not change the data base. Instead, the binding environment is used for finding the substitution of a variable in terms of access to the data base through the procedure's input parameters. The tree shown in Fig. 9.3 is constructed and linked to the corresponding steps in the plan diagram. The root of the tree is entered in the root slot of the internal representation of the DIFF-IND procedure.

A CHECK with a closed variable or constant as target is translated as follows:

```
(CHECK (a b C) <present-code> <absent-code>) =>
  (cases [ (= (get a b ) C) <trans-of-present-code>]
         [T <trans-of-absent-code>])
```

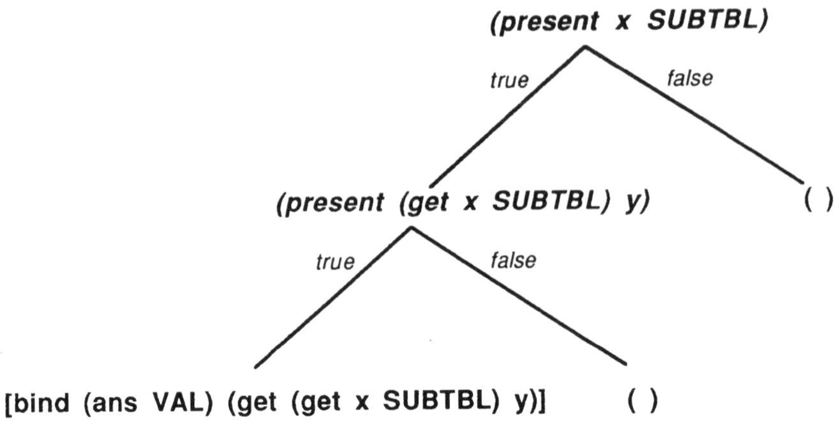

FIG. 9.3. Tree showing relevant cases in DIFF-IND procedure.

where <trans-of-*form*> is the translation of <*form*> to the symbolic internal representation.

A step containing a call to a user-defined procedure in some environment db-in is translated as:

(<user-proc-name> <arglist>) =>
  (db-out (<user-proc-name> <arglist> db-in))

Here (db-out <form>) denotes the output environment produced by the symbolic evaluation <form> which will be expanded in-line.

A useful rule for simplification of user procedure calls is:

(db-out <user-proc-name> <arglist> {binding> . <env>})) =>
  {<binding> (db-out (<user-proc-name> <arglist> <env>)) }

which is applied whenever it can be shown that the user procedure does not depend on <binding>.

The simple example above only contains CHECK statements with triples having an open variable as the target. CHECK with a closed variable (e.g. *X), an input parameter or a constant produces a node in the tree with an identity predicate. For example, a CHECK with the triple [a b C] leads to the predicate.

(= (get a b) C)

A step containing a call to a user-defined procedure will create a special node in the tree that gets expanded when the procedure definition is known. Then the effect of the procedure is retrieved and its input parameters are substituted by the arguments. An attempt is made to simplify the resulting expression.

2.4 Effect Description Analysis

2.4.1 Mapping the Data Base Onto Domain Functions

The typical output of symbolic evaluation will be a highly-nested cases statement with get-compositions embedded in the predicates and environment. Unless we can assign meaning to these get-compositions, we cannot interpret this as a solution to the student's task, because the student may have chosen from a variety of data representations, each requiring special access and data-base change operations. To take a rather simple example, the student may have asserted triples like [9 COMPL 1], [8 COMPL 2], etc. If we knew that these triples represented a 10-complement function, we could parse (get x COMPL) as (10-complement x) for any x. DAN has a repertoire of low-level, domain-specific library plans (DSLPs) which extract this knowledge from the student's data base for each possibly useful function or predicate in the subtraction domain (e.g. add1, sub1, val-of, geq).

The student may have chosen from among a wide variety of table or procedural representations, as indicated in Fig. 9.4. We represent these as a class hierarchy, which for each class has the associated rule for rewriting the user's effect description into diff. <DIFF> is an arbitrary symbol invented by the user.

If we take account of argument reversals, there are 10 possible ways of organising subtraction tables. Each indirect-table subclass has two triples

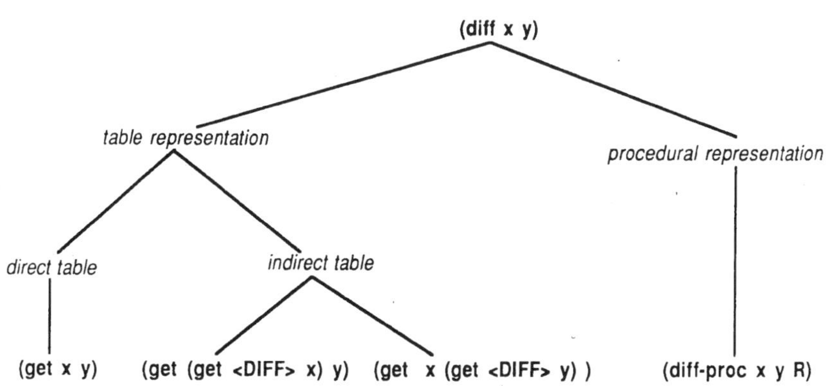

FIG. 9.4. Alternative ways of looking up (or computing) the difference between x and y.

as parts which are mutually constrained (the outer and inner get) by the difference predicate. We hypothesize a particular table-class, and seek confirmation until we can decide on the actual class used by the student. Then we look for all the entries of the table and create an object DIFF which has associated with it the code to recognize (diff a b) [e.g. as (get (get a SUB) b)]. Data base analysis reveals the frequent error-type of missing or inconsistent entries in the data base. Triples which belong to no pre-defined class, but partially match some class (i.e. because they contain a known link-name) are categorized as inconsistent and the user is informed about them.

2.4.2 A Formal Description of the Data Base

The concepts of "direct table" and "indirect table" have the following formal descriptions:

```
direct-table ==
[a table with
  name: (an integer)
  base: (my name)                      %base & name are coreferential
  content: (an alist with
            typical-pair: [left: (an integer)
                           [right: (an integer) ] )
  variety: (one-of add sub mult)
  constraint: apply [ (my variety)
                      { (my base)
                        (the left from
                             (any pair --->p) of (my content) ) ) } ]
                      = (the right from p) ]


indirect-table ==
(a table with
  name: (the target from (a tableptr with source: (my base) ) )
  base: (an integer)
        (the source from (a tableptr with target: (my name) ) )
  content: <as in direct-table>
  variety: <as in direct-table>
  constraint: <as in direct-table> ]
```

Using the direct and indirect subtraction tables for the number 7 shown earlier, we may interpret these descriptions as follows: a direct table has a number base which happens to be the same as its own name ("7", in this example). The direct table consists of an association list, which is just pairs of integers. A constraint which must be fulfilled is that if we apply a function (e.g. "sub" or "add") to two arguments – the base (e.g. "7") and the left element of some pair (e.g. "2") – then the result should be equal to the right element of that pair.

The interpretation of indirect-table is almost identical, with one crucial exception – the relationship between its "name" and "base" slots. The name is some item which is specified by saying that it is the *target* (i.e. the thing pointed to) from some particular *tableptr* whose source is the integer base ("7", in this example). A *tableptr* is a subclass of a *triple* which relates an *integer* to a *table*. Thus, the relational structure (7 SUBTBL 7SUBTBL.) is an instance of a *tableptr*.

2.4.3 Instantiating an Appropriate Plan

In analyzing the student's data base each subclass of table is hypothesized in turn as a possible data representation, and confirmation of these hypotheses is then sought. In this example, our student is in fact using an indirect-table representation, and the description-matcher confirms that hypothesis since table has an associating matching function:

```
(lambda (obj)
        (satisfies (obj
          (! [obj name] !name)
          (! [obj alist] !content)
          (obj !constraint) ) )
```

Next, DAN examines the intent-specification of DIFFERENCE. It is the task of DAN to generate a particular manifestation of the detailed plan, *based upon an analysis of the data representation the student has already chosen*. If our student used indirect-tables, DAN would generate an idealized plan which uses the indirect style of fetching exhibited by the SOLO DIFF-IND procedure shown earlier.

The intent-specification of a difference-plan as found in the plan library is illustrated:

```
difference ==
[a plan with
   input1: (an integer) ---> X
   input2: (an integer) ---> Y
   input3: (the access-of Y) from
                       (a table with variety: sub
                                     base: X) )
]
```

The expression (access-of Y) means that there is an if-needed procedure attached to the "access-of" slot of the table which will specify how to perform the retrieval. For direct and indirect tables the "access-of" method attached to their schemata is:

```
access-of i =>
    (the right from
            (the pair from
                    ( (my content) with left: i) ) )
```

To illustrate the use of this method, suppose the direct-table representation for "7" includes the pair (2 5). If we want to access some element indexed by "2", then we do that by retrieving the right half of the pair whose left half is "2". In this case, the pair (2 5) has a right half "5", so if we sent the message "access-of 2" to the instance of direct-table whose name was "7", the result would be "5".

From this method DAN first constructs a description of the intended effect of accessing each type of table. For a direct table the intended effect is:

```
(the target from
  (a triple with source: X
                 rel: Y) )
```

For an indirect table the intended effect is shown in Fig. 9.5.

DAN knows that an instance of fetch will handle the "outer form" shown in the rectangle above, so when it processes the intended effect of an indirect-table, it produces the following effect description:

```
F1 ==
[a fetch with
  input1: (the target from (a tableptr with source: X) ) ---> T
  input2: Y
  output: (a node) ---> A
```

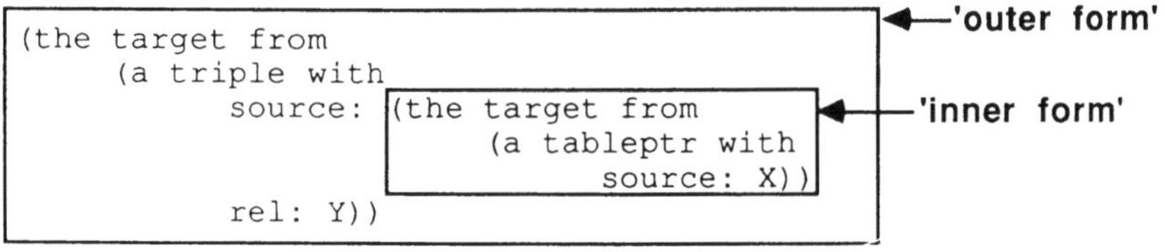

FIG. 9.5. Intended effect of an indirect table.

The "inner form" is processed analogously, leading to the following effect description:

```
F2 ==
[a fetch with
  input1: X
  input2: SUBTRACTION
  output: (a node) ---> T
```

DAN knows that the final output from a plan can be achieved either by a print or an "assert" operation, so one possible final representation for the idealized plan includes, in its "effect" slot, the following:

```
the effect from
  (an assert with
        arg1: (a constant)
        arg2: (a constant)
        arg3: (the output from
                 (a fetch with
                  input1: (the output from (a fetch with
                                          input1: X
                                          input2:SUBTRACTION))
                  input2: Y) ) )
```

The idealised effect description serves as the DAN's driving force. That is, the effect description derived from the user's own algorithm and data representation is systematically compared against DAN's own idealised description. The interactive debugging session is directed by a possibly encountered mismatch between these effect-descriptions, and works towards the goal of reducing the difference, as described next.

2.4.4 Mapping User Code Onto Domain Functions

Once these low-level, domain-specific library plans (DSLPs) are recognized, we can do a top-down analysis similar to that of Ruth (1976), starting from a high level DSLP which is pre-defined by us for each particular task. Given the definitions of SETUP and ANSWER which impose the layout shown earlier, the DSLP functions as a grammar which can be used to recognize all possible variations in the actual effect description of the user's code. For 2 column subtraction the DSLP has the following definition (omitting db-out for brevity):

```
2-COL-SUB (A B C D E F db-in) =
  (cases [ (geq (val-of B) (val-of D) )
             (cases [ (geq (val-of A) (val-of C) )
                        { [bind (val-of E) (diff (val-of A) (val-of C) ) ]
                          [bind (val-of F) (diff (val-of B) (val-of D) ) ]
                          .db-in} ]
                      [t (fail 2-COL-SUB) ] ) ]
          [t { [bind (val-of E) (borrowed-from (val-of A) (val-of C) ) ]
               [bind (val-of F) (borrowed-by (val-of B) (val-of D) ) ]
               .db-in} ] )
```

Suppose now that the student wrote the following program for two column subtraction, similar to the code presented in section 1.2, but this time storing the initial values directly with particular nodes in the data base (A, B, C, D, and E) rather than passing in integers as parameters, and with a buggy definition of DIFF-IND:

```
TO SUBTRACT /A/ /B/ /C/ /D/
1 NOTE A---VAL---> /A/            %e.g. A---VAL---> 7
2 NOTE B---VAL--->/B/
3 NOTE C---VAL--->/C/
4 NOTE D---VAL--->/D/
10 DIFF-IND B D F                  bug! should use /B/ and /D/
20 CHECK BORROWFLAG---IS---> SET
  20A If present: DECREMENT A; CONTINUE
  20B If absent: CONTINUE
30 DIFF-IND A C E
40 RESPOND
DONE
```

```
TO DIFF-IND /X/ /Y/ /ANS/
10 CHECK /X/---SUBTBL --->?T          %fetch tablename
  10A If present: CONTINUE            %found it
  10B If absent: EXIT                 %oops, it's not there!
20 CHECK *T---/Y/--->?R               %e.g. 7SUBTBL---6--->1
  20A If present: CONTINUE            %go on to step 30
  20B If absent: EXIT                 %no borrowing!!
30 NOTE /ANS/---VAL--->*T             %should be *R instead
DONE
```

DAN recognizes this as a function at the top of the definition hierarchy and symbolic evaluation expands it by inserting the effect descriptions of the called functions (and so on recursively for these). The resulting effect description is a large composition of gets, which ideally should be matched by 2-COL-SUB.

Recognition now proceeds top-down, involving the sub-plans of val-of, geq, diff, borrowed-from, and borrowed-by. Each of these sub-plans is itself re-written to conform with the particular representation adopted by the student. For example, the sub-plan for dealing with a borrowed-from column containing the digits x and y can be re-written in two ways:

```
borrowed-from (x y) == (diff (subl x) y) |
                       (diff x (add1 y) )
```

Similarly, the diff plan (which implements $x - y$ for $x \geqslant y$) must be re-written in terms of primitives which the student may have elected to use. The difficulty here is that the student may have chosen to implement "diff" in terms of tables in the data base or a recursive counting procedure. We will consider both representations.

2.4.5 *Comparing the Actual Effect With the Ideal Effect*

A variety of user programs for a given task can be recognized as having the same effect description as a pre-stored plan. The reduction to a canonical form allows the user to (1) invent arbitrary names, (2) order steps arbitrarily, (3) break up procedures arbitrarily into sub-procedures, (4) pass values through intermediate nodes of the data base, and (5) invent his or her own data representation.

Our goal is to give the students as much help as possible in detecting the underlying cause of an error. Here the effect descriptions are useful too: by using the library plan to generate the get-compositions corresponding to their data-representations, we can compare the terminal nodes of both their and DSLP's effect description for each condition. (DAN takes care of situations in which nested cases must be re-ordered for both trees to match.) A collection of standard error conditions can now be trapped by DAN and described to the user, as presented next.

Name Subtitution. A very frequent error which can be detected by comparing effects at terminal nodes is name-substitution (e.g. the student writes w and means v). DAN compares the bindings added or deleted at each terminal branch of DSLP (goal bindings, g_i) with those of the user program (actual bindings, a_i). Assume it finds a mismatch of two bindings at some terminal branch:

```
goal binding:   g = [bind (g1 g2) g3]
actual-binding: a = [bind (a1 a2) a3) ]
```

For example, if in line 30 of DIFF-IND the code is NOTE/ANS/VAL *T instead of NOTE/ANS/VAL *R, so a critical part of its effect description is:

{ [bind (ans VAL (get x SUBTBL)] . env} %*actual*

instead of

{ [bind (ans VAL (get (get x SUBTBL) y)] . env} %*goal*

as described earlier (lower right hand node of Fig. 9.3).

We go up in the symbolic evaluation tree to the place where *a* was achieved using variable *w* (i.e. line 30 of DIFF-IND using variable T). If the mismatch was in pair $\{a_i, g_i\}$, and in the local environment some other variable was bound to g_i, we can propose substituting it for the one used in the code. In our example the mismatch was in $\{a_3, g_3\}$ with a_3 being T, and g_3 being R, so a substitution of R for T at line 30 is suggested to the student.

If g_i is not bound locally, we look at the CHECK (or procedure call) where w was bound and recursively search for the goal of binding w to g_1. In case of success, we ask the student whether they want to accept the proposed renaming.

Step Insertion. If variable renaming fails, we try step insertion, because another typical source of errors in SOLO is students forgetting a level of indirectness (i.e. using the source of a triple, instead of the target along some link). Lines 10 and 30 of SUBTRACT (as presented in section 2.4.4) manifest this error, given the implementation of DIFF-IND presented alongside it.

A CHECK step can be inserted to correct that, if by substituting (get s K) for some subexpression s in a_i (where K is some constant link) a_i can be made equal to g_i. In SUBTRACT the actual effect is:

(diff-ind B D F) % *actual*

whereas the goal in 2-COL-SUB (section 2.4.4, numbered line 4 of 2-COL-SUB definition) ultimately gives:

(diff-ind (get B VAL) (get D VAL) F) % *goal*

and thus K = VAL. The insertion of two CHECK statements of the form CHECK B VAL ?BVAL and modification of the calls of DIFF-IND in lines 10 and 30 is suggested. The more elegant patch of simply passing the parameters /A/ /B/ /C/ and /D/ through directly (two at a time) to the successive calls of DIFF-IND can also be suggested, in which case the four lines of NOTE (1–4) are detected as "uncovered" (*possibly* redundant) code.

Reversed Branches. If step insertion fails also, we look at the possibility of reversed present and absent branches (cf. Ruth, 1976). This manifests itself in the effect description such that the correct data base change has occurred, but at the wrong branch of the tree. In such cases, the user is queried about whether the clauses of the CHECK statement should be reversed.

Counterexample Generation. If CHECK clause reversal fails also, our last resort is to look for a branch of the tree where the conditions are correct, but there is a disagreement in the effect. DAN chooses a counter-example that would run through this branch of the tree, and asks the student to try that example on his program.

Consider line 20B in DIFF-IND. The student did not consider the case where (geq x y) does not hold. The effect description for SUBTRACT has no effect where it should match lines 7–9 of 2-COL-SUB. We collect the case predicates that lead to this leaf of the symbolic evaluation tree, and see that under the condition:

```
(and (present (B SUBTBL))
     (not (geq (val-of B) (val-of D) ) ) )
```

SUBTRACT would fail. Since DAN knows that (val-of B) and (val-of D) are digits, it generates values which fulfill this condition and asks the student to try his program with those.

3. ANALYSING RECURSIVE PROGRAMS

3.1 Programs Which Produce One Net Effect

Using add1 and sub1, the student may have written a recursive procedure to implement "diff". Since a SOLO procedure can only have an effect by side-effecting the data base, the DSLP for a procedural implementation has to change slightly. Any function f, which is represented procedurally as f-proc will be transformed in the library plan as follows:

```
{ [bind (val-of x) (f <arglist>) ] . env} =>
          (f-proc <arglist> N env) )
```

where N is the node to be side-effected.

The following example shows a typical student implementation, together with the effect description produced by DAN:

```
TO DIFF-REC /X/ /Y/ /ANS/
1 CHECK EQUALS /X/ /Y/
  1A If present: NOTE /ANS/ VAL 0; EXIT
  1B If absent: CONTINUE
2 CHECK /X/ SUB1 ?X1
  2A If present: DIFF-REC *X1 /Y/ /ANS/; CONTINUE
  2B If absent: EXIT
3 CHECK /ANS/ VAL ?V
  3A If present: CONTINUE
  3B If absent: ERROR; EXIT
4 CHECK *V ADD1 ?V1
  4A If present: NOTE /ANS/ VAL *V1
  4B If absent: ERROR; EXIT
DONE
```

Symbolic evaluation first produces:

```
diff-rec (x y ans db-in) ==
     (cases [ (= (get EQUALS x) y)
                { [bind (ans VAL) 0] . db-in} ]
              [ (present (get x SUB1) )
                { [bind (ans VAL) (get (get ans VAL) ADD1) ) ]
                    (self (get x SUB1) y ans db-in) } ] )
```

This matches a recursion pattern for which there is a DSLP. The binding being affected in the terminating case (ans VAL) is identical to that of the post-recursive step, which means that (ans VAL) is successively rebound. The DSLP simplifies this to an instance of a prototypical data base entry:

```
[db-entry value      [bind (ans VAL) g007]
          init       ( (g007 . 0) )
          rec-rel    ( (x . (get x SUB1) )
                           (g007 . (get g007 ADD1) ) )
          term-if    (= (get EQUALS x) y) ]
```

It says that the value is an (ans VAL) binding whose target can be computed by substituting for g007 the init value and then stepping through the rec-rel a-list substituting for g007 until term-if is true. This representation has the advantage that other recursive implementations (i.e. a tail-recursive one) can be mapped to an equivalent db-entry. The DSLP for diff-proc will match this db-entry instance modulo renaming and substituting (sub1 x) for (get x SUB1).

3.2 Programs Which Have a Composite Net Effect: Using Temporal Abstraction

The concept of "temporal abstraction" was developed by Waters (1976; 1979), and Rich and Shrobe (1978) to describe the variables enumerated in loops as a *set* of objects which could be manipulated as a whole. We apply this principle to recursive procedures operating on threaded data structures and use it to understand *compositions* of several side effects.

In a recursive procedure such as INFECT (section 1.1), a side effect (conditional or unconditional) may occur logically at any of five locations, depending on the juxtaposition of the side effect, the recursive call, and the termination test. Here is a skeleton of the INFECT procedure, with the five possible locations of side-effect occurrences shown in bold (not all five can coexist, and the SOLO user must make careful use of the control-flow keywords CONTINUE and EXIT to obtain certain combinations):

TO INFECT /X/
. . .
<**initial**>
. . .
CHECK /X/---KISSES--->?Y
  If present: <**pre-rec**>; INFECT *Y; <**post-rec**>
  If absent: <**termination**>
. . .
<**final**>

These occurrences are depicted schematically in Fig. 9.6, which shows a recursive procedure P partitioned into its possible constituents. The effect of each solid box in the figure, in accordance with the notion of temporal abstraction, is to add or delete some *set* of triples. The overall effect of P will be the composition of these. In the figure, "rec" is short for recursion, "self" is the actual recursive invocation of P, and "get-next" is an implicit emumeration function which retrieves the next node in the thread (this happens automatically during pattern-matching in SOLO, e.g. when Y is bound to BARBARA, then COLIN, then DIANA, the nodes shown in Figs. 9.1a and 9.1b).

Any of the effect steps may be conditional, composite, or missing altogether. The restrictions for recognizing a program as an instance of this schema are: (1) P has a parameter x which is the beginning of a thread; recursive invocations of P thus enumerate successive nodes along the

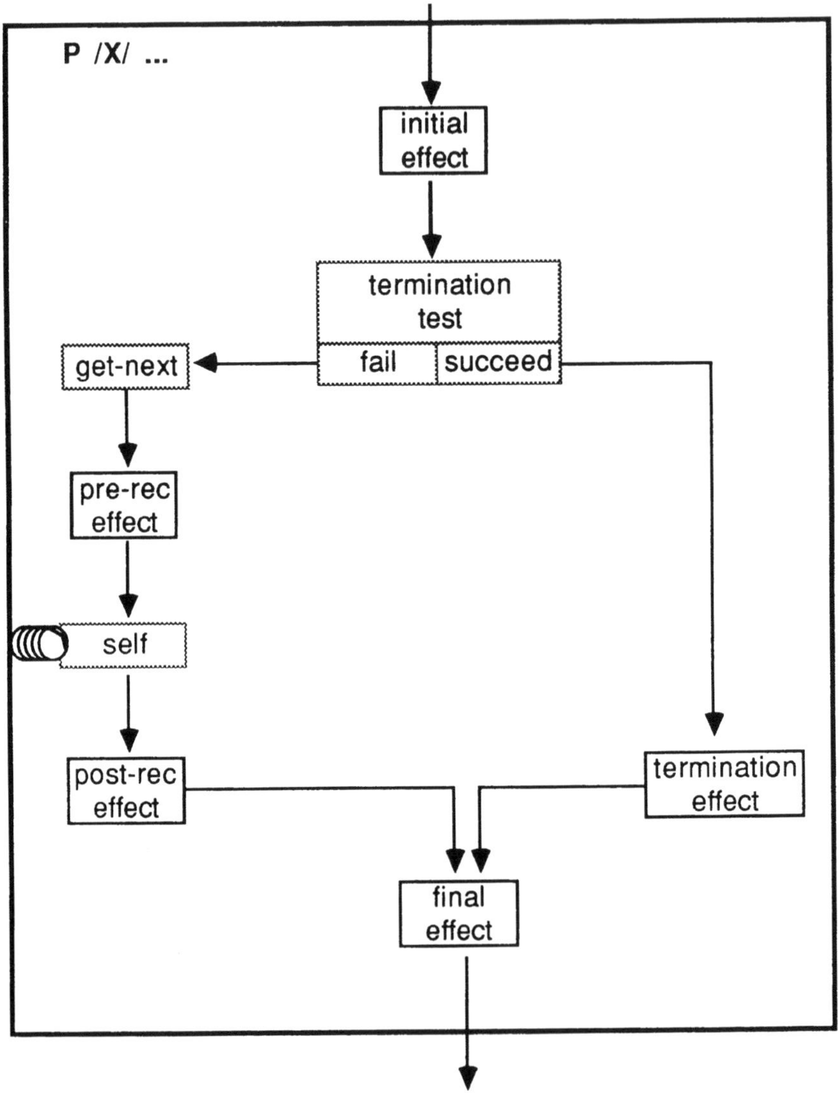

FIG. 9.6. The recursion schema for thread enumeration.

thread; (2) the recursion and termination steps involve the enumerated node and relation R, where R is non-cyclic and one-to-one or many-to-one in the data base (we don't deal with one-to-many mappings of R, which would exist if, say, the triples [ANDY KISSES BARBARA] and [ANDY KISSES DIANA] were both present in the data base); (3) the effects do not alter the thread and the side-effected node can only be reached from the enumerated node via one-to-one relations.

The effect steps can be classified according to time of execution and range of nodes on which the effect occurs, as shown in Fig. 9.7.

The important insight of temporal abstraction is that the nodes enumerated during recursion can be dealt with as a *set*. Thus, any of these steps has an effect which can represented as a set of triples (called db-set). The termination step is the degenerate case of a singleton set. We describe db-sets as follows:

[db-set
typical member: (<filter> => <side effect>)
init: (<enumerated node> . <first value>)
rec rel: <thread link>
termination: (ABSENT [<ref> <thread link> ?])]

time of execution of effect

range of enumeration	*descent*	*ascent*
entire thread	initial effect	final effect
butlast of thread	pre-rec effect	post-rec effect
last of thread	termination effect	

FIG. 9.7. Different kinds of side-effect steps, depending upon time of execution and range of affected nodes.

where

```
<filter> ::= T |
            <simple filter> |
            (OR <conjunctive filter> . . .)
<simple filter> ::= (PRESENT <triple>) |
                    (ABSENT <triple>)
<conjunctive filter> ::=
            (AND <simple filter> . . .)
<side effect> ::=
            (+ [<enumerated node> <link> <node>] ) |
            (− [<enumerated node> <link> <node>] )
<ref> ::= <enumerated node> | (get <ref> <link>).
```

By (get <node> <link>) we denote the reference from <node> via <link>. Thus <ref> is the n-fold composition of the reference from the <enumerated node> (called e) along <link>.

For example, the node BARBARA in Fig. 9.1 can be referred by:

(get ANDY KISSES)

whereas the node DIANA can be referenced by the composition

(get (get (get ANDY KISSES) KISSES) KISSES)

An instantiated schema does not, of course, refer to specific nodes in the data base, but rather to a generalised description of a typical node along the thread.

How are the db-sets derived from an instantiated recursion schema? We fill the slot "typical member" from the effect of the step (e.g. a NOTE of some triple is a + with its source replaced by a <ref> involving e). If the effect is unconditional, the filter is T else the condition is taken as the filter. The "init" slot is the first value that e will take. Enumeration stops when termination is true. Steps which work on the entire thread have:

(ABSENT [e <thread link> ?]),

while those working on the butlast of the thread have:

(ABSENT [(get e <thread link>) <thread link> ?])

as their termination.

Consider the instantiated schema for SOLUTION-1 of section 1.1, repeated here for convenience:

```
% SOLUTION-1

TO INFECT /X/
1 EXAMINE /X/
2 CHECK /X/ KISSES ?Y
  2A If present: INFECT *Y; EXIT
  2B If absent: EXIT
DONE

TO EXAMINE /X/
1 CHECK /X/ IS INOCULATED
  1A If present: EXIT
  1B If absent: NOTE /X/ GETS FLU; EXIT
DONE
```

The code contains only a conditional initial effect whose description is as follows:

```
[db-set
  typical member: ( (ABSENT [e IS INOCULATED] ) => (+ [e
    GETS FLU] ) )
  init: (e . x)
  rec rel: KISSES
  termination: (ABSENT [e KISSES ?] ) ]
```

3.2.1 Composition of Recursive Sets by Symbolic Evaluation

In general, a recursive procedure may comprise any *combination* of effect steps. To describe the net effect of the entire procedure, the individual effects must be composed. For instance, the addition of a set of triples followed by the conditional deletion of some elements should have the composite effect of asserting some elements of the set conditionally upon the negation of the condition for deletion (e.g. see SOLUTION-2 below). This simplification is done during symbolic evaluation.

Although the db-set for each step is a temporal abstraction (and hence ignores the order in which the nodes are enumerated), compositions of side-effects are sensitive to temporal order. Thus, we first compose those effects which occur on the descent and then those which occur on the ascent. The effects are still dealt with as db-sets (i.e. the inner details of the enumeration sequence are ignored). All we need to worry about is whether the db-set is of the "descending" or "ascending" variety, which we know from its position in the instantiated schema.

Composition proceeds as follows: At a node in the symbolic evaluation tree (called S-node) where a db-set is to be asserted, we grow a branch with a description of the range of values that could be taken by the enumerated node. The range {e | e in R*(x)} says that e can take the value of all the nodes in the transitive closure of R starting at x. At the S-node at the end of this branch, the typical member of the db-set is asserted. If there is a (non-T) filter, we split into two branches, one with the condition and the other with its negation, and add the side effect to the S-node at the end of the branch where the condition is true.

The next db-set is dealt with in the same way at all terminal S-nodes grown so far. If it has a filter, we test it at each S-node: if the sets have the same range, it may be possible to show either that the condition must always hold or that it can never hold, thus saving the split. If the ranges overlap, we introduce one branch for the overlapping range and others for the non-overlapping parts. On the overlapping sets it is then possible to test conditions or apply rules for cancellation (i.e. a NOTE followed by a FORGET of the same triple has no net effect) and overwriting (i.e. a NOTE following another NOTE with the same triple has no further effect).

Finally, starting from the terminal S-nodes we collect effects and conditions for all nodes with the same net-effect into one db-set with the appropriate filter. The result is the description of the program used for comparison with the ideal effect description.

3.2.2 Examples

Here are two alternative solutions to the problem posed in section 1. One has a bug.

```
%SOLUTION-2 (Successive sweeps)


TO INFECT /X/
1 CONTAMINATE /X/
2 DECONTAMINATE /X/


TO CONTAMINATE /X/
1 NOTE /X/ GETS FLU
2 CHECK /X/ KISSES ?Y
  2A If present: CONTAMINATE *Y; EXIT
  2B If absent: EXIT
DONE
```

```
TO DECONTAMINATE /X/
1 CHECK /X/ IS INOCULATED
  1A If present: FORGET /X/ GETS FLU; CONTINUE
  2B If absent: CONTINUE
2 CHECK /X/ KISSES ?Y
  2A If present: DECONTAMINATE *Y; EXIT
  2B If absent: EXIT
DONE
```

%SOLUTION-3 (Ascending conditional side effect)

```
TO INFECT /X/
1 CHECK /X/ KISSES ?Y
  1A If present: INFECT *Y; CONTINUE
  2B If absent: EXIT
2 CHECK /X/ IS INOCULATED
  2B If present: EXIT
  2B If absent: NOTE /X/ GETS FLU; EXIT
DONE
```

In SOLUTION-2, the plan diagram for INFECT matches a schema for a conjoined effect. The plan diagram for the first of these, CONTAMINATE, matches the recursion schema for thread enumeration: an unconditional side-effect occurring only in the initial effect slot of the schema. It thus has the net effect:

```
for all {e | e in KISSES*(x) }
  (+ [e GETS FLU] )
```

The second of the conjoined effects, DECONTAMINATE, matches the same schema, except that a conditional side effect occurs at the initial effect slot. This yields the following net effect description:

```
for all {e | e in KISSES*(x) }
  (PRESENT [e IS INOCULATED] ) => (- [e GETS FLU] )
```

During symbolic evaluation, the two S-nodes are recognized as having the same range, so the evaluator simplifies their combined effect to be:

```
for all {e | e in KISSES*(x) }
  (ABSENT [e IS INOCULATED] ) => (+ [e GETS FLU] )
```

which is precisely the intended effect of the ideal INFECT procedure.

SOLUTION-3 has a plan diagram which matches that of the recursion schema with just a (conditional) "post-rec" effect. Notice that in this solution the first thing that normally happens is the recursive invocation of INFECT (step 1A), which means that the side effect only happens when ascending. Our schema knows that a "post-rec" effect on its own fails to reach the final node in the thread (in this case due to the EXIT at step 1B). This is instantiated from the schema's canned effect description as follows:

for all {e | (get e KISSES) in KISSES*(x) }
(ABSENT [e IS INOCULATED]) => (+ [e GETS FLU])

That is, the conditional side-effect is perpetuated only on the "butlast" of the thread running from x via KISSES. For the example of Fig. 9.1, SOLUTION-3 happens to work. However, a counter-example can be generated for the student in the following way: generate a thread in which the final node (f) of the thread satisfies the condition specified in the schema's effect description, i.e. (ABSENT [f IS INOCULATED]). In such a case, SOLUTION-3 will fail. This counter-example can be used to point out the inherent flaw in the student's solution.

Temporal abstraction provides us with a powerful mechanism for reasoning about side effects on sets of data objects. Our method of composing several such sets lets us analyse recursive procedures involving side effects on threaded data structures. Static set descriptions, which are the essence of temporal abstraction, can be combined using simplification rules derived from symbolic evaluation techniques. A library of recursive schemata enables us to analyse a range of students' programs, to combine set descriptions in a sensible way (e.g. composing descending and ascending effects in the right order) and to generate tailor-made counter-examples for programs which might work by accident.

4. CONCLUSIONS

Our work demonstrates how a combination of domain-specific knowledge and symbolic evaluation techniques can be applied to building a help facility for novice programmers. Writing programs in an elementary assertional data base language like SOLO is experienced by our students as a simple and natural entry point into programming. However, automatically coping with the sorts of bugs which arise through programming by side-effect requires extensions to earlier work on program understanding and debugging. The techniques we have employed give the students a fair amount of freedom in choosing their own representations, a fact which reflects one of the main goals of the course they are taking (i.e. understanding computer modelling and knowledge representation).

REFERENCES

Bobrow, D. & Winograd, T. (1978). An overview of KRL-O. *Cognitive Science, 1*, (3), 3–46.

duBoulay, J. B. H., O'Shea, T., & Monk, J. (1981). The black box inside the glass box: Presenting computing concepts to novices. *International Journal of Man-Machine Studies, 14*, 237–249.

Laubsch, J. (1979). *ObjTalk: Eine auf semantischen Netzen basierende objekt-orientierte Sprache zur Darstellung von Wissen.* MMK-Memo 12, Institut fuer Informatik, Universitaet Stuttgart.

Papert, S. (1980). *Mindstorms: Children, computers, and powerful ideas.* Brighton, England: Harvester Press.

Roberts, R. B. & Goldstein, I. P. (1977). The FRL manual. *AI memo*, MIT AI Laboratory, Cambridge, MA.

Rich, C. (1981). A formal representation for plans in the Programmer's Apprentice. *Proceedings of the Seventh International Joint Conference on Artificial Intelligence (IJCAI-81)*, Vancouver, BC, Canada, 1044–1052.

Rich, C. & Shrobe, H. (1978). Initial report on a LISP programmer's apprentice. *IEEE Transactions on Software Engineering, SE-4:6*, 456–467.

Ruth, G. R. (1976). Intelligent program analysis. *Artificial Intelligence, 7*, 65–85.

Waters, R. (1976). A system for understanding mathematical FORTRAN programs. *AI memo 368*, MIT AI Laboratory, Cambridge, MA.

Waters, R. C. (1979). A method for analyzing loop programs. *IEEE Transactions on Software Engineering, SE5:3*, 237–247.

Wertz, H. (1982). Stereotypical program debugging: An aid for novice programmers. *International Journal of Man-Machine Studies, 16*, 379–392.

Young, R. M. (1981). The machine inside the machine: User's models of pocket calculators. *International Journal of Man-Machine Studies, 15*, 51–85.

10 Syntactic Debugging of Procedural Programs

Tony Hasemer
Human Cognition Research Laboratory, The Open University, Milton Keynes, England

OVERVIEW

Analysis of program code, according to the syntax of the programming language used, can be more powerful as a debugging aid than is sometimes supposed. Its potential advantage over algorithmic debugging is that it involves no assumptions about what programmers intended to do, but rather concentrates purely upon what they should have done. In this chapter a simple programming language with extremely regular syntax (SOLO; see Chapter 1) is used as an example environment in which to explore the possibilities of syntactic analysis, and the debugging systems described (under the generic title AURAC) have been implemented. They worked correctly within their specified limits.

1. INTRODUCTION

The work described here was the subject of my PhD thesis in 1983 and relied upon what is often called the Existence Proof: "Here is my machine, it does work, and from the fact that it works I can derive certain hypotheses about the debugging process in general". Since 1983, and especially since the advent of high-performance graphics workstations, research into debugging strategies has undergone a fundamental change, it now being possible to show visual descriptions of program execution, and even visual descriptions of bugs. The suite of programs together referred to as AURAC were purely textual in their responses: their operations and their results could have been displayed on a mechanical teletype terminal and contained no graphics at all. Nevertheless the principles underlying AURAC remain valid and interesting from the point of view of debugging strategies in general.

1.1 Empirical Justification

It may seem odd to claim that syntactic analysis alone can yield large amounts of debugging information, when anyone who has ever tried to find the bug in someone else's program knows that the hardest task of all is to work out what the program was intended to do. We programmers tend to assume that the most effective debugging strategy will be top-down, perhaps because we write our programs in that manner. AURAC tackles the problem bottom-up, and in fact never reaches the top.

I studied a group of fellow-tutors of SOLO debugging actual SOLO programs written by our students. The vast majority of those students were initially completely computer-naive, and none had previous experience of SOLO. On the other hand the tutors, having taught the same course over several years, knew full well that the overall purpose of any program would be to complete one of a small range of projects, the same ones every year, but they did not know precisely which one. Under these circumstances some of the tutors displayed clear bottom-up strategies, whilst others were quite happy to debug without initially knowing the program's purpose. They showed that debugging was taking place in essentially three stages:

1. "Skim" the faulty code in much the same way as one might "skim" a newspaper article, looking for salient points. In this case the saliences are syntactic errors, including missing or inappropriate data.
2. Recheck the code looking for errors in higher-level segments of it, here identified as programming "clichés".
3. Check the code again, attempting to follow data flows in order to establish that these "make sense", and identify the effect of sections of the code in terms of the program's overall purpose, if known.

These three strategies were not necessarily carried out in the order given, nor were they necessarily applied to the whole of the faulty code at once.

Each of AURAC's three modules closely model the behaviour of the tutors at times when they could reasonably have been said to be employing one or other of the above strategies. AURAC III in particular sets up a series of expectations as it works through the code, assuming for example that if some triple is NOTEd into the data base then there should at some later point in the code be a corresponding CHECK command, involving the same triple. This strategy will be explained in more detail later; the interesting point to make here is that it was derived directly from the tutors' experimental protocols.

My conclusion from these experiments was that several forms of syntactic debugging strategy are clearly observable in the behaviour of programming experts, and I assume – without a shred of evidence other than the anecdotal – that the same strategies are employed outside the possibly special context of my experiments. Thus, AURAC is in a real sense a cognitive model, albeit a model of the behaviour of a small and select group of human beings: SOLO experts. It was important to me to build a machine whose debugging strategies were human-like, even if it approached its problems in a more step-by-step, organised way than most of us humans do.

The following sections introduce AURAC and discuss its three modules in terms of the levels into which I divide syntactic errors. These levels are somewhat arbitrary, being based as much upon the programming techniques necessary to trap any given error, as upon any connection between the level of error and the student's degree of understanding (see Chapter 1 for a treatment of the main features of SOLO).

2. AURAC

Using SOLO students can and have built cognitive models, sometimes of considerable sophistication, as part of the Open University undergraduate course in Cognitive Psychology. For example they might model the conclusions drawn by Collins and Quillian (1969) during their studies of the hierarchical nature of human memory. The students, being novice programmers, naturally make large numbers of mistakes, from the level of simple typos up to a misunderstanding of the necessary algorithms. The purpose of AURAC is as far as possible to classify these errors and to deal with them automatically. This does not mean that AURAC corrects errors automatically; whilst parts of AURAC are interactive in real time and query the user immediately about any suspected error, other modules are intended to be used as debugging tools, after execution (and failure) of a procedure or program.

AURAC is embedded in an improved re-implementation of SOLO, named MacSOLO because it was implemented in MacLisp. The improvements consist mainly in a larger range of more human error messages, an on-line and intelligent HELP system which can automatically produce help appropriate to whatever the student is doing, a range of syntactic autocheckers including part-word recognition and completion, and a spelling checker (see Chapter 1).

2.1 Simple Syntactic Errors

Simple syntactic errors are those errors which occur at the level of a typing-mistake. They are assumed to be in principle accidental and not to indicate any failure of understanding on the user's part; this may not always be the case, as in the difference between ?WHO/*WHO but as already mentioned the classifications given here are approximate.

Accidental mistakes should not need much explanation, but merely a warning of the fact that a mistake has occurred. The user should know at once how to put it right. MacSOLO's syntax checkers, epitomised by the spelling checker, will interrupt the user in mid-entry to ask, for example, "When you typed ?WHO did you mean *WHO ?". The spelling checker in its final form is highly context-sensitive and is able to ask that exact question intelligently – say, during procedure-definition within SOLO's editor. Incidentally, the HELP system is always at hand for users who can't understand the complaints of the syntax checkers. The above are all implemented as demons: they contain very little knowledge and in most cases have no intelligence. They simply perform the checks they are designed to perform, and carry out no analysis of the code. When subsequently a procedure written in the MacSOLO environment fails to execute correctly, AURAC is called upon to analyse the code during a re-run of the same procedure (or program if the procedure was part of one) under the same input conditions.

2.2 Higher-Level Syntactic Errors: AURAC I

AURAC 1 is in essence a rule-based production system whose rules (there are twelve of them) encapsulate a considerable amount of knowledge about SOLO syntax. In particular it knows about loops, nested loops, conditional forms, and the permissible combinations of these. It takes each line of the user's code in turn, analyses it, and passes it on to the normal run-time MacSOLO interpreter. The results of its analysis are stored for later presentation to the user.

Any error found at the higher syntactic level is recorded at the moment of its discovery in an error frame, a standardised data structure having slots for various items of information concerning any error. Here is a very simple SOLO procedure containing a single error:

```
TO DEMO
10 CHECK FIDO THINKS ?THOUGHT
   10a If present: CONTINUE
   10b If absent: CONTINUE
20 NOTE TONY HAS *THOUGHT
```

MacSOLO would announce the run-time error, and execution would halt:

> "Procedure execution halted in DEMO because of:
> Unbound variable – *THOUGHT has no value on line 20 of DEMO.

The user now calls upon AURAC to debug this procedure. When it has done so, it prints the following further messages:

> "An error on line 10 of DEMO at level 1:
> Your code (CHECK FIDO THINKS ?THOUGHT) is activated and that CHECK-triple does not exist in your data base. So there is also . . .
> An error on line 20 of DEMO at level 1:
> Your code (NOTE TONY HAS *THOUGHT) is activated and that contains an unbound variable. This caused your run-time error.

The terminology of these messages from this module of AURAC may seem odd, but was familiar to the students for whom the system was designed. Notice how two errors (the failure of the binding and the subsequent failed reference) are chained. This shows in the "So there is also . . ." segment between the two main messages. After storing each of the two errors it detects as error frames, AURAC is able to explain that the earlier error caused the later, run-time, error. The error frames will be described in detail later, but first of all I want to discuss AURAC II because it makes use of the same error frames.

2.3 Cliché Analysis: AURAC II

A programming cliché is a fragment of code which performs a recognisable task and which appears repeatedly in the code of independent programmers. A simple SOLO cliché is:

```
10 CHECK A B C
  10a If present: FORGET A B C; CONTINUE
  10b If absent: NOTE A B C; CONTINUE
```

This cliché deletes the triple A B C if it is already present in the data base but writes it into the data base otherwise. It might typically be used to set and reset a data base flag. A cliché is not necessarily confined to one line of code: AURAC can detect eight of the most common SOLO clichés, of up to four lines in length.

It is not necessary that individual lines of a multi-line cliché be contiguous; they can be spread even over several procedures within a program. Detecting them could therefore be an expensive process. AURAC gets partially around this problem by seeking to match code against clichés in two stages: it looks first for sections of code that match cliché "skeletons", and if a match is found it goes on to analyse that section of code in terms of a richer description of the corresponding cliché.

A skeleton may be thought of as a template, or as resembling formal programming constructs such as the Lisp LOOP. That is, the skeleton contains the invariable parts of the cliché, leaving out for example the names of any user-supplied tokens or variables. Here is the skeleton for the above cliché:

```
MAINLINE    :        CHECK
FORSUBLINE           :
A SUBLINE   :        FORGET
B-SUBLINE   :        NOTE
A-CONTROL   :        CONTINUE
B-CONTROL   :        CONTINUE
```

In attempting to find this cliché in the user's code, AURAC would try to match that skeleton against the code, line by line. In order to limit the possibility of combinatorial explosion, it allows only mismatch (say an EXIT control-statement instead of one of the CONTINUEs). If more than one mismatch occurs, AURAC abandons the attempt. In the case of multiline clichés one mismatch is allowed per line.

The skeletons are stored in a library (inevitably called the Cupboard) along with more detailed schematics of the corresponding clichés. When a skeleton matches, AURAC tries for a match between the same segment(s) of code and the schematic. The schematic for the current example is:

```
((CHECK >N >O ?P)
(FORGET <N <O *P & CONTINUE)
(NOTE <N <O *P & CONTINUE))
```

Matching now allows the temporary variables N, O and P to be bound so as to store the arguments to the CHECK instruction, and these values are compared with the arguments to the FORGET and NOTE instructions in order to ensure that the three user-entered triples are the same. Similarly, the matcher can accept ANY to represent tokens or control-statements whose precise form is irrelevant to the cliché. The symbols N, O and P are unrestricted, and may appear in any number of different clichés without confusing the matcher. ?N would mean the same as >N, and <P would

mean the same as *P; the different forms are provided merely to make it easier to write the cliché library.

When a match or very close match is found, AURAC remembers it until all lines of the procedure or program have been analysed. Subsequently it goes through all of the remembered matches again, and where only part of a multi-line cliché has been found it rejects all the matches concerned. Thus, so long as two clichés differ by more than one item per line, they can reliably be distinguished from one another. AURAC always picks the cliché which most corresponds to the user's code.

Here, in code form, is a four-line cliché which replaces one data base triple with another, the second being inferred from the first:

```
TO DEM1
10 CHECK FIDO LIKES ?V
   10a If present: CONTINUE
   10b If absent: EXIT
20 CHECK *V BROTHER *P
   20a If present: CONTINUE
   20b If absent: EXIT
30 FORGET FIDO LIKES *V
40 NOTE FIDO LIKES *P
```

Suppose now that the user had inadvertently typed *V instead of *P on line 40. The typical message from this module of AURAC would be:

> "Your procedure DEM1:
> Lines 10 of DEM1, 20 of DEM1, 30 of DEM1 and 40 of DEM1
> seem to be intended to remove one triple from your
> data base and to replace it with another,
> but on line 40 of DEM1 you have written *V
> where perhaps you meant to write *P.

This message is composed of canned fragments, AURAC has no English-language abilities. The procedure name is given along with the number of each code-line in the cliché because, as mentioned, naive users may spread clichés across procedure boundaries within a program. This is particularly true when they are not aware that what they have written is a cliché!

Other lines of code might well have appeared in the definition of DEM1, interspersed with the lines comprising the cliché, hence the need for line numbers, which are not part of SOLO itself but are added by AURAC.

2.4 Error Frames

The error frame recording any error found at the syntactic or cliché level is simply a data-structure with named slots. There are seventeen slots in any frame, and a description of these now follows.

Cause/Effects. When an attempted variable-binding fails, as when the line CHECK FIDO LIKES ?V is executed in the absence of any corresponding data base triple, that fact is temporarily stored in AURAC's working memory, and an error frame is created. Later reference to the same (unbound) variable causes a second error frame to be created, and the data in working memory allows the two errors to be related in a cause/effect chain. These two slots record the existence of any such chain, for later report to the user.

Type. AURAC 1 can detect thirteen distinguishable errors in looping/conditional constructs. Each of these is a type, and when one of them is found in the user's code it is recorded in this slot as an error message segment such as "CHECK triple does not exist in your data base".

Unreached. If a control-statement error occurs such that the user's code contains unreachable lines or subprocedures, their line-numbers and procedure-names are recorded here.

Evaluated/Code. These slots are merely for completeness in the subsequent printouts, so that the message-printers can tell the user how SOLO evaluated any particular line of code, where that line contains variables, and where in the light of any earlier errors that code can be evaluated. For example, the Code slot might contain CHECK FIDO ISA ?WHAT whilst the Evaluated slot contained CHECK FIDO ISA DOG.

Line/Procedure. The data here identifies the line of user code to which the current error frame refers.

Recursion/Altprocs/Altnodes. These slots hold the information necessary to explain endless recursion. Remember that in MacSOLO twenty levels of recursion are allowed: any excess is treated as an error. If the error arises its Type will be "uses up more than twenty LEVELS", which MacSOLO users will understand when it subsequently appears in AURAC's report. The *Recursion* slot will contain one of five sub-types, each of them again being a message segment:

1. "Your chain of data base nodes is too long."
2. "Your series of subprocedure calls is too long."

3. "Self-recursion."
4. "Data loop."
5. "Procedural loop."

AURAC calls itself recursively to handle subprocedure calls, and maintains its own push-down stack of data relevant to itself. Amongst this data are records of each subprocedure call and its arguments. When the recursion limit is reached, the data allows distinctions to be made between the five subtypes:

1. An otherwise correct recursive procedure may run past the twenty-level limit. For example a recursive procedure may follow a chain of data base nodes; if the chain consists of more than twenty nodes, this sub-type of endless recursion is signalled.
2. Subprocedures may be nested more than twenty deep, which of course again infringes the limit of twenty recursive levels.
3. When AURAC detects the same procedure with the same arguments recurring at sequential levels, it assumes a procedural error in the user's code. In the unique case where a recursive procedure follows a data base chain containing only JOHN KISSES JOHN, the difference cannot be detected by AURAC (see e.g. in Chapter 7).
4. Sometimes a procedure and its arguments will be repeated identically after a series of intervening calls to the same procedure. This would happen if a recursive procedure were applied to a data base containing circular data, as in JOHN KISSES MARY . . . <a chain of several other triples> . . . LIZ KISSES JOHN.
5. Finally, a whole sequence of procedures and their arguments may be repeated.

Thus, sub-types 1 and 4 will be accompanied by extra data in the *Altnodes* slot to identify the data base nodes concerned, and sub-types 2 and 5 will carry information in the *Altprocs* slot specifying the offending procedure-names.

Level. Information as to the recursive level at which the current error occurred is derived from AURAC's working memory and stored here.

Cliché. The name of the cliché concerned if the current error has been identified as a cliché error. This name is purely an internal marker, and is never shown to the user.

Altlines. Line-numbers and procedure names of all lines comprising the current cliché, if any.

Word/Symbol. Cliché errors are atomic. That is to say, AURAC suggests patches consisting of only a single word of code. The *Word* slot holds the user's (incorrect) version; the *Symbol* slot holds the correct version inferred by AURAC.

Announce. The boolean value of the contents of this slot specifies whether or not this error frame needs to be passed to the message printers. Where only some of the lines of a multi-line cliché are found in the code, the error-frames associated with those lines will be redundant and so need not be announced.

An important feature of this style of representation is that error frames created during early analysis may later be modified, or discarded altogether, during analysis of later code. Once AURAC has completed its analysis and so has fully refined its remaining error frames, it passes the whole set to its message printers, which read the error frames and output messages accordingly.

2.5 Data Flow Analysis: AURAC III

Data flow analysis involves the setting up of expectations, and their subsequent satisfaction. The result conceptually resembles a flow-chart. For example, a CHECK instruction involving a wildcard (SOLO variable) sets up the expectation that the variable will be referred to again later in the code. Similarly, if there is a call to a user-defined procedure, there is the expectation that the procedure's formally declared parameters will be referred to as execution proceeds. In either case the expected items (bound variable, formal parameter) can be equated to the cause of the expectation (call to CHECK, argument to the procedure call). AURAC keeps track of both expectations and satisfactions so that at any point during analysis a variable or parameter can be traced back to the point at which it entered the program (often via the original top-level call).

Ideally, it should not be the case that a SOLO program makes any permanent changes to the data base. A correct SOLO program normally consists of a SETUP procedure to establish initial data base conditions, then the program proper, and finally a CLEANUP procedure to restore the data base to normal. Therefore, each NOTE instruction sets up two expectations: that the NOTEd triple will be referred to later via a call to CHECK, and that there will be a call to FORGET involving the same triple. However, it is perfectly legal SOLO usage to put the CLEANUP procedure before the program proper, and the SETUP procedure at the end (messy, but legal). Because of this it is possible for the FORGET expected by a NOTE lexically to precede the NOTE itself. This is where AURAC's method is superior to symbolic evaluation techniques such as those of Laubsch and Eisenstadt (1981; see Chapter 9): the latter would derive the wrong overall net effect from such an inversion of the expected order of operations.

Of course, it is not actually illegal to write a SOLO program which does make permanent changes to the data base – for example a simple model of learning would need to do so. For this reason any imbalances which AURAC finds in its records of expectations and satisfactions are merely pointed out to the user, and are not counted as errors. Typical message segments from this module might be:

> ". . . and also the triple NOTEd on line 20 of DEMO is never CHECKed. . . . and also the triple NOTEd on line 20 of DEMO is never FORGOTten."

Expectations are placed on a stack as they are generated, in a standard form which specifies the place (procedure-name, line-number) where the expectation arose together with a descriptive token such as the word NOTE or the name of a newly-bound variable. When this expectation is later found to be satisfied in the code (in the case of NOTE, as already mentioned, it is possible for the satisfaction to have been detected previously and so to be already present, waiting to be expected!) it is deleted from the expectations stack, but a copy of the same information is placed on the satisfactions stack. A bound variable or a formal parameter may change its name as it is passed into a subprocedure, or if it occurs along with a wildcard in a loop or conditional triple. Therefore, the satisfaction just placed on the stack also carries a note as to the variable's current name. At the end of its analysis, AURAC simply reports on any left-over expectations. The information recorded in the satisfactions stack can also be put to good use, since AURAC is able to look down it so as to trace the execution-path of any particular item of data. Notice that AURAC is not concerned with the value of any variable or parameter: this last part of its analysis remains lexical, (i.e. syntactic).

2.6 Canonical Algorithms

Bringing in algorithms does necessarily violate the assertion made earlier that AURAC has no need to know the purpose of a program in order to analyse it. For this reason the ability to detect algorithms was always seen (by me) as an add-on extra to AURAC, but the technique is nonetheless interesting.

In the kind of programs written by users of SOLO, it is very often the case that one line of code corresponds directly to one step in the written algorithm. For example, the algorithm for two-column subtraction could be (see also Chapter 9):

1. Subtract the bottom "units" digit from the upper "units" digit. If this gives a positive result, go to 4. Else go to 2.
2. Add ten to the upper "units" digit. Go to 3.
3. Subtract 1 from the upper "tens" digit. Go to 1.
4. Subtract the lower "tens" digit from the upper "tens' digit.

The equivalent SOLO program consists of four lines of code in two procedures, each line corresponding exactly to one of the above steps, including a recursive call for step 3:

```
TO SUBTRACT /BT/ /BU/ /TT/ /TU/
10 CHECK /TU/ /BU/ ?ANSU
  10a If present: CONTINUE
  10b If absent: BORROW /BT/ /BU/ /TT/ /TU/; EXIT
20 CHECK /TT/ /BT/ ?ANST
  20a If present: PRINT "Answer is:" *ANST *ANSU; EXIT
  20b If absent: EXIT

TO BORROW /BT/ /BU/ /TT/ /TU/
10 CHECK /TU/ PLUS10 ?NEWTU
  10a If present: CONTINUE
  10b If absent: EXIT
20 CHECK /TT/ 1 ?NEWTT
  20a If present: SUBTRACT /BT/ /BU/ *NEWTT *NEWTU: EXIT
  20b If absent: EXIT
```

The lines of SUBTRACT represent steps 1 and 4 of the algorithm, and the lines of BORROW correspond to steps 2 and 3. The number-bonds necessary for subtraction of single columns are present in the data base (e.g. the triple 7 4 3 represents the fact that seven minus four equals three).

AURAC treats algorithms much as it treats clichés, and is able to detect the individual steps regardless of how large and rambling the program itself might be. It does this by combining the knowledge stored in an algorithm library with its data flow analysis. Library entries are very similar to cliché schematics and also contain variables to which to bind the user's tokens:

```
(subtract      (check /tu/ /bu/ ?ansu)
               (check /tu/ plus10 ?newtu)
               (check /tt/ 1 ?newtt)
               (check /tt/ /bt/ ?anst)
```

Whatever form the original (input) data may take as program execution proceeds – bound variables/parameters or components of data base triples – there must at some point in a subtraction program be a line of code which contains, say, the equivalents of both digits in the units column in the format necessary for them to be compared with the number bonds in the data base: CHECK /TU/ /BU/ ?ANSU. AURAC's usefulness here is to recognise this line as an algorithmic step.

Provided that it can detect the above four lines in the user's code, and regardless of whatever else may also be there, AURAC can say that in some sense the program is correct (i.e. it does carry out the steps of the algorithm). An expert could write a program which satisfied AURAC but which subtracted incorrectly – for example by including lines which temporarily altered the stored number-bonds – but it would still be fair to say that the subtraction process itself was properly coded. It might also occur to an unfriendly user to try to alter the value of one of the SOLO variables directly, for example by adding CHECK *NEWTT 5 ?NEWTT; but this causes an error to be signalled by MacSOLO, which will not allow such an entry on the grounds, for its novice users, that that would be a clear mistake. In practice, AURAC can spot algorithmic equivalents in users' code over a range of different types of program.

In the above SUBTRACTION example, there is no need for the recursive call. The code of SUBTRACT could have repeated in BORROW with no loss of effectiveness or correctness. Therefore, AURAC has to allow for (to have in its library) algorithm variants. These cannot be generated automatically by AURAC, and must be entered by hand.

Combining the detected algorithm-lines with data-flow analysis enables AURAC to ask for example:

> "Was /A/ in the title line of SUBTRACT intended to represent the digit on the top row, tens column? (Y or N)"

If the user's answer is Yes, the equivalence between the user's token /A/ and the algorithm's token /TT/ is established. This may in turn allow AURAC to establish equivalence between the entire line of user code and, say, line 3 of the algorithm. It is not in fact always necessary to ask the questions: the range of likely user tokens is limited, and variable-names such as /TOPTEN/ are in fact detected by a "typical mnemonic variable-name recogniser". When AURAC succeeds in identifying lines of code corresponding to all of the lines in the algorithm, it announces that the program will achieve a certain objective (two-column subtraction in this case):

> "Your program will SUBTRACT."

If one or more of the expected lines is missing, AURAC poins this out to the user:

"There is no line in your program which repays the borrowed ten."

3. CONCLUSIONS AND CRITIQUE

My conclusions have to be drawn in today's context, rather than being merely a repetition of what I thought of AURAC at the end of 1983. It seems obvious now, though it did not then, that in an ideal world all possible syntactic analysers/debuggers would be built into any worthwhile programming environment. If one could rely on any program to be free of syntactic errors, then the task of debugging would be greatly simplified and speeded up (although the average bug would take longer to track down!). Many modern computing environments – and here the Macintosh™ operating system deserves a special mention – use icons, office metaphors, templates or intelligent help systems in an effort to reduce syntactic errors at all levels to a minimum.

To my mind, AURAC remains interesting for three reasons. One is that it categorises errors in terms of what can or should be done about them. This happens to correspond fairly closely with the intuitive idea that the more complex an error, the more serious the student's misunderstanding – and, of course, vice versa.

The second reason is that it demonstrates the possibility of cleaning programs of syntactic errors, leaving only conceptual errors to be handled. One of the most time-wasting and frustrating aspects of learning to program, both for the student and the teacher, is the constant necessity of hunting down obscure syntactic mistakes, and to be able to do this automatically would be as great a boon as the spelling checker is in a word-processing environment.

And the third reason is the remarkable degree to which AURAC is able to criticise and to suggest patches for a program, without any need to know the program's purpose. The clear distinction it makes between syntactic errors, which can be expected to lessen with practice, and conceptual errors which may need a tutor's help, is a very important one for both novices and those who teach them.

In practice, AURAC did ask its users at the start of its analysis which of the available programming projects they were attempting. However, this information was used solely to select the relevant parts of the algorithm library. Exhaustive matching of every code line against every algorithm line, as in the cliché-recognition system of AURAC II, turned out to be too computationally expensive. However, the actual matching is in both cases essentially a parallel process carried out on a serial machine. The expense of AURAc's approach is a criticism of the available equipment rather than of AURAC itself.

An important aspect of AURAC, which may be considered a failing, is that it only works on code which is already nearly correct. One cannot type just any old junk into it and expect to get a perfect program out. AURAC's design concept was that it was one step beyond MacSOLO: the latter would more or less force a user to type a nearly-correct program, and then AURAC would do the rest.

Also, it has to be admitted that the add-on algorithmic analysis worked only over a limited range of pre-defined programming topics. It would obviously be impossible to expand the algorithm library to include all algorithms and variants for all possible SOLO programs. Outside a teaching environment this ability on AURAC's part is probably useless.

4. FUTURE WORK

As mentioned at the beginning of this chapter, AURAC's outputs were purely textual. During its design phases, however, I visualised it in highly diagrammatic terms, drawing coloured lines on sections of code to show expectations and their subsequent satisfactions, for example, and treating each user-defined procedure as a separate, self-contained box. The most abidingly useful principle of AURAC is that it presents debugging information strictly in terms of the code which the user has written; students learning to program in, say, Common Lisp often complain that its basic error-traps supply messages which do not seem to bear any relation to the actual bug. But AURAC talks directly about "your code on line N of FOO", and does not inflict even more load on its users by talking in terms of its own internal representations (see also Chapters 2 and 6 on this point).

Now that high-definition graphical representations of program execution are possible, a new implementation of AURAC would provide very different-looking outputs, able to show the whole of a program's execution (up to the detection of a bug) rather than a series of canned verbal comments concerning the details of individual lines of code. A series of tools would allow the user to inspect these details at will, at any point in the displayed execution. I am currently working on such an environment for Common Lisp, but the basic principles of AURAC have not been forgotten.

REFERENCES

Collins, A. M. & Quillian, M. (1969). Retrieval time from semantic memory. *Journal of Verbal Learning & Verbal Behaviour*, *8*, 407–423.

Laubsch, J. & Eisenstadt, M. (1981). Domain specific debugging aids for novice programmers. *Proceedings of the Seventh International Joint Conference on Artificial Intelligence*. Vancouver, B.C.: Canada 964–969.

11 Plan Diagrams as the Basis for Understanding and Debugging Pascal Programs*

Rudi Lutz
School of Cognitive and Computer Sciences, Sussex University, Sussex, England

1. INTRODUCTION

The research described here aims to create an intelligent system capable of aiding programmers in the task of debugging programs. As computer hardware becomes cheaper the cost of producing and maintaining software is becoming the major factor in most applications. In addition, the decreasing costs and increasing power of hardware means that projects are becoming increasingly more ambitious and complex, and hence more error-prone and indeed there appears to be a complexity barrier past which it is very difficult if not impossible to go (Winograd, 1973). It is, therefore, becoming increasingly necessary to use the computer itself to aid the programmer in producing correct software. One approach to this is the attempt to build fully-automated, program-synthesis systems (Barstow, 1979; Manna & Waldinger, 1979). These would only require the programmer to provide a very high-level specification of what the program is to do and the synthesis system would automatically generate a correct program to carry out the programmer's intentions. Although much interesting work has been done on automatic program synthesis it seems unlikely that really usable systems will become available in the near future.

An approach much more likely to lead to a working system in the foreseeable future is that of the "programmer's apprentice" (Hewitt & Smith, 1975; Rich, 1981; Rich & Schrobe, 1978; Waters, 1982). Such a system has a large amount of knowledge about programming. For instance

*This work was supported in part by SERC/ALVEY Grant No. GR/D/57355-IKBS/156.

it knows the various standard ways of sorting a list numbers. It also has knowledge about common data structures and implementation techniques. The system can then use this knowledge to relieve the programmer of many of the details associated with implementing various algorithms. However, it would expect the programmer to supply the high-level algorithm to be used. It could also check code given by the programmer for consistency with what it knows.

An intelligent debugging system is more modest in its aims than a full programmer's apprentice. However it is clear that a debugging system needs to be able to understand and (possibly) suggest edits to a program in exactly the same way as a programmer's apprentice system. One can therefore quite easily imagine enlarging such a debugging system to a full programmer's apprentice.

2. A CATEGORISATION OF BUGS

It is possible to distinguish several different types of error that can occur in programs, and several authors have attempted to categorise these. A new taxonomy will be presented here which includes some of the categories and ideas from previous work. Before doing this, however, a brief description of previous taxonomies will be given for comparative purposes.

The main distinction underlying the different taxonomies is between those motivated by an interest (i) in the psychological processes which cause programmers to make errors, and (ii) in automatically identifying and repairing the errors, although there is of course some overlap between these. The work of Youngs (1974), and Shneiderman (1980) typifies the former, while that of Goldstein (1974) and Miller and Goldstein (1977) typifies the latter. The work of the Cognition and Programming Project at Yale (Johnson, Soloway, Cutler, & Draper, 1983; Spohrer et al., 1985) falls into both camps to some extent but, as their work is primarily aimed at novice programmers and deals with the misconceptions novices have, it does not fully address the kinds of errors more expert programmers make.

Youngs (1974) classifies programming errors into syntactic, semantic, logical, and clerical errors. Syntactic errors are errors in the use of the syntax of the programming language and are easily detected by compilers. Semantic errors occur when a program requires the computer to do something either impossible or contradictory (e.g. read from a closed file). Normally such errors would give rise to run-time error messages. Logical errors occur when the program is a valid program which runs to completion without any obvious errors but the program does not in fact do what it is supposed to. Clerical errors are due to such things as mistyping, or using a text editor carelessly. The distinction between semantic and logical errors could form the basis for a debugging system (e.g. an expert system using run-time error message information) but, as will be seen later, the definition of semantic errors can be widened to encompass many of the bugs Youngs would classify as logical, leading to a clearer relationship between the kinds of bug in a program, and the techniques needed in order to debug it.

Shneiderman's (1980) taxonomy depends much more on a psychological model of the programming process. In his model, programmers begin by forming a mental model of the problem and its solution (the internal semantics), and then bring general programming knowledge, and knowledge of the specific programming language being used, to convert this internal description into an actual program to solve the problem. Shneiderman also makes the distinction between syntactic and semantic errors, and also assumes that syntactic errors are easily caught by compilers. In his taxonomy semantic errors include all other kinds of bug that can occur in programs, and he subdivides these into two further categories. The first of these corresponds to errors in the conversion process from the internal semantics to the actual program, and the second to an incorrect conversion from the problem to the internal semantics. Shneiderman points out that the first type of error is much more easily debugged than the second, which may involve a complete redesign of the solution, or of the programming strategy.

Goldstein's (1974) bug taxonomy is based on a theory of programming as a planning activity. This views programming as a process of finding a plan (a sequence of steps) which achieves some goal. Each step in the program may in turn have prerequisites that need to be true before the step can be carried out, thus giving rise to subgoals that need to be planned for. Under this view several kinds of bugs can occur. The first of these is what Goldstein terms a *linear main-step failure*, and occurs when a sub-plan in the program fails to achieve the goals it is supposed to, independently of the other steps in the program. This kind of bug can be fixed by repairing this sub-plan in isolation. The second type of bug is what he terms a *preparation error*. This corresponds to the situation when the sub-plan concerned does solve its goals under certain assumptions about the program state on entry to the sub-plan, but these assumptions are not necessarily always true. To fix this kind of bug it is necessary to insert a new step which sets up the conditions assumed by the faulty sub-plan. The third kind of bug is what Goldstein terms a *non-linear main step failure*. This type of bug arises from non-linear interaction between sub-plans, and in general is very hard to fix. Sometimes this kind of bug can be fixed by suitably interleaving the steps of the sub-plans, or by adding extra steps to one or both of the sub-plans which are not strictly necessary to achieve the goals the sub-plan is designed to achieve, but which are there to eliminate the unwanted interaction. In addition, Goldstein distinguishes between what he terms *theory bugs*, and what he terms *procedure bugs*. Theory bugs correspond to the case where the initial goals as derived from the problem statement are in error, often because of misunderstandings about the problem domain. Procedure bugs are bugs in the implementation of a program to solve the problem. All the above types of bugs are special cases of procedure bugs. To fix theory bugs an automatic system would also have to have knowledge of the domain, not just general programming knowledge.

Miller and Goldstein's (1977) taxonomy has much in common with that just described. They also view the programming process as a planning activity. However, they provide a planning grammar which specifies how plans may be combined to provide higher-level plans. Given their planning grammar, they then distinguish between syntactic, semantic, and pragmatic bugs. Miller and Goldstein use the term *syntactic* to describe the case where the basic plan grammer is violated. For instance, the grammar may specify that a particular plan needs a particular type of sub-plan at a particular place in a plan, and if this is missing then there is a syntactic error. Note that this is not the same as an error in the use of the syntax of a particular programming language. It really falls into one of the categories that Youngs or Shneiderman would term semantic or logical. Semantic bugs, according to Goldstein and Miller, occur when a syntactically (in their sense) optional component is missing from a plan, but is required by the nature of the problem the program is attempting to solve. These bugs fall roughly under Youngs' notion of logical error since they give rise to a fully functioning program which simply does not do what it is supposed to. Finally, pragmatic bugs occur when an inappropriate choice (with respect to the problem) of plan has been made. Again, this type of bug falls under Youngs' notion of logical error.

We use the taxonomy shown in Fig. 11.1. The simplest distinction it makes is that between syntactic and semantic errors. Syntactic errors are, as we have seen, easily caught by compilers. Semantic errors correspond to the case where the program in some sense does not do what it is supposed to. To arrive at this taxonomy it has been assumed that programmers, when confronted with a problem, come up with some sort of solution, or high-level design, corresponding to Shneiderman's internal semantics. Now there are two cases – either their design is correct, or it is not (cf. earlier taxonomies). In either case they now attempt to implement their design as a program. In the case where their design is indeed correct but they mis-implement it, there are two types of error that can occur:

Type 1. These errors manifest themselves as internal inconsistencies of one kind or another between parts of the program. Simple examples are trying to read from a closed device, or passing an unsorted list through to

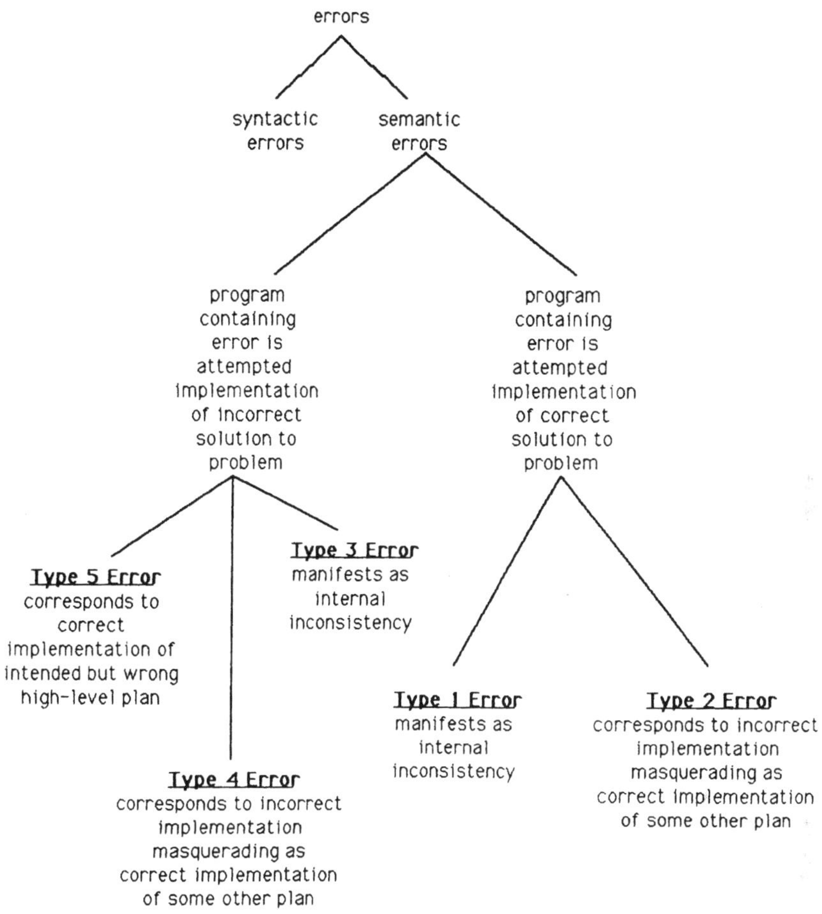

FIG. 11.1. A taxonomy of errors.

some piece of code implementing an algorithm which expects a sorted list as input.

Type 2. Programs containing (only) this type of error manifest themselves as correct (internally consistent) programs for some other problem. An example might be if the programmer was trying to write some code to sort some numbers into ascending order, but used "<" instead of ">" so that the program sorted into descending order. The code would be a perfectly valid solution to a different problem from the one intended.

On the other hand, if the programmer's high-level plan does not in fact solve the problem, there are again several ways in which errors can manifest themselves:

Type 3. These errors also manifest themselves as internal inconsistencies in the program. The programmer is trying to implement the design (even though it will not turn out to be the solution to the problem) and has made similar kinds of errors to those of type 1. Thus the design contains a theory bug, but type 1 procedure bugs have also been made.

Type 4. These errors are similar to those of type 2. The programmer has inadvertently managed to implement a different plan from the one intended. In this case the design contains a theory bug, but type 2 procedure bugs have also been made.

Type 5. This corresponds to the case where programmers actually implement their proposed (faulty) solution correctly.

Notice that these error types are in increasing order of difficulty with respect to their location and correction. Type 1 and type 3 errors are in some sense errors whatever the purpose of the program. Because of this it seems reasonable to try to locate these types of errors completely automatically. If it is assumed that the programs being debugged are not by novices, then it is likely that the program will be a reasonable attempt at an implementation of the programmer's intentions, and hence if a program contains only type 1 errors then it can quite possibly be debugged automatically into a correct program. At worst automatic debugging may turn the program into one with a type 2 error (which may or may not have been there initially). Programs with type 2 errors can be debugged by interacting with the programmer. This is because the programmer knows the intended high-level plan and hence should be able to give information about what various parts of the program should be doing. In contrast, although type 3 errors can also be automatically detected, correction will leave a program with type 4 or type 5 errors. Again the type 4 errors may be corrected by interacting with the programmer, but only to a program with a type 5 error. Type 5 errors will be very hard to fix, even for skilled programmers. This is because the program will not do what it is supposed to, in the sense that it does not solve the original problem, but all parts of the program do what the programmer expects since the program is a correct implementation of the design.

3. SOURCES OF KNOWLEDGE FOR PROGRAM UNDERSTANDING AND DEBUGGING

In order to debug a computer program it is necessary to develop an understanding of the program and to use this understanding to pinpoint the places where what the program actually does differ from what one would expect knowing the purpose of the program. It is helpful to think of an intelligent debugging system as an experienced programmer whose advice may be sought when one is faced with a bug one does not understand in a program. Such an expert programmer will use several techniques and sources of information to help understand and debug the program. These include the following:

Plan recognition – this is the technique where by recognising the form of all or part of a program one can recognise what it does (i.e. this is "programming cliche" recognition).
Symbolic evaluation of a piece of code – this involves actually analysing code to see what it does.
Reasoning backwards from the manifestation of an error to its source.

In applying these techniques the programming expert will use information from the following sources:

Interaction with the program's author.
Meaningful variable names.
Comments in the program.
Program segmentation into functions and procedures.
Data input to and output from the program.
Run-time error messages.
Trace output.

Plan recognition and symbolic evaluation are used by the expert to gain an understanding of the program. This means that the programmer would then be able to:

Describe the program in terms of some high-level plan of which the program is an implementation.
Describe how the various parts of the program are implementations of sub-plans.
Describe how these sub-plans interact to achieve the overall goal (plan) of the program.

Conversely, if programmers can do these three things one would then say they have an understanding of the program, and it is in this sense that the term "understanding" will be used from now on.

It is clear from this definition that the process of plan recognition is really the key to program understanding. When experts look at a piece of code which, say, sorts a set of numbers, they do not try known plans at random until one is found which fits. The process of plan recognition is clearly guided by clues, and these clues come from the sources of information listed above. In particular, things like the use of a procedure name "sort" should suggest that as a first attempt one should look at all the methods one knows for sorting. Obviously, program comments, information supplied by the program writer as answers to questions about the program, and the way the program is segmented can all provide useful information to guide the process of plan recognition.

However it is possible that some pieces of code might not match any plans known to the expert. In this case the expert would almost certainly try a process of symbolic evaluation to try and see what that piece of code does. It may then become apparent that the piece of code does perform some known function, albeit in a different fashion to previously-encountered methods. One can then say that the expert programmer has again recognised the plan for which this code was an implementation, the only difference being that this time the plan was recognised by evaluating the code rather than just matching against a library of previously known plans.

When debugging programs there are essentially two processes used by expert programmers. The first of these is really an application of the process of program understanding described above. If, while attempting to understand the program, the expert finds examples of code which almost match known plans then an error has almost certainly been located, particularly if this near-match occurs where there is some inconsistency in the use of known plans. In this case, edits can be suggested which would correct the plan. Alternatively, a piece of code may be recognised as the implementation of some plan but this plan does not achieve what the program's author says it should. In this case code which implements the desired plan can possibly be suggested. At the very least the mismatch can be pointed out. This debugging method can be used to locate errors of types 1 and 3 in programs.

The other debugging method uses the remaining sources of information available to the programmer (i.e. the data input to and output from the program, system generated run-time error messages, and trace information). The first debugging method which uses plan recognition alone is really only used by programmers on smallish programs. When debugging larger and more complex programs the advice-giving expert will use the input/output data and trace information together with information from the program's author and/or the run-time error messages to locate the places in the code an error first became apparent. The expert would then attempt to reason backwards from this place to the place in the code which originally caused the error. This reasoning backwards process is really one of isolating only that code which could have affected the place where the error became apparent (Weiser, 1982), and one can then reason about this subsection of the code using all the techniques of plan recognition. Expert programmers will often assume parts of the code to be correct and reason about the rest of the code using these assumptions. Only if the error cannot be found, or if some piece of evidence leads to a contradiction will these parts of the code be examined in detail. In addition, certain run-time error messages will suggest very specific errors to experts which can be found and corrected quickly.

4. THE INTELLIGENT PASCAL DEBUGGER PROJECT (STAGE I)

Work is currently in progress on building an intelligent debugging system (IDS) for Pascal programs. The long term aim of this research (Lutz, 1984a) is to build a system capable of helping the programmer to locate and fix errors of types 1 to 4 in programs. IDS will attempt to integrate all the previously described methods and sources of information rather in the way an expert programmer does. However, the work described here is an initial attempt at a debugging system using only the basic techniques of plan matching and symbolic evaluation (Lutz, 1984b) to arrive at a high-level description of what the program (or part of it) does and how it does it. Where logical inconsistencies (type 1 or type 3 errors) are found suggestions can be made as to how to correct the code. At the moment no attempt has been made to use information implicit in variable names and so on. Despite this these techniques are powerful enough to duplicate the capabilities of other debugging systems (Johnson, 1986; Lukey, 1978; Soloway, Ehrlich, Bonar, & Greenspan, 1982) for Pascal programs, except for where these systems make use of problem specific knowledge. More importantly, the power and generality of the representation methods used enables IDS to deal with programs involving such things as recursive and non-recursive procedure calls, value and reference parameter passing, records and pointers, as well as the full range of data types available in Pascal. Thus, IDS can deal with programs involving dynamic data structures implemented using pointers and records, and indeed an example of this will be described shortly. IDS attempts, where possible, to be language independent so as to facilitate the application of any techniques developed to other programming languages. In doing this it draws heavily on the work of Rich, Schrobe, and Waters (Rich, 1981; Rich & Schrobe, 1978; Waters, 1978; 1979; 1982) whose development of the Programmer's Apprentice project at MIT represents a major attempt at representing the knowledge underlying programming. To a lesser extent it draws on the work of Eisenstadt and Laubsch (1980 and Chapter 9) whose work on an intelligent debugger for SOLO programs bears some similarities to that described here.

4.1 Surface Plans

As in the MIT work, the program is represented not by its source code but by a surface plan. This is essentially a representation of the program in terms of its control and data flow. By representing this graphically we can think of the surface plan as a control and data flow graph. For example Fig. 11.2 shows the surface plan corresponding to the following code:

```
n:=1;
while n <=10 do
            begin
                  writeln(n);
                  n:=n+1;
            end;
```

In this diagram, control flow is represented by hashed arrows and data flow is represented by ordinary unhashed arrows. Basic operations such as applying a function (@function) are shown by boxes with the operation indicated inside. Tests are shown as boxes, with the relevant relation (e.g. ">") or predicate (e.g. =nil) indicated and the YES/NO subpartitions of the box indicating which way control flow will go, depending on the result of that test. Data flow between two such boxes indicates that data values produced by one are used as inputs to the other. Control flow between two boxes indicates that the first box is to have its action performed before the action corresponding to the second box. We will adopt the convention, however, that control flows will not be shown when they are actually implied by the data flows. One way of interpreting such boxes is to regard each box as being a processor in its own right. Such a processor is activated when it has received input on all its incoming data flow arcs, and it has also received a control flow token on its incoming control flow arc if it has one. When it is activated it outputs suitable values on its output data flow arcs and outputs a control flow token on its output control flow arc if it exists. These values and tokens then pass along the arcs to activate other boxes. Where an arc subdivides the value on the arc is transmitted along all branches of the arc. Processors corresponding to tests generate a control flow token on either the YES output or the NO output depending on the values of the inputs to the test and the actual test applied. The reason for applying tests to data is generally so that one can generate different values depending on the result of the test and then use these values later in the program. To enable later processors to make use of whichever values are actually generated after a test we need somehow to make all of these available as potential inputs to other processors. This is done using join-outputs boxes which reconnect the separate data flows corresponding to divergent control flow routes at tests.

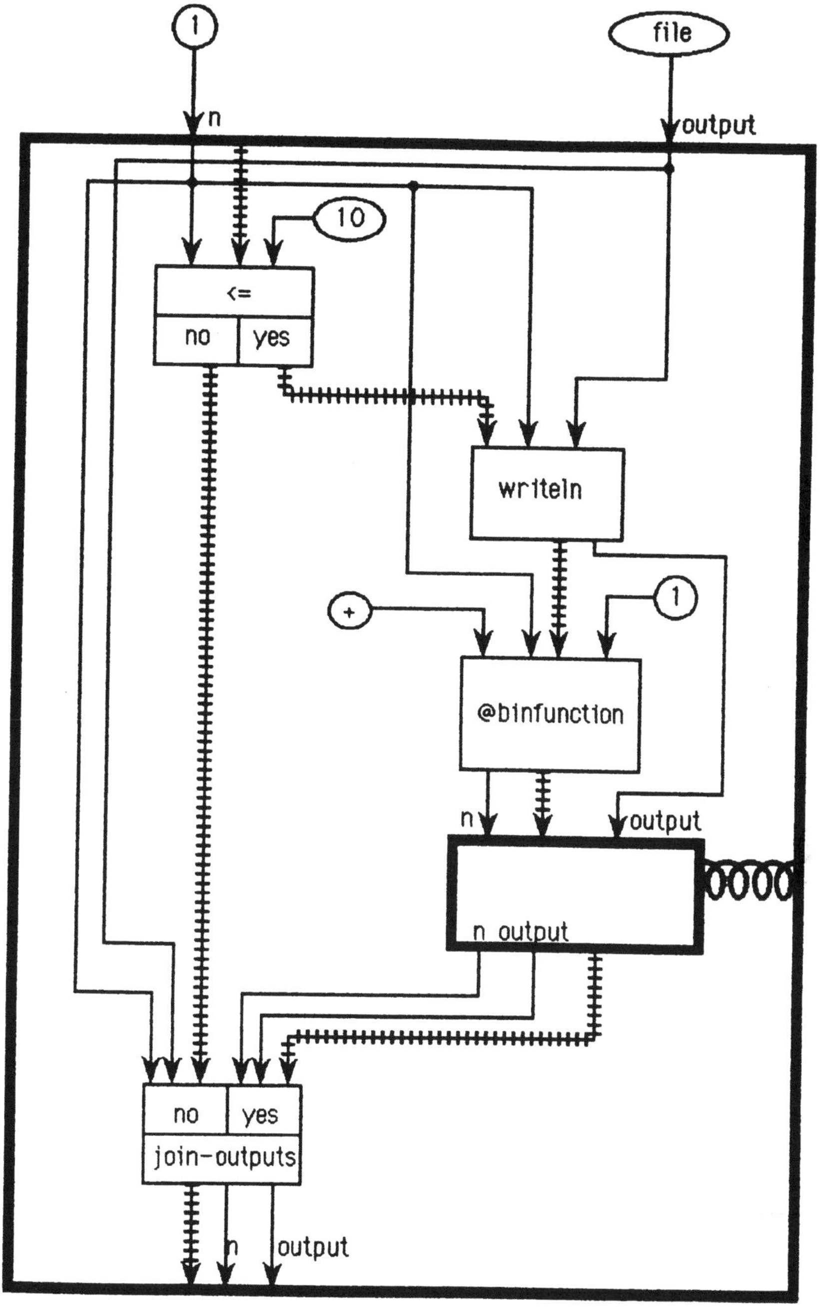

FIG. 11.2. A surface plan.

Program segments are also indicated by boxes. However these boxes perform a more complicated operation than basic ones. Subsegment nesting is shown by the nesting of boxes. Looping constructs have been translated to a recursive representation. For example, a **while** statement of the form:

while condition **do** action;

will be interpreted as if it were just a procedure call:

loop(......)

where the procedure loop was defined by:

```
procedure loop(......);
begin
    if condition then
                begin
                    action;
                    loop(......);
                end
end;
```

This has the advantage of removing cycles from the surface plan thus making subsequent analysis easier. An example of this representation of loops can be seen in the **whileloop** segment (Fig. 11.2) which contains a nested occurrence of itself. This kind of recursive subsegment nesting is indicated by a spiral line connecting the outer segment to its inner recursive copy. Labels corresponding to variable names in the original Pascal program have been attached to the data flow arcs as an aid to understanding the diagram and in order to enable IDS to converse with uses and suggest edits in terms of the variable names with which they are familiar.

Such surface plans can then form the basis of a hierarchical system of representations of the program. To go from a lower level to a higher level in such a hierarchy it is necessary to recognise some sub-graph at the lower-level representation as performing some known function. The subgraph can then be replaced by a segment quite explicitly representing the function performed. In this way the program is progressively represented by higher and higher level segments, until at the top level the program is represented by a simple graph (possibly a single segment) performing the overall function of the program. Using this and the technique of temporal abstraction (Waters, 1978; 1979; Rich, 1981) which enables one to reason about a set of sequentially generated items as a single collection it is possible to recognise that Program 1 (see Table 11.1, p. 262) reads numbers from the terminal (or a file), sorts them into ascending order using a list structure, and then outputs the sorted set of numbers.

4.2 The Plan Library

In order to do the hierarchical recognition just described a library of commonly occurring programming clichés (whole algorithms and even code fragments) is needed, stored in the same plan diagram formalism. The present system uses Rich's (1981) plan library, with some new additions. In principle, such a plan library can be used in two ways:

1. To enable programmers to specify their code at a high level in terms of plans in the library, leaving the system to actually implement the code in the desired language.
2. To analyse code written by a human programmer giving the system a high-level understanding of what the code does and how it does it; in terms of what the overall goal of the code is, and which parts of the code achieve which sub-goals.

Although there has been some success at the first of these uses (Waters, 1982), the second has until recently been frustrated by the lack of a suitable plan recogniser which could analyse plan diagrams into their constituent plans (but see Brotsky, 1984; Wills, 1986). Here, a generalisation of traditional chart parsing techniques is developed (Lutz, 1986; 1989; Thompson & Ritchie, 1984).

The plan library contains several different kinds of information:

1. Definitions of primitive operations. For example, @**function** which takes as input a function and an object in the domain of the function and applies the function to the object producing an object in the range of the function. Similarly, @**binfunction** takes a binary function and two objects as inputs. In addition there are definitions of common operations on various types of object. For example, **set-add**, a binary function taking a set and an object as inputs and producing a new set, with the object added to the old set as output. Another commonly used operation is **newarg**, which takes as input a function and two objects. Its output is another function equal to the input function in all ways except that its value when applied to the first of the two objects is equal to the second of the two objects. This is used for representing things such as array updating, record-field updating, list surgery and so on.

2. Definitions of primitive objects and their properties known to the system (e.g. built-in functions, predicates, binary function and relations).

An example is the binary function for addition, **plus**, with the definition specifying such things as type information for its inputs and outputs, the facts that it is associative and commutative, and that it has identity element 0, and so on. Other functions specified here are such things as **car** and **cdr**.

3. Definitions of primitive data-types (e.g. **integer** and **binfunction**).

4. Temporal plans specifying algorithms or commonly occurring code fragments. Each such plan not only has control and data flow information associated with it but also preconditions and postconditions. Preconditions are conditions that must be satisfied by the inputs and/or parts of a plan for a use of it to be valid. Postconditions are conditions satisfied by the outputs of a plan given that its preconditions have been satisfied. Note that in general we will consider control flow constraints to be preconditions on a plan considered as a pattern of data flows. In this way irrelevant control flow information occurring in actual programs will be ignored, since the plans will only specify essential control flow constraints. A good example of a temporal plan is **trailing generation and search**, shown in Fig. 11.3. This plan captures the data flow pattern common to code which searches data structures for an object satisfying some predicate, keeping track of both the object it is currently examining, but also the previous object.

5. Data plans specifying how compound data-objects are built up out of more primitive ones. Typical examples of this are plans such as **iterator** and **labelled thread**. An **iterator** consists of an object, and a function whose domain and range are both equal to the type of object. Such a data object can be used to generate an entire sequence of objects, starting with the initial object, applying the function to it to get the second, applying the function to the second to get the third and so on. This is a remarkably common construct in programming. For instance, using the number 1 as the initial object and the function **one-plus** (which adds one to its argument) gives an interator which generates the natural numbers. Alternatively, starting with a list as the initial object and the Lisp function **cdr** as the function lets one generate successive tails of a list as is so often done in programming. The **labelled-thread** data-type also consists of two parts – a function, and another compound data-type, a **thread**. A **thread** consists of a set of objects and a second injective function mapping the set to itself. The set should be thought of as a set of nodes, and the second function as a successor function which takes a node and returns its successor. So a **thread** is really a linear graph-like structure. The other function needed with the **thread** to make a **labelled thread** is the labelling function. Its domain is the set of nodes in the **thread**, and it produces values to be associated with each node. A typical example of a **labelled thread** is a Lisp list. The dotted pairs can be thought of as making up the set of nodes, the **cdr** function is the successor function, and the **car** function gives us the value associated with each node. Again the definitions of such data types specify constraints that

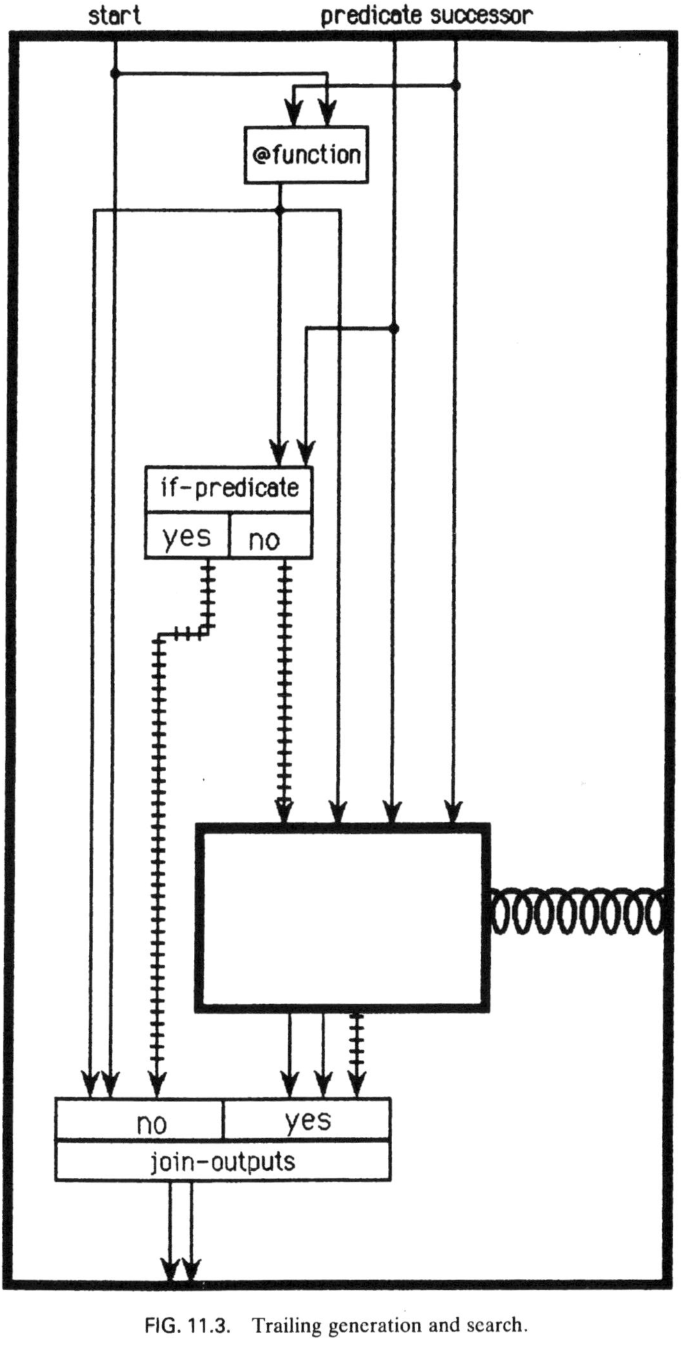

FIG. 11.3. Trailing generation and search.

must be satisfied by the parts of the structure. These could be just simple type information, or could be more complex relationships (e.g. that a **thread** must *not* have a cycle).

6. Data overlays specifying how some data object may be viewed as an implementation of an object of some other type. These specify how it is possible to view one type of data object as another. For instance, the data overlay **iterator->thread** specifies that an iterator can be regarded as a thread by treating the set of objects generated by the iterator as the set of nodes in the thread, and the function part of the iterator as the successor function for the thread. This overlay and others like it, play a crucial role in **temporal abstraction**, which bridges the gap between temporal sequences of objects as produced by loops, and iterators and other non-temporal data structures such as threads, lists, and directed graphs. In many of the diagrams that follow no distinction has been made between iterators and threads, in that an initial object and a successor function have been grouped together as a single object and treated as a thread. This is purely to avoid having to show multiple levels of analysis in diagrams which are already complicated enough.

7. Temporal Overlays specifying how a temporal plan may be regarded as an implementation of some operation. A good example of this is the overlay **trailing generation and search->internal thread find**. This overlay captures the idea that the pattern code in **trailing generation and search** can be used to implement an **internal thread find** operation which given a thread and a predicate as input returns the first node in the thread satisfying the predicate (it also returns the previous node). Now of course it should be noted that the **trailing generation and search** plan makes no reference to threads. So the overlay has to specify which objects being input to the searching plan can be viewed as constituting a thread, and in what way. This is shown in Fig. 11.4, where the constraint underneath the diagram indicates that the start object and the successor function input to the **trailing generation and search** plan can be grouped together as an iterator which, when viewed as a thread using the **iterator->thread** overlay, forms the input to the **internal thread find** operation.

Temporal abstraction was one of the most important notions introduced by Rich and Waters and subsequently further developed by Laubsch and Eisenstadt (1982). It enables one to view a series of data objects computed in a temporal sequence (e.g. the values of a variable as a loop is executed) as a single data object. This is similar to the point of view programmers have when considering a sequence of reads from a file – they can switch between regarding the file as a single stream-like object, or they can think of the temporal sequence of values produced by the reads. It is the formalisation of this reasoning which enables the Programmer's Apprentice to take a really high-level view of many programs and to recognise the common

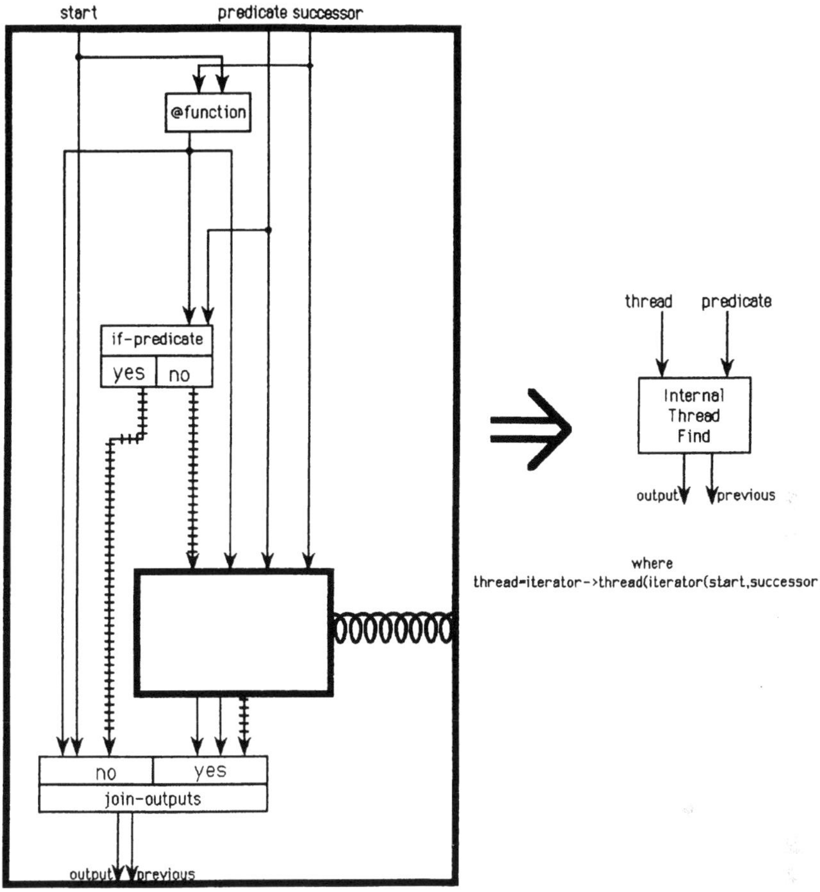

FIG. 11.4. Trailing generation and search-->internal thread find.

pattern (e.g. filtered iteration) behind many different programs and implementation techniques.

There are several advantages to this method of representing programs and plans in terms of their control and data flow. First, the program representation is no longer dependent on the specific variable names chosen by the programmer. Therefore, at least one type of superficial variation between programs has been removed. It should be noted that from a theoretical point of view variables in a programming language are just a device for ensuring a desired data flow – it is the data flow that is important, not the variables.

Second, many, but not all, structurally different programs can be represented by the same surface plan. Thus, some other superficial differences between programs can be eliminated by this technique. Of course, it is not possible for any representation to be completely canonical with respect to program equivalence. If it were we could use the representation to solve the program equivalence problem (by translating the programs into the representation, and then checking that the representations are the same) which is a well-known non-decidable problem.

Third, it is a language-dependent representation. Therefore, a lot of the reasoning applied to a program is applicable to programs in any language. There does, however, need to be a language-dependent translation process to go from the source code to the surface plan of a program. In order to be able to suggest edits and so on, a language-dependent plan to source code translator is also needed. Apart from these two modules, most of the rest of the plan recognition system is written in a language-independent fashion.

Fourth, plans can be combined in a linear fashion to form new plans without the component plans interfering with each other. All that needs to be done is to connect the output data (and control) flows from the first plan to the appropriate input data (and control) flows of the second, and provided that any special constraints required by the plans (e.g. type restrictions on the inputs) are satisfied the resulting plan will be a valid combination of the two original plans.

Fifth, plans can easily be combined in such a way that they share common sub-plans. This makes it easy to represent and reason about the common programming practice of not recomputing values which have already been computed.

This ability to easily combine plans enables one to form a library of commonly occurring plans which can then be put together to make up programs. The recognition process is then primarily one of seeing how a given program is actually built up from combinations of these known plans, and debugging can partly be seen as the attempt to understand the program using the above recognition technique, noting any near matches to known plans. The following sections will describe these processes in some detail.

5. UNDERSTANDING PROGRAMS USING PLAN DIAGRAMS

Before showing how a combination of plan recognition and symbolic evaluation on plan diagrams enables IDS to find type 1 (and type 3) errors in programs it is instructive to see how plan recognition is actually done in practice. This has previously been described in a variety of papers (Rich, 1981; Schrobe, Waters, & Sussman, 1979; Waters, 1978; Wills, 1986), but the process is not as entirely straightforward as their descriptions would suggest. Many of the difficulties arise from the fact that the programs considered here have not been written using KBEmacs (Waters, 1982) so that the particularly close match between the programs and the plan library that Rich and Waters have in the first place does not exist in our case. In addition, as mentioned earlier, it is not possible to have a completely canonical representation of programs, and a certain amount of what are essentially program transformation techniques have to be used to get round some of the differences between the actual surface plans that arise in practice and the plans in the plan library. Furthermore, the language being used has an affect on the way people not only do, but even can, write their code, and this leads yet again to the actual surface plans differing in significant ways from the plans in the library. So the process of understanding a correct program will be shown first, and in the next section it will be shown how this differs in the case where the program has a bug in it. In what follows reference will be made not only to the plans and overlays already discussed, but also to many from Rich's library, using his original terminology (see Rich, 1981, for details).

The program we will consider is Program 1 (see Table 11.1), a fairly simple program which reads in numbers from a file or terminal (one per line) until the end of the file, and outputs the numbers in ascending order. It does this by use of a linked list which holds the numbers, each new number being stored in the appropriate place in the list. The program contains a couple of user procedures – **findplace**, which finds the correct place in the sorted list where a new number is to go, and **addtolist**, which actually adds in a new number to the list. We will begin by considering the procedure **addtolist**. Its surface plan is shown as Fig. 11.5. The understanding (via plan recognition) process proceeds in several steps (not necessarily in the order given):

Step 1. An instance of a **spliceafter** plan is recognised, resulting in Fig. 11.6.

Step 2. The plan **spliceafter+newarg** is recognised. This plan consists of the **spliceafter** just recognised and the **newarg** at the top left of Fig. 11.6. An overlay **spliceafter+newarg->internal labelled-thread add-after** is then used. As part of this overlay head and ^.next are recognised as forming an **iterator** which can be viewed as a **thread**, but additionally this **thread** and the ^.numb function are grouped together as a **labelled thread**. This **labelled thread** is regarded as a single object which is one of the inputs to the **internal labelled-thread add-after** operation. The recognition of this operation corresponds to realising that this part of the code (corresponding to the **spliceafter** plan) can be viewed as inserting a new node (whose label is the value of n) into a **labelled thread** after the node given by t.

Step 3. Similarly, a **new labelled root** operation is recognised, implemented by the rightmost **newarg**, and the top left **newarg**, which it shares with the **internal labelled thread after-add** operation. It is partly this ability of the plan diagram formalism to share parts of plans (and of the chart parsing recogniser IDS uses) which makes it so powerful. Again, head ^.next, and ^.numb are required to be a **labelled thread**. The plain diagram

TABLE 11.1
A Sample Program

```
program  sort(input,output);
type  listelement = record
                        numb : integer;
                        next : ^listelement;
                    end;
      plist = ^listelement;
var   head, p : plist;
      n : integer;

procedure  addtolist(n : integer; t : plist);
var  p : plist;
begin
   new(p);
   p^.numb:=n;
  if t = nil then
     begin
        p^.next := head;
        head:=p;
     end
  else
     begin
        p^.next:=t^.next;
        t^.next:=p;
     end;
end;
```

Program 1.

```
procedure  findplace(n:integer; var p:plist);
var t : ^listelement;
    found : boolean;
begin
   if head^.numb > n then
     p:=nil;
   else
     begin
        p:=head;
        t:=p^.next;
        found:=false;
        while not found do
           if t <> nil then
              if t^.numb <= n then
                 begin
                    p:=t;
                    t:=t^.next;
                 end
              else  found:=true
           else  found:=true;
     end;
end;

begin
   head:=nil;
   while not eof do
      begin
         readln(n);
         findplace(n,p);
         addtolist(n,p);
      end;
   p:=head;
   while p<>nil do
      begin
         writeln(p^.numb);
         p:=p^.next;
      end;
end.
```

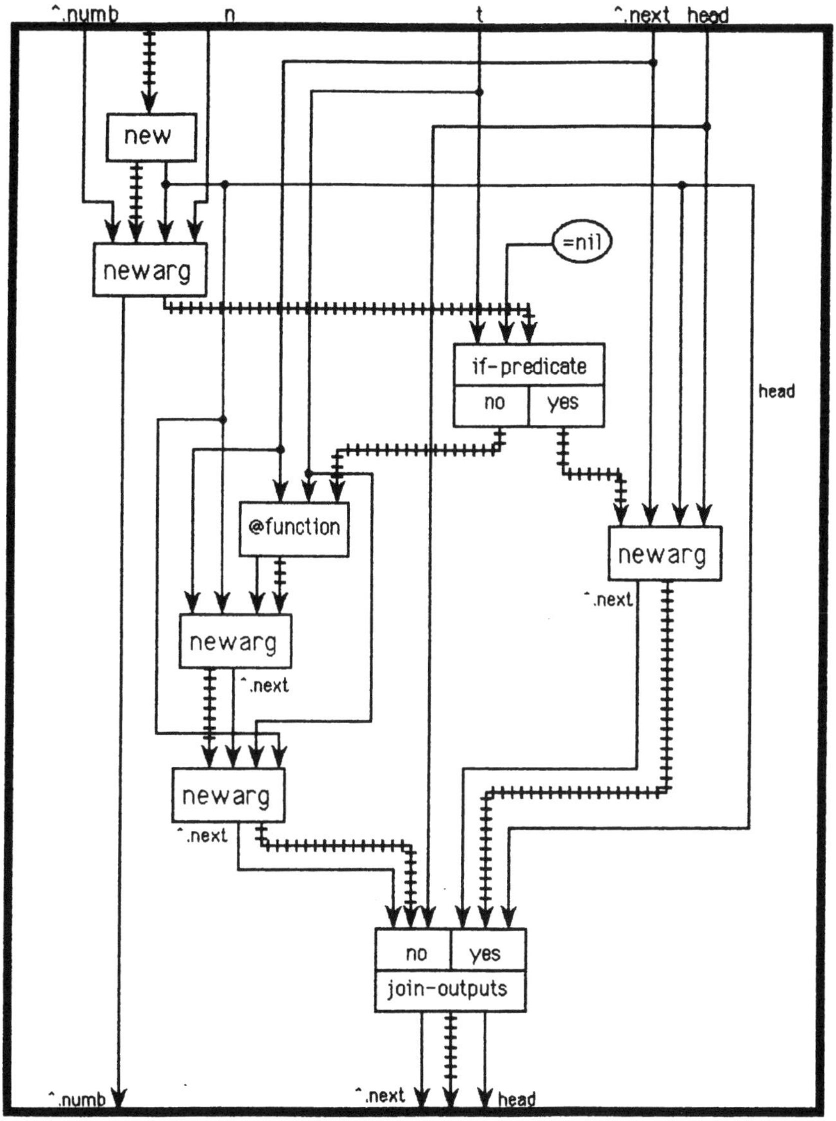

FIG. 11.5. Addtolist surface plan.

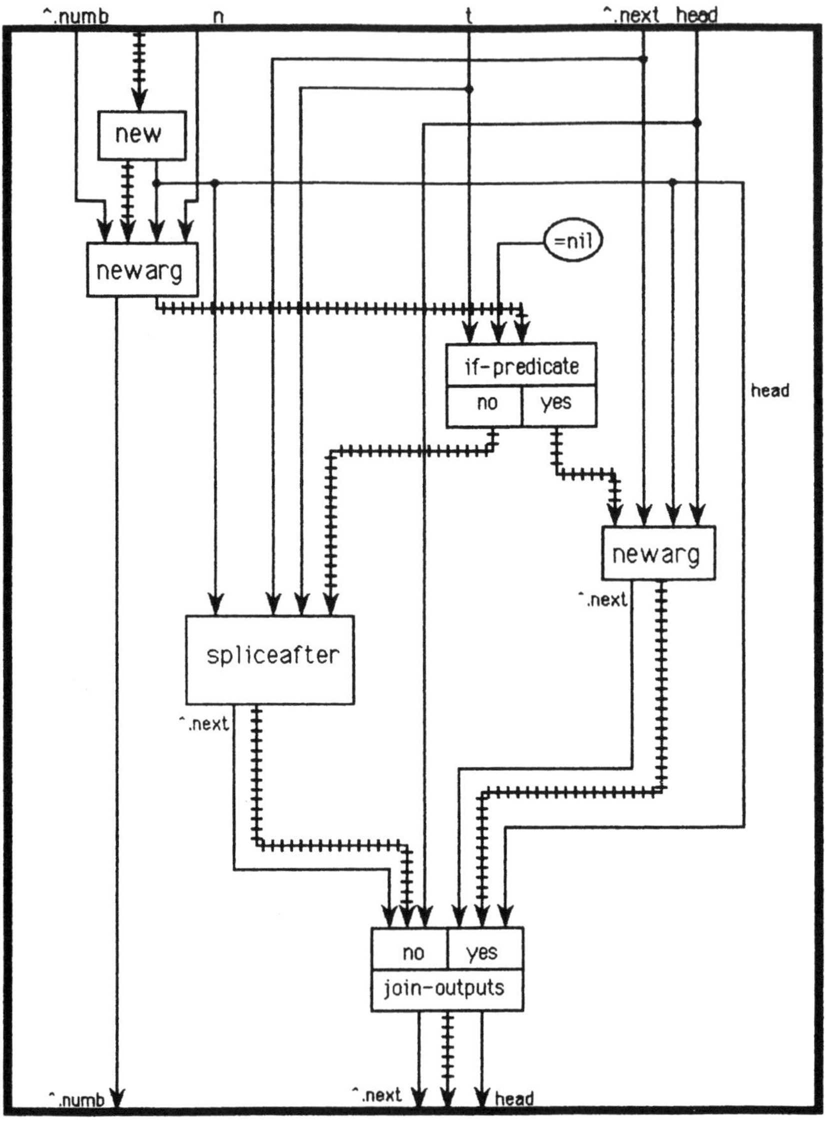

FIG. 11.6. First steps in building the surface plan of addtolist.

for **addtolist** after these last two steps is shown in Fig. 11.7. The grouping of objects into single compound objects is shown by shaded ovals round the appropriately grouped objects. Such shaded objects are then treated as single objects which can be inputs to (and indeed outputs from) computations in plan diagrams.

The analysis of **findplace** is complicated by the fact that its surface plan (shown as Fig. 11.8) needs to be transformed until it is in a sufficiently standard form for the recognition to proceed. IDS contains a library of program transformations, represented as graph transformation operations. An example is **enflag + deflag expansion**. **Enflag**ging is the plan library form of the common programming trick of using some variable (the flag) to hold a value coding up which way control flow actually went at a test. Later parts of the program can test this flag and take appropriate action (**deflagging**). **Enflag + deflag expansion** can easily be understood by looking at Fig. 11.9 which shows a fairly general form of this operation. At first sight, it would appear that rewriting plans like this would actually make matters worse, but the expansion is not normally done in the generality shown. IDS actually uses a heuristic rule stating:

If a **deflag** is found immediately after an **enflag**, and the succeed action of the **deflag** is empty **then** use **enflag + deflag expansion**.

This heuristic avoids copying actions, which would make the plan larger and more complicated. Additionally, in practice the **deflag** test can often (usually) be removed after the expansion as a result of further analysis.

Additionally, IDS contains other heuristic rules, such as:

If an action in the outer (non-recursive) part of a loop has constant inputs and so can be evaluated, but the corresponding inputs to the recursive part of the loop are not constant, **then** move the action outside the loop, and then evaluate.

Implicit in the statement of this rule is the idea that parts of surface plans whose inputs are known constants can be evaluated, and replaced by the results of the evaluation. Also note that moving an action out of a loop entails also moving it out of the recursive call to the loop into the outer part of the loop.

By applying these and other similar transformations, the surface plan for findplace is first of all transformed into a comparatively standard form. The analysis then again proceeds in several steps:

Step 1. Recognise complex predicates. By this is meant the process of recognising that a condition like:

$f(x) < n$

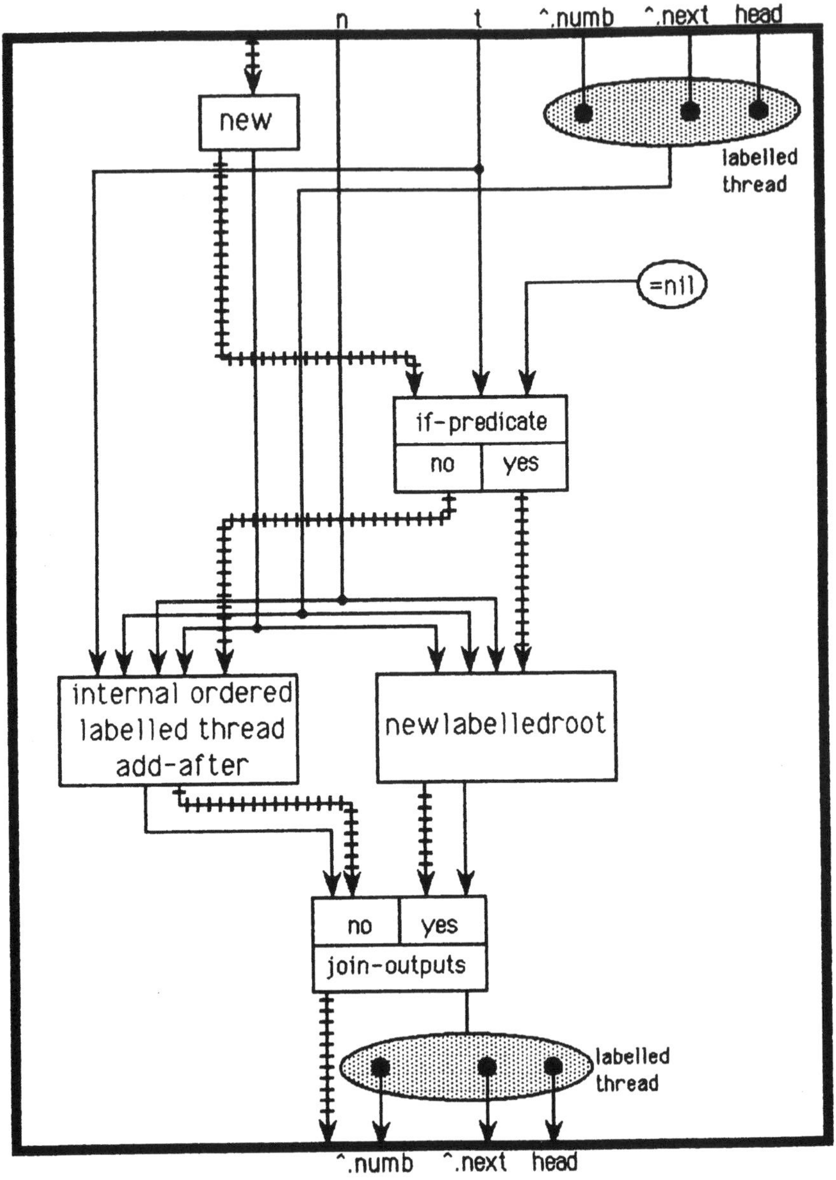

FIG. 11.7. Step 3 in building the surface plan of addtolist.

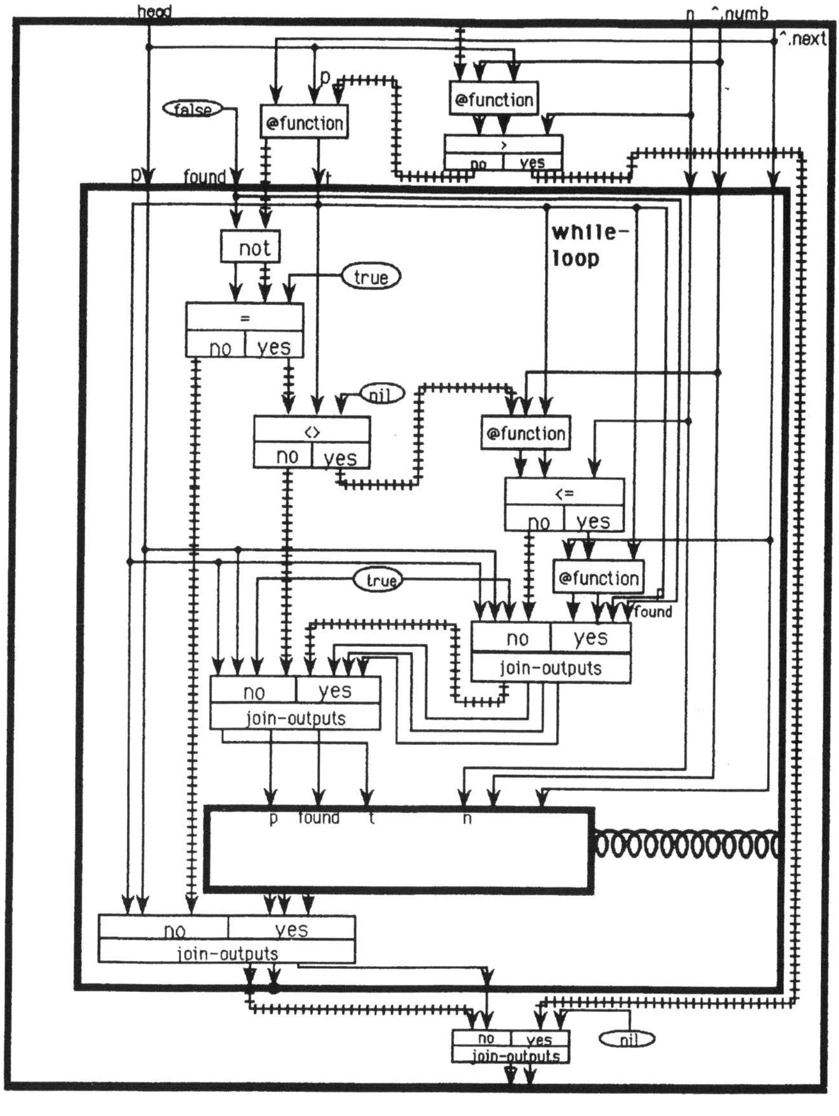

FIG. 11.8. The surface plan representation of findplace.

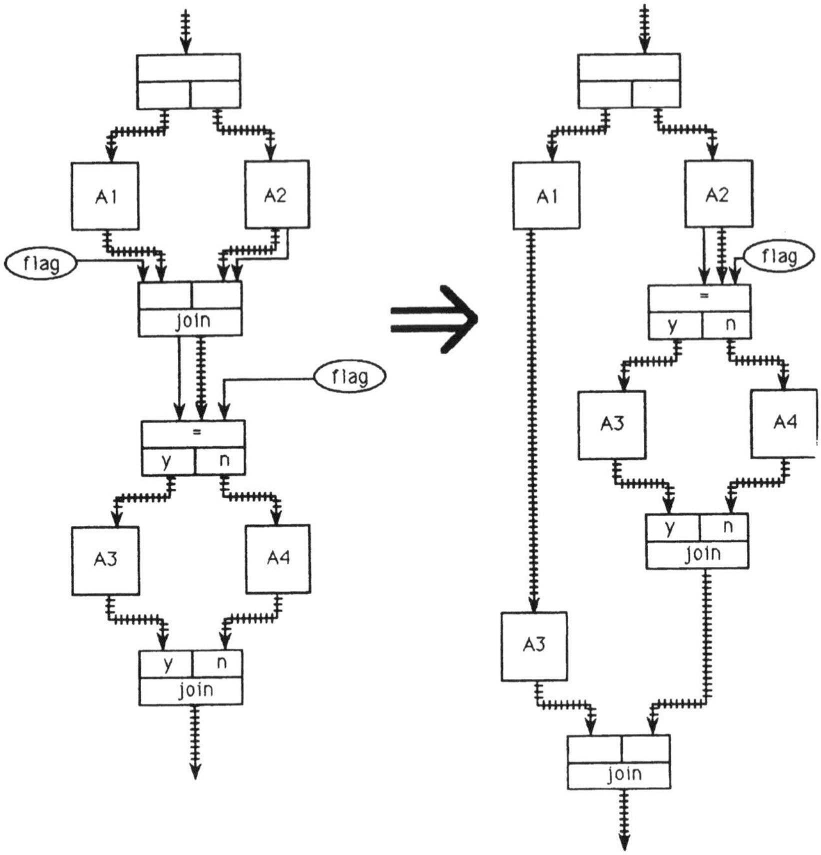

FIG. 11.9. Enflag+deflag expansion.

can be regarded as a complex predicate of x by first of all regarding the combination of a binary relation (in this case <) and a fixed value (in this case n) as a predicate g defined by:

$$g(y) = \text{true if } y < n, \text{ and } g(y) = \text{false otherwise}$$

and then regarding the combination of a function (in this case f) and a predicate (in this case g defined above) as a compound predicate h, defined by:

$$h(y)=g(f(y))$$

If such complex predicates have an obvious or easily understood name (such as =nil) then this has been used, otherwise the grouping is again

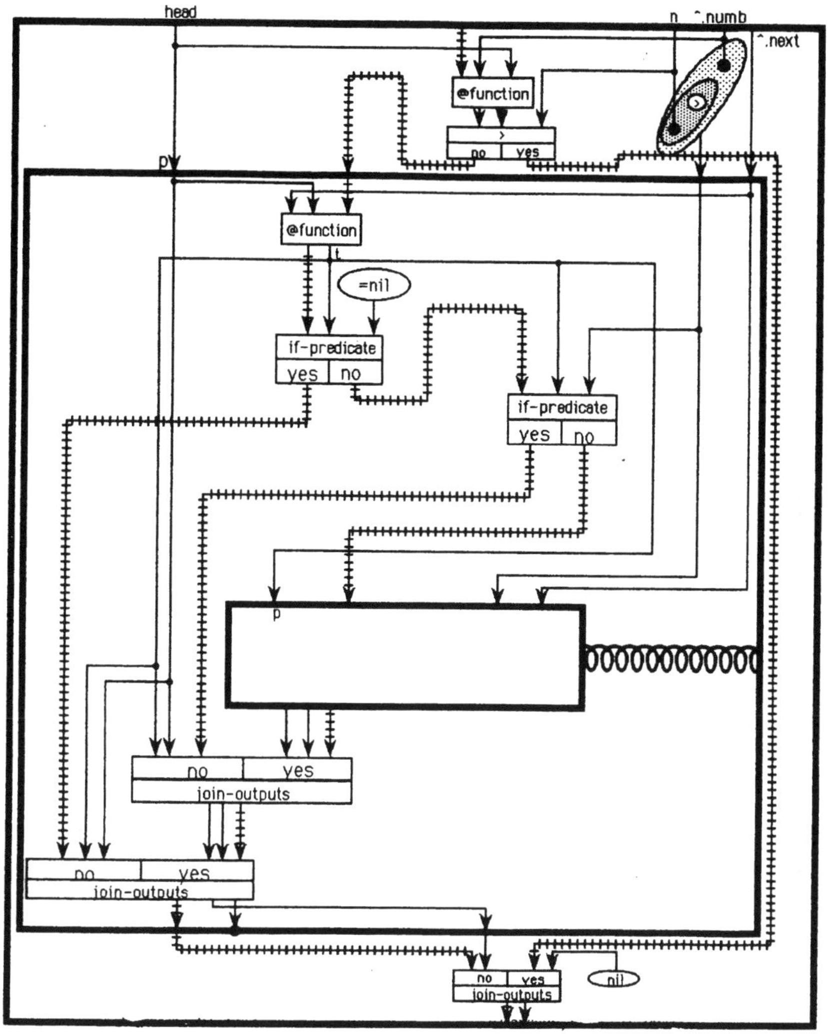

FIG. 11.10. The plan diagram for findplace after step 1.

shown by shaded ovals round the appropriately grouped objects. This is all done using overlays such as **@function + predicate->predicate** from Rich's library. The plan diagram resulting after this has been done is shown in Fig. 11.10.

Step 2. The standard plan, **terminated iterative generation and search** (a variant of **iterative generation and search** discussed earlier), is now recognised, resulting in the plan diagram Fig. 11.11.

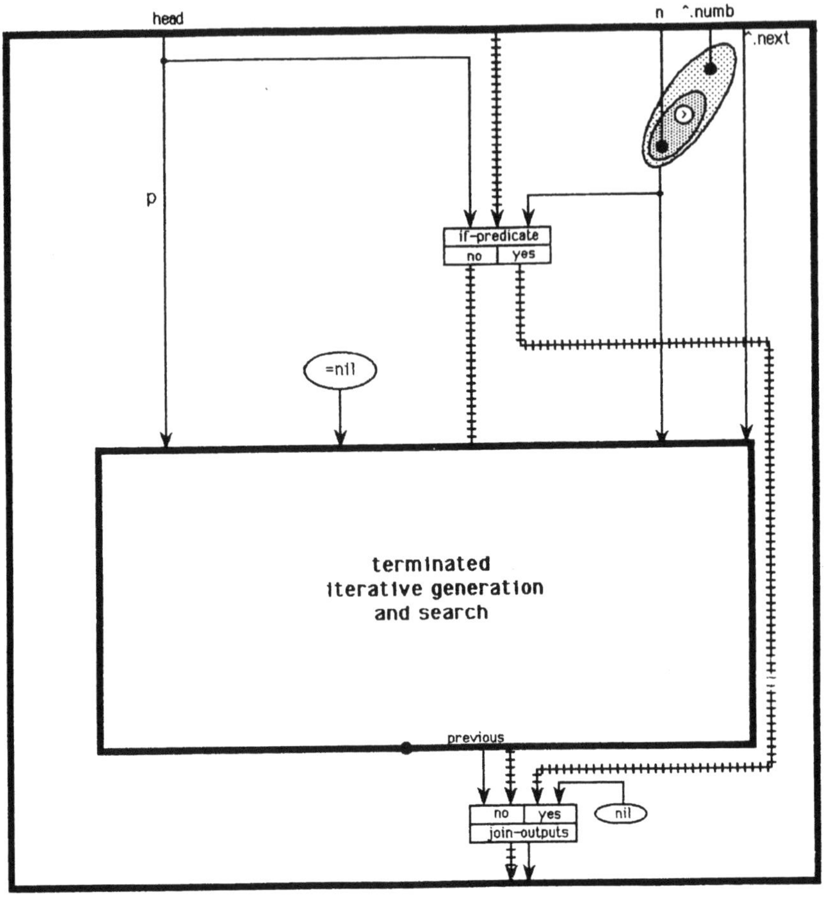

FIG. 11.11. The plan diagram for findplace after step 2.

Step 3. Now IDS uses an overlay to recognise that the above plan can be viewed as implementing the **internal thread find** operation discussed earlier, with a **nil-terminated thread** as input. This **nil-terminated thread** essentally is that obtained by iterating down the data structure starting from head, and using ^.next as the successor function. In this way we arrive at Fig. 11.12.

Step 4. Finally IDS is able to recognise that this pattern of code actually implements an **Internal Labelled Thread Find** operation, corresponding to its recognition that **findplace** finds the first node in its input thread whose label is greater than n (the resulting plan diagram is shown as Fig. 11.13).

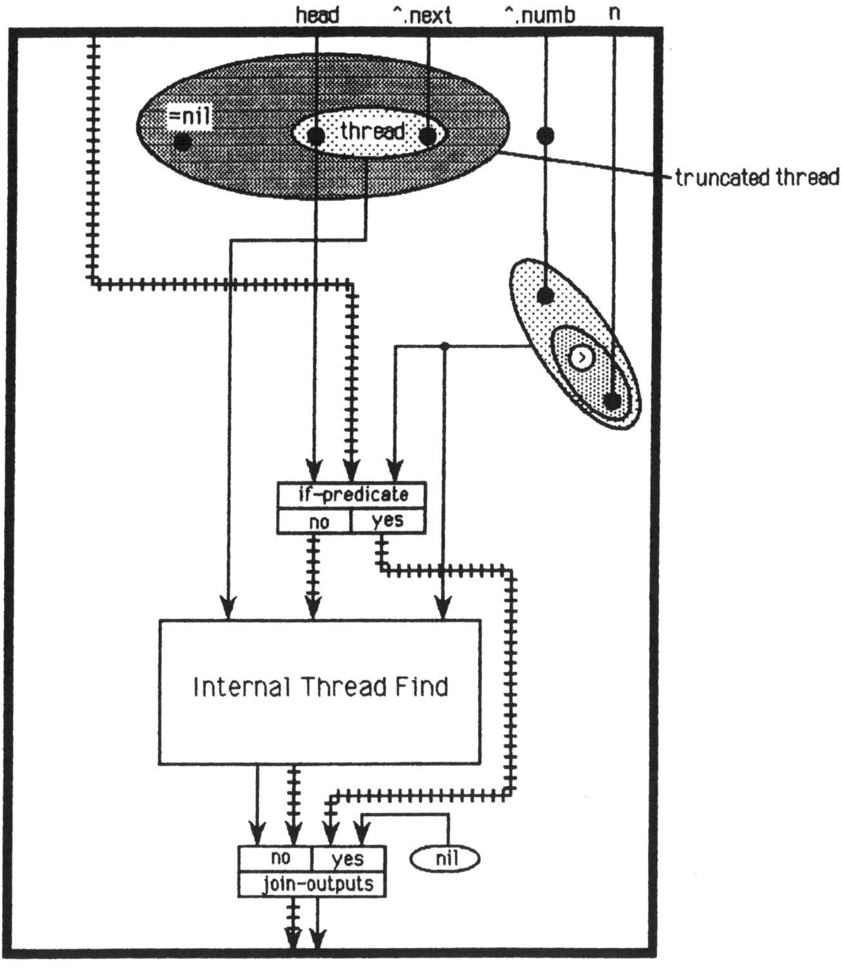

FIG. 11.12. The plan diagram for findplace after step 3.

Having analysed both procedures to the best of its ability IDS now turns its attention to the main program. Its surface plan (or at least most of it) is shown in Fig. 11.14. To analyse this, it substitutes its understanding of the user procedures **findplace** and **addtolist** in place of the boxes representing the calls to these procedures. Note that this is done with its high-level accounts of what the procedures do, so it is a considerable improvement on just replacing procedure calls by the body of the procedure (with appropriate substitutions) as is done in Wills, (1986). When this replacement is done, clearly part of the resulting diagram consists of the final diagrams for

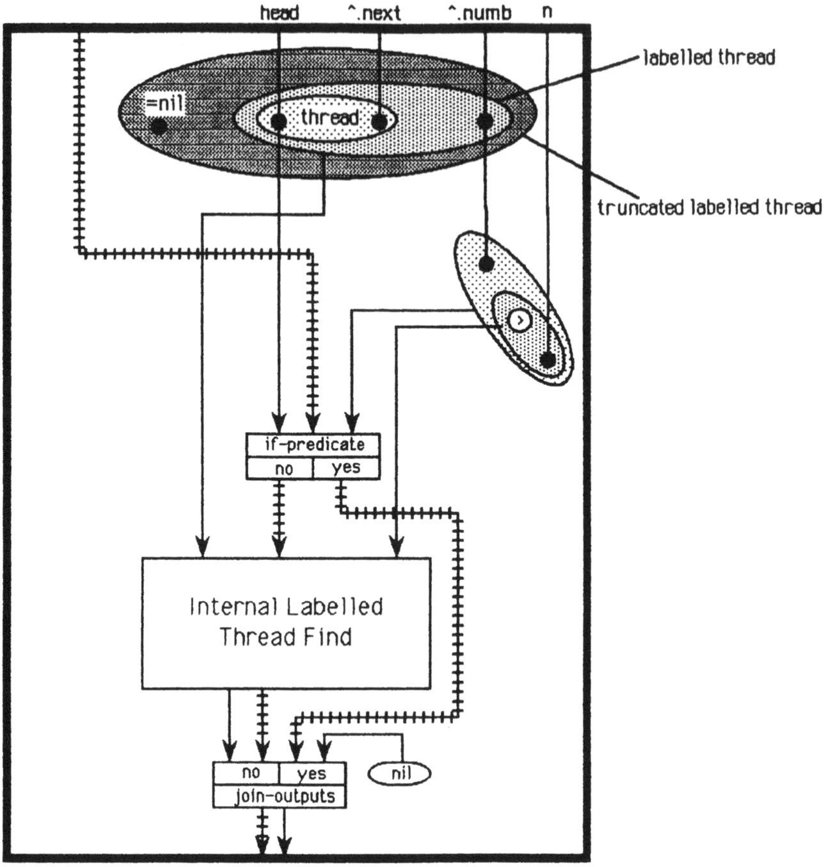

FIG. 11.13. The plan diagram for findplace after step 4.

findplace and **addtolist** (appropriately joined). IDS then notices that the nil value output by **findplace** when it fails to find a suitable item in the list is an example of an **enflag**ging operation, tested for by **addtolist**. IDS therefore again does an **enflag + deflag expansion**, followed by removal of the test in a similar fashion to that described during the understanding process for **findplace**. The resulting diagram (for this part of the main program's surface plan) is shown in Fig. 11.15. IDS now recognises another standard plan, that for inserting a new item into a finite (nil-terminated) ordered labelled thread (ordered by > in this case), resulting in Fig. 11.16. Notice how this plan actually comes from two procedure calls – parts of the cliché come from one procedure and other parts from the second. The resulting surface plan contains two standard plans. The first of these is **terminated**

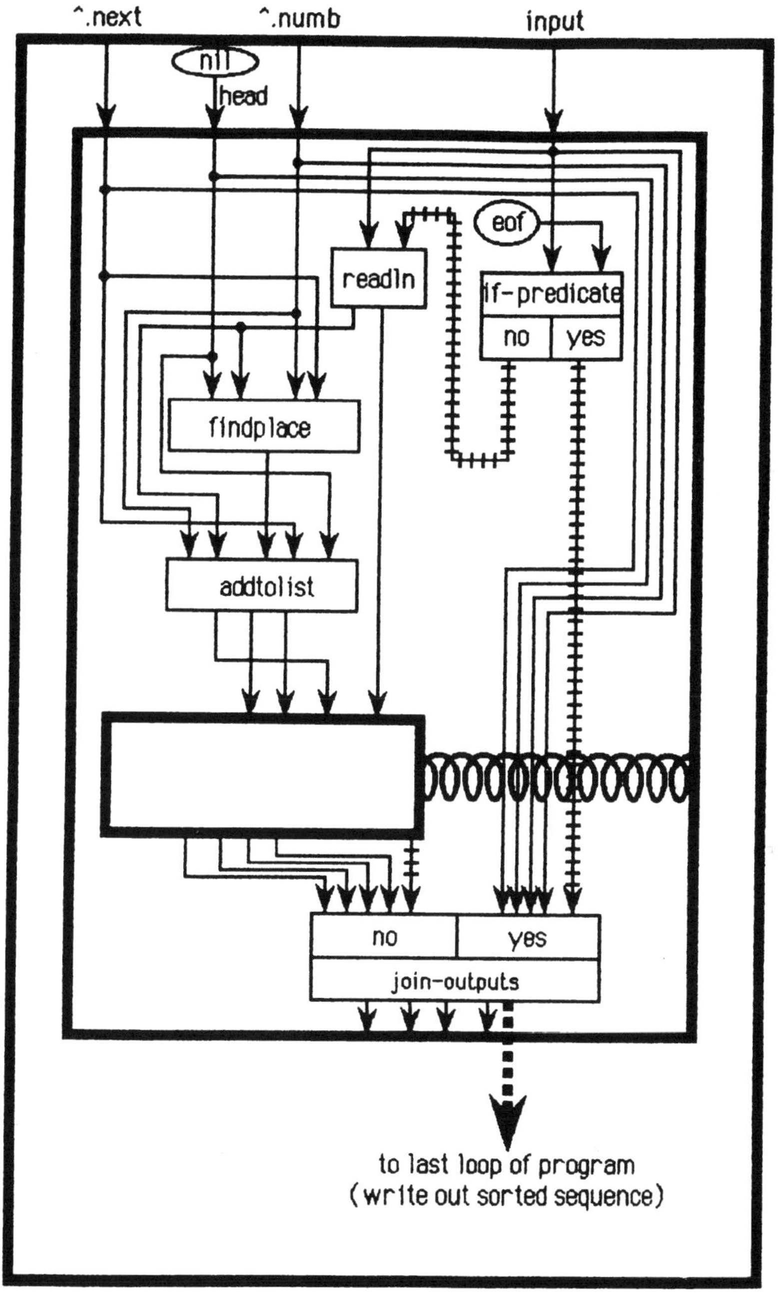

FIG. 11.14. The main program surface plan.

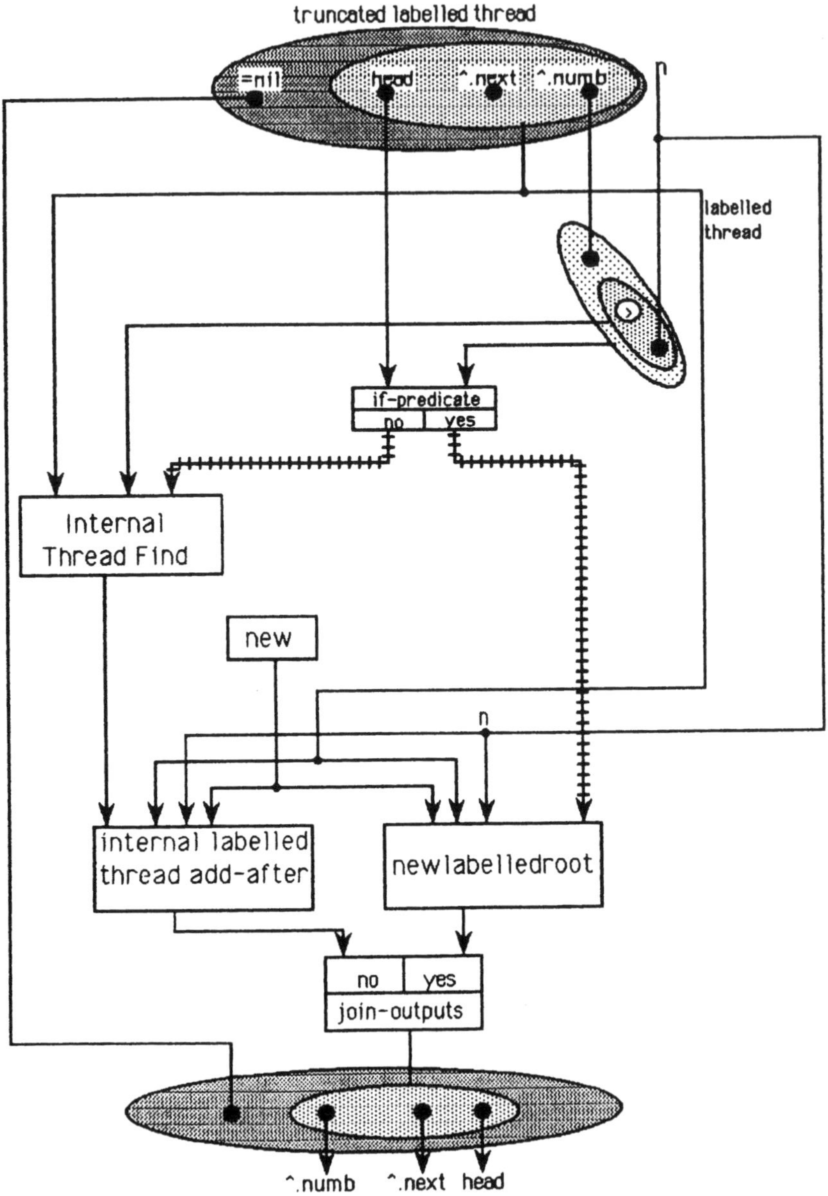

FIG. 11.15. The findplace and addtolist of the main program's surface plan.

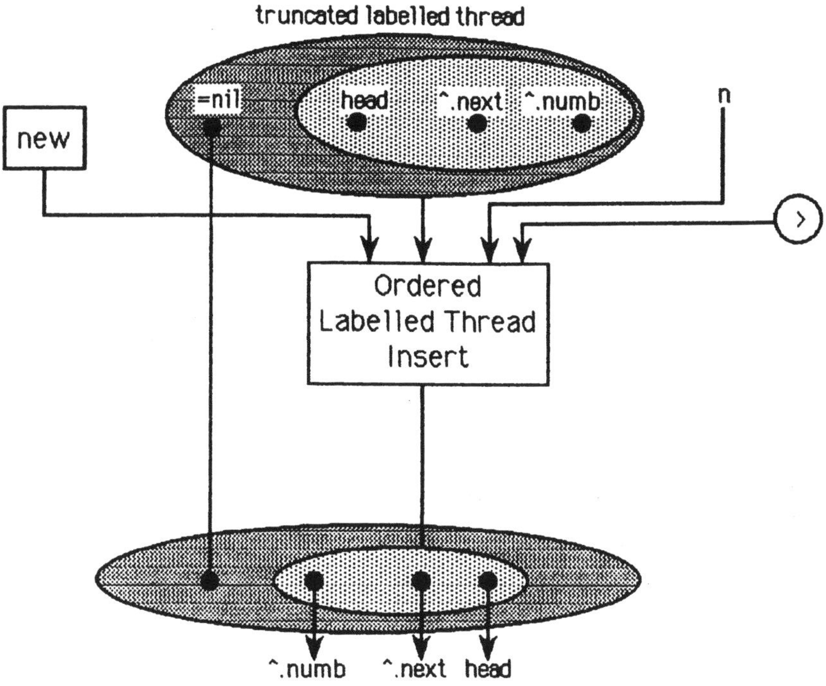

FIG. 11.16. A further step in building the plan diagram of the main program.

iterative read, a plan for reading items out of a file until some condition (in this case end-of-file) is reached. Temporal abstraction enables one to view the objects read temporally out of the file as a sequence, and an overlay enables IDS to view this plan as implementing a **readall** operation which takes a file as input and produces a finite sequence as output. The other standard plan recognised is **iterative ordered labelled thread insert**, which IDS then uses as an overlay to recognise an implementation of a **sort** operation, temporally abstracting the items input to the **ordered labelled thread insert** operation (which are the same items produced by the **iterative read**) as the sequence input to the **sort**, and viewing the labelled-thread output from the **iterative ordered labelled thread** plan as the ordered sequence output by the **sort**. Similarly, the final loop is seen to be implementing a **writeall** operation, which takes a sequence and writes it to a file. Thus the whole program is finally represented by Fig. 11.17. As a final stage, IDS checks that all the preconditions for all the various plans and overlays involved in this analysis of the program are satisfied.

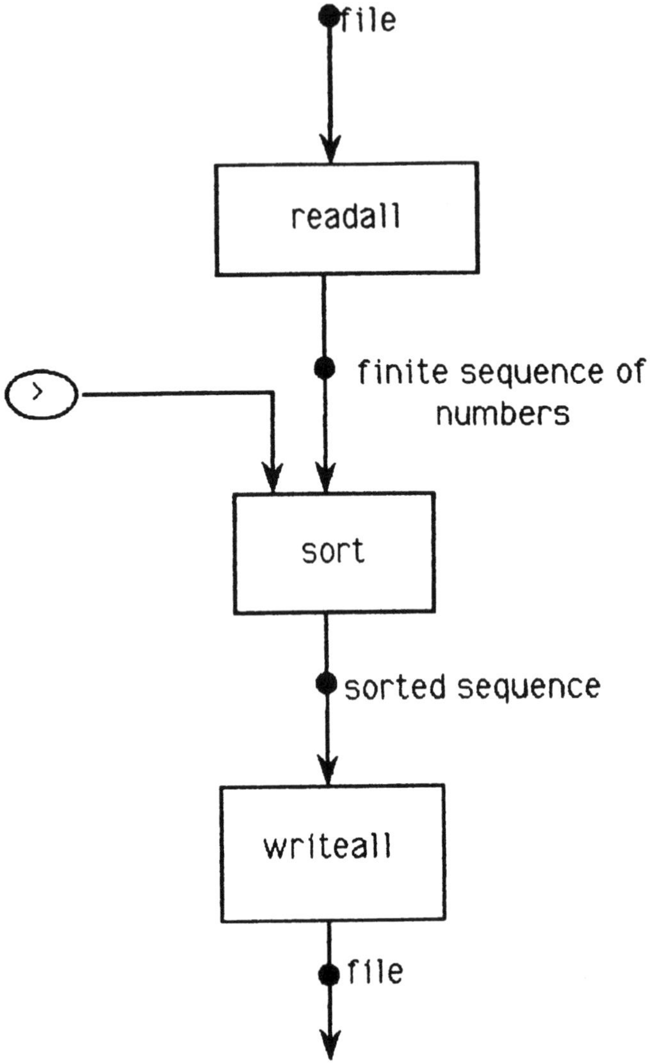

FIG. 11.17. The final stages of analysis.

6. DEBUGGING PROGRAMS USING PLAN DIAGRAMS

The strategy used by IDS to debug programs is the following:

1. Translate the program into its surface plan.
2. Try to understand the program by recognising all occurrences of library plans, as described above. Make a note of any "near" matches.
3. Symbolically evaluate any remaining (i.e. unrecognised) parts of the surface plan.
4. Check for broken preconditions of any of the recognised plans.
5. Use near match information and broken precondition information to try and repair the program.
6. Translate the debugged surface plan back into the source language.

So suppose that, instead of being correct, the program just analysed had contained a bug, and in particular suppose that procedure **addtolist** had been the following instead of the earlier correct version:

```
procedure addtolist(n : integer; t : plist);
var p : plist;
begin
     new(p);
     p^.numb:=n;
     if t = nil then
                    begin
                         p^.next := head;
                         head:=p;
                    end
     else
                    begin
                         t^.next:=p;
                         p^.next:=t^.next;
                    end;
end;
```

The bug in this procedure is that the two lines responsible for splicing in the new element into the list have been given in the wrong order, resulting in the kind of behaviour shown as Fig. 11.18. How does IDS detect and correct this bug?

It starts by trying to understand the program as before, and of course its analysis of **findplace** is identical to that described earlier. However when it tries to analyse **addtolist** it recognises the **new labelled root** plan as before,

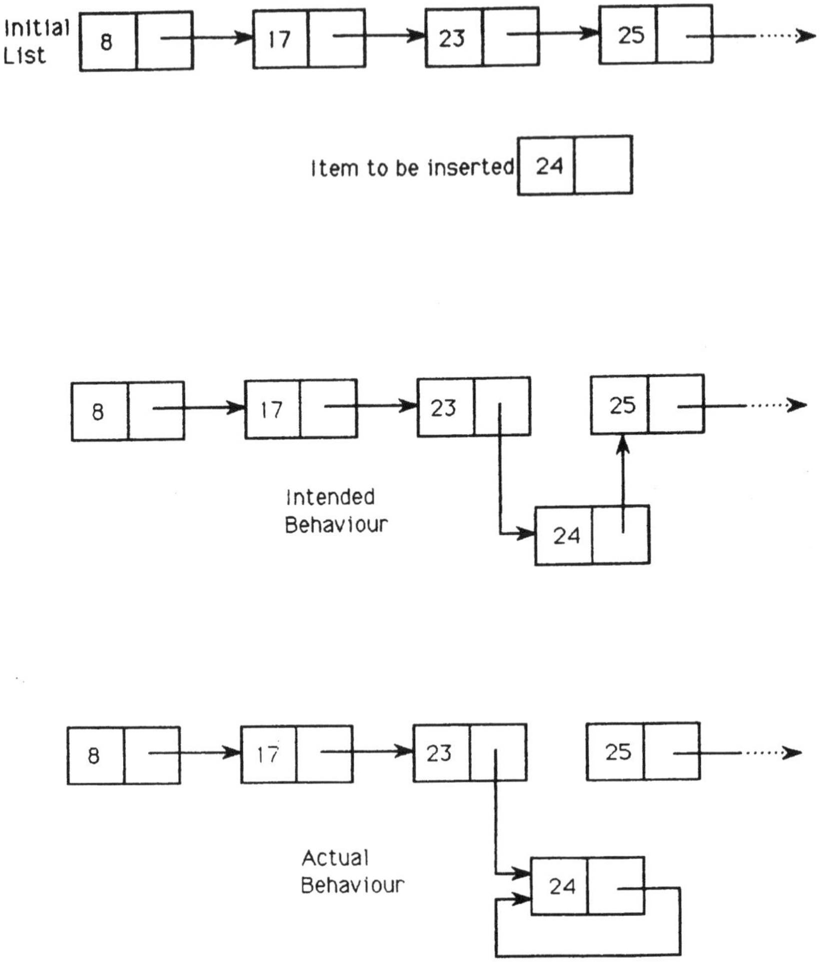

FIG. 11.18. The buggy program's behaviour.

but is unable to recognise the **internal labelled thread add-after** plan. However, as IDS is using a generalisation of chart parsing to do plan recognition, it also builds up information about partial plans that it recognises. In particular, it finds the partial **spliceafter** plan shown in Fig. 11.19. In this figure, plans are represented as lists of their components, each component being represented as a three-element list. The head of the list is the type of the component (e.g. **@function**), the second element is an ordered list of its inputs, and the third component is an ordered list of its outputs. A value occurring both in the output list of some component and

Correct Spliceafter

Buggy Spliceafter

t^.next:=p;
p^.next:= t^.next;

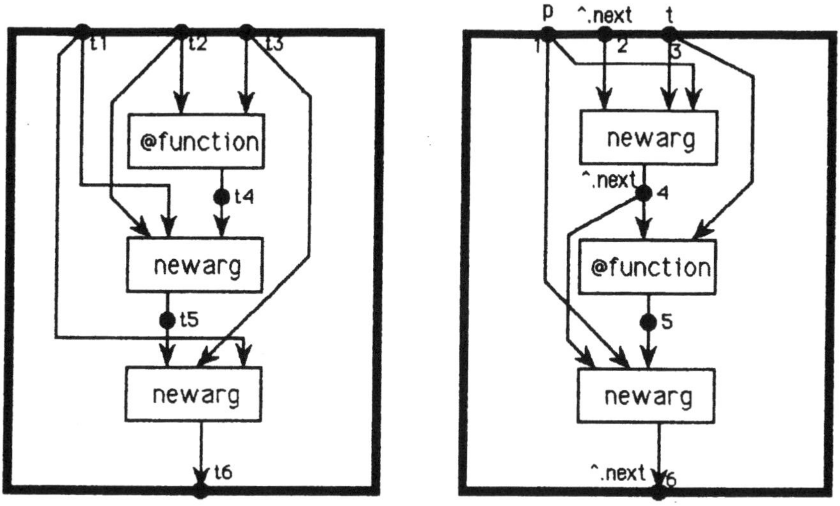


```
[spliceafter [?t1 ?t2 ?t3][?t6]] =>

 [ [@function [?t2 ?t3][?t4]]
   [newarg [?t2 ?t1 ?t4][?t5]]
   [newarg [?t5 ?t3 ?t1][?t6]]
 ]
```

```
[  [@function [4 3][5]]
   [newarg [2 3 1][4]]
   [newarg [4 1 5][6]]
]
```

Matching process gives best partial match as:

```
[spliceafter [1 4 3][?t6]] =
   [ [@function [4 3][5]]
     [newarg [4 1 5][6]]
   ]
```

and needing to find an object matching

```
[newarg [6 3 1][?t6]]
```

to complete the match.

FIG. 11.19. Alternative spliceafter plans in addtolist.

the input list of another indicates data flow between the appropriate ports of each of the two components. Variables have been used in the input and output lists for library plans, and integers (i.e. instantiated values) in actual surface plans. The figure shows the partial match to **spliceafter** found by IDS, and what would be needed to make it a complete instance of **spliceafter**. This partial match is close enough for IDS to recognise it as a

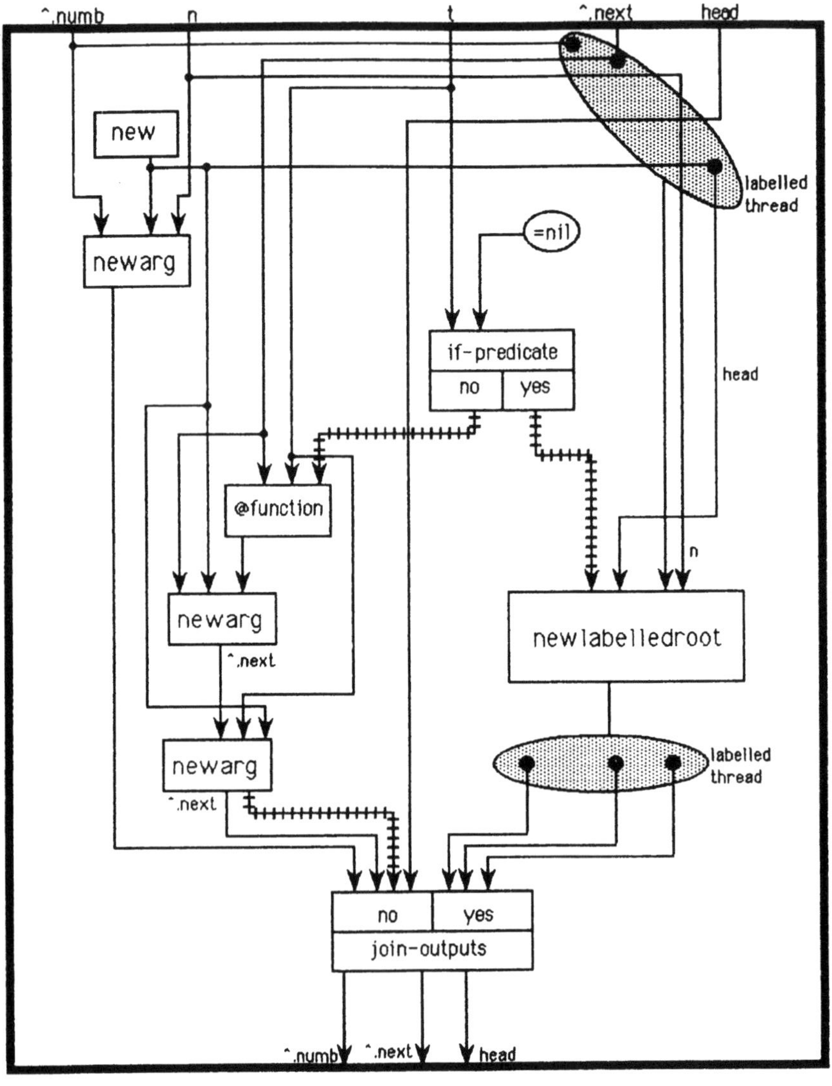

FIG. 11.20. The plan diagram of the buggy addtolist.

near miss. However, at this point IDS does not categorise this as a bug – it merely makes a note of the near miss for future reference. So, at this point the analysis of **addtolist** is Fig. 11.20 rather than Fig. 11.7 as earlier.

Now, IDS begins analysis of the main program as before. When it starts analysing the concatenation of **findplace** and **addtolist** it finds that it cannot really go any further after doing **enflag + deflag expansion** leading to Fig. 11.21. So, for the moment it assumes that it has finished its analysis, and starts trying to verify all the preconditions for the various plans and overlays. As part of this process it tries to verify that the preconditions for **internal labelled thread find** are satisfied. Now there are actually two places it has to check these preconditions – on entry to the loop, and on entry to its tail recursive component. This double checking corresponds to doing inductive reasoning. One of the preconditions that has to be satisfied is that the object input to the **internal labelled thread find** be a thread. In the outer part of the loop this is of course (trivially!) satisfied by the null thread. However the input to the **internal labelled thread find** in the recursive part of the loop comes from **addtolist** in the outer part. So, IDS has to check that ^.numb, ^.next, and head coming from **addtolist** form a thread. Now these values come from a join-outputs box, so it has to check that the values input on the success side, and on the failure side of the join-outputs form a thread. This is clearly true on the success side (they come from a **newlabelledroot** plan). However, on the other side they come from the part of **addtolist** that IDS was unable to recognise. Therefore, IDS symbolically evaluates (King, 1976) the unrecognised part of the plan (the part that should be the **spliceafter** in this case) and deduces that:

^.next(object1) = object1

where object1 is the input labelled p in the diagram (note that we are treating ^.next as the name of a composite function). This clearly contradicts the definition of a thread (part of which states that there are no cycles in a thread) and so IDS has located an internal inconsistency in its analysis of the program, and hence has located the bug. Even in the case where IDS cannot now go on to suggest a fix, pointing out where the bug lies could be of great use to the programmer. However in this case IDS can actually suggest how to fix the bug. It does this by first of all noticing that the piece of the surface plan it couldn't recognise has (partly) been recognised as a partial **spliceafter** plan. In addition, it notices that the best way to turn the unanalysed part of the plan into a complete **spliceafter** is to delete (refer to Fig. 11.19 for the notation):

[newarg [2 3 1] [4]]

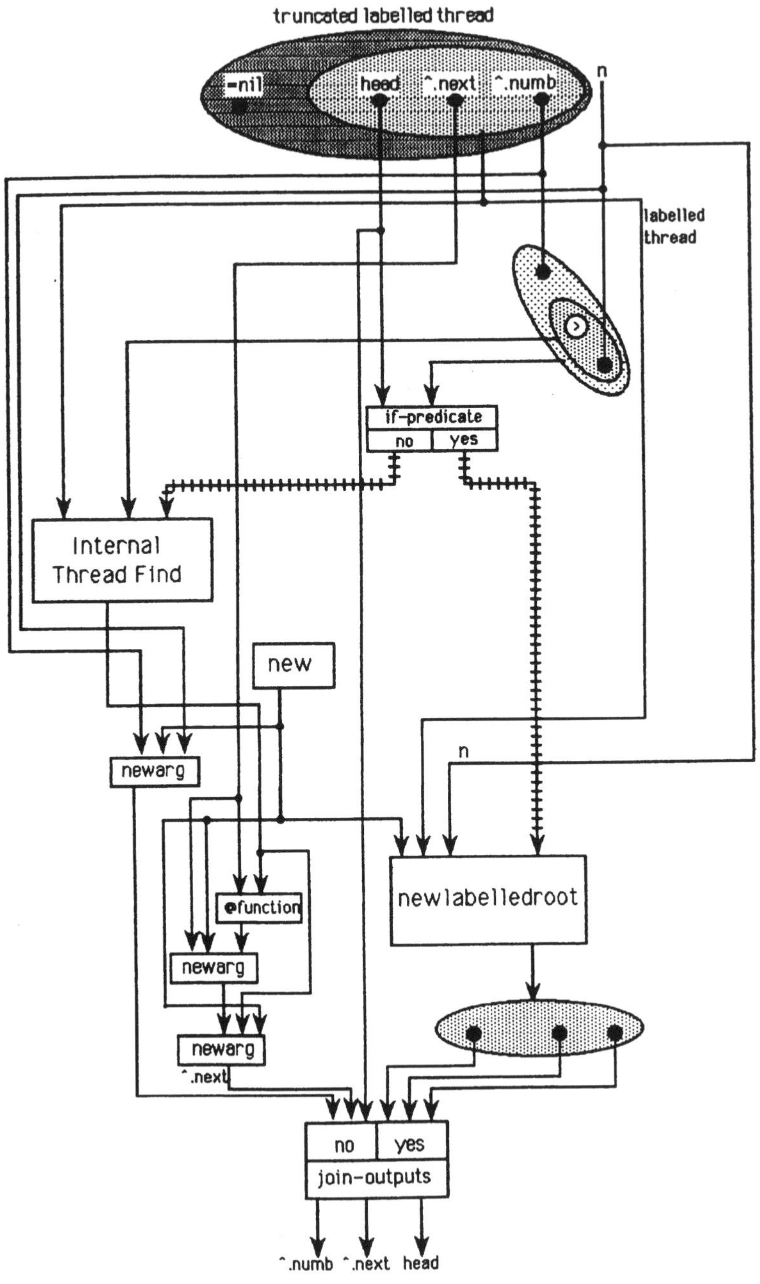

FIG. 11.21. Addtolist after enflag+deflag expansion.

from the plan and replace it by a new **newarg** operation:

[newarg [6 3 1] [7]]

where 7 is a new connecting point. This would give rise to a **spliceafter** plan:

[spliceafter [1 4 3] [7]].

The question then arises as to how this should be connected up to the surrounding graph in place of the original unrecognised parts of the plan. Although the question of how to do this in general is still an ongoing topic of research, in this case it does it by noticing that the new node 7 (the output of the plan) is replacing node 6. So it connects node 7 to everything node 6 was previously connected to. Similarly it notices that the only new input is node 4, replacing node 2. So it connects everything that was connected to node 2 to node 4. IDS then notices that, if it did this, the analysis can continue (in fact exactly as described earlier for the original correct program) and IDS arrives at the same analysis of the program, with no broken preconditions. So it can ask the user if the program is indeed trying to sort the input numbers, and if so, can correct the plan accordingly. By keeping track of the variable names associated with all the dataflows involved IDS can even generate the correct code, with the right use of variable names. Note that at present no attempt is made to point out (or even recognise) the fact that the error was really just having two lines in the wrong order. But, IDS does point out the incorrect lines, and the correct versions of them. Also, if IDS had not had the plan for sorting in its library it could still in fact correct this bug, by noticing that once it has recognised the **spliceafter**, and hence the **labelled thread add-after** plan, it would find that the broken precondition was no longer broken. The difference would be that it would query the user about the program at a lower level. Instead of asking if the program was trying to sort, it would have to ask if a particular piece of code was trying to splice a new item in at a particular place in a linked list structure.

The question of how to generate correct code in terms of variables the user will recognise is enormously complicated by the fact that the piece of amended code may have been through a long sequence of the program transformation operations. It is still an area of ongoing research as to how this can best be dealt with in general.

7. CONCLUSIONS AND FUTURE WORK

The work of Rich, Schrobe and Waters at MIT has laid the groundwork for a very solid theoretically based representation of the knowledge underlying programming. Their system is aimed at helping programmers develop complex LISP programs, but is actually also suitable for use by any system that needs to understand and debug programs. Due to the language independent nature of the plan diagram formalism, their work is applicable to any language provided a translator from that language to the surface plan representation is available. Such translators exist for LISP (Rich & Schrobe, 1978). FORTRAN (Waters, 1978), and COBOL (Faust, 1981). A translator for Pascal has been implemented in our system using the techniques of (Hecht, 1977; Chow & Rudmik, 1982). It is hoped that the work reported here has shown that this formalism can form the basis of a debugging system for Pascal. Further work needs to be done to try and make the system interact more with the programmer to enable it to be a useful tool in tracking down type 2 and type 4 bugs, and to find a good set of program transformation heuristics, a good set of heuristics for rejoining amended subgraphs (corresponding to repaired parts of surface plans) to the surrounding plan diagram, and a good set of heuristics for retranslating amended plan diagrams back into Pascal.

REFERENCES

Barstow, D. R. (1979). *Knowledge-based program construction.* New York: North Holland.

Brotsky, D. C. (1984). An algorithm for parsing flow graphs. *Technical Report AI-TR-704.* MIT Artificial Intelligence Laboratory.

Chow, A. L. & Rudmik, R. (1982). The design of a data flow analyser. *Proc SIGPLAN '82 Symposium on Compiler Construction.* Boston Mass.: USA 106–113.

Eisenstadt, M. & Laubsch, J. (1980). Towards an automated debugging assistant for novice programmers. *Proceedings of the Artificial Intelligence and Simulated Behaviour Conference (AISB-80).* Amsterdam.

Faust, G. G. (1981). *Semiautomatic translation of Cobol into Hibol.* MIT Laboratory for Computer Science MIT/LCS/TR-256.

Goldstein, I. P. (1974). Understanding simple picture programs. (PhD Thesis), *Technical Report 294.* MIT Artificial Intelligence Laboratory.

Hecht, M. S. (1977). *Flow analysis of computer progams.* New York: Elsevier North-Holland Inc.

Hewitt, C. & Smith, B. (1975). Towards a Programming Apprentice. *IEEE Trans. on Software Engineering, 1,* 26–45.

Johnson, W. L. (1986). *Intention-based diagnosis of novice programming errors.* Pitman: London.

Johnson, W. L., Soloway, E., Cutler, B., & Draper, S. (1983). Bug catalogue I. *Technical Report YaleU/CSD/RR #286.* Department of Computer Science, Yale University.

King, J. C. (1976). Symbolic execution and program testing. *CACM, 19*:7 July 385–394.

Laubsch, J. & Eisenstadt, M. (1982). Using temporal abstraction to understand recursive programs involving side effects. *Proc. American Association of Artificial Intelligence (AAAI-82).* Los Altos: Morgan Kaufmann 400–403.

Lukey, F. J. (1978). *Understanding and debugging simple computer programs.* PhD Thesis, University of Sussex.

Lutz, R. K. (1984a). Towards an intelligent debugging system for Pascal programs: A research proposal. *Technical Report No. 8.* Open University Human Cognition Research Laboratory, England.

Lutz, R. K. (1984b). Program debugging by near-miss recognition and evaluation. *Proc. ECAI 1984*, 529.

Lutz, R. K. (1986). Diagram parsing – A new technique for artificial intelligence. *Cognitive Studies Research Paper No. 54*, Cognitive Studies Programme, University of Sussex.

Lutz, R. K. (1989). Chart parsing of flowgraphs. *Proc. IJCAI*, Detroit, USA 1989, 116–121.

Manna, Z. & Waldinger, R. (1979). Synthesis: Dreams => Programs. *IEEE Trans. on Software Engineering SE-5:4*, 294–328.

Miller, M. L. & Goldstein, I. P. (1977). Overview of a linguistic theory of design. *AI Memo No. 383A*. MIT Artificial Intelligence Laboratory.

Rich, C. (1981). Inspection methods in programming. *AI-TR-604*. MIT Artificial Intelligence Laboratory.

Rich, C. & Schrobe, H. (1978). Initial report on a Lisp programmer's apprentice. *IEEE Trans. on Software Eng. SE-4:6*, 450–467.

Schrobe, H. E., Waters, R. C., & Sussman, G. J. (1979). A hypothetical monologue illustrating the knowledge underlying program analysis. *AI Memo 507*. MIT Artificial Intelligence Laboratory.

Shneiderman, B. (1980). *Software psychology. Human factors and information systems*. Cambridge, MA: Winthrop Publishers, Inc.

Soloway, E., Ehrlich, K., Bonar, J., & Greenspan, J. (1982). What do novices know about programming. *Research Rep. No. 218*. Department of Computer Science, Yale University.

Spohrer, J. C., Pope, E., Lipman, M., Sack, W., Freiman, S., Littman, D., Johnson, L., & Soloway, E. (1985). Bug catalogue: II, III, IV. *Tech. Rep. YaleU/CSD/RR #386*. Department of Computer Science, Yale University.

Thompson, H. & Ritchie, G. (1984). Implementing natural language parsers. In O'Shea T. and Eisenstadt, M. (Eds), *Artificial Intelligence: Tools, Techniques, and Applications*. London: Harper and Row 245–300.

Waters, R. C. (1978). Automatic analysis of the logical structure of programs. *AI-TR-492*. MIT Artificial Intelligence Laboratory.

Waters, R. C. (1979). A method for analysing loop programs. *IEEE Trans. on Software Eng. SE-5:3*, 237–247.

Waters, R. C. (1982). The programmer's apprentice: Knowledge based program editing. *IEEE Trans. on Software Eng. SE-8:1*, 1–12.

Weiser, M. (1982). Programmers use slices when debugging. *CACM*, *25*, 7, 446–452.

Wills, L. M. (1986). *Automated program recognition*. MSc Thesis, MIT Electrical Engineering and Computer Science.

Winograd, T. (1973). Breaking the complexity barrier (again). *Proc. ACM SIGIR-SIGPLAN Interface Meeting*.

Youngs, E. A. (1974). Human errors in programming. *International Journal of Man-Machine Studies*, *6*, 361–376.

12 An Automated Programming Advisor

John Domingue
Human Cognition Research Laboratory, The Open University, Milton Keynes, England

OVERVIEW

This chapter describes a system (ITSY) developed to help students learn Lisp. The work described in this chapter has been built up from other work within HCRL. Previous research within HCRL (Lewis, 1980; Eisenstadt, 1983; Hasemer, 1984), using the SOLO programming language, has shown that novice programming students can benefit from relatively small changes to their programming environment and from "intelligent" help. The motivation for the present research was the hope that we could do the same for Lisp.

1. INTRODUCTION

1.1 Why Lisp?

LISP has become one of the most commonly-used programming languages in research and commercial Artificial Intelligence (AI). As a result there are an increasing number of conventional programmers who want to become competent Lisp programmers. Unfortunately, because AI is still a young science, there are relatively few expert Lisp programmers and therefore few Lisp tutors. It is hoped that ITSY will help fill the gap.

ITSY is designed for professional conventional programmers wishing to convert to Lisp. By professional conventional programmer we mean a person who is currently employed as a programmer and has at least two years experience in the field. Professional programmers are likely to have negative transfer from their first programming language because of the unusual features of Lisp. For example, most conventional programming languages do not have the toplevel interpreter that is present in Lisp.

1.2 The Approach Adopted and System Characteristics

The first step in building ITSY was to study novice Lisp programmers. About 130 hours of data were collected from professional programmers learning Lisp (see Domingue, 1987, for details). Three things arose from this study:

1. The subjects made a substantial number of errors; (i) 35% of the lines typed by the subjects contained an error, (ii) subjects spent most of their time attempting to get their code to run (i.e. getting the syntactic and semantic bugs out).
2. The errors made by the subjects fell into relatively few categories.
3. A substantial amount (12%) of the errors were caused by the environment.

The first two of these findings suggested that our system should be error-based and exploit the error-cliché methodology. A cliché is a standard form of code (Brotsky, 1981). An error cliché is, therefore, a standard form of code which is incorrect. We have designed ITSY to trap these error clichés and explain the misunderstood concept to the student. To deal with the last finding, we also decided to improve the environment.

The basic approach used in this thesis is to collect a library of error clichés from students learning in the domain. These error clichés constitute a theory of the buggy knowledge that novice programmers are assumed to have. Then to determine what misconception a student must have in order to produce a particular error cliché. The next step was to build a system that is able to match error clichés against student input and then explain the misconception that the student must have.

ITSY has been designed to be used with a set text, Lisp (Winston & Horn, 1984), in order to remove the need to duplicate text and exercises. ITSY provides help in two different ways: Tutorial advice when a student makes an error; a friendly environment – including coaching on available Lisp tools.

1.3 An Example

The best way to gently introduce ITSY is to show an example. Suppose that the student has typed in the following function definition, in an attempt to create a synonym for CAR:

```
(defun buggy-first (l)
  (car (l)))
```

Once the student has loaded the function BUGGY-FIRST and typed in the form:

```
(buggy-first '(a b c))
```

Lisp gives an error [the reason for the error is that the L in (CAR (L)) should not be surrounded by brackets]. Instead of entering the debugger ITSY displays the buggy piece of code written by the user and a set of message frames to explain the source of the error to the student. These outputs are achieved in several stages: (i) the user's code is transformed into an internal form used by ITSY, (ii) this representation is matched against known error clichés, and (iii) the error-ridden code is found, highlighted and error messages printed out.

1.3.1 Transforming User's Code.

The first part of spotting the error is transforming the students' code into an internal form. The internal form used in ITSY is close to the surface plans used the Programmer's Apprentice (Waters, 1985). Figures 12.1 and 12.2 show the internal representation used by ITSY. Each labelled box represents a segment of code (usually a function). The arrows show dataflow. Figure 12.1 shows the internal representation of the form (BUGGY-FIRST '(A B C)). The box labelled *Function Application* represents the application of the function BUGGY-FIRST. The input to this function is the QUOTE function; represented by the box labelled *Quote*. The input to QUOTE is the list (A B C).

As ITSY analyses the toplevel form it also analyses any functions, defined by the student, that are called. The network shown in Fig. 12.2 diagrams the definition of the function BUGGY-FIRST. The box labelled *User Defined Function* represents the function BUGGY-FIRST. The input to the function is represented by the line labelled L. Notice this line does not lead to any of the internal boxes as the parameter L is not used within the function body. The function CAR is represented by the box labelled *CAR*. The input to this function is the box labelled *Function Application*. The Function Application box represents the function call L, in the student's code, which of course is undefined.

The error cliché matcher then tries to match one of the error clichés against this network (comprising of Figs. 12.1 and 12.2), starting from the toplevel form and working in the same way as the evaluator. As the error

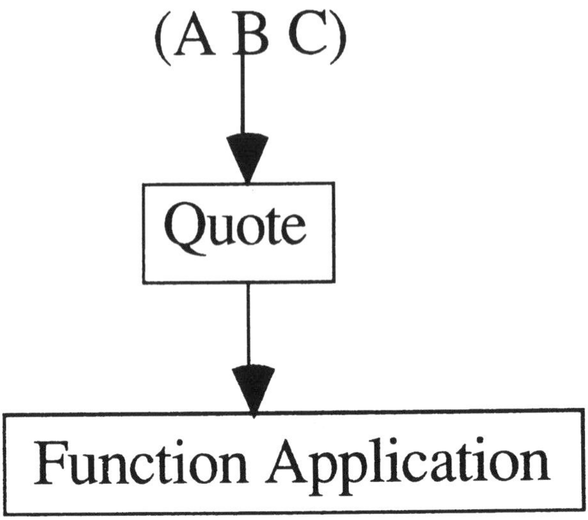

FIG. 12.1. The plan diagram of the form (BUGGY-FIRST '(A B C)), in which function application represents the application of the function BUGGY-FIRST.

cliché matcher traverses the network each error cliché actively tries to match itself against a section of the network. The surface plan representation and the error clichés are implemented in an object-oriented manner. The nodes in the network are implemented as objects, the labels on the boxes refer to the type or class of the object. The error clichés are implemented as messages.

The error cliché, which is called *brackets around a variable*, matches. This error cliché has the form:

Error Cliché Name:	Brackets Around a Variable
Surface Code Segment:	Function Application
Criteria:	Function is undefined
	The "name" of the function is the same as one of the input ports of the function definition the segment occurs in.
Other Checks:	The "name" of the function is not a function.

In each error cliché the slots deal with (i) the name of the error cliché, (ii) the type of object that the error cliché can match against, (iii) criteria which are tests that need to be satisfied in order for the error cliché to match, and (iv) other checks that are tests to prevent false alarms in cliché matching. The above example of an error cliché matches against the

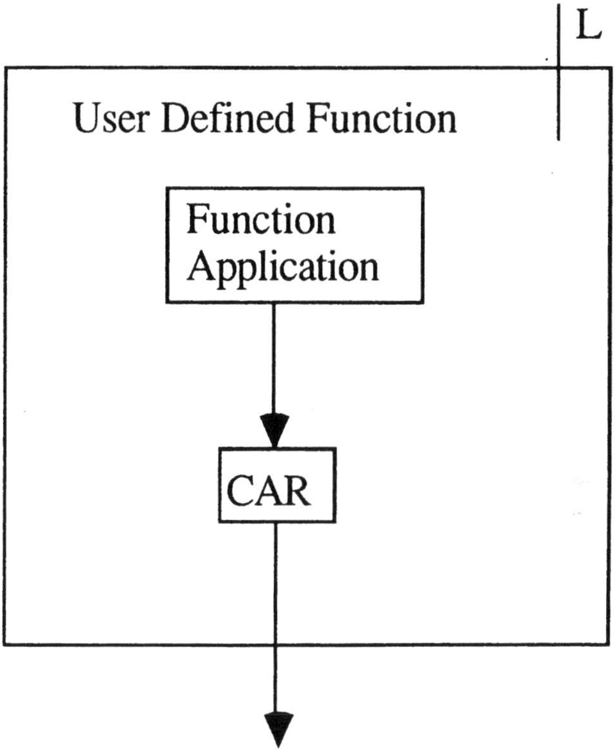

FIG. 12.2. The plan diagram of the definition of the function BUGGY-FIRST.

function application object in Fig. 12.2. Each surface code segment (shown as a labelled box in Figs 12.1 and 12.2) is represented as an object which has various slots to be filled. The criteria and other checks test the slots of these objects.

Once the error has been found ITSY checks the student model. In this case the model indicates that the student needs to be tutored. The student model consists of an unconnected graph. Each node in the graph can have one of several states (see some possible states in Fig. 12.3). Finally, a code highlighter uses various information (e.g. the buggy piece of code and the function in which the buggy piece of code occurs) to bring the function to the top of the screen and highlight the buggy piece of code. ITSY then displays a set of message frames to explain the source of the error to the student. The error cliché finder is used to fill in various slots of these messages. In the above example the name of the function that the error occurred in (i.e. BUGGY-FIRST) and the name of the variable surrounded by brackets (L) are inserted into different slots in the messages.

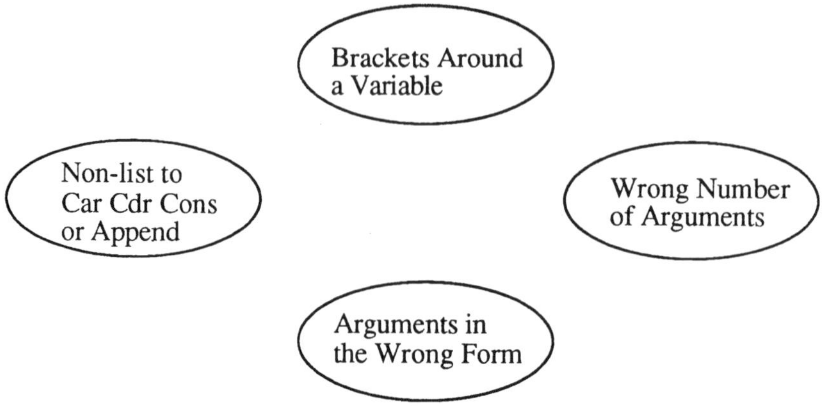

FIG. 12.3. Some possible states in ITSY's student model.

In the following sections we will consider the various parts of ITSY in more detail, after we have first reviewed related work in this field. These sections deal with (i) how the user's code is transformed into plan diagrams, (ii) the mechanics of error cliché matching and (iii) the nature of the student model. In conclusion, we consider some plausible extensions to ITSY.

2. RELATED WORK

ITSY grows out of related work in two different areas. The first area is that which deals with Intelligent Tutoring Systems and Computer Aided Instruction, while the second is that area concerned with Automatic Program Analysis and Debugging.

2.1 Intelligent Tutoring/Computer Aided Instruction

2.1.1 Spotting Errors

Traditional CAI packages compare a student's answer with a correct version. Typically the answers are simple yes/no type or multiple choice. The BIP system (Barr, Beard, & Atkinson, 1976) simply compared the output of student programs with a correct version. A more interesting method was used in WEST (Burton & Brown, 1979). WEST compared the students' answers with those of an expert, then assumed that the students lacked all of the skills needed to produce the optimum answer, unless they had used that skill recently. WEST would then tutor the student on one of these skills.

GREATERP (Anderson & Reiser, 1985) used production rules to implement both an expert and a buggy novice LISP programmer. These rules are implemented in GRAPES (Goal Restricted Production System). Every time a student types a LISP symbol GREATERP decides what rule would have to fire in order to duplicate the input. If the duplicating rule is in the expert set then GREATERP does nothing, but if the duplicating rule is in the buggy set then GREATERP gives the student a short tutorial. As long as the student writes ideal code GREATERP stays in background. There is a flaw in this strategy however. If a student is writing a variation of the solution that GREATERP does not know about then the student will get confusing advice.

The approach taken by GREATERP is different to that of ITSY. GREATERP inspects each symbol as the student types it in and proceeds to tutor the student if the symbol is incorrect. ITSY is less restrictive. The student is allowed to write the whole of their program before ITSY examines it. GREATERP has the advantage that it is able to tutor the student as soon as the error occurs. One of the disadvantages is that the student does not have a chance to write a whole program at once. Nor does the student practice debugging programs.

Ideally, the expert should be a glass box or articulate (Goldstein & Papert, 1977); non-articulate or black-box experts only being used where no theory exists on how to build one, or for reasons of efficiency. The expert in ITSY is an intelligent debugger because our pilot study showed that students spend most of their time debugging code.

2.1.2 Presentation Method

There are two main methods that CAI packages use in order to communicate with the student: displaying stored chunks of text; using natural language generators to create text. Barr, Beard, and Atkinson (1976) have pointed out that storing chunks of text limits the amount of branching possible and so makes the system inflexible whereas natural language generators have a limited vocabulary and consequently their communications with students tend to be dry and unmotivating. ITSY uses a combination of stored chunks of text and annotated graphic examples, because natural language generation is considered beyond the scope of this project.

2.1.3 Student Model

O'Shea and Self (1983, p. 143) describe a student model as follows: ". . . any information which a teaching program has which is specific to the particular student being taught. The reason for maintaining such information is to help the program to decide on appropriate teaching actions".

A student model is needed in ITSY to determine when a student has made an interesting error, as any error that occurs may be due to a fundamental misconception, or may just be a trivial slip. BIP (Barr, Beard, & Atkinson, 1976) used a counter for each elementary skill in BASIC programming as a student model. Each time a student successfully completed a task the counters for all the skills needed in that task were incremented. If the student failed to complete the task the corresponding counters were decremented. A problem that Wescourt, Beard, Gould, and Barr (1977) found with this scheme was that the faster students sometimes leap-frogged over the simpler tasks and then failed on a difficult task. Because they missed out a lot of the simpler tasks, they may have met some of the simpler skills only once. If such a skill was then needed in a difficult task, and they failed on this task, the counter for this skill would be decremented to zero. The model then contained the inaccuracy that the student did not have this skill. This student modelling problem was overcome in BIP-2 (Westcourt et al. 1977). Skills were represented by finite state machines rather than counters. The finite state model used was hierarchical, each skill being on a different level. The model had five possible states, the current state depending on how well a particular skill had been learned.

Guidon (Clancey, 1979) modelled the student as a subset of the system's expert, this is called an overlay model. The expert knowledge was represented as a set of rules (actually the expert was Mycin; see Shortliffe, 1976). Guidon's student model has three parts:

1. A record of the rules that the student knows.
2. A probability that a student will apply a particular rule in a specific case.
3. A probability that a student would mention a rule if asked to support a partial solution.

In LMS (Leeds Modelling System; Sleeman & Smith, 1981) problems are grouped into levels. If a student is able to complete problems at level I and then fails at a problem at level I + 1 LMS generates, from the existing student model, a set of new possible student models. This set is narrowed down by presenting the student with more problems from level I and deleting from the set those that did not predict the student's answer.

ITSY uses a non-hierarchical graph to represent the student's knowledge. Each node in this graph relates to a particular Lisp concept. There are two reasons why the model is non-hierarchical. Firstly, students who use ITSY may have encountered some parts of Lisp before, and each student may have some knowledge about a different part of Lisp. Secondly, students using ITSY are free to try the exercises in any order. This will mean that they will encounter concepts in a different order.

2.1.4 Path Selection

In traditional CAI packages the student is given a selection of tasks to complete. The student can proceed along a number of fixed routes through the system. In both (Burton & Brown, 1979) the students totally controlled their path through the system. In BIP-1 (Barr, Beard, & Atkinson, 1976) the system chose the next problem for the student. The method by which to choose a problem for a student raises questions such as:

1. How many new skills should be present in the next task? Should the system try to find a task with the maximum number of new skills at a particular level or just one?
2. Should the number of new skills presented change as the student progresses, or depend on the type of student? If so how?

Westcourt et al. (1977) tried to answer these questions by using various types of simulation. The method they used in BIP-2 changed the number of new skills presented according to how well the student was doing.

TRILL (Cerri, Fabrizzi, & Marsili, 1984) uses a socratic search strategy to find the erroneous concept that caused the student's error. In order to carry out this search TRILL uses a semantic network representing the syntactic knowledge needed correctly to use Lisp concepts such as ATOM, LIST, CAR, CDR. This network guides control in the search for the concepts that the student needs in order to avoid making the mistake.

IMPART (Elsom-Cook, 1984) embodies a specific model of teaching interaction. Elsom-Cook states that the goal of any teacher is to provide the student with a model of the domain which is at least as powerful as that of the teacher. Since the student has the clearest understanding of their state of knowledge and the teacher is the expert in the domain, in IMPART teaching is carried out by a negotiation between the student and teacher.

The students will choose their own tasks when using ITSY. Because of this they will not have to follow a fixed route through the system.

2.2 Intelligent Program Analysers and Debuggers

When students make an error, ITSY will have to classify the error so that the right tutorial package can be chosen. ITSY uses several of the techniques from intelligent automatic code debuggers and analysers to classify the bugs. Automatic debuggers falls into three broad categories:

Debuggers that work in a limited context (e.g. Adam & Laurent, 1980; Laubsch & Eisenstadt, this volume; Hasemer, 1984; Johnson & Soloway, 1985; Ruth, 1976).
Debuggers that work in a general context, but need a program specification as well (e.g. PUDSY, Lukey, 1980; MYCROFT, Goldstein, 1975).
Debuggers that work in a general context without using a program specification (e.g. PHENARETE, Wertz, 1982).

Those debuggers that work in a limited context, have a high-level description of the task that the students are attempting. Adam and Laurent (1980, p. 78, 79) say that there are two possible ways of describing the task. Either statically, using a set of assertions, or dynamically having some general encoding of the algorithm. Ruth (1976) uses a dynamic description called a program-generating model, which is described below. Adam and Laurent (1980) describe the program solution dynamically using graphs; transformations of the graph are used to prove the equivalence of the student program and the correct program. These transformations are similar to but more powerful than those used by Ruth (1976). Any irreducible mismatches between the high-level description and the student's code are taken to mean that there is a bug in the code.

PROUST (Johnson, 1985) is an intention-based PASCAL debugger. Programming knowledge in PROUST is frame-based and is contained in problem descriptions which consist of programming goals and sets of data objects. Programming goals are the principal requirements that must be satisfied and the sets of data objects are the data manipulated by the program. Data objects can either be constant-valued or variable-valued. Goal statements consist of a name of a type of goal followed by arguments. The problem descriptions describe what the programs must do but not how they are supposed to do it, these are described by plans. Johnson claims that debugging requires knowledge of the intentions of the programmer. Currently, ITSY has no knowledge of the intentions of the programmer. This is because over 80% of the errors found in the pilot study required no knowledge of context in order to be fixed. However, as we shall see later, it is possible to give ITSY context knowledge.

PLANs (Waters, 1978) and the plans used in PROUST are similar but there is a subtle difference. The plans used in PROUST are derived from a psychological theory of programming plans being developed at Yale whereas PLANs are a program representation optimised in its utility for automatic systems. The main goal of PLANs is to represent a program completely, making as much information as possible explicit.

Plans are stereotypic methods for implementing goals. Plans are compared to the students program to determine which fits best. Plans contain a template slot which describe the form the PASCAL code should take. Plan templates consist of PASCAL statements, subgoals and labels. This representation is low-level and PASCAL-dependent. Johnson's reason for this is (Johnson, 1985, p. 85):

> If concrete plan and program representations are used, then some high-level errors are harder to identify, because the syntax gets in the way. If abstract representations are used, some low-level errors are impossible to identify, because relevant evidence has been abstracted away. Given the choice, a concrete representation must be used, since PROUST must be able to identify as wide a range of bugs as possible.

ITSY uses PLANs, these can be as concrete or as abstract as needed, so that both low- and high-level errors can be spotted.

PROUST parses a student's program into a tree. It then selects, from the problem description, one goal at a time. The values of any data objects known at this point are substituted into the goal description. PROUST then tries to match each of the goal's plans in turn with the parse tree, using the plan's template slot. This is analysis by synthesis; PROUST generates possible implementations and matches these against the student's. If PROUST is unable to match a plan with the student's code then a bug is present. PROUST tries to interpret these plan differences using bug rules. Each bug rule has a test part which matches against the differences if the rule applies, and an action part which explains the plan differences.

The debuggers which need a program specification use the specification as a static description of the program, to try and spot any inconsistencies between this description and programs written by students. The specification takes the form of assertions (given by the student) in propositional calculus. This, whilst bringing in additional information, can lead to problems if the students give incorrect assertions, and also requires that students learn an additional "language" (the program specification language). MYCROFT (Goldstein, 1975) also uses the output of the program (i.e. the pictures that the program drew), to gain extra information.

Debuggers like PHENARETE (Wertz, 1982) that do not work in a small domain or use any sort of specification, look for a certain class of errors. These errors are typically syntax errors, unreachable statements, endless recursion and non-terminating loops. The errors that are spotted are not deep semantic or conceptual errors; finding such errors requires knowledge about the actual task being attempted. Programs that will run, but do not give the correct output fall into this latter category.

There are two distinct stages to debugging: analysing the code and either fixing or reporting the errors. These are discussed in turn below.

2.2.1 Analysing the Code

Most systems break up the analysis stage into several passes. The first pass involves looking for syntactic and simple semantic errors (i.e. potential run-time errors detectable syntactically such as $3 \div 0$, or calling an undefined function). Wertz (1982) calls these surface errors. Compilers for languages such as PASCAL, ALGOL, Lisp and C are able to detect errors of this type.

A typical debugger takes one of three actions on spotting the error.

1. The system, like a compiler, just reports the error.
2. The system interacts with the user, suggesting a simple change in the code such as substitution of a word, deletion of an argument or addition of brackets. The user usually answers yes or no, depending on whether they agree with the change.
3. The system makes simple changes to the code and then notifies the user (e.g. PHENARETE, Wertz, 1982).

The next stage in analysing involves producing a canonical form of the code. This can then be compared with either a library of clichés (Brotsky, 1981; Hasemer, 1984) or a library of plans (Rich, Shrobe, Waters, Sussman, & Hewitt, 1978), or a general form of the solution in the limited context debuggers. The canonical representation of code, used in the seminal MIT work, was the language-independent, plan diagram representation (Rich et al. 1978).

The plan diagram represents code segments as boxes, each box giving a specification for the code segment. Control flow and data flow are represented by hashed and solid lines respectively. So, for example, the LISP code below is represented in Fig. 12.4:

```
(cond ((< x y) x)
      (t (+ x y)))
```

The function + is shown as a box. The two arguments, x and y, are represented by the two solid arcs connected to the top of this box. The output of the function is represented by the solid arc coming out of the bottom of the box. The predicate < is represented by the box containing the symbols <, T and F. The two possible paths for control flow, after the predicate, are represented by the two hashed lines from the T and F sections of the box. The lowest box represents a join. A join specification is a mirror image of a predicate specification. Unlike the predicate specification, however, the join does not represent any real computation. Joins are used to rejoin the two control-flow branches of a predicate block.

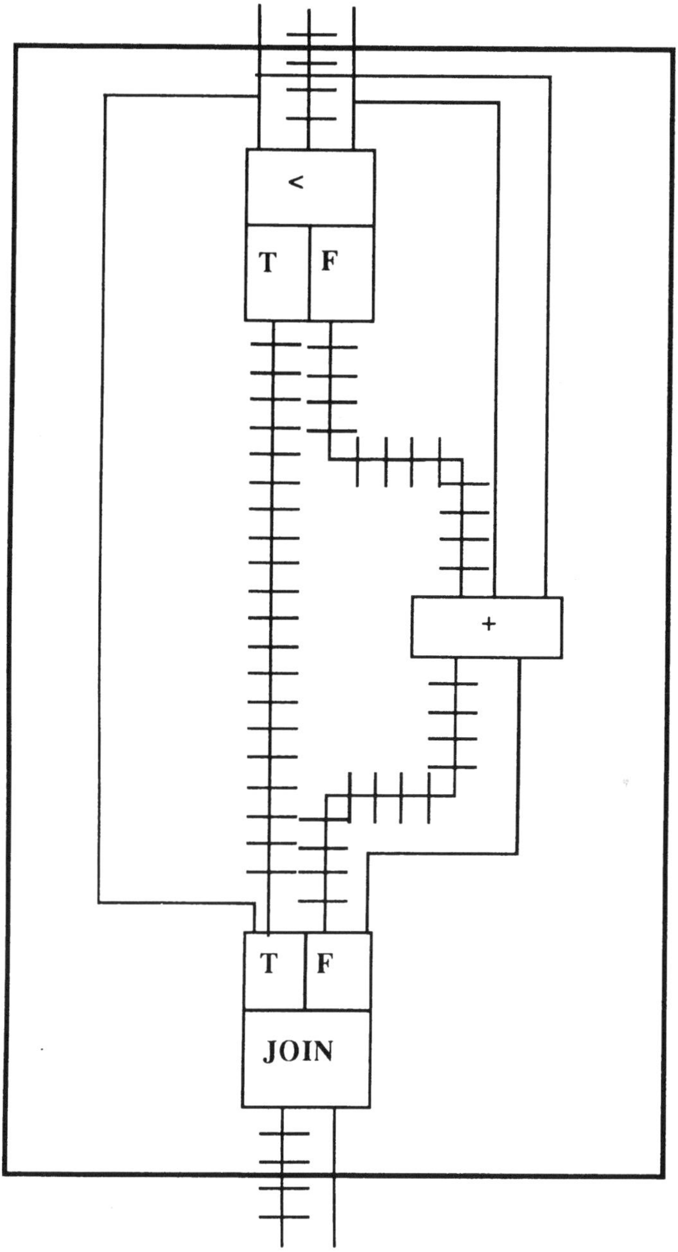

FIG. 12.4. Plan diagram of (COND ((< X Y) X) (T (+ X Y)).

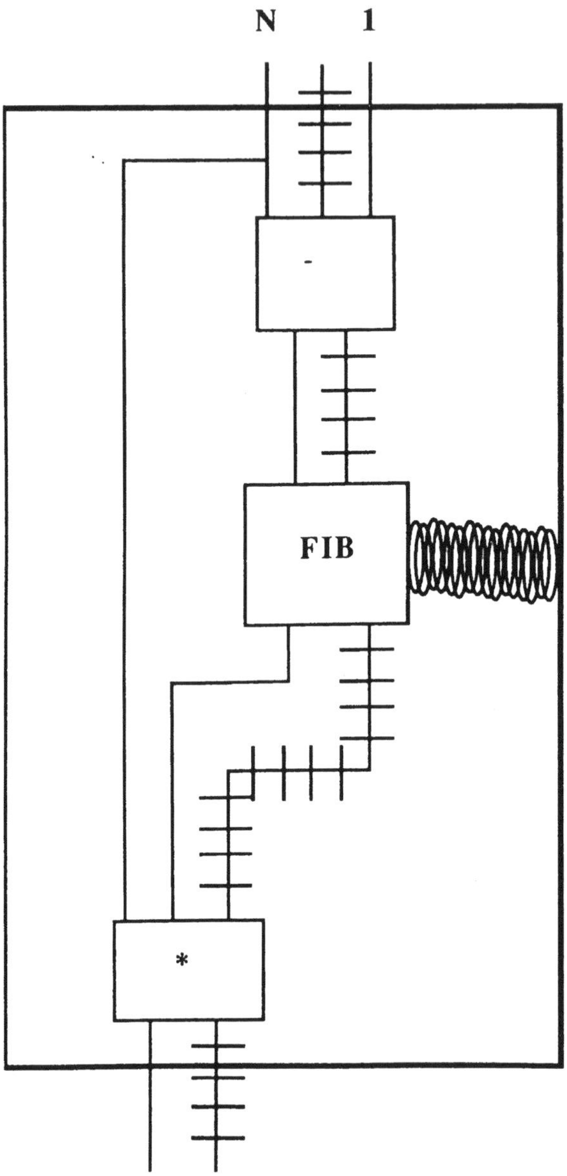

FIG. 12.5. Plan diagram of (DEFUN FIB (N) (* N (FIB (– N 1)))).

Recursion is represented as a looping line to the outside of the box. Figure 12.5 represents the (infinitely recursive) code:

```
(defun fib (n)
  (* n (fib (- n 1))))
```

Iterative loops are converted into their tail-recursive counterparts, and temporal decomposition is then applied (Waters, 1979). Temporal decomposition is a technique for abstracting iterative loops or tail-recursive functions. Each operation in the loop becomes a vector operation that acts on a vector of data objects. A vector of data objects is a vector where each element contains the values of all the variables of the loop for a particular iteration (see Chapter 9 for an application of this to SOLO). The boxes in the plans can also be high-level plans, allowing plans to be as abstract as needs be.

The Recognizer (Zelinka, 1986) is a system that performs the program recognition by parsing. Programs are converted into a PLAN-like graph representation. The library of structures to be recognised are translated into a graph grammar (currently performed by hand) and the program is parsed using the grammar. The graph parser is an extension of Brotsky's flow-graph parser (Brotsky, 1981). The extensions cope with some of the features of PLANs. Other features of PLANs, which cannot be dealt with by these extensions, have been transferred to attributes on the nodes and edges of the flow graph.

Another method of analysing code is to transform the code into a graph and then normalize the graph. Normalization transforms the graph into a standard form. An example of a transformation used might be – if a variable is used for two different purposes then a new variable is generated. This makes the matching process easier. This technique is primarily used by debuggers that store a version of the answer to the particular exercise attempted by the student (e.g. LAURA, Adam & Laurent, 1980).

Code may also be understood by means of meta or symbolic evaluation. PHENARETE uses meta-evaluation to analyse the students' code. The main difference between evaluation and meta-evaluation is that in meta-evaluation every possible branch of the code is taken. PHENARETE meta-evaluates the code, until every branch has either terminated, or has come to a repetition. This method is often combined with others, to work on pieces of code that another method has failed to analyse.

2.2.2 Finding the Bugs

Once the code has been transformed into a suitable form, the next step is to find the bugs. Bugs are found by looking for mismatches between a high-level description of the student code, and a high-level description of the correct code.

MYCROFT (Goldstein, 1975) and PUDSY (Lukey, 1980) used a specification as the high-level description of the correct code, and matched the output of the students' programs against a specification. MYCROFT was able to find errors in LOGO programs which drew shapes. The specification used in debugging described the relationships between the components of the shapes drawn. The bug was then deemed to be in the section of code that constructed the part of the drawing that conflicted with the specification. PUDSY also used debugging clues such as re-assignments to variables before the old value was used. Ruth (1976) used a program generating model to try and generate the student program. The generator was a high-level description of the correct program, and was only able to generate the student's code if the code was correct. If it could not do so it then tried to match on simple variations of the code. Variations might include code with the arms of conditionals swapped, or the signs in algebraic expressions switched. Laurent's system LAURA matched the normalized graph against the model answer. As in Ruth (1976) if it was not possible to obtain a perfect match then the student graph was altered until either a match was made or no more variations were left.

SNIFFER (Shapiro, 1981) uses a cliché finder, a time rover and sniffers to find bugs in a program's execution history. Each sniffer contains information about a particular type of bug. This information is represented by a set of rules. A sniffer will use the time rover to obtain the value of a variable at different times during the evaluation. The program's execution history is recorded by a time rover. This stores all the intermediate states of variables and the effects of side-effecting functions (enough information is stored so that the program could be run backwards if required). The cliché finder identifies algorithms by recognising patterns in a plan diagram representation of the code. The cliché finder acts in the same way as the code analyser in the Programmers' Apprentice (Waters, 1985). As we have seen, ITSY finds bugs by trying to match sections of a plan-diagram-like description of the code against error clichés.

2.2.3 *Fixing the Errors*

One of the major problems when fixing a bug is that the edit may interfere with another part of the program, so causing another bug. Goldstein (1975) specified a certain order in which to fix bugs in programs that drew pictures so as to cause the least interference. Some examples of the heuristic-order rules are:

Fix the bugs in the properties of the picture parts before bugs in relations between the picture parts.

Fix the bugs in the intrinsic properties of a picture part before the bugs in the extrinsic properties.
Use the edit that has the maximally beneficial side-effects. This is because several errors can be caused by the same bug.
Use the edit that causes the minimum changes to the user's code.

PUDSY (Lukey, 1980) tested each possible edit to make sure that the edit did not cause another bug to appear in the program. This test consisted of comparing the amended program with the program specification.

TALUS (Murray, 1986) is a Lisp debugger able to detect and correct errors at the algorithmic, functional and implementation level. TALUS takes student program and a reference program and tries to prove them equivalent using a theorem prover. TALUS is a debugger that works in a limited context and has eighteen task descriptions stored in a task library. Debugging takes place in four stages:

Program simplification – a theorem prover is used to simplify the code eliminating constructs such as COND.
Algorithm recognition – the simplified code is parsed into frames which are matched against the frame representations of the various algorithms stored in the task structure.
Bug detection – the equivalence of the reference and student program forms a conjecture. If the conjecture cannot be proved then the student's program is considered buggy.
Bug correction – once the bug has been detected TALUS inserts the minimum amount of reference code to restore the proof of equivalence.

As TALUS uses a theorem prover which can only deal with a subset of Lisp, student programs are first simplified. There are some constructs which TALUS cannot simplify however:

Free variables in function definitions.
Side effects in conditional tests.
Side effects in the actual arguments of lambda expressions.
Destructive functions such as NCONC. TALUS replaces NCONC with APPEND when the arguments are fresh list structures (that is lists that have been CONSed up within the program). When the arguments are not fresh list structures TALUS has to rely on heuristics.

In debuggers there seems to be a trade-off between generality and complexity. In order to find deep semantic and teleological errors context-knowledge is needed. In areas such as programming we cannot expect novices to provide this knowledge so it must be built into the system. Built-in context knowledge limits the generality of a debugger as it will only be able to debug those programs the built-in context knowledge covers.

ITSY spots errors using a variant of the code analyser in the Programmer's Apprentice. A certain part of the analysis within the Programmer's Apprentice involves replacing segments of code by a smaller number of segments, or by a single segment. This involves matching segments of code against a pre-stored cliché. In an analogous fashion, ITSY attempts to match segments of code against a pre-stored error cliché.

Notice that the matching process can occur at either a low or high-level code abstraction. In the Programmer's Apprentice code is transformed into surface plans and then by matching these against clichés, plan diagrams are produced. The plan diagrams can be matched against clichés to produce further (more abstract) plan diagrams. This process can occur as many times as necessary, each time a deeper understanding of the code is achieved. The same can occur with error clichés. When matching occurs more than once each new round of matching produces the source of deeper errors.

In subsequent sections we consider some key aspects of ITSY in more detail.

3. TRANSFORMING THE CODE INTO PLAN DIAGRAM FORM

In this section we discuss how ITSY transforms the student's code into ITSY surface plan form. At the instant when this transformation takes place, the student has written a piece of code, usually intended to test a user-defined function, directly into the Lisp toplevel. Whilst evaluating this code the interpreter signals an error, and ITSY attempts to discover the cause of this error. In order to do so, ITSY transforms the student's code into surface plans (here implemented as objects) and compares the plans with its library of error clichés.

3.1 The End Product – Internal Representation of the Code

In the Programmer's Apprentice (Waters, 1985) code is first translated into a surface plan. Once the surface plan has been constructed programming clichés from the cliché library are matched against chunks of the surface plan to form more abstract plans. ITSY translates student programs into a surface plan form and then tries to match Error Clichés from the Cliché library against segments of the surface plan.

The differences between surface plan representation used in the Programmers' Apprentice and the internal representation used in ITSY are quite minor. In the surface plan representation segments are represented in terms of lists. The control and data flow links are represented explicitly stating which segments are connected. In ITSY's internal representation segments are represented as objects. The control and data flow links are represented implicitly by setting a control or dataflow slot of an object to another object. In surface plan representation the segments have a type. This type determines how the segment interacts with control flow. Splits in the control flow are achieved by setting the type of a segment to split. In ITSY's internal representation there is only one type of object that can split the data flow – the pred. Pred objects have a test slot. The test slot holds the predicate that will split the control flow.

3.1.1 Representation of Lisp Objects

Different types of Lisp objects are represented in ITSY by different classes. The classes form a hierarchy: at the top of the tree there is the most general Lisp object; at the bottom there are objects such as individual functions and constants. Figure 12.6 shows part of the complete tree of classes. The lightly filled in boxes show the parts where the analyser is partially implemented. The heavily filled in boxes show the parts where only the class exists (i.e. the analyser is not implemented).

Each object contains the following slots:

Name – holds the name of the object.
Control-in – this is the controlflow input port.
Control-out – this the controlflow output port.
Input – this is the dataflow input port.
Output – this is the dataflow output port.
Expectations – points to an entry in a hash table. This entry contains a prototypical object. This holds information such as the expected number and type of arguments and the type of output.
Code – this slot contains the code represented by the object. This is needed so that ITSY can give the tutorial in terms of the student's own code.
Code function name – the function, if any, the code occurs in. This is used by ITSY's highlighting module.

Just below the top of the tree are symbols, numbers, functions, and bind local vars. The first three denote the obvious types of objects. Bind local vars refers to objects that represent any Lisp function able to locally bind variables, such as LET or DO. Below the functions are the connectives and non-connectives. The connectives of a language are the primitives that implement control and dataflow (e.g. SETQ, COND and DO).

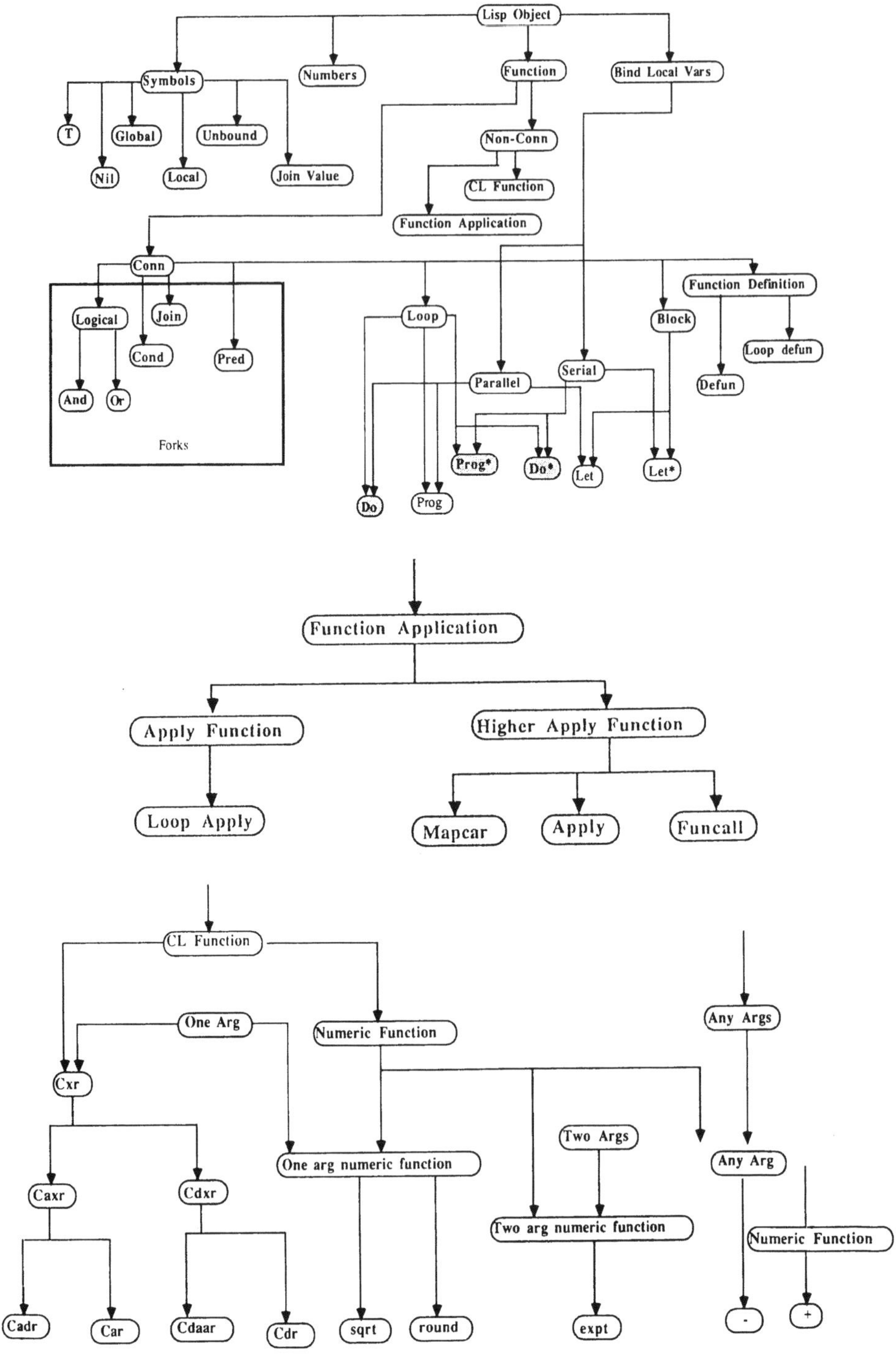

FIG. 12.6. (a, b & c) The hierarchy of Lisp objects used in ITSY.

3.1.2 Connectives

There are no variables as such in plan diagrams. Variables are replaced by a pointer to their value. SETQs change the position of the pointer. This removes variations due to using variables to store temporary values. The two segments of code:

```
(defun one (x y z)
  (append (list (+ x y)) z))

(defun two (x y z)
  (setq x (list (+ x y)))
  (setq z (append x z))
  z)
```

would be represented as Fig. 12.7. Only the last s-expression in a function is represented in the surface plan representation. The other s-expressions in a function exist only for side-effect purposes. The representation of function TWO is in fact the representation of the variable Z. The two previous s-expressions in TWO are there to side effect the values of the variables X and Z. Notice that the effect of SETQs (controlling dataflow) is abstracted away.

Below the connectives in Fig. 12.6a are forks, function definitions, blocks and loops.

Forks. Forks include the constructs concerned with branching control flow, such as COND and OR. These are changed into pred and join objects. Pred objects have three parts: a test, a true output port and a false output port. The test holds the predicate of the fork. Note that the value of a test slot can be any object, even if it represents a non-predicate function. In the representation of the following code:

```
(or (> x y) (print "X is greater") x)
```

two pred objects would be created. The first pred object's test slot would be connected to a > object and the second pred object's test slot would be connected to a PRINT object. The true output port holds the control flow path followed if the test is true. Similarly, the false output port holds the control flow path followed if the test is false. So, for example, the following code would be represented as Fig. 12.8:

```
(cond ((> x y) (+ x y))
      ((= x y) (+ x 1)))
```

Notice there is no COND object in this diagram. Each test part of a clause has been replaced by a pred object, the test part connected an object

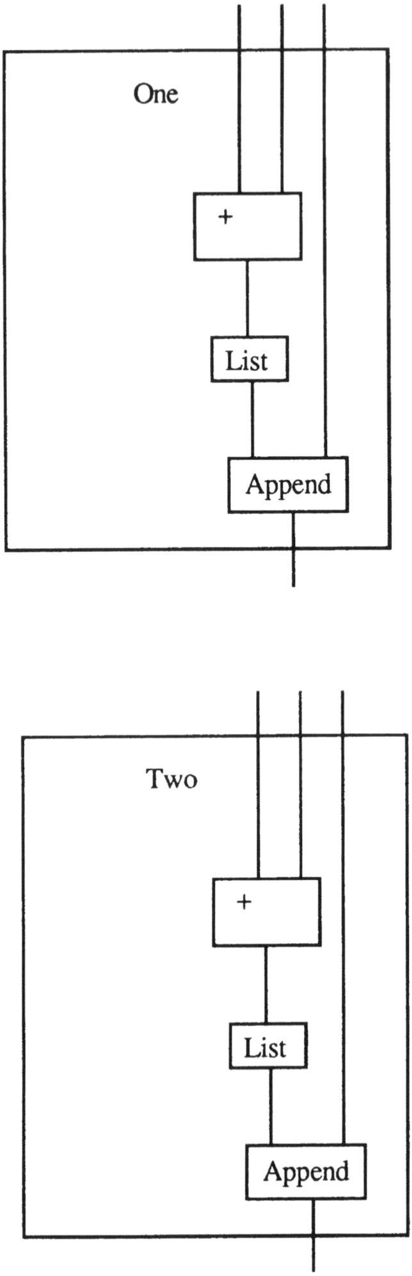

FIG. 12.7. The plan diagram of the ONE and TWO functions.

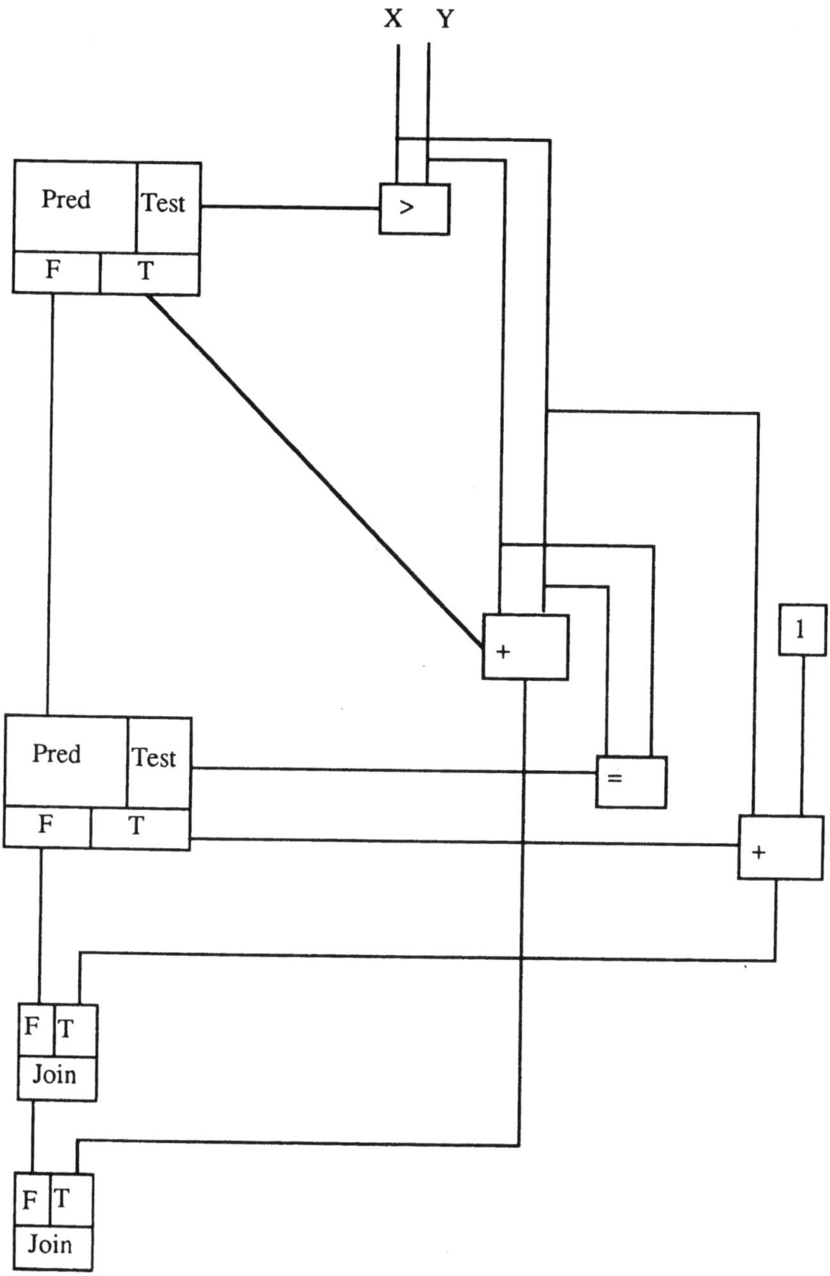

FIG. 12.8. The plan diagram of a conditional.

representing the test function. The test for the first clause, (> X Y) is represented by the first pred object and the > object connected to the pred's test slot. The result part of the first clause, the s-expression (+ X Y) is represented by the + object. This is connected to the true output port of the pred object.

The test part of the second clause (= X Y) is represented by the second pred object and the = object connected to the pred object's test slot. The result part of the second clause (+ X 1) is represented by the + object with X and a 1 object connected to its input ports. The top join object connects the two control flow paths of the lower pred object. The lower join object connects the two control flow paths of the top pred object.

The following code:

```
(or  (and (> x y) (+ x y))
     (and (= x y) (+ x 1)))
```

would be represented as Fig. 12.9. Notice that there are no OR or AND objects in the diagram. A pred object is created for every s-expression except the last in ORs and ANDs. This is because the control flow can split in every s-expression except the last in an OR or AND. The surface plan representation of each s-expression except the last is connected to the test slot of a pred object. The last s-expression in an OR clause is connected to the false output port of pred object representing the penultimate s-expression. The last s-expression in an AND clause is connected to the true output port of pred object representing the penultimate s-expression.

The top left pred object is created when the OR is analysed. The test slot of this pred object is connected to the surface plan representation of the first s-expression in the OR, (AND (< X Y) (+ X Y)). The false output port of this pred object is connected to the surface plan representation of the last s-expression in the OR, (AND (= X Y) (+ X 1)).

The top right pred object is created when the first AND is analysed. The test slot of this pred object is connected to the surface plan representation of the first s-expression in the first AND, (> X Y). The true output port of this pred object is connected to the surface plan representation of the last s-expression in the first AND (+ X Y). The top join object connects the two control flow paths of the top right pred object.

The lowest pred object is created when the second AND s-expression is analysed. The test slot of this pred object is connected to the surface plan representation of the first s-expression in the second AND, (= X Y). The true output port of this pred object is connected to the surface plan representation of the last s-expression in the second AND, (+ X 1). The second lowest join object connects the two control flow paths of the lowest pred object.

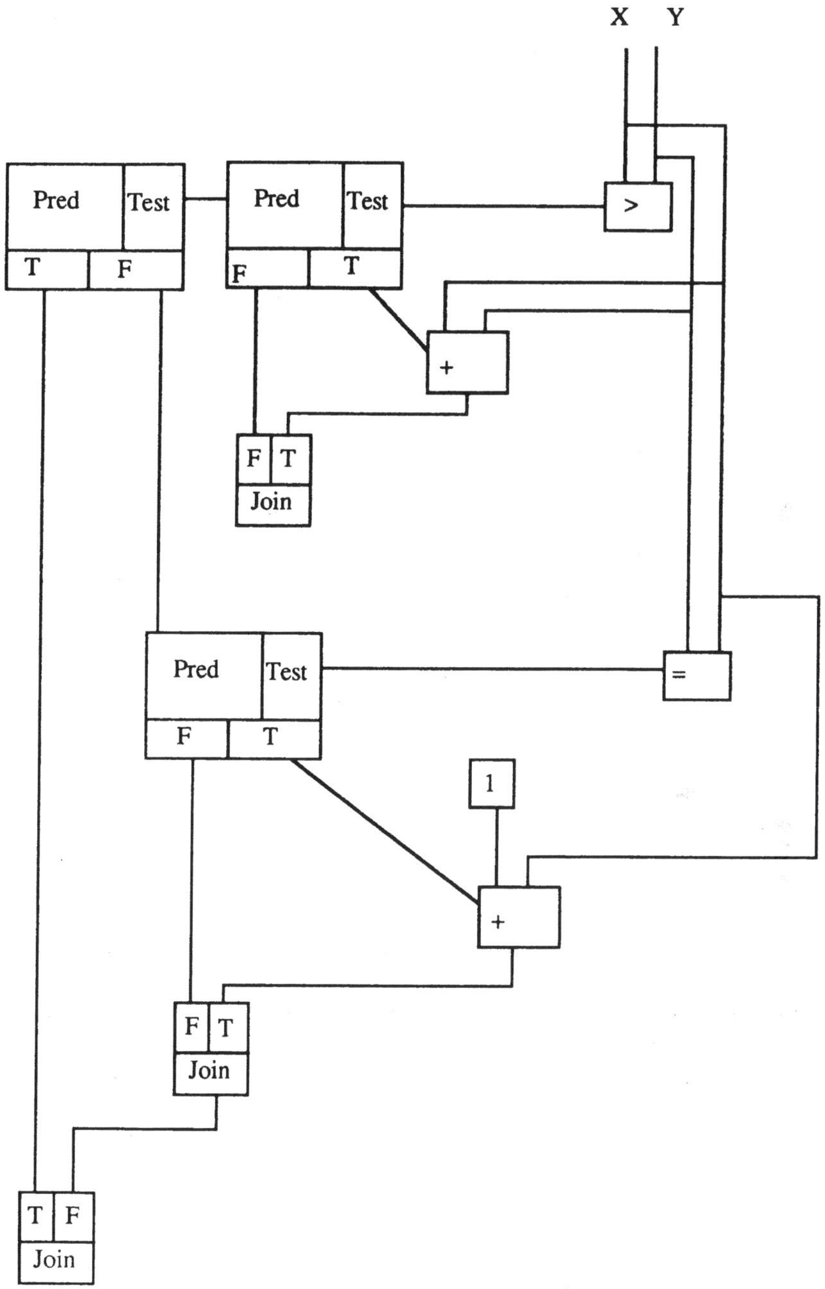

FIG. 12.9. The plan diagram of a form involving a disjunction and two conjunctions.

The lowest join objects connects the two control flow paths of the top left pred object. Note that if either a true output port of the false output port of a pred object is connected directly to the corresponding join then the output of the join is the test of the pred object. In Fig. 12.9 the true output port of the top left pred object is connected directly to the true input port of the lowest join object. The true output of this join is the test of the top-left pred object, which is the surface plan representation of (AND (< X Y) (+ X Y)).

Notice that many of the differences in the code have been abstracted away. The reason why not all the differences have been abstracted away is that the two pieces of code are not really isomorphic. If the s-expression (+ X Y) returned NIL then the COND expression would return NIL, and the second clause would not be tried. In the OR version the second clause would be then tried, as the first returned NIL.

Function Definitions. Function definitions include functions defined by DEFUN and loop functions (see Fig. 12.6). User defined functions are analysed and stored away in a hash table. A user-defined function is represented by an object with the following extra slots:

Function name.
Parameter list.
Global variable list.
Code and objects.

The function name (obviously) contains the name of the function. The important part of function definitions are the parameter list and the global variable list (could be called the port list or the io-port list). The parameter list contains the arguments (input ports) to the function. The global variable list contains the global variables side-effected in the function (i.e. altered by SETQ). This is the only side effect a user defined function can cause in the subset of Lisp that we are considering. The code and objects slot contains a mapping between each object and the code it represents, this is used by the highlighting module.

Loop functions are used in the analysis of loops. These are similar to user-defined functions except that scoping within the function is dynamic and there are no local variables. So, for example, the following code:

```
(prog (a)
   (setq a 2)
   lp
   (setq a (+ a 2))
   (go lp))
```

would first be translated into the following:

```
(prog (a)
   (setq a 2)
   (lp))
(loop-define lp ()
   (setq a (+ a 2))
   (lp))
```

The body of the loop (between the tag and the go tag) have been converted into a function. LOOP-DEFINE creates this function. The code is then converted to plan diagram in Fig. 12.10.

Loop function objects are used to represent the LOOP-DEFINE section of code – the second segment containing the + is a loop function object. The fact that the two LP objects are connected by a spring means that the inner LP object is a recursive call to the outer LP object.

Loop. Loop objects are Lisp constructs that allow looping. No objects of this type are actually created. This is used to differentiate between the Lisp constructs that allow loops and those that only allow linear control flow e.g. PROG and LET. Currently, PROG is the only Lisp looping construct that ITSY can analyse.

Blocks. Blocks represent constructs that allow linear sequences of code without loops. As with loop, objects of this type are not created. There are two such constructs that ITSY can currently analyse, LET and LET*.

Bind Local Vars. Bind local vars represents constructs that allow local variables to be bound. Parallel and serial represent the two different ways this can happen. If local variables are bound in parallel all the values for the variables are evaluated before binding any of them to the variables. If local variables are bound serially, the variables are bound as the values are evaluated one after the another.

3.1.3 Non-Connectives

The non-connectives consist of two parts function applications and Common Lisp functions. Function application represents the application of user defined functions to their arguments. Loop apply is used in the analysis of loops. Higher apply-functions represent the application of functions using a higher-order function, that is a function that takes a function as an argument. Examples of higher-order functions include MAPCAR and APPLY. Function application objects contain a type slot.

This is set to the type of the function call. This slot can have one of three values; normal, recursive and undefined (see Fig. 12.6b).

Common Lisp functions cover the non-connective Common Lisp functions. One arg, two args and any args are used to specify the number of arguments a function requires (see Fig. 12.6c).

3.2 The Transformation Process

The actions of this module of ITSY are in some ways similar to the Lisp evaluator. The transformation process begins with the form typed into ITSY's toplevel. At any time there is exactly one active object. Initially, a pointer object is created and made the active object. The input to this object is the toplevel form. At this stage of the analysis the input slot of the object is just the code itself rather than any representation.

If the toplevel form is an atom, the input to the pointer is replaced by an object representing the value of the atom. When a variable is analysed the surface plan representation of the variable's value is stored in a hash table under the variable's name. This is manipulated when the Lisp environment changes, such as inside a function or a LET.

If the toplevel form is a list, the first element of the list is considered to be a function and the analyser creates an object that represents the function. The inputs to this new object are the arguments to the function.

If the function is user-defined the analyser creates a Function Application object. The analyser then checks if the function definition has been analysed. The analyser carries out this check because the definition of user-defined functions are only analysed once. As the function application appears in the toplevel form the function definition will not have been analysed. The definition is analysed and stored in a hash table under the function's name. If no definition exists for the function the type slot is set to undefined. The new object created then becomes the active object and the process starts again.

As the transformation process runs, the segments of raw code in the active object's input slots are replaced by ITSY's internal representation. As a code segment is translated into plan diagram form the code is stored, to be used by the tutorial frame presentation package. After analysing all of the code we end up with a network of connecting objects.

Each object has an expectations slot. There is a hash table containing prototype versions of each Lisp function. Whenever a Lisp construct is met this slot is filled with the prototype versions stored in the hash table. The prototype version used carries information such as the number of arguments a function should be given. This is used by the error-cliché matcher.

The transformation process described above is carried out in two independent contexts. The first context is the toplevel context. This is either

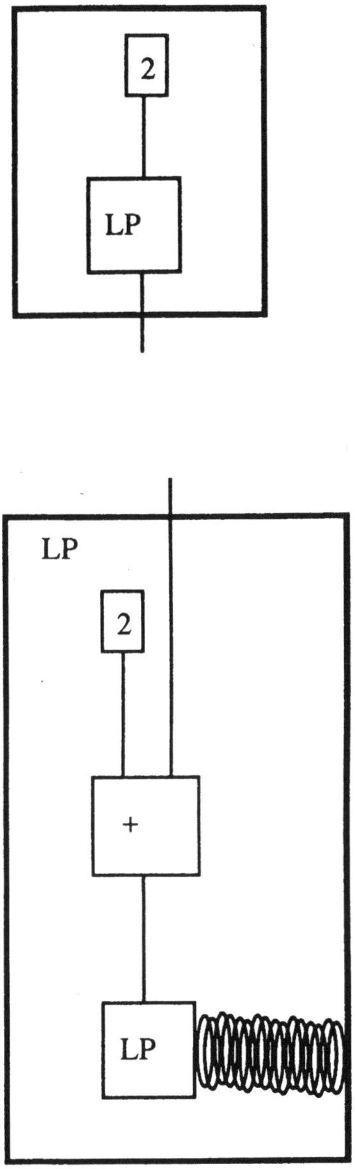

FIG. 12.10. The plan diagram of a loop construct.

toplevel or inside a function. When code is analysed within a function definition the toplevel context is inside a function, otherwise it is toplevel. The second context used is the embedded context. This context is either normal or inside a fork. This is used in the analysis of forks.

3.3 Current Limits of Analysis

As mentioned earlier the only loop construct that ITSY can currently deal with is PROG. Extra code to transform the other constructs into the equivalent of PROGs is needed. In most cases the addition of a new Common Lisp function would involve adding a new type of object in ITSY's Lisp Object Hierarchy. Special forms would also require the addition of code in order to be parsed. The functions that would create the most difficulty would be the destructive functions. This is not too great a problem as these functions are generally not used by novices, or are used when the novice has had a fair amount of exposure to Lisp.

4. MATCHING ERROR CLICHÉS AGAINST THE TRANSFORMED CODE

This section describes in detail how ITSY matches an error cliché against the transformed code. Each error cliché has the following four parts:

1. Error Cliché Name – the name of the error cliché.
2. Surface Code Segment – the "type" of object that the error cliché can match against.
3. Criteria – criteria that need to be satisfied in order for the error cliché to match.
4. Other checks – tests that prevent false alarms.

The matching process is carried out by two distinct modules. The plan diagram traversing module and the error cliché matching module. The plan diagram traversing module traverses the network of objects created by the code transforming module (describing in the previous section). The error cliché matching module is activated each time the plan diagram traversing module comes to a new node. The error clichés are active – that is they actively attempt to match themselves against a segment of the network of objects. Error clichés are in fact implemented as messages, the Error Cliché Name corresponds to the name of the message and the Surface Code Segment corresponds to the class of objects the message can be sent to. The error cliché matching module fires each error cliché in turn. The error cliché then actively tries to match itself against the current node in the network. This process stops when either an error cliché has matched itself against part of the network or all of the nodes have been examined.

4.1 Traversing the Transformed Code

The output of the code analyser is a network of plan diagram segments represented by objects. This module walks through the network. For example, in the surface plan representation in Fig. 12.7, the + is matched against the error clichés, then LIST is matched, then APPEND.

This method of matching means that ITSY will not always find the same error that the evaluator would. In the following code:

```
(append (list (car 1)) 2 3)
```

ITSY would find the error "2 is the wrong type of argument for APPEND" whereas the Lisp evaluator would report "1 was the wrong type of argument for CAR". One might think that a simple cure for this would be to proceed in a depth-first manner. However, if the traverser were altered to proceed in a depth-first manner then ITSY would have problems with the following code:

```
(appen (car 1) 2 3)
```

ITSY would report "1 was the wrong type of argument for CAR" whereas the Lisp evaluator would report "APPEN is not a defined function". The real cure for this is to divide the error clichés into two halves. Each node in the network would be visited twice. The traverser would visit a node, fire half of the error clichés then visit the nodes below the current node in a depth-first manner. After visiting all of the nodes below the current node the traverser would then fire the other half of the error clichés. The first half would contain error clichés that match against errors concerning the actual function being called (such as the Bracket Around a Variable error cliché), the other half would contain error clichés that match against the errors concerning the arguments to a function (such as Argument of the Wrong Type error cliché). This would have to be implemented in future versions of ITSY.

When possible ITSY gives a tutorial on a single error. There are two reasons for this. Firstly, the student would be confused if they were to be tutored about several different topics at once. Secondly, there is a chance that any errors yet to be discovered may have been caused by the student having the same misconception. The student is given a second chance to fix the other errors before receiving a tutorial about them.

The surface-plan network is traversed until either an error cliché is found to match a segment of code, or all the code has been traversed. Each different type of plan diagram segment has its own built-in code traverser. As the network is traversed each plan diagram segment's traverser becomes active, once all parts of the segment have been inspected the traverser passes activity to another plan diagram segment's traverser. The different type of plan diagram segment traversers are described in turn below.

Two steps have been taken to make ITSY's messages coincide with the Lisp error messages if there is more than one error in the student's code. Firstly, the error clichés have been ordered. This ordering is based on the order in which the Lisp evaluator evaluates Lisp forms. The wrong number of arguments error cliché is before the wrong type argument error cliché, so in the following example:

```
(car 1 2)
```

the wrong number of arguments error cliché matches first. Some of the error clichés have been artificially raised. The error cliché bracket around a variable is one such error cliché to have been raised. This error cliché matches one level above it normally would. By level I mean what is commonly called list depth, so in the list:

```
((((a b) c) d) e f (((g))))
```

e and f are at level 1, d is at level 2, c is at level 3, and a, b and g are at level 4.

The following example will help explain, consider:

```
(+ (a) 'john)
```

(A is a variable). If the error cliché bracket around a variable were to match at the level of the s-expression (A), the error cliché wrong type argument [which matches at the level (+ (A) 'JOHN)] would match first. This is because the + segment is checked before the arguments. The error cliché bracket around a variable has been "raised" so that it matches at the level of (+ (A) 'JOHN).

4.2 Matching a Code Segment Against an Error Cliché

As each part of the network is traversed an attempt is made to match each of the active error clichés in turn. The members and order of the active set is determined by the type of error signalled. Common Lisp errors as implemented on the 3600 Symbolics series have a type. ITSY uses this type to select the active set. For example, an error of the type "undefined function" excludes a "wrong type" error cliché.

When ITSY is trying to find an error cliché to match against a segment two rules are used:

Try to match the most complex error cliché first.
Try to match as high up as possible, that is at the highest level.

Matching has to proceed in a certain order as some error clichés subsume others. This can best be explained using an example. There are error clichés Arguments in the Wrong Form and Wrong Number of Arguments Given to a Function. The first error cliché matches against sections of code such as:

```
(expt (2 3))
```

where the arguments to the function EXPT have been presented in the wrong form. The Wrong Number of Arguments Given to a Function error cliché would match against this section of code because the function EXPT has been given the wrong number of arguments, but Arguments in the Wrong Form is the error cliché that applies in this case.

4.3 An Example of Matching

In order to make clear some of the concepts discussed earlier we shall describe in detail a match with the error cliché Arguments in the Wrong Form. Consider the following code:

```
(defun my-add (x y z)
  (+ (x y z)))
```

When the student types the s-expression:

```
(my-add 10 20 30)
```

at toplevel the surface plan diagram in Fig. 12.11 is generated.

The error cliché finder first looks at the function application to make sure it is a defined function then the arguments are traversed. None of the error clichés match up against the arguments or the function application so the function definition is traversed. During this process the function + is traversed. At this point the error cliché Arguments in the Wrong Form matches against the surface plan segment for +. The function + satisfies the criteria for the error cliché Arguments in the Wrong Form1 with the surface code segment CL Function that is: the function + has only been given one argument in the definition of MY-ADD and the function does not only take one argument. The argument to the function + satisfies the subcliché Arguments in the Wrong form Subcliché that is: the function "10" is not defined and the other checks are satisfied.

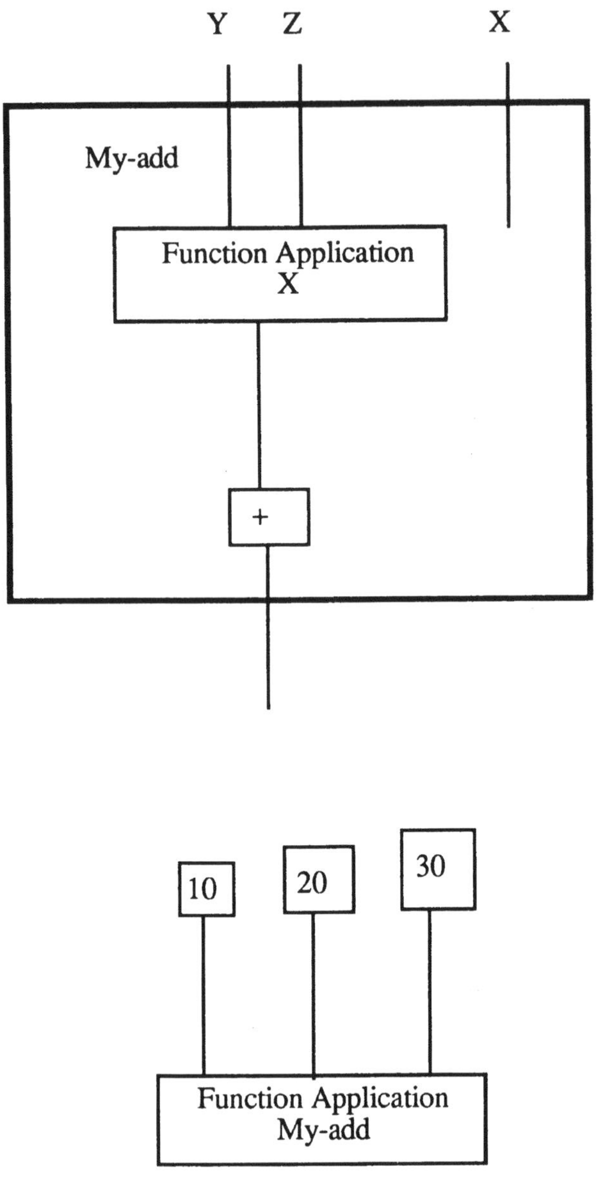

FIG. 12.11. The plan diagram for the MY-ADD case.

4.4 The Error Clichés

Each error cliché is represented as a collection of rules. For each type of surface plan segment there is a rule that determines whether or not that particular segment could match the error cliché. A rule has four parts:

Error Cliché Name – the name of the error cliché.

Surface Code Segment – the type of surface plan segment that the error cliché can match against. Note that the error cliché can also match against all children of the type of surface plan segment. For example, an error cliché with Surface Code Segment Function Definition could also match against surface plan segments of type Defun and Loop Defun.

Criteria – a set of criteria that need to be satisfied.

Other Checks – a set of checks to make sure that this is not a false alarm. This is needed because sometimes the student can make several errors at once. For example, one of the manifestations of the Arguments in the Wrong Form error cliché is that it traps errors when the student gives a list argument as separate quoted atoms:

```
(cons 'a '(b c d))
```

is written as:

```
(cons 'a 'b 'c 'd)
```

but the student could have meant:

```
(cons 'a (list b c d))
```

if B, C, and D are variables. This manifestation of the error cliché checks quoted atoms to make sure that none are bound variables so as to distinguish between these two cases.

Some error clichés use sub-clichés. These have the same format as error clichés but are not error clichés in their own right. These are used when an error cliché extends over several surface plan segments. Sub-clichés can refer to the error cliché (or any part of the error cliché) that uses them by using the term super cliché (see Domingue, 1987, for a full list of the error-clichés used in ITSY).

5. THE STUDENT MODEL

Student models are used to determine how student input should be interpreted. In ITSY the task of the student model is to determine whether the student should receive a tutorial once the cause of an error has been found. Because of this the student model is closely tied to the error clichés.

The student model consists of a graph. Each node in the graph represents a LISP concept associated with each of the error clichés in the library, that is to say there is a node in the graph for each error cliché. An error cliché matches against a segment of code that contains an error. Behind this error is a Lisp concept that the student did not understand, otherwise the student would not have made the error. There is a node in the student model that represents how well the student understands this concept. For instance, a type of error that students make is to try and use a lambda variable declared in the argument list of a function. A student could type the following:

```
(defun foo (a b c)
  (setq a 1)
  (setq b 2)
  (setq c 3))

(defun bar ()
        (plus b c a)) ; a, b, and c are NOT bound here
```

Associated with this type of error is the error cliché Wrong Scope. The student model will have a node associated with this error cliché. Each node has four states:

1. Concept has not yet been encountered.
2. Concept has been seen but not learnt.
3. Concept has been partially learnt.
4. Concept has been fully learnt.

All of the nodes are initially in state 1. When a student sees a concept for the first time, the corresponding node changes state. If the student successfully applies the concept, the node moves to state 3, otherwise the node moves to state 2. For example, if the first s-expression a student typed in was:

```
(car 1)
```

The node for the error cliché Argument of the Wrong Type would move

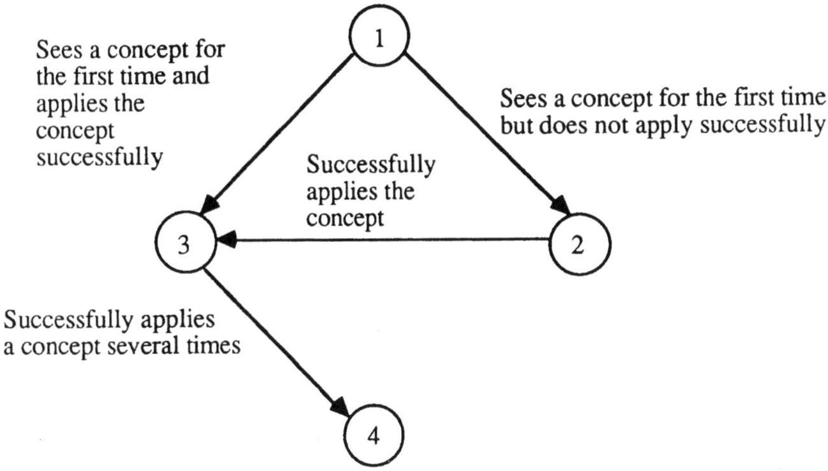

FIG. 12.12. The states and transition paths of a student model.

from state 1 to state 2, but if a student had typed in:

(car '(a b c))

The node would have moved from state 1 to state 3 (see the transition paths in Fig. 12.12).

5.1 Representation

The nodes are represented by objects. Each object holds the current state of the node. The objects are stored in a hash table under the name of the error cliché. Each node has its own upgrade and downgrade handlers which alter the state of the node. The node's new state depends on the original state and what just happened.

5.2 Updating the Model

Updating the model is carried out in a similar way to matching an error cliché against a student's code. The transformed code, that is the student's code in surface plan form is traversed in a similar way to the code traverser used by the error cliché finder. There are two main differences. Firstly, student model clichés instead of error clichés are matched against the transformed code. Secondly, the whole graph of objects is traversed rather than stopping when a student model cliché matches.

The four states are represented by the intergers 1–4 (see Fig. 12.12). The link between states 3 and 4 is achieved by adding an increment (less than one) to the current value. The current state is then the current value rounded down. The smaller the increment the more times a student has to successfully apply the concept. Currently the value is 0.1 (i.e. it takes 10 goes to advance from 3 to 4).

5.2.1 Student Model Clichés

Student model clichés are derived from error clichés. An error cliché matches a segment of code that contains a certain type of error. The type of error corresponds to a Lisp concept that the student does not understand. It is this concept that links a student model cliché to an error cliché. A student model cliché matches against any segments of code that show that the student understands this concept. Consider the error cliché No Bracket Function Call:

Error Cliché Name:	No Brackets Around a Function Call
Surface Code Segment:	Symbols
Criteria:	The symbol is unbound.
	The symbol is the name of a function.
Other Checks:	None.

the associated student model cliché is:

Student Model Cliché Name:	No Brackets Around a Function Call
Surface Code Segment:	CL Function
Criteria:	None.
Other Checks:	None.

You might think that the student model clichés could be just correct code clichés, but they are not because they are the correct code of which the error cliché is an erroneous form. In other words they apply to places where the student could have made an error, but did not.

Below is a description of a Null Student Model Cliché. These student model clichés are an artifact of the hierarchy of Lisp Objects described in Fig. 12.6. Each student model cliché can not only match against objects the same type as specified in the Surface Code Segment but all the children of this type. Null Student Model Clichés are used to prevent a child of a type of object inheriting the student model cliché.

A Null Student Model Cliché does not have Criteria or Other Checks slots. This describes exceptions to student model cliché rules. This means that the surface code segment which is called Quote cannot match against student model cliché No Brackets Around a Function Call. Unless specified it can be assumed that every Lisp object has a Null Student Model Cliché. The equivalent of these (Null Error Clichés) also exist, but they were not shown in order to make the error clichés readable.

Null Student Model Cliché Name:	No Brackets Around a Function Call
Surface Code Segment:	Quote

Objects of type Quote inherit from the type CL Function. If it were not for this Null Student Model Cliché every time a student quoted an a Lisp s-expression the node corresponding to the error cliché No Brackets Around a Function Call would change state. This node should only change state when a student correctly applies a function.

Student Model Cliché Name:	No Brackets Around a Function Call
Surface Code Segment:	Function Application
Criteria:	Type of function application is normal or recursive
Other Checks:	None

5.2.2 Action Taken on Different Values of the Student Model

Whenever ITSY traps a student error the student model node associated with the error cliché is checked. The value of the node determines ITSY's next action. It was decided that the student should always have access to a tutorial, in case the model was inaccurate. The action carried out under each value is described below:

1. Concept has not yet been encountered.
   The tutorial is given.
2. Concept has been seen but not learnt.
   Extra help is given. This is not actually implemented yet. The extra help would be provided in the form of extra frames.
3. Concept has been partially learnt.
   The student is asked if a tutorial is wanted.
4. Concept has been fully learnt.
   No tutorial is given, but a present tutorial option is added to the Lisp menu and the student notified how to obtain a tutorial. The present tutorial option would remain until the next student input to the Lisp toplevel window.

6. CONCLUSIONS

This chapter describes research where the concept of a programming cliché has been inverted and used as a basis for an automated programming advisor. The help given to students is based on the bugs they make. This is different from systems in which the student is measured in terms of an expert (e.g. WEST, Burton & Brown, 1978).

One of the aims of ITSY is to give students enough help so that they can use the bare system unaided. This is why the error messages generated by the Lisp system have been left in. ITSY sits in the background until a student has written a program, only giving help when the student tries the program out. This is to get the student used to the normal cycle of developing Lisp software. One of the problems with this, however, is that ITSY cannot offer any help if the student is completely stuck (e.g. if the student has trouble developing an algorithm or specification).

At present ITSY uses the relatively low-level surface plan representation of code. The reason for this is that novice Lisp programmers make syntax errors. However, ITSY has the potential to handle the dilemma between dealing with low- and high-level errors.

The power of the PLANs representation is that they allow higher-level PLANs to be built up from low level PLANs. Figure 12.13 shows how ITSY could use the full power of the PLAN representation to detect bugs and algorithmic errors from both complete Lisp novices and more advanced students.

Another possible extension to ITSY would be the addition of a student history. This would use a push-down stack of previous events. An event would be the analysis of the student's input (including the analysis of any functions referred to) and any error clichés that matched against the input. The stack would be weighted so that the more distant in time an event occurred the less influence it would have on the current input. ITSY would then use the stack to focus its search for an error. The stack would be used when ITSY was unable to match an error cliché against the student's input.

ITSY's approach could be extended to experts in the form of an advanced Program Debugging system. Since PLANs are language-independent the debugger could cope with any programming language that had an analyser (analysers exist for Lisp, Fortran and PL1; see Waters, 1985). As we cannot restrict expert programmers to work in a restricted context or burden the programmer with the need to supply specification, the system would only be able to detect a certain class of errors. This class would include errors such as: unreachable statements, endless recursion and non-terminating loops. It would not be possible to detect deep semantic or conceptual errors. Such errors require knowledge about the actual task being attempted.

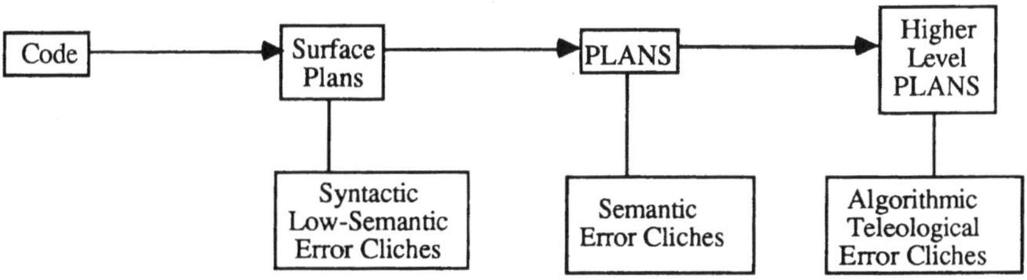

FIG. 12.13. Schematic diagram of an ITSY system that could deal with Lisp novices and experts.

In order to increase efficiency not all the error clichés would be active for any error. The set of error clichés activated would depend on the type of error signalled, this would tie the debugger closely to the normal program debugger. For example, the error stack overflow would trigger the endless recursion error cliché, but not the incorrect loop initialisation error cliché.

Expert error clichés for Lisp could include:

Placing mixins to Flavors in the wrong order.
Surgically changing a list (using one of RPLACA, RPLACD, NCONC etc.) that will be used later.
Using a THROW when not inside a CATCH.
Bad style clichés such as using inefficient code.

These are just some of the directions that could be taken from this line of research.

REFERENCES

Adam, A. & Laurent, J. P. (1980). LAURA, a system to debug student programs. *Artificial Intelligence*, *15*, 1980, 75–122.

Anderson, J. R. & Reiser, J. B. (1985). The LISP tutor. *BYTE: The Small Systems Journal*, *10*, 159–175.

Barr, A., Beard, M., & Atkinson, R. C. (1976). The computer as a tutorial laboratory: The Stanford BIP project. *International Journal of Man-Machine Studies*, *8*, 567–596.

Brotsky, D. (1981). Program understanding through cliché recognition. *Working Paper 224*. MIT Artificial Intelligence Laboratory.

Burton, R. R. & Brown, J. S. (1979). An investigation of computer coaching for informal learning activities. *International Journal of Man-Machine Studies*, *11*, (1), 5–24.

Cerri, S. A., Fabbrizzi, M., & Marsili, G. (1984). The rather intelligent little lisper. *AISBQ*, *50*, 21–24.

Clancey, W. J. (1979). Tutoring rules for guiding a case method dialogue. *International Journal of Man-Machine Studies*, *11*, 25–49.

Domingue, J. (1987). ITSY, an automated programming advisor. *Tech. Report No. 22*, Human Cognition Research Laboratory, Open University, Milton Keynes, U.K.

Eisenstadt, M. (1983). A user-friendly software environment for the novice programmer. *Communications of the ACM*, *26*, 1058–1064.

Elsom-Cook, M. T. (1984). *Design considerations of an intelligent tutoring system for programming languages*. Warwick: Doctoral dissertation, Department of Psychology, University of Warwick.

Goldstein, I. P. (1975). Summary of MYCROFT: A system for understanding simple picture programs. *Artificial Intelligence*, *6*, 249–288.

Goldstein, I. P. & Papert, S. (1977). Artificial Intelligence, language, and the study of knowledge. *Cognitive Science*, *1*, 84–123.

Hasemer, T. (1984). A very friendly software environment for SOLO. In M. Yazdani (Ed.), *New Horizons in Educational Computing*. London: Ellis Horwood, 84–100.

Johnson, L. W. (1985). *Intention-based biagnosis of errors in novice programs*. Doctoral Dissertation, Yale University, May 1985.

Johnson, L. W. & Soloway, E. (1985). PROUST: An automatic debugger for Pascal programs. *BYTE The Small Systems Journal*, *10*, 179–190.

Laubsch, J. & Eisenstadt, M. (this volume). The automatic debugging of recursive side-effecting programs. In M. Eisenstadt, M. T. Keane, & T. Rajan, *Novice Programming Environment: Explorations in Human-Computer Interaction and Artificial Intelligence*. Hove: Lawrence Erlbaum Associates Ltd.

Lewis, M. (1980). Improving SOLO's user interface: An empirical study of user behaviour and proposals for cost-effective enhancements to SOLO. *Technical Report No. 7*. Computer Assisted Learning Research Group, The Open University, Milton Keynes, England.

Lukey, F. J. (1980). Understanding and debugging programs. *International Journal of Man-Machine Studies*, *12*, 189–202.

Murray, W. R. (1986). *Automatic program debugging for intelligent tutoring systems*. Texas: Doctoral dissertation, Artificial Intelligence Laboratory, The University of Texas at Austin.

O'Shea, T. & Self, J. (1983). *Learning and teaching with computers*. Harvester Press.

Rich, C., Shrobe, H. E., Waters, R. C., Sussman, G. J., & Hewitt, C. E. (1978). Programming viewed as an engineering activity. *MIT Artificial Intelligence Laboratory, A.I. Memo 459*, January.

Ruth, G. R. (1976). Intelligent program analysis. *Artificial Intelligence*, *7*, 65–85.

Shapiro, D. G. (1981). Sniffer: A system that understands bugs. *A.I.Memo No. 638*. MIT Artificial Intelligence Laboratory.

Shortliffe, E. H. (1976). *Computer based medical consultations: MYCIN*. New York: American Elsevier.

Sleeman, D. H. & Smith, M. J. (1981). Modelling student's problem solving. *Artificial Intelligence*, *16*, 171–188.

Waters, R. C. (1978). Automatic analysis of the logical structure of programs. *Technical Report No. TR-492*. MIT Artificial Intelligence Laboratory.

Waters, R. C. (1979). A method for analysing loop programs. *IEEE Transactions on Software Engineering*, *SE-5*, 237–247.

Waters, R. C. (1985). KBEmacs: A step toward the programmer's apprentice. *Technical Report 753*. MIT Artificial Intelligence Laboratory.

Wertz, H. (1982). Stereotyped program debugging: An aid for novice programmers. *International Journal of Man-Machine Studies*, *16*, 379–392.

Westcourt, K. T., Beard, M., Gould, L., & Barr, A. (1977). Knowledge based CAI: CINS for individualised curriculum sequencing. *Technical Report No. 290*. Inst. for Mathematical Studies in the Social Sciences, Stanford University, Stanford, California.

Winston, P. H. & Horn, B. (1984). *Lisp*. Addison-Wesley.
Zelinka, L. M. (1986). *Automated program recognition.* MSc Thesis. MIT Electrical Engineering and Computer Science.

Author Index

Subject Index